THE PILGRIM'S GUIDE

To Santiago de Compostela

INCIPIT LIBER IIII SCI IACOBI Apli.

ARGVMENTVM beati calixti pp.

Siueritas apro lectore nris uoluminib; req̄rat̄ in hui̅ codicis serie. ampucato estacionis scrupulo secure intelligat̄; Que eñi meo scribit̄ur; multi ad huc uiuentes uera ē restantur;

Capto. i. de uiis s. iacobi; f̄. cle iii
Capto. ii. de dietis aplici itineris; f̄. cle iii
Capto. iii. de nominib; uillaru itineris ei; f̄ cle iii
Capto. iiii. de tribz bonis edibz mundi; f̄ cle iii
Capto. v. de nominibz uiatoz sci iacobi; f̄ cle iii
Capto. vi. de amaris i dulcibz aq̄s itineris ei; f̄ c cle iii
Capto. vii. de quitatibz terraru ⁊ generis itineris eius; f̄ cle v
Capto. viii. de scōr corporibz req̄uiedis i itinere ei ⁊ de passiõe eor
Capto. ix. de qlitate ciuitatis ⁊ ecclie s. iacobi; fone s eucropii;
Capto. x. de distencione oblacionu̅ altaris. s. iacobi; f̄ cle iii
Capto. xi. de pegriniis. s. iacobi digne recipiendis; f̄ cle iii

Cap i.

Qvatvor uie sunt que ad sēm iacobu̅ tendentes in unu̅ ad pontē regine in horis yspanie coadunantur; Alia per sēm eidiu̅ ⁊ moinē pesulanu̅. ⁊ cholosani ⁊ portus aspi tēdit̄ alia p sčm ona aiaz podii. ⁊ sčm fidecis cōquis. et sčm petru̅ de moissaco moedit̄ alia p sčm oratiā. macda leuā uiziliaci. ⁊ sčm leonardu̅ lemouicensem. ⁊ urbē petragoricensem pgit̄. alia p sčm martinu̅ turonense. ⁊ sčm ylariū pictauensem. ⁊ sčm iohem angliacensem. ⁊ sčm eutropiu̅ sčonensem. ⁊ urbē burdegalensem uadit̄; Illa que p sčm

THE PILGRIM'S GUIDE

TO SANTIAGO DE COMPOSTELA

WILLIAM MELCZER

ITALICA PRESS
NEW YORK
1993

ITALICA PRESS, INC.
595 Main Street
New York, New York 10044

Library of Congress Cataloging-in-Publication Data
Melczer, William.
    The pilgrim's guide to Santiago de Compostela / William
    Melczer. p. cm.
    Includes bibliographical references and index.
    ISBN 0-934977-25-9
    1. Codex Calixtinus. Liber 5. 2. Christian pilgrims and
pilgrimages—Spain—Santiago de Compostela. 3. Cathedral of
Santiago de Compostela. 4. Santiago de Compostela (Spain)—
Religious life and customs. 5. Christian shrines—France.
6. Christian shrines-Spain. 7. Spain—Religious life and
customs. 8. France—Religious life and customs. I. Codex
Calixtinus. Liber 5. English. 1993. II. Title.
BX2321.S3M45 1993
263'.0424611—dc20   93-18623
                                                               CIP

Third (Revised) Printing
Printed in the United States of America
5 4 3

For Deena and Andrew,
who have just set out on life's longest pilgrimage

Santiago. Cathedral of Santiago. Nave. Late XI-early XII
C. In foreground, trumeau of the Pórtico de la Gloria, 1168-
1188.

CONTENTS

ILLUSTRATIONS

PREFACE

The uncommon interest that the pilgrimage road to Santiago de Compostela and its monuments in stone and parchment have generated in the last half century or so is parallel to the concomitant interest awakened during the same period by Romanesque form-culture. While the rise and evolution of the latter obeyed a number of heterogeneous factors, it was soon understood that the internationalization of the pilgrimage to Compostela and its early development in the eleventh and twelfth centuries constituted one of the avenues of expansion of the Romanesque. Pilgrimage-culture and Romanesque form-culture were perceived as organically intertwined.

The extent of that linkage, however, has remained a matter for debate, as much debated as the line of influence of the various great architectural monuments of the pilgrimage road. The passions of the past, fueled by ever-present national interests, have by now largely subsided, in part due to the sobering effects of ever-more rigorous historical methodologies, and in part due to the rather ecumenical climate which took hold of western Europe with the close of the hostilities of World War II.

In the background of this great revival of interest in the pilgrimage road and its monuments lie the vast hagiographic and ecclesiastico-historical works of the seventeenth and eighteenth centuries: Mabillon, Croiset, and Flórez only prepared the way for the nineteenth-century monuments of the Bollandists and Migne. Indeed, speaking to us from a past still anchored in the ancien régime, hagiography was the first avenue to become explored in depth, only to be forgotten one or two generations later. It is with such works in mind that López Ferreiro's lasting masterpiece of erudition of the years 1898–1911 concerning the Cathedral of Compostela must be evaluated. The great merit of López Ferreiro is that he undertook nearly single-handedly the study of a wide range of subjects concerning the pilgrimage, the route, and its monuments: he has become an indispensible reference up to our own times.

In the years between World Wars I and II Gómez Moreno, on the one hand, and Arthur Kingsley Porter, on the other, made deep inroads into the elucidation and interpretation of the monuments and sculptural representations of the pilgrimage road. While the Spanish scholar provided us with descriptive texts of these monuments, the Harvard art historian advanced theories which, though often invalidated by subsequent findings, proved instrumental in promoting significant debate and counter proposals: Kingsley Porter's Hispanic-centered, often idealistic, positions were, in fact, countered by a whole array of precisely documented and dated, mainly French, contributions: Gaillard, Lambert, Conant, and many others belong to this splendid historic school, which made virtue of the analytic study of precisely defined subjects. With Durliat, Moralejo, Williams, and Naesgaard this art-history school reached into our own days.

A somewhat parallel evolution occurred in the historical studies concerning the pilgrimage and the text of the *Codex Calixtinus*, too. Vázquez de Parga's multi-volume work on many aspects of the pilgrimage has remained highly valuable to our own times. Already Gaston Paris at the turn of the century, and Joseph Bédier and Menéndez Pidal more specifically later zeroed in on the, originally, fourth book of the *Codex*, the *Pseudo-Turpin* and its connections with the vast epic literature of the medieval West: the pilgrimage to and from Compostela was conceived as the great oral vehicle for the propagation of the *chansons de geste*. Such an engaging perspective too was destined to undergo considerable historical modulations.

Next in line came the material and historical infrastructure of the pilgrimage routes and of the pilgrimage itself – roads, bridges, hospices, supporting institutions, services, food, apparel, as well as the specific historical, social, economic, juridical, and medical aspects of the vast society of pilgrims, no less than symbolic, religious, liturgical, musical, and iconographic considerations related to the pilgrimage and to the cult of St. James. In these specific analytical studies La Coste-Messelière has shown us the way, followed subsequently by a whole army of prolific historians. Within the frame of such a new historicism, the text of the *Codex Calixtinus* was also submitted to incisive analytical study. Labande and David in France; Pérez de Urbel, Filgueira Valverde, and Díaz y Díaz in Spain; Schmugge, Plötz, and Herbers in Germany; Caucci von Saucken in Italy; and many others did much to set Jacobean studies upon firm historical tracks.

My own contribution has found its *Lebensraum*, on the one hand, in a specifically analytical reading of the text of the *Guide*, and, on the other, in the particular attention devoted to the hagiographical aspects of the account. The former endeavor generated the many notes as well as the Gazetteer; while the latter generated the Hagiographical Register as well as many other observations embedded in the general notes. By degrees the notion grew upon me that the medieval pilgrims saw in the route to Compostela a kind of Broadway of saints, of relics and of

PREFACE

reliquaries. The elaboration upon the notion of a Broadway of saints is one of the modest contributions of the present labor.

At this point a few observations concerning the structure and methodology of this work as well as suggested indications for its usage might be in order. The seven chapters of the Introduction in Part I are meant to be just that, introductory remarks that provide the reader with some ideologico-historical background in order to better understand the phenomenon of the pilgrimage to Compostela as a whole and of the *Pilgrim's Guide* in particular. This portion of the volume opens with a discussion of the fundamental interdependence of relics and pilgrimages and is followed by introductory chapters on the early history of St. James and the beginning of his cult in Spain; the historical coordinates that tied James to the Spanish *Reconquista* and to the French interests along the international pilgrimage route to Santiago; on the system of these routes in France and in Spain; on the structure of the *Liber Sancti Jacobi*; on the material, administrative, and juridical culture underlying the pilgrimage; and on the iconography of Santiago. The notes to Part I are mostly bibliographic, and in most cases they refer to works in the bibliography, using an abbreviated citation. Occasional cross-references lead to the notes to the text of the *Guide*, to the Hagiographical Register, or to the Gazetteer.

Part II opens with the English translation of the *Guide* and is followed by the corresponding notes. As to the translation, I have endeavored to produce a readable text and at the same time to preserve the outlandish idiosyncrasies of the original. The author of the *Guide* himself drew from several uneven sources, particularly for the long chapter 8 where he writes about the French saints along the road. Chapter 9, which contains a rather detailed description of the Cathedral of Compostela, is plagued by architectural expressions of doubtful or ambiguous meaning. For convenience sake, I have given section headings to the long gallery of French and Spanish saints in chapter 8. It should be noted too that the chapter headings that appear in the table of contents at the beginning of the *Guide* do not always correspond exactly to the chapter headings in the actual text. I have edited these to make them consistent.

The notes to the text of the *Guide* constitute the lion's share of this labor of love. Many of the notes deal with the interpretations of the text, and hence, they are of a philological nature. Others are concerned with historical, geographical, hagiographic, and art-historical matters. Whenever the need arises those notes are cross-referenced.

Since the text of the *Guide* places such an emphasis on saints, relics, and reliquaries, it seemed convenient to establish a Hagiographic Register of most of the saints mentioned. For these entries

XI

mostly French and German sources were utilized. Each entry is provided with a specific bibliography. The Gazetteer, on the other hand, collects practically all geographical terms of the *Guide* that relate to France and Spain. For the sake of clarity toponyms and geographical terms have been left in their original French or Spanish spelling. So too, the names of churches, monasteries, and ecclesiastical institutions. The names of saints, on the other hand, have been rendered in their common English version.

The bibliography is necessarily select: emphasis was placed, on the one hand, on ideological and historical contributions, and, on the other, on art-historical works. For the benefit of an English readership, as many works in English as possible were included. For the sake of brevity, each bibliographic term is provided with an abbreviation that has been used throughout the work. The rich hagiographic literature was included in the bibliographic entries throughout the Hagiographic Register. There has just appeared a comprehensive annotated bibliography on medieval pilgrimage in general.

The volume is so articulated that it is able to provide convenient access for a variety of readers: those mainly interested in the geography of the road shall focus on the corresponding chapters of the *Guide*, on the Gazetteer, as well as on some related notes; those chiefly interested in hagiography, the cult of relics, and reliquaries will turn to chapter 8 of the *Guide* and then to the Hagiographic Register; those interested in the description of the Cathedral of Santiago and in related art-history subjects will turn to chapter 9 of the *Guide* and the plentiful related notes; finally, those interested in a variety of other subjects will be able to find their way by the index as well as through the cross-references throughout the volume.

If this work is lucky enough to find at least some measure of sympathetic reception in the English-speaking world, and if it succeeds in awakening an interest in some aspect of this centuries-long human epic on the pilgrimage routes of Santiago de Compostela, then it will have accomplished its purpose. May the benevolent reader, not unlike the pilgrims on the road to Compostela approaching their longed-for goal, turn to the pages that follow with their hearts in their hands and the spark of Santiago in their eyes.

ACKNOWLEDGMENTS

The long-standing interest I have had in the pilgrimage route to Santiago de Compostela goes back to the early 1970s, a time when I had the good luck of becoming acquainted with the later Walter Muir Whitehill, in those years the Director of the Boston Athenaeum and *factotum* of a small but generous foundation that helped me out in the first two medieval bronze-door campaigns I have conducted. Walter Muir Whitehill set me on the track of the *Codex Calixtinus* of the Cathedral Archives of Compostela, a text of which he had already published a Latin transcription in the forties, and opened up for me generous vistas leading to the splendid Romanesque art of Santo Domingo de Silos and especially of the pilgrimage route proper to Santiago.

From the many challenges that the route to Santiago offered me over the years, I have developed an early and abiding interest in the iconography of Romanesque form-culture – the relief sculptures and wall paintings along the route. I have, in fact, been collecting for many years now a substantial documentation on the scenes of the Christological cycle of the pilgrimage routes, much of which is relatively little known. An ancillary interest, however, concerning the *Pilgrim's Guide* and the rich historical and artistic material contained in it soon developed. Foremost among these concerns was the notion of the medieval pilgrimage route to Compostela as a kind of Broadway of saints, relics and reliquaries that even for today's cultural standards – let alone for medieval tempers and levels of expectation – dazzles the visitor. Thus I soon saw myself embarked on the translation and annotation of the *Guide,* a task which, simple as it looked at the outset, grew ever more complex as the work progressed. The translation, as all translations, turned into interpretation, and the interpretation into commentary and a large set of background documentation. Projected as a one-year labor, it took nearly three.

Many were those who assisted me in this long endeavor. In the first line I remember the brotherly help and Franciscan care of the late Father Elías Valiña Sampedro, the living spirit of Cebrero. Father Elías had tended the Hispanic portion of the pilgrimage route at a time when few seemed to notice it, only to see himself outflanked when the road started to attract a new generation of enthusiasts. To him goes my admiration and my unqualified gratitude.

Next, I wish to express my deep thankfulness to the Reverend Canon Father José Maria Díaz Fernández, Archivist and Librarian of the Cathedral of Santiago de Compostela, who has generously made available to me over the years the *Codex Calixtinus* and who introduced me to the welcoming circle of the canons of the cathedral. Fathers Jesús Precedo, Alejandro, Celestino, Jaime, Manuel Silva, Silveiros, and others, to say it with a metaphor, have made of the cathedral a home for me.

On the western shores of the ocean, the support I have received over the years was no less generously committed. My colleagues at Syracuse University, Dr. Gershon Vincow, the Vice-Chancellor; Dr. Samuel Gorovitz, the Dean of the College of Arts and Sciences; Dr. Ronald Cavanagh, the Vice-President for Undergraduate Studies; Dr. Benjamin Ware, the Vice-President for Research and Graduate Studies; Mrs. Nirelle Galson, the Director of the Division of International Programs Abroad; Prof. Harold Jones, the Chairman of the Department of Languages and Literatures – they have all liberally assisted me in the necessary travels and research. To each of them, and to many other colleagues too numerous to name here, goes my sincere gratitude.

The stations of the route to Santiago have also offered me, whenever needed, their disinterested support: the *confrères* of the Abbey Church of Conques have always been magnanimous with the treasures in their jurisdiction; Dr. Denis Milhau, the Director of the Musée des Augustins in Toulouse, has been more than generous in providing me with free access to the magnificent ensemble of capitals in his collections; Don Abadia Armando Urieta, the Mayor of Jaca, and his right hand, Ms. Maria Carmen Castán, have supported me in a variety of ways over the years; the Reverend Father Miguel Lafonte, Director of the Cathedral Museum of Jaca, has generously opened his doors for me; the Reverend Father Juán Mariscal of Carrión de los Condes has at all times lent me a brotherly hand; Doña Amelia Valiña Sampedro and Doña Maria del Pilar Armesto Valiña of Cebrero have been like sisters to me; Don Gerardo Estébez, the Mayor of Santiago de Compostela, has shown me his benevolence on numerous occasions; finally, Prof. Flint Smith, the Director of Syracuse University's Study Center in Madrid, has lent me along the Hispanic portion of the road encouragement and brotherly assistance beyond the call of duty. To all these colleagues and friends, I wish to express here my sincerest thanks.

Before closing, I would like to thank Prof. Donald Mills of Syracuse University and my son John Melczer for having assisted me in the translation of some arduous expressions, and furthermore remember the librarians and the bibliographers without whose cooperation and kindness this work would never have seen the light. Dr. David Stamm and Dr. Metod Milaç, respectively the Director of the Syracuse University Libraries and the Curator of its Special Collections; Ms. Amy Blumenthal, Assistant Librarian at Cornell University Libraries; Mr. Javier Rey Souto, Assistant Librarian at the Archives of the Cathedral of Santiago de Compostela; Miss J. Warcollier, Secretary of the Société des Amis de Saint Jacques de Compostelle in Paris; Ms. Patricia Quaif and Ms. Lori Dennet of the Confraternity of Saint James of London; and Prof. Guillermo Bercerra, Administrative Director of Syracuse University's program in Madrid – have all been of a help too precious to adequately describe here.

Finally I turn with gratitude to Dr. Eileen Gardiner and Dr. Ronald Musto of Italica Press in New York City who have shown a Carthusian patience and understanding for my incorrigible Germanisms and Latinisms and who are responsible for any virtue that the ensuing text may have. Needless to say, inaccuracies, incongruencies, and errors are nobody's but mine.

In closing, my thoughts revert to those who have always been with me on this long pilgrimage of life: Eugenio and Magdalena, my parents, long since gone to sleep; my mother-in-law, Anna Kaltenbrunner-Bachzelt, also resting in the Lord; and Elisabeth, my faithful companion, without whose constant support and encouragement not only this labor but most of my other undertakings would have been futile. It was she, Elisabeth, who had first conceived the work that presently sees the light. At long last, as always, I am grateful to our sons, Peter, Andrew, and John, to whom I remain indebted more than I will ever be able to repay. This volume, in fact, is dedicated to one of the three, Andrew, together with the companion he chose for his pilgrimage in life, Deena.

Arles. Abbey Church of Saint-Trophime. Facade. Late XI C.

Saint-Gilles-du-Gard. Abbey Church. Facade. Late XI C.

Saint-Gilles-du-Gard. Abbey Church. Facade, partial view.
Late XI C.

Conques. Abbey Church of St.-Foy. Late XI C. General view from northeast (above). Tympanum sculpture of Last Judgment (below).

Santiago. Cathedral of Santiago. St. James as Santiago
Matamoros. Tympanum relief above fenestration. South
transcept. Early XII C.

Léon. Pantheon of the Leonese kings attached to San Isidoro.
Late XI C.

Santiago. Cathedral of Santiago. View of Facade, c. 1657.

Santiago. Cathedral of Santiago. Transcept. Late XI-early
XII C.

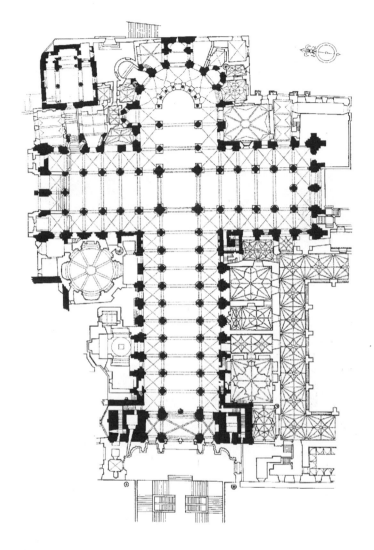

Santiago. Cathedral of Santiago. Floor Plan.

Santiago. Cathedral of Santiago. Pórtico de las Platerias.
Early XII C.

PART I – INTRODUCTION
RELICS AND PILGRIMAGES

The belief in and the reliance, to various degrees, upon enti-
ties, powers, and affinities in ways that utterly transcend understanding – that is to say, a mystic bent of mind – has been
a constant of human existence. Humanity, indeed, is a race of
individuals capable not merely of mental abstractions but also
of mystic abstractions. And medieval men and women were
more overtly and more explicitly so.[1]

The fundamentally mystic bent of the medieval mind conditioned its attitudes towards cult, devotion, and religious
practices; but it also conditioned its attitudes, no less prominently, towards the everyday pursuits of life. While the general desacralization ensuing from the Enlightenment and the
French Revolution turned away many from habitual devotional practices, within the province of everyday pursuits
we continue to be the sons and daughters of prehistoric
mystic rites: don't we all wear rings on our fingers? don't
we all sit *around* a table *partaking* from the same dish? and
don't we keep a framed photograph on our night table, an
imago standing for and reminding us of our beloved ones?
Medieval mysticism, thus, is not so far from the twentieth
century as one might often think. Furthermore, the mystic
bent of mind, and particularly devotional and religious mysticism, are not necessarily part and parcel of humanity's conscious self. Quite to the contrary. While granted that there
was and still is a highly conscious aspect of mystic rituals,
most such practices are eminently subconscious: they are the
children of life-long and even generation-long habits, which
we never question because they have been with us forever
and because everybody else practices them. Medieval men
and women, no less than their contemporary colleagues, did
most of what they did because it had been done by so many
and for so long.

The future is mortgaged on present expectations. The
bodily contact with material, physical objects variously
thought of as sacred, constituted perhaps the single over-

1

riding expectation, the brightest hope of Western medieval individuals. The underlying notion was that the sacred consecrates its immediate environment: hence the need to share that environment, the need for an unmediated contact with the sacred. The desire for consecration is then the reason that the medieval Christian partook of the Eucharistic sacrament, literally *incorporating* Christ, and thereby becoming Christ-like; and that is why they surrounded themselves with images whose faithfulness to the sacred prototypes assured their own sacredness. That is also the reason why they undertook pilgrimages to visit relics.[2]

The notion of sacred relic may be best described in terms of a cultural overlapping: on the one hand, the cult of the dead, widespread since prehistoric times; and, on the other, the belief in the thaumaturgical powers associated with personages held sacred. A vital component of the theory is the collateral notion according to which the earthly remains – hence *reliquiae*, that is to say, relics – of variously understood sacred figures are in themselves efficacious, thaumaturgical, and hence miracle-producing. Relics, therefore, are venerated twice: as part of the general cult of the dead and as a source of spiritual power and, hence, of miracle.[3]

But relics, as wine, do not travel well. In one of the oldest and, no doubt, fundamental Judeo-Christian rites, perpetuated to our own days, the dead are buried. And the tomb, which is a kind of a house of the dead, is always firmly localized, anchored to a specific place. It follows that the earthly remains of saints, their relics, are likewise localized, firm, unmovable. The best proof for the recognition of the essential immovability of relics is the medieval juridical notion of *furta sacra*, sacred thievery, the theft of saintly remains. Medieval theory held that if a stolen relic did not return to its original location, that was because it felt *comfortable* in its new one. Vis-à-vis the reality of the forced mobility and location change through stealth, the juridical code reaffirmed the right of the relic to permanence in its new home.[4]

Pilgrimage and relic are the two sides of the same coin. The one is conditioned by the other: the essential mobility of the pilgrimage is a function of the essential immovability of the relic; and the fixedness of the latter is predicated upon the mobility of the former. The ultimate goal of the pilgrimage is a visual and actually tactile contact with the sacred relic: the ideal pilgrim makes his weary way to see the saintly remains, to touch them. And if the relic itself cannot be touched – either because it is too ephemeral, like one single hair of Mary Magdalene, or too precious, like the entire earthly remains of an apostle – then the reliquary casket becomes a surrogate for the relic: one touches the casket or the sarcophagus instead of touching the relic. But the act of touching remains essential, of paramount significance: for all thaumaturgical powers, whether of a living saint or of his or her remains, become active, efficacious at the concrete physical, bodily contact. The physical presence, therefore, is a condition sine qua non: an age-old synagogue practice mandates the kissing of the Torah; Muslim *prostratio* assures a five-point contact with the surface of the earth because the spirit of Allah, having descended among his faithful, is dwelling on the surface of the earth; Christ's hand grazes the eye of the blind; St. Peter cures with his shadow. The mode of the physical contact may be variable; but its principle knows no compromise. Now, at the end of his journey and facing the relic, it is up to the pilgrim to take the last step, to establish the decisive contact. The moment when, after weeks and months of marching, he finally sees and touches the holy relic, he feels that the spiritual presence of the sacred is transferred, no matter to what minimal degree, into his own spirit, mind, intellect, and body. His feelings may be confused; but the presence of the sacred, remains for him a poignant, unmistakable reality. Our pilgrim has come to venerate: as he turns homeward, however, he himself becomes the great beneficiary of the process of veneration.[5]

The question arises: which relic should the pilgrim pursue? Whose saintly remains should he or she visit? Saints are as numerous as pebbles on the seashore. To whom to turn? In this regard, the Christian world of the Middle Ages, whether in the East or the West, was in no way at a loss: a precisely defined Christian hierarchy was eventually established – a densely populated celestial militia, arranged as if within a huge pyramid, on the top of which Christ Himself is enthroned; immediately under him we find the Virgin, and then the Twelve Apostles, St. John the Baptist and the most famous saints, such as Francis of Assisi, Anthony of Padua, Benedict of Aniane, Isidore of Seville. At the bottom of the pyramid, on the other hand, we find the humblest, the least famous, the barely local saint or merely virtuous personage who may be known merely in a village or two, perhaps only to a family or two. Between the top and the bottom of this celestial pyramid there are hundreds and thousands of martyrs, abbots, bishops, popes and prelates of all ranks, virgins, fathers of the Church, patriarchs, at times prophets, and an endless throng of saints. The theory governing this vast celestial militia is of a disarming simplicity: the principle of intercession. The faithful turns in prayers and invocations to the local martyr or saint, who then conveys the supplication upwards, through the endless hierarchical ranks, turning always to the next in line, until the pious message reaches Christ. At times Christ Himself, in a delicate interpretation of the Trinitarian principle, forwards the supplication to God the Father. To put it differently, the celestial militia operates much the same way as the ecclesiastical hierarchy of the Church on earth. Now it becomes evident why the faithful tries to place his or her supplication on the hierarchical ladder of relics as high as he or she possibly can.[6]

Theoretically, the highest relic – the earthly remains of Christ is, of course, a theological impossibility: after the Resurrection, the Lord ascended to heaven *in corpore*. If the earthly remains of Christ were thus out of the reach of the faithful, there was always the city whose very stones had felt the weight of His body and whose walls had witnessed his agony. Jerusalem, in fact, held a place of unquestioned pre-eminence among all pilgrimage sites. This was due partly to an old Hebrew tradition that harked back still to the times of the Temple of Solomon and the Second Temple of Zerubbabel. Jews used to come up to the Holy City bringing with them to the Temple the expected sacrifices.

Once Christianity became sufficiently well established, and not before the fourth century, Christian pilgrims – *palmers,* for the palm leaves they carried – started to arrive at the Holy City, never in large numbers but in a rather steady flow. Egeria, probably a native of Galicia, did so in the years 381–384. With the rise of Islam in the seventh century, matters came to a near halt. But in the later Middle Ages the flow of pilgrims picked up once again. Jerusalem was the site of the triumphal Entry of Christ, of the Last Supper, and of the Passion of the Lord. Nothing could match the level of interest and of devotional commitment to these events and to the sites and monuments associated with them. And then there was the Holy Sepulcher itself, the sarcophagus with its famous peeking holes through which pilgrims could indeed ascertain that it was empty: appropriately, a relic of the highest rank.[7]

But immediately after Christ and the monuments associated with His life and Passion – and quite apart from the Virgin Mary, whose veneration constitutes a problem sui generis, with a genial solution of its own – we have the magnificent, powerful and inspiring figures of the Twelve Apostles. The direct disciples of Christ, the bearers of his *mandatum*, the apostles have commanded the highest level of devotion since the early days of the Church. Their remains, in fact, were destined to be among the most sought-after relics in Christendom. Almost overnight, thus, Rome became a pilgrimage center of the utmost importance: apart from the Pontifical See itself, which was naturally interested in fostering its own visibility, the tombs of Peter and Paul were preserved in the Eternal City. Peter the Apostle ranked always first among the disciples of Christ; and it was upon his shoulders that the Ecclesia was destined to be erected. Paul, on the other hand, though without being, *stricto sensu*, among the original twelve, was rightly considered the Apostle of the Gentiles, equal in rank to the others. Thus, the place of Rome as a most significant repository of holy relics, and hence of pilgrimages, became firmly secured: *romeros* have flocked to the Eternal City ever since.[8]

Now, to be sure, the entire remains of one, and only one other apostle were known to be buried within the broader boundaries of western Europe: those of St. James the Greater, the son of Zebedee, whom a long tradition had intimately associated with Galicia and particularly with Santiago de Compostela. The place of eminence of James within the College of the Apostles is well established: together with Peter and John, they formed the inner circle of the twelve, those who had witnessed, even if under considerable stress, the theophany of the Transfiguration on Tabor. This alone would be more than sufficient to make Santiago de Compostela a pilgrimage center of the first order. But there is an additional reason why the pilgrimage road to Compostela has acquired over the centuries a nearly mythical reality of its own: it is organically integrated, more perfectly than the pilgrimage to either Jerusalem or Rome, into the cosmic cycle of seasons.[9]

We have left our ideal pilgrim at the moment of his turning homewards, himself the greatest beneficiary of his pilgrimage. He had been preparing himself for months, years, for a lifetime, for the great mystic encounter. Once that centerpiece of hope, fear, and expectation is over, enriched, elated, fulfilled with an acquired spiritual reality, he is ready to undertake his journey back.[10]

For pilgrimages are circular. Like sacred processions – whether around the Ka'aba in Mecca or with the Torah scrolls in the synagogue or around German country-churches at Christmas – they are progressions in a circle – one comes in order to return, not in order to stay; one fills oneself with the sacredness transpiring from the relic and one departs home. No one can stand for long the overbearing presence of the sacred: Moses descends from Sinai as soon as he possibly can; the three apostles are nearly blinded by the Transfiguration on Tabor; the soldiers must *necessarily* fall asleep in order to eschew witnessing the great mystery of the Resurrection. All in all, the circular quality of the pilgrimage, of any pilgrimage, presupposes, on the level of human experience, nature's essentially cyclic mode of regeneration: the two-beat alternation of death and renewal or, with the pilgrimage to Santiago de Compostela in mind, even the fourfold sequence of the seasons of the year.

Considering the pilgrimage from such a nature-governed cosmic perspective, winter and summer are metaphorically transmuted into home and abroad, the latter, to be sure, the much longed-for site of the sacred relic. Spring and fall, on the other hand, become the two legs of the journey: the former, towards the sacred site and the sacred contact with the miraculous relic; the latter, back to the village, the hamlet, back to everyday, often marginal, existence. If we consider for a moment that pilgrimages to Santiago from the distant central-European lands, as well as from Germany, took a span of time in the neighborhood of one year, that the most convenient seasons for the three to four months of marching each way were precisely spring and fall, and that it was reasonable to avoid a sojourn in Galicia during the cold winter months, it follows that spring was usually selected for eminently practical reasons too for the long journey to the far-off land. The cosmic wheel of the cycle of seasons, itself the daughter of nature, went thus hand in hand with considerations of practical feasibility. The pilgrim's progress in space and time became thus organically integrated into the larger cosmic progression of the four seasons.

We are ready now to proceed to the early history of St. James as well as to the consideration of the historical forces in the background of the pilgrimage to his tomb, forces that were interested in converting his relics into a focal point of national rally no less than international mass-movement.

THE ORIGIN OF THE CULT OF
ST. JAMES THE GREATER IN SPAIN

The origin of the cult of St. James in Galicia is wrapped in a shroud of darkness. Apart from a few scriptural and hence incontrovertible facts of his life, the early Hispanic connection of the saint, and, subsequent to his death, the *translatio* of his body, its burial and, centuries later, the rediscovery of his lost tomb are all part of a puzzle-work of quite incredible magnitude and complexity. Even for medieval historical standards for which clarity and reliability are not precisely a hallmark, the story of the cult of St. James – if relying on the documents at hand – is extremely confusing.[11]

As it clearly transpires from numerous passages in three of the four Gospels, James the Greater or the Major, the son of Zebedee and the brother of John, is one of the Twelve Disciples of Christ, one of the faithful fishermen of Galilee. In fact, when Christ encounters him for the first time, James, together with John, is mending his nets. Beyond his general participation in the Christological events however, together with Peter and John, James belongs to the most weighty and significant among the followers of Christ, to the inner circle of the apostles. The Lord surnames him and his brother "Sons of Thunder" and, early enough, responsibilities of particular weight will be placed upon his shoulders. At exceptionally delicate moments of His ministry, Christ allowed no one close to Him except Peter, James, and John. The two brothers are, significantly enough, present at the miraculous fishing; later, however, when the Master is asked to allow James and John to be seated at his right and left in

7

His Glory, the Lord does not hesitate to teach them a lesson in humility (Matt. 20.20–28). It is only after these preparatory steps, as is to be expected, that the three of the inner circle witness, even if fallen on their faces and scared, the great and overwhelming theophany of Mount Tabor; and similarly, heavy with sleep, they bear testimony to the agony of the Lord in the Garden of Gethsemane.[12] James the Greater's martyrdom is conveyed in the Acts of the Apostles in the briefest and starkest terms: "King Herod...beheaded James, the brother of John." It was then AD 42.[13]

From the third and fourth centuries stem the first narratives expanding upon the gospel accounts concerning James. By degrees, a considerable *amplificatio* is effected, in the main upon the single moment of his martyrdom, which now becomes extraordinarily enriched.[14] In the fifth and sixth centuries the *Passio Jacobi* comes thus into being cast finally in its written mold somewhere in southeastern France, probably in the Languedoc or along the Rhône. Subsequent to the story of fervent proselytizing and preaching in the Holy Land, the account of the martyrdom proper is taken up together with the events that led to it, the whole segmented along complex narrative lines.

James converts the dreadful magus Hermogenes who previously had quite indiscriminately exercised his dark powers, as well as his pupil Philetus. Word of the strange occurrences reaches the ears of the establishment. Arrested by Lysias and Theocritus, commanders of the centurions in Jerusalem, James is thrown into prison. Even from behind bars he relentlessly pursues proselytizing: intervening as well as he can in a discussion taking place outside the prison, he converts several disputants. For the authorities, evidently, he is rapidly turning from an embarrassing, occasional nuisance into a threatening public danger. Abiathar, the high priest, decides now to step in. He contrives a scheme in order to eliminate James. A vociferous and rebellious demonstration is organized in the Holy City, and soon after the blame is put at James's door. Accused of seditiousness, James is brought before Herod Agrippa with a rope around his neck held fast by the scribe Josias. Herod pronounces the guilt sentence and hands out the orders for James's execution. On the way to his decapitation James meets a cripple and heals him. Upon seeing this miracle, Josias is moved to the bottom of his heart, and he too converts. Once the execution ground is reached, both are beheaded.[15]

The account of the martyrdom of James, lengthy as it is, follows in several of its episodes accepted typological patterns of Christian martyrdom: the scheming establishment trying to concoct some legal justification, no matter how transparent, for the execution; the miracle performed on the way; the conversion of one of the henchmen; the chain reaction elicited by the miracles of the would-be martyr; and the multiplication of the martyrdom.[16] The portion of the account covering the conversion of Josias appears already in Clement of Alexandria, and nearly the whole of it in the *Historia ecclesiastica* of Eusebius of Caesarea. The martyrdom of James the Greater had thus been established beyond any reasonable doubt.[17] Now the region of his evangelizing campaign must be determined.

But the accounts on James's evangelizing are not as univocal as those on his martyrdom. His proselytizing activities in the Holy Land are seen as the prelude only for more portentous undertakings. The original Twelve Disciples of Christ had a mission to fulfill. Christ's pronouncement at the time of the Washing of the Feet, *mandatum novum do vobis* ("I give you a new mandate"), has always been interpreted *sensu lato* as the injunction to spread the Good Tidings throughout the world. The very term used for the disciples, *apostle*, carries in its Greek etymology – *apostello*, to send forth – the very essence of their existence. When, at Pentecost, tongues of fire descended on them and each began to speak a foreign language, the groundwork was laid down for their mission to the far corners of the world. It remained to be determined where each one would direct his steps. The apocryphal *Gospel of the Twelve Holy Apostles* establishes that Latin had fallen into James's lot. Latin, as a matter of course, was a generic pointer towards the West. This would have to be further refined to make it refer to Spain.[18]

But things are not as simple as that. Paul's Epistle to the Romans speaks of his seeing his brethren "on his way to Spain," and later he states even more explicitly that he "shall set out for Spain." Paul's supposed journey to the far European west, denied in some quarters and accepted in others, had a Roman epicenter.[19] There was, however, a second and even more tightly Rome-centered tradition that claimed for

Peter himself the honorific task of the evangelization of Spain. The emphasis on Peter and hence on the episcopal see of Rome sought, in the years after Alaric's devastation of the Eternal City, to restore the prestige of Rome. It was precisely Innocent I, in the early fifth century, who sponsored the notion of Peter's involvement in the Iberian peninsula, involvement to which an ancillary tradition was at times conjoined, that of the seven preachers sent by Peter and Paul to Spain. Even King Recaredo's efforts to strike a balance between his desire for independence of the national Visigothic Church and the necessary submission to Rome ratified in the famous Council of Toledo of 589, must be understood within the framework of the pontifical Curia's attempts at Roman apostolic predominance.[20]

There are, on the other hand, a number of entries in various important ecclesiastical documents or otherwise works of ecclesiastical purport that propound precisely the pioneering apostolate of James the Greater in the evangelization of Spain. The *Breviarium apostolorum* of the sixth or seventh century, a Latin text derived from a Greek original written somewhere in the Byzantine realm, speaks of the preaching, martyrdom, and burial of James:

> Jacobus qui interpretatur subplantator filius Zebedei frater Johannis. Hic Spaniae et occidentalia loca praedicatur et sub Herode gladio caesus occubuit sepultusque est in Achaia Marmarica VIII. kal. Augustas,

that is to say, "James, whose name should be interpreted as the one who follows, the son of Zebedee, the brother of John, preached in Spain and in the western regions; struck with a sword, he died, under Herod, and was buried in Achaia Marmarica on July 25." Leaving aside for a moment the question of the place of burial, the *Breviarium* keeps intact the tradition of the martyrdom of James in Judea, proposes for the apostle a necessary journey to and from Spain, a journey which had to take place by a tacitly agreed-upon logic before the martyrdom.[21] The mentioning of the tacitly agreed-upon logic is here no tongue-in-cheek remark: following a later and most venerable tradition, the body of James will travel to Spain a second time after the martyrdom, and the saint himself will physically reappear at the head of his faithful, mounted on a white horse, and will lead them to the victory of the *Reconquista*.[22] It is then this notion of James's first

travel to Spain that will be taken up in a number of eighth-
and ninth-century works, with collateral subjects occasionally added to it depending upon the individual idiosyncratic
treatment.

Aldhelm of Malmesbury, who died in 709, in his *Carmen
in duodecim apostolorum aris,* amplifies the bare notion of
preaching: James converts the Spanish nations.[23] A text attributed to Isidore of Seville, *De ortu et obitu patrum,* received
in the eighth century an interpolation that speaks of the
preaching of James throughout Spain, of his burial, and of
a letter sent by the saint to the Twelve Tribes in the disper-
sion. This last reference seems to carry a double significance:
on the one hand, for the Twelve Tribes of Israel in the
diaspora; and, on the other, for the converted Jews, that is
to say the Christians of Jewish origin.[24] The celebrated *Commentary on the Apocalypse* of Beatus of Liebana, one of the
most famous and popular works of the eighth century in
the northern regions of Spain, and to a considerable extent
also elsewhere in the West, contains an inventory of the
provinces of the world, each with its corresponding evangelizing apostle. Within such *divisio apostolorum,* Spain is
allotted to the cares of James the Greater.[25] A particularly
important witness for the consolidation of the notion of the
Hispanic Jacobean connection is the hymn, also from the
eighth century, *O dei verbum patris,* which is at times also
attributed to Beatus of Liebana, though lately such assignation has been proved misdirected or at least dubious.
The hymn constitutes a highly complex piece of writing
ascribed to December 30, the feast of St. James in the
Visigothic-Mozarabic Church.[26]

Interest in this hymn lies in the parallel it proposes between twelve precious stones and the Twelve Apostles. The
catalogue of the twelve stones corresponds to the four rows
of three stones each decorating the ephod of Aaron's priestly
robe in Exodus. The precious stones of Aaron, quite naturally, stand for the Twelve Tribes of Israel. The allegorical
correspondence between stones and tribes had been considerably expanded before the *O dei* hymn in a Syriac hom-
ily, authored possibly by one Marutha, that included also
the apostles. There are several other early sources propos-
ing the analogy with the apostles, with or without the
tribes.[27]

11

A second interest of the hymn rests in the apportion-
ment of the regions or provinces of the world to the various apostles, and in particular in the definition of the role
of James. He is not merely enumerated next to his corresponding province, as it happens with the rest of his companions but, left to the very end, is first defined as *potius
Ispania*, the conqueror of Spain, and subsequently given a
full strophe of praise. There, among others, James the
Greater is called *caput refulgens aureum Ispanie*, and furthermore, *tutorque nobis et patronus vernulus*, our protector and patron helper. This amounts to something close
of declaring St. James the Patron of Spain. The pairing of
apostles with provinces occurs in most cases observing
established relationships. In the case of a few apostles,
however, considerable idiosyncratic treatment, and even
sui generis interpretation is evident: the inclusion or omis-
sion of Thaddeus is often a problem; the identity of Judas
with Thaddeus is another; Matthias is at times confused
with Mattheus; and there are more. The position of James
the Greater as the evangelizer of Spain in the eighth-century texts quoted above, on the other hand, is fairly firm,
though from time to time James the Lesser is confused
with our James. This is not to say that if we scrutinized
broader chronological parameters we would not find at
times an occasional discordant voice: as early as the fourth
century, Ephrem the Syrian, in his commentary on the
Diatessaron of Tatianus, sends James to Gaul and Paul to
Spain; and Ado of Vienne, of whom more will be said later,
will do something similar at a surprisingly late date, in
the middle of the ninth century.[28]

Apart from a few differing inflections though, by the end
of the seventh century and to further degree by the eighth,
James became, by and large, accepted as the evangelizer of
Spain, and his return to the Holy Land was tacitly understood in order to square his proselytizing activities in
Hispania with the evangelical account of his martyrdom in
Judea. There remained the problem of the *translatio* of his
body. This matter is addressed by a number of ninth-century texts. Ado of Vienne, in his revision of the *Martyrologium*
of Florus of Lyons, as well as in the *Libellus de festivitatibus SS
Apostolorum*, both mid-century texts, speaks of the *translatio*
of the remains of James to Spain, their burial close to the

British sea – this cannot be anywhere but in Galicia – and their subsequent veneration:

> Hujus beatissimi apostoli sacra ossa ad Hispanias translata et in ultimum earum finibus, videlicet contra mare Brittanicum condita, celeberrima illarum gentium veneratione excoluntur.[29]

The famous *Martyrologium of Usuard*, of the third quarter of the century, and Notker Balbulus of St. Gall, a little later, report the *translatio* in terms similar to those of Ado. The line of transmission of the notions included in these accounts, as well as the transmission of the texts themselves, are by no means clear. In particular, it is not certain whether Usuard borrowed directly from Florus or from Ado's revision of Florus. There is also the good possibility that the above-quoted passage from Ado is a somewhat later interpolation, for in a work written *after* his revision of Florus's *Martyrologium*, the *Chronicon*, he ignores James and returns to the theory of the apostolate of Paul. But, be that as it may, it can be said in general terms that most of these important ninth-century texts speak in confident terms of James's *translatio* and his burial in Galicia.[30]

It was under Alphonso II, king of Asturias and Galicia (792–842), and under Bishop Theodemir of Iria Flavia that the long-forgotten tomb of James was claimed to have been rediscovered. Alphonso II readily understood the political significance of the discovery and eagerly seized upon it, in the first line, for the sake of the consolidation of his fragile kingdom. A few years earlier, the author of the above-cited *O dei* had tried to do something similar by providing the hymn with an acrostic in honor of the usurper king of Asturias, Mauregatus. But the poet of the *O dei* had been operating among the relative abstractions of wishful reflection fueled by pious theological or religious intentions. Now Alphonso II had something more concrete, something tangible and visible in his hands: the tomb, a definable geographic location, the beginning of a cult.[31] The old Greek sources had spoken of a toponym, *en polei tes Marmarikes*, in the city of Marmarikes, where, at some point, the remains of James the Greater had been buried. It is not to be excluded that some intermediate stop on the long way of the *translatio* might be hidden in this toponym, though nothing certain can be demonstrated: perhaps the Monastery of St. Catherine in the Sinai built by Justinian, or the famous Coptic Monastery of Mennas near Alexandria, or some point in Cyrenaica further to the west. The fact remains that the designation became, with the passing of time, corrupted by degrees into *achaia marmarica,* and from there into *arce marmarica* or *in arcis marmaricis* or *sub arcis marmaricis.* The corruption occurred not merely on the literal but also on the conceptual level: the toponym ended up being understood as a designation for an architectural description, a marble tomb under an arch, possibly in a vaulted chamber.[32]

With the rediscovery of the tomb of James the Greater we are entering into a period of relative historical concretion, of relative historicity. Such historicity, in terms of what we like to call *facts,* is however no less defined by the reading we make of them than the earlier reviewed documentary accounts are defined by the meaning we attach to them. The facts will become subjected now to the impact of interpretations and these will depend on local as well as larger international ideologico-political forces whose intent will be to capitalize on the fortunate discovery. The overlapping of myth upon history, the fruitful exchange between them, as well as their conversion into each other provide thus for the more recent period of the *traditio Sancti Jacobi* a particularly fertile breeding ground for historical attitudes and motivations.

MYTH AND HISTORICAL REALITY IN THE TRADITION OF ST. JAMES

In 710 or 711, when at the head of Islamized Berber tribes, Tarik-Ibn-Zaid crossed the strait to which he gave the name – from Jebel el-Tarik, the mountain of Tarik, derives Gibraltar – he could have hardly realized that he had opened the single most crucial chapter in Hispanic history. None of the weighty historical developments of earlier times – the Roman conquest and the Visigothic, as well as the other Barbarian invasions – or, for that matter, of later epochs, had on Spain the profound and lasting impact that Islam imprinted on its history and its culture. The influence of over eight centuries of Islamic presence in Spain was in itself of the highest significance – enough if we think of the remarkable socio-economic and religious tolerance among

Muslim, Christian, and Jewish communities in the cities of al-Andalus. The ultimate impact of Islam, however, must be measured also in terms of the political developments that its presence in the peninsula brought in its wake. Foremost among these is the centuries-long Christian drive toward the south in a politico-religious effort to eliminate the foothold of Islam from the peninsula – what is called, in short, the *Reconquista* – itself integrated at a later point into the wider parameters of the crusade against the infidels. The rediscovery of the long-forgotten tomb towards the end of the eighth century occurred, tellingly enough, at a time when the Christian political fortunes in the land were at their lowest ebb; it occurred at a time when the living presence of a religious-national figure of apostolic grandeur, who would be capable of rallying around himself the Christian forces at bay, was a dire need. The presence of Saint James – Sanctus Iacobus, that is to say, Santiago – no matter to what extent mythical and legendary, fulfilled, indeed, such a historical necessity.[33]

Only the northernmost regions of the peninsula, beyond the fruitful central high plains, remained unconquered by Islam: the harsh and cold climate, forbidding mountainous nature, and hostile environment, all contributed to their exclusion from the domains of al-Andalus. It is little wonder that in these northern provinces opposition to Islam struck its first roots.

The provincial kingdom of Asturias was the very first to rally itself to the call.[34] As so often in such circumstances, however, the targeted foe soon multiplied: on the one hand, the powerful Islamic dominions in the south and foremost the mighty Caliphate of Córdoba; on the other, the well-entrenched ecclesiastical establishment of Toledo. The external foe found itself in the company of an unexpected internal partner with whom to share the burden of enmity. The antagonism vis-à-vis the former needed no particular justification. The infidels were a thousand-faced monster on whom any number of disparaging epithets could be hanged. But the opposition to the ecclesiastical establishment in Toledo did need one.

Ever since the times of the great Barbarian migrations, Toledo had been the undisputed metropolitan of the Visigothic Church. It is there that many church councils had been held; it is there that St. Eugene, the city's first bishop,

had been beheaded; it is there that King Recaredo had renounced in 589 some of the Visigothic ideological prerogatives and bowed to Roman Catholic preeminence; it is there
that the Virgin herself appeared in 666 to St. Ildephonsus
bestowing upon him the famous bishopric chasuble and
thereby extending to the city her particular protection. But
now Islam had engulfed most of the Hispanic territories and,
of course, Toledo itself; and the Visigothic capital, as if nothing had happened, continued to sit tight on its ecclesiastical
privileges; except that the Visigothic hierarchy, in a characteristic deference to, but also compromise with, the new
masters had been, so to speak, supplanted by a Visigothic-
Mozarabic one. *Mozarabs*, in fact, carried in their very designation the second class political citizenship they were condemned to bear. Such dependence and compromise, which
from the outside smacked of servility vis-à-vis Islam, was
looked upon askance and with distaste by Oviedo, the
Asturian capital that saw itself as the newly-born paladin of
the *Reconquista*. Yesterday was yesterday, but today is today,
the Asturians must have muttered. A theological bone of
contention was readily found: adoptionism – the theory according to which Christ was the adopted Son of God. Now,
perhaps conveniently enough, adoptionist theories were
sustained by somebody as highly placed as the Primate Archbishop of Toledo, Elipandes. Both the theories and their promoter were violently impugned and indicted by the great
ideological representative of northern Visigothic circles, the
Beatus of Liebana. The theological controversy, however, only
concealed more tangible matters: hierarchical prerogatives
and ecclesiastical power.[35]

It was not in eighth- and ninth-century Asturias, however,
but in tenth- and eleventh-century Aragón, Navarra, and
León that a political game of higher stakes was destined to
be played out. The overlords of these territories – kings of
various political weight, from ephemeral to substantial to
heavy – had understood that any chance for success in re-
gaining some of the territories lost to Islam was predicated
upon ultramontane collaboration. Such a collaboration took
up three main forms. One of these was interested political
marriage: Alphonso VI, at the time already king of León,
Castilla, and Galicia, led to the altar Constance, the daughter of the duke of Burgundy, Robert the Elder; and the daughter of Alphonso, Urraca, followed suit by her union, in first

marriage, to Raymond, a count of the same Burgundian house. Several of the Aragonese kings were also looking towards the east for advantageous wedlocks. Sancho Ramírez espoused the sister of a great baron of Champagne, and Pedro I, the daughter of Guillaume VIII, the powerful duke of Aquitaine.[36]

The second form of collaboration, a direct counterpart to the above dynastic connections, was military assistance. In this case too, not only the Spanish recipients but their providers too were interested partners: military support has at all times constituted a handy way of asserting influence – this time French influence on the peninsula. Already Sancho el Mayor of Navarra had entertained more than friendly relations with the count of Bearn, the duke of Aquitaine, and even with Robert the Pious, king of France. Such a Francophile opening was continued by Sancho's son, Ferdinand I, and by his grandson, Alphonso VI. The lordship of the former over the northern and northeastern portions of the meseta was not attained without French auxiliary contingents, and the ever-vaster territorial conquests of Alphonso, including the conquest of Toledo, would not have been quite possible without the attending Burgundian cavalry. The reconquest of the fruitful valley of the Ebro, including Huesca and Zaragoza, for long the primary goal of the Aragonese kings, was made a reality only after the active assistance of French troops was assured.[37]

With the *Reconquista* of territories came also the protracted but vitally important process of the *repoblación*, the resettlement of land, villages, and towns. Alphonso and his colleagues soon learned to take advantage of two closely integrated socio-economic ingredients resulting from the bonanza of the *Reconquista*: on the one hand, the pilgrimage route, or better routes, as a mainly transversal axis of stability within the newly conquered territories; and on the other, the foreign, mainly French, *Landsmannschaften* that settled in particular quarters of towns and villages, not without enjoying considerable economic advantages offered to them quite liberally by the Hispanic administration.[38]

The third form of ultramontane collaboration, perhaps less eagerly sought after than offered, took the form of ecclesiastical and particularly monastic penetration. The old idea of the Asturian kingdom of carving out for itself a Visigothic Church not subject to the dictates of the

Visigothic-Mozarabic hierarchy of Toledo was seized upon once again and forcefully pursued by Ferdinand I of León, Castilla, and Navarra, the son of Sancho el Mayor. At the epicenter of this idea lay the struggle for hierarchical supremacy and hence for ecclesiastical power in its manifold manifestations. Mutually favorable relations with the great reformed Benedictine Order of Cluny had been started already by Sancho el Mayor and continued under his son and grandson, no doubt as a political leverage of considerable weight. The politico-military entente alluded to earlier played no little part in the establishment of such monastic linkage.[39]

Under Sancho el Mayor a reform was undertaken at the great Monastery of San Juan de la Peña, a reform that reminds us, in so many ways, of Cluny: increased economic activity, emphasis on the divine service, charitable undertakings of many sorts, including hospitals and hospices. Independence was jealously guarded, but sympathies for the spirit of the Cluniac reform went unconcealed. San Juan de la Peña, itself a pioneering settlement, became the head of a chain of monasteries. One of its elected abbots had previously resided for years in the famous Burgundian abbey. In 1071 the Roman Catholic rite substituted the Visigothic one in the Aragonese monastery, and in 1080 that same rite was declared mandatory throughout all the liberated territories.[40] In the reorganized episcopal sees French ecclesiastics were often appointed: such were Pons, formerly a monk of Sainte-Foy of Conques, and Raymond, formerly prior of Saint-Sernin of Toulouse. As San Juan de la Peña in Aragón, so Sahagún in León: both monasteries obtained political and ecclesiastical exemptions. Sahagún also surrounded itself with a string of dependent monastic settlements. Here too, one after another, French monks were appointed as abbots of important abbeys. One of these, Bernard de Sedirac, would eventually become the archbishop of Toledo subsequent to the fall of the city into Christian hands in 1085. It is at that point that Alphonso VI, crowning a semi-independent Spanish drive for the *Reconquista*, also crowned himself by assuming the imperial title.

It is by realizing the depth and the extent of the French involvement in the early phases of the *Reconquista* that we might better understand the concomitant French interests in sponsoring the cult of St. James. As the *Reconquista* identified itself with its patron saint, Santiago, so the ultramontane interests in a general anti-Islamic stand turned supportive of the, by now, Galicia-centered apostolic cult. To these general politico-religious propensities, economic interests, whether real or envisaged, were in due time also associated. Furthermore, the bishops of Gaul, as well as the powerful monastic reform movements of Cluny and Clairvaux, had always been on the lookout for ways of counteracting, at least in part, the hierarchical preeminence of Rome. The gradual consolidation of the Hispanic cult of St. James provided a splendid opportunity for pursuing such a policy of diversification: next to Peter and Paul in Rome, James would shine henceforth in Galicia. Connected to such ecclesiastico-political concerns, the strictly economic advantages for France, on French territory, of an international mass pilgrimage to Galicia could not have escaped at least some of the Gallic minds. German pilgrims would henceforth traverse the vast French plains to reach the Pyrenees. The preeminence of Roman and, via the Italian ports, the Jerusalem pilgrimages would thus be at least in part counterbalanced and perhaps even held in check.[41]

The French involvement with the *Reconquista* and the cult of St. James had a further source from which it was able to derive inspiration and strength: Charlemagne. The emperor represented an inexhaustible trove of imaginative wealth that kept feeding for centuries the minds of the large masses on both slopes of the Pyrenees. Central to the Carolingian contributions is the story of Charlemagne's army withdrawing from the peninsula after a successful military operation against the infidels. In the narrow mountain passes of the Pyrenees the Christian contingents were suddenly attacked by a Muslim army in an unequal and unchivalrous engagement. A handful of paladins, the rearguard of the army under the leadership of Roland, put up a heroic struggle in the course of which all of them were slain. But the bulk of the army, in the meanwhile, contrived to cross the mountains and reach the safe plains on the French side.

The story is simple enough. But magnified a thousand times by the force of a magnificent epic-poetic masterpiece, the *Chanson de Roland*, the story had become for centuries the ultimate symbol of the medieval Christian West. The fact that what actually was an insignificant melee with Basque irregulars is exalted to the level of an apocalyptic confrontation between Christians and Muslims, between good and evil, does not detract from the value of the story. Quite to the contrary: what is essential is whatever settles in the mind of the masses, whatever becomes living, invigorating, active myth, capable of feeding the spirit and strengthening the will and the arm. In the repeated enactment of this monumental epic tragedy on the roads and in the minds of the West, the emperor is exalted as the safeguard of Christianity; Roncevaux or Roncesvalles, where the supposed battle had taken place, becomes a geographical relic; Roland and his paladins turn into uncanonized saints whose remains are visited at Blaye; Roland's mythical sword, the rock parted by its blows, his battle horn become like many displayed relics. An indication of the widespread international influence of the Carolingian legend may be gathered from the fact that on Spanish soil we find quite a number of relief representations of the hand-to-hand engagement of Roland and an infidel knight, and that in Germany a large number of gigantic Roland figures have become symbols of civic fortitude: we find them on the exterior wall of city halls.[42]

The connection of this Carolingian tradition with St. James is apparent already from the fact that both sites, Roncesvalles and Blaye, were made part of the route to Santiago. Furthermore, Charlemagne's campaign and Roland's combat against the infidels were understood as a contribution to the drive of the *Reconquista*. But there is a further and more direct link between the Carolingian emperor and St. James: it is the famous dream of Charlemagne. St. James appears in a dream before the astonished emperor and promises him the possession of Galicia; Charlemagne sees a starry way on the sky and is told to follow it in order to get to the saint's tomb. At times the representation of the legend includes further episodes, such as the scene before the walls of Pamplona where the emperor implores the help of St. James and, when the latter appears, the walls of the city cave in.[43] The dream of Charlemagne capitalizes on the mythical stature that the emperor enjoyed in Gallic consciousness, no less than on the deep biblical and Constantinian reverberations evoked by the very notion of a dream. The starry way in the sky, for its part, reminds the medieval mind of the stars the shepherds saw over the wondrous site in Galicia which alerted them in the first place to some miraculous occurrence. The tradition of Charlemagne's double link to St. James – his place in the struggle against the infidels and his miraculous dream, not to speak of a further story that makes him the first pilgrim to Santiago – went a long way to providing a convenient historical and mythical cushion for later French interests in St. James and in the pilgrimage road to his sanctuary.

We have arrived now to the point in which we ought to turn our attention once again back to the tomb of St. James. Subsequent to the miraculous *inventio* of the tomb in the first half of the ninth century by Bishop Theodemir of Iria Flavia who was summoned to verify the stellar portents in the sky noticed by the shepherds, a first chapel was built over the sepulcher by Alphonso II. Theodemir's central role played in the *inventio* is attested, at least in part, by his tombstone bearing the date of his death in 847, found lately in excavations in the cathedral. The geographic site, Compostela, in one of its possible etymological derivations, is made to hark back to *campus stellae*, the field of stars that appeared to the eyes of the astonished shepherds. There are, however, other alternatives for the etymology of the toponym: from *composita*, well-dressed ground; or from the syncopated form of *compositum*, derived from *componere* in its meaning of "to bury." Be that as it may, the cult struck roots. By the end of the ninth century Alphonso III saw himself compelled to turn the chapel into a three-aisled pre-Romanesque church which was consecrated in 899. Nearly a century later, in 997, Al-Mansur raided Santiago de Compostela, burned the city, destroyed the south aisle of the church and carried off its bells to Córdoba. Al-Mansur's intervention was terrible but short-lived. Bishop Pedro Mezozo initiated the reconstruction immediately.[44]

It was, however, towards the end of the eleventh century, under the bishopric of Diego Peláez, that a conscious and aggressive program of dignifying the apostolate of James and of exaltation of the city of Santiago as a "second Rome" took place. Diego Peláez was harsh, outspoken, and without the necessary subtleties required by a delicate political game that put forth a guarded attitude vis-à-vis Rome and at the same time pursued a fierce line of independence from Cluniac and Burgundian influences. Soon he found himself committed on too many fronts and on none of them advantageously. In the meanwhile, though, some important advances did take place. In 1078, as the last of the large pilgrimage churches, the building of the vast Romanesque Cathedral of Santiago was begun: it would, henceforth, proclaim its magnificence until our own day. In 1095, furthermore, under Urban II, the bishopric see was transferred from Iria Flavia to Santiago.[45] At that critical point someone was needed with a very particular combination of vision, energy, sense of reality, and political finesse: only he would be able to draw together the many dangling ends as well as, by a mighty last drive, to provide an appropriate Compostelan framework for the extant tradition of the cult of St. James in Spain. That statesman turned out to be Diego Gelmírez.

Chancellor of the count of Galicia, chief administrator of the diocese of Santiago, bishop in 1100 and archbishop in 1120, Diego Gelmírez controlled ecclesiastical politics in Galicia until his death in 1140. In contradistinction to Peláez, Gelmírez reactivated the old connection with France and particularly with Burgundy so strenuously pursued by former kings and in particular by Alphonso VI.[46] Such a connection proved to be of the utmost importance as leverage at home and abroad. The Burgundian sympathies turned out to be of the greatest advantage when Guy, archbishop of Vienne and brother of the deceased count of Galicia, Raymond, ascended to the papal throne as Calixtus II.[47]

Throughout his long leadership at the helm of the church and later of the Cathedral of Santiago, Gelmírez dived sufficiently into royal dynastic affairs, no less than controversies, and was able thereby to accrue political advantages for the archiepiscopal see. Even more importantly, while championing a general allegiance to the Roman Curia, he knew how to assure privileges and commissions for Santiago de Compostela and, thanks to his special relationship to Calixtus II, to obtain for the Galician apostolic see the coveted metropolitan title previously held by Mérida. True that he was unable to forestall the secession of Portugal from Galicia and León, and that he tried in vain to force the hand of Toledo to release its grip from the primateship it had been holding for so long; but, capitalizing on French and Cluniac connections, he bolstered Santiago as a kind of a second epicenter of Western Christendom and realistically evaluated the pilgrimage to St. James – in his time already a mass movement – as perhaps the most important tool of power at his disposal.[48] Two documentary writings of great importance came down to us concerning the vast undertakings in, around, and centering upon Santiago de Compostela during the forty or so years that Gelmírez was active in the city: the *Historia compostelana*, a work of apologetic and glorifying nature, and the *Liber Sancti Jacobi*, a compilation concerning St. James, the pilgrimage to his relics, and the Carolingian connection. These works are part of a historical reality in the making, to which Gelmírez had contributed no small measure.

That is the way history advances, in leaps and bounds: at times constructing bulwarks of reality from which ideals, projects, programs, but also beliefs and persuasions eventually rise – what are these if not mythical components of the future? – and at others building on legendary accounts lost in the unfathomable well of the past out of which, in due time, new historical realities are forged. The history of the cult of St. James in Spain is made up of such disparate components, some mythical, others factual, intimately interacting with and feeding on each other. All told, the legends of the distant past and the hopes associated with an unknown future were the mythical forces that fueled the reality of the cult of St. James, a cult that was focused upon the concrete parameters of an urban center around the rediscovered tomb, as well as upon a mass movement of pilgrims that from the Christian West, channeled through the four French roads, made their weary way to Santiago de Compostela.

THE ITER SANCTI JACOBI

The Road to Compostela is nothing but a metaphor.[49] By the mid-eleventh century western Europe, including eastern and northern Spain, was crisscrossed by a complex network of roads, partly ancient Roman pavements, partly high-medieval itineraries that served, among many other purposes, to facilitate the pilgrimage to the Galician shrine. At the same time, with the increasing focus of interest on Santiago in the late eleventh and early twelfth centuries, a number of specifically Jacobean roads came into being, most of them dirt surfaces, with their own appropriate infra-structure of hospices, bridges, chapels, and reliquary churches. The hermit Domingo, before the turn of the century, had repaired a portion of the old Roman road between Nájera and Redecilla del Camino. Moreover, pilgrimage roads were submitted to periodic inspection. One *Petrus peregrinus* was charged with the specific task of restructuring the mountain road leading into Galicia between Rabanal del Camino and Puertomarín. As time went on and pilgrimages multiplied, the powerful reformed Benedictine Monastery of Cluny was given in trust a number of key sites along the way: first in Nájera, Palencia, and Burgos, and later on in Sahagún. The monks of Saint Géraud d'Aurillac, on their part, would not lag behind: they established a pilgrim's refuge on the heights of Cebrero.

The *iter Sancti Jacobi* described by the *Guide* corresponds to what we otherwise also know of the specifically Jacobean roads.[50] Four of these traverse vast areas of central and southern France in order to converge towards the western Pyrenees. The northernmost road, excelling all others in importance, is the *via turonense*. This was considered, on the whole, the *magnum iter Sancti Jacobi* which, initiating in Paris, in the proximity of the venerated relics of St. Dionysius, left in its wake so many toponymic references in the French city. In fact, Paris served as the natural gathering point for the Belgian, some Flemish, as well as the German pilgrims that had come in through the imperial city of Aix-la-Chapelle on the so-called *Niederstrasse*.[51] Notwithstanding, the name designating this first road, the *via turonense*, evokes not Paris but the city of Tours with its once magnificent reliquary church of Saint-Martin. Born in Szombathely, Hungary, the evangelizer of the Loire valley was destined to become one of the favorite saints along the pilgrimage route to Galicia. The splendid Romanesque church of San Martín in Frómista and the homonymous chapel in the very Cathedral of Santiago de Compostela are eloquent testimonies of his prestige. The *via turonense*, moreover, is remarkable otherwise too: besides promoting the veneration of the remains of saintly figures as renowned as Hilary of Poitiers and Eutropius of Saintes by offering the pilgrims access to their holy shrines,[52] it allowed pilgrims to visit also some of the relics of a parallel tradition conveniently intertwined with the Jacobean pilgrimage: the Carolingian epic stories and songs concerning Roland. In Blaye, in fact, the remains of Roland could be visited, while in Bordeaux, one could admire his famous Olifant – a miraculous horn the echoes of which were still reverberating in the ears of many a susceptible pilgrim.[53]

The *via lemovicense,* named after Limoges, had its own relics to offer. At Vézelay, at the fountainhead of the road, within a marvelously luminous Romanesque basilica, the body of Mary Magdalene could be seen, touched, and worshipped. The sinner that had made it good, a beloved distinctive paradox in Christianity, has since times immemorial stirred the imagination of the faithful. The German, Flemish, and, of course Burgundian pilgrims who flocked this way continued subsequently towards Limoges and Périgueux, not without visiting also the famous relics of St. Leonard of Noblat. An alternate route reached also Limoges passing through Bourges, whose famous cathedral would boast, a little later, splendid stained glass windows dedicated to the story of St. James. The *via podense,* in its turn, started at Notre-Dame-du-Puy in the rather impenetrable Massif Central, and gathered pilgrims from Auvergne, Bourgogne, and portions of southern Germany. It offered them the haunting relics and the famous treasures of Sainte-Foy of Conques in the roughness of the Rouergue, as well as the legendary shrine of Saint-Pierre of Moissac bordering the fertile alluvial plains of the Garonne.[54]

The southernmost route of the four, the *via tolosana,* started at the prehistoric cemetery of Alyscamps in Arles. The magnificent collection of paleochristian sarcophagi, which even today greets the visitor of the city, must have produced a striking impression upon the pilgrims embarking on their long way on which they were to meet the relics of so many saints and martyrs. The Italian,[55] Provençal, and Languedocian pilgrims of this route, as well as the Germans venturing down from the *Oberstrasse,* marched through Saint-Gilles-du-Gard and Montpellier before reaching the large and venerable city of Toulouse. St. Giles fed by a doe and St. Saturninus dragged down the steps of the capitol by a bull provided the intellectual as well as devotional highlights of the way. By the time the Pyrenees were within reach, pilgrims felt sufficiently well prepared, both spiritually and physically, to undertake the second and by far most arduous portion of the route through the mountains and high plateaus of Spain.

But first the Pyrenees had to be crossed. From late fall until the spring thaw the mountain passes were uncrossable; during the rest of the year they were wrought with hardship. Except for the Landes on the *via turonense* south of Bordeaux – a one-hundred-kilometer-long stretch of hopeless sand dunes – the marchers to Santiago had never before encountered anything as formidable and forbidding as the chain of the Pyrenees. The first three northernmost roads met at Ostabat and from there they proceeded together to Saint-Jean-Pied-de-Port where the actual climb started. Through Valcarlos the pilgrims reached the Pass of Cize (Ibañeta) at a height of 1057 meters, from which point they descended to Roncesvalles or Roncevaux, a drop of some one-hundred meters towards the valley.[56] By the middle of the eleventh century a refuge had been built on the height of the Cize which, however, soon proved inadequate to withstand the winds and the icy cold spells of the pass. After a while the facilities were transferred to Roncesvalles, which had the ideological advantage of expressly incorporating the Carolingian and Rolandian traditions, tenuously present already in Valcarlos and on the Cize. Pilgrims could rest now in relative comfort in the proximity of the stone parted by Roland's mythic sword Durandel; they could also sleep in the immediate vicinity, and actually in the shadow, of the so-called *silo* of Charlemagne, a graveyard reputed to hold the remains of at least some of Roland's rear guard as well as of the rank and file of Charlemagne's army. The notion of sleeping in the proximity of a saint was important: some medieval churches have preserved until our own days *elevated* reliquary caskets, actually tombs, *under* which pilgrims used to spend the night protected by the beneficial influence of some saintly remains.[57]

From Roncesvalles the road winds down to Pamplona and from there to Puente la Reina. At the magnificent medieval bridge built by Queen Doña Mayor, consort of King Sancho el Mayor, whose five arcades proudly proclaim even today the will to reach the still distant Galicia, the *via tolosana* too joins her sister routes. The Toulouse road, in fact, having left behind the magnificent Languedocian capital with her most splendorous ensemble of Romanesque monasteries anywhere in Christendom (Saint-Étienne, Saint-Sernin, la Daurade), followed the ample and lush plains of the Garonne and then made its way into the outer Pyrenees by way of Oloron. The pilgrims of this southern route, via Barce, had to climb to a height of 1632 meters in order to reach the Somport Pass, considerably more exposed than the Cize. Shortly after the pass, however, the Santa Cristina hospice, one of the largest and best-equipped stations on the route, greeted the pilgrims.[58] From here, through Canfranc, the marchers descended to Jaca, a stopover soon to become a leading urban center irradiating Romanesque form-culture, and from there, through Tiermas and Monreal, they reached Puente la Reina. Of the two passes, Roncesvalles was destined to acquire over the years an ever greater importance. Partly because Somport was impassable for longer seasons, and partly because of the will and even explicit political interest to capitalize upon the Carolingian connections of Roncesvalles, more and more pilgrims of the *via tolosana* were re-routed at the level of Oloron towards Saint-Jean-Pied-de-Port.

At Puente la Reina there were still over 600 kilometers awaiting the pilgrim. The Hispanic portion of the route, the *iter Sancti Jacobi* proper, paradoxically also called *camino francés*, provided little relief for the wayfarer. Hot in summer days, cold during the nights of the intervening seasons, crisscrossed by streams that were liable to suddenly become impetuous torrents, wrought with dangerous mountain routes skirting deep precipices – the mountains of Navarra, the mesetas of Castilla and of León, and then again the mountain chains of Galicia were, all in all, a bitter trial for the already overtaxed and often exhausted pilgrims. Also, populations were scarcer here than on the French side, occasional food and shelter less available, casual meetings with passersby more unpredictable, aimlessly roaming vagrants ready to become bloodthirsty on the first occasion more numerous, organized brigandage more widespread – all the signs of frontier regions that, in the later eleventh century, were embarked on their first politico-social consolidation and resettlement. In consequence, the pilgrims had to rely more heavily than ever on explicitly organized assistance in the significant pilgrimage centers on the route – Puente la Reina, Estella, Nájera, Burgos, Frómista, Carrión de los Condes, León, Astorga, and Cebrero in Galicia, to name the best known.[59] On this long road that seemed never to come to an end, pious and encouraging didactic legends, as the one of the unjustly hanged pilgrim in Santo Domingo de

la Calzada,[60] were interwoven with the heroic narratives of
Roland, Charlemagne, and their paladins in Roncesvalles and,
with the theologically timely and colorful stories of miracles
in Cebrero and elsewhere. In fact, it was only when the pilgrim was finally standing on the windswept heights of Cebrero
and was gazing towards the much longed-for goal of his pilgrimage – still invisible in the distance, over 140 kilometers
away – that the ultimate reality of belonging to the great nation of the marchers to Santiago must have dawned upon him.
That last week or so on the rough Galician terrain thus was
something of an anticlimactic relief. That is the reason why,
when he finally reached the Cathedral of Compostela through
its north portal, he probably entered it, as Master Matteo would
do later at the Portal de la Gloria, on his knees.[61]

THE LIBER SANCTI JACOBI

A central document within the medieval tradition of St.
James and in particular in the protracted process of the establishment and subsequent development of the pilgrimage route to Santiago de Compostela is the *Liber Sancti Jacobi,*
a precious text of which a number of manuscript copies
have come down to us,[62] and of which the most complete
and important is the one preserved today in the library-
archive of the Cathedral of Santiago de Compostela. The
Liber Sancti Jacobi, as we have it today,[63] is a collection of
five compilations, actually books, on various subjects connected, though far from uniformly, by a double unifying
thread – the glorification of the Apostle St. James the Major, and the French and particularly Carolingian contributions to that glorification. In time-honored medieval fashion, a letter-preface attributed to Pope Calixtus II (1119–24)
introduces the *Liber.* Hence is the manuscript also known
as *Codex Calixtinus.* The addressees of the letter-preface on
the other hand – the abbot of Cluny and Guglielmus, patri-
arch of Jerusalem (1139–45) – serve as pointers to the interests centering upon, or irradiating from, Compostela:
Cluniac interests in expanding the French monastic sphere
of influence over the pilgrimage road, and Compostelan
interests in matching the reputation of the other great Christian pilgrimage centers, and particularly of Rome. As to

the temporal parameters of the compilation as a whole, these oscillate between the year 1139, the date of the last miracle recorded in the *Liber*, and 1173, the year in which the text was transcribed by a monk of Ripoll.[64]

The first book, of considerable proportion, is a collection of liturgical pieces of various sorts and for various uses, but chiefly meant to serve for the cult of Santiago on the two days specifically designated for his worship: July 25, the day of his martyrdom, and December 30, the day of his *translatio*, the miraculous translocation of his remains from Jerusalem or Judea to Spain.[65] The liturgical texts comprise an important collection of antiphones, hymns, and tropes – from which comes the musical relevance of the *Liber*: the hymns and tropes, in particular, are variously attributed to important ecclesiastical personages of Chartres, Jerusalem, Poitiers, and Rome – once again the emphasis is placed on the great pilgrimage centers of Christianity as well as on some of the important stations on the Compostela road. Chartres, like Bourges, preserves a splendid, though later, stained-glass window dedicated to the story of Santiago. A number of homilies and sermons are also included in the first book. Of the latter, many are attributed once again to Pope Calixtus. One sermon, *Veneranda dies*, for December 30, bears a particular relevance: it constitutes an outspoken exaltation of the pilgrimage to Santiago de Compostela. Due to the comprehensiveness, single-minded purposefulness, and organic unity of the liturgical texts, these have often been considered as the original centerpiece of the codex to which, subsequently, the various other portions have gradually been added.

The second book, the *Liber miraculorum*, is a collection of twenty-two miracles of St. James, patterned according to medieval books of miracles, each book dedicated to one of the rather important saints. Pope Calixtus appears here too, conspicuously enough: eighteen of the miracles are said to have been collected by him. As to the dating of the miracles, all but one occur between 1080 and 1110, a short and concentrated time-frame corresponding precisely to one of the key periods in the development of the pilgrimage tradition on the route to Compostela. The last miracle registered is, according to the text of the codex, of the year 1135, a date usually considered as the *terminus post quem* for the compilation as a whole. Most of the miraculous stories occur in France, Italy, and Germany, with the French playing a conspicuously prominent role in most of them. Even more significantly, almost all toponyms variously associated with the miracles are nothing but the great French pilgrimage sites on the route to Compostela: Bourges, Vézelay, Poitiers, and Toulouse. And even in the case of miracles occurring already on Hispanic soil, the beneficiaries of the thaumaturgical interventions of Santiago turn out to be for the most part French. Though an international perspective is certainly present in the compilation, the *Liber miraculorum* seems to speak foremost to the centrality of St. James's preoccupation with his French devotees, rather than to the exaltation of the universality of the *patrocinium* of the saint.[66]

The third book contains various texts whose common denominator is the glorification of the cult of St. James and particularly the fostering and upgrading of the bishopric see of Santiago de Compostela in whose domain the saintly relics are guarded. At the close of the book, the thaumaturgical effects of shells – a prominent Jacobean symbol – receive considerable attention. The central concern of this compilation, however, always within the above-mentioned glorification, is the emphatic narration of the *translatio* of the saintly relics from Jerusalem to the shores of Galicia first and thereafter to its present site in Santiago de Compostela. That the episode of the *translatio* must have held the highest degree of long-lasting significance for the compiler, one may infer from the fact that *two* versions of the *translatio* are reported and furthermore, that the authority of *two* popes are invoked in order to authenticate the account. Pope Calixtus II, who is, of course, present throughout the entire *Liber*, introduces the episode with a preface, and a certain Pope Leo seconds him with something like a certification letter. This Leo has traditionally been glossed as Pope Leo III (785–816), whose early dates fit the Carolingian orientation forced by the French with such insistence upon the tradition of the pilgrimage to Santiago in general and, as we shall see in a moment, particularly by the compiler of the fourth book of the codex, the Pseudo-Turpin.

The earliest report concerning the *translatio* is contained in the *Martyrologium of Usuard,* a completed version of which saw the light not before 867. Usuard already reports, at such an early date, on the devotion of the faithful to the relic: "The most holy relic of St. James, carried from Jerusalem to Spain and deposited in the far-away regions of this land, are devoutly honored by the continuous veneration of the faithful of the country." The attribution to Pope Leo III is, therefore, with all certainty, nothing but a pious, though hardly disinterested, wish. Borrowing from earlier sources, the *epistola leonis episcopi* is actually an eleventh-century composition subsequently elaborated and finally incorporated, for reasons of evident convenience, into the third part of the *Liber*. It is still later that the account of the *translatio* will enter the *Golden Legend*.

The fourth book, the *Historia Turpini* or *Pseudo-Turpin*, is the best known portion of the *Liber* and the one that has been the most studied. A letter-preface of Turpin, presented as "archbishop of Reims and faithful companion of Charlemagne in Spain" serves as an introduction to the *historical* account. The connection with the administrative and ecclesiastical hierarchies of the emperor is secured through the addressee of the letter, Liutprand, dean of Aix-la-Chapelle. The *Royal Chronicles of St. Denis* had already dealt generically with the campaigns of Charlemagne. The *Historia Turpini*, for its part, purports to serve as a kind of supplement to the chronicles: Bishop Turpin appears in the narration as an eyewitness-historian of the exploits of Charlemagne in the Iberian Peninsula. While the heroic rear-guard action of Roland and his paladins remains much the same as we have it in the *Chanson de Roland*, the emperor is introduced here as the deliverer of Spain, and particularly of Galicia, from the Saracen infidels. An even more significant innovation vis-à-vis the *Chanson* lies in the distinctly Jacobean angle of the Turpin story: the Apostle Santiago is presented now as explicitly inspiring and encouraging Charlemagne.[67]

Nowhere is the Jacobean motivation of the emperor, strongly present in so many other ways too, more forcefully and at the same time more poetically expressed than in the famous episode of the "dream of Charlemagne": the emperor sleeps and in his dream he sees the Milky Way whose ultimate meaning, however, he fails to understand. At that point the Apostle Santiago appears to him and explains to the astonished monarch the significance of the road of stars: it is the road to the saint's tomb presently impassable for being overrun by the infidels. Before the end of the vision, the apostle spurs Charlemagne to deliver the lands

invaded by the Saracens and thereby to open up the pilgrimage to his holy tomb. By specifically making Charlemagne
the benefactor of the pilgrims to Santiago, the *Pseudo-Turpin*
proposes, in particularly forceful terms, an ideological orientation otherwise also present in the *Liber Sancti Jacobi:* this is
an orientation whose main beneficiaries are not so much the
apostle and his pilgrims, but rather French national and ecclesiastical interests in Carolingian garb.[68]

The fifth book of the *Liber* is the *Pilgrim's Guide to Santiago
de Compostela,* the very subject of the present volume. Of its
actual author-compiler we know next to nothing for certain.
A candidate for the authorship has been one Aimery Picaud
from Parthenay-le-Vieux in the Poitou, to whom one of the
hymns of the compilation is ascribed and who otherwise
too is mentioned in the letter of Pope Innocent II that closes
the *Liber*, as the donor of the *Codex* to the Cathedral of
Santiago. But the letter of Innocent is almost certainly spurious, and the other traces we have of Aimery's presence in
the work are of indicative value only. All told, nothing firm
may be said at this point of him or of anybody else as the
author of the compilation.[69]

The *Guide* itself, no doubt one of the most precious documents in the early medieval literature of voyages, like the
Liber Sancti Jacobi, is eminently uneven in the presentation
of its material to the reader. After an initial brief declaration on the veracity of the subsequent text ensued by a bare
table of contents, eleven chapters follow, unequal in length
and in the extension, interest, and depth of the subjects
treated. The first six and the last two chapters are extremely
short, at times only a brief paragraph, often not amounting
to more than one or two cursory statements. The first chapter speaks of the four French roads up to their meeting point
in Puente la Reina; the second, of the stations of the journey from the Somport Pass on; the third, of the regions and
cities traversed on Spanish soil; the fourth, of the hospices
on the three major pilgrimage routes of Christianity:
Mount-Joux at the Great Saint Bernard Pass on the way to
Rome, Jerusalem, and Santa Cristina at the Somport Pass;
the fifth, of road maintenance and those virtuous souls
who do the repair work; the sixth, of rivers, a constant
preoccupation of the pilgrims; the tenth and the eleventh
chapters, finally, speak respectively of the canons of the

Cathedral of Santiago and of the welcoming accorded to, and deserved by, pilgrims. All in all a meager crop.

Sandwiched between these extremely short and often quite disappointing paragraphs, there are three extremely long chapters which turn out to be the essential marrow of the *Guide*. It is for these that we have been waiting, and it is these that will speak to us of lands and people, of relics and reliquaries, and of Santiago de Compostela – though perhaps not quite the way we thought they would.

We must take them one by one. The seventh chapter describes the regions and occasionally the cities that the pilgrims are bound to cross on their way to Santiago. The old historical region of Poitou, in Central France, receives an extraordinarily positive review: Poitevains are vigorous, handsome, courageous and generous; they are good-natured because their land is fertile and happy. The old Latin motto, *pratum ridet* – the meadow smiles, seems to be lurking in the background. Surprisingly, the rest of the French regions are handled, though with a sympathetic eye, quite unceremoniously. Once on the other side of the Pyrenees, however, the views of the author become suddenly negative, vicious, opinionated. Particularly the Basque and the Navarrese fare badly in the review: the former are barbarous, the latter bark like dogs. Also, the Navarrese sleep and copulate with their animals, howl like wolves, and do everything in order to lay their hands on the purse of poor defenseless pilgrims. As these proceed towards the west, conditions become gradually more supportable. The plains of Castilla are rich and fertile, we learn, but it is a treeless country, as it is still today, and its inhabitants are malign and vicious. Galicia, towards the end of the long march, is the only Spanish region that does well in the account. The reason is simple: their people are the closest to the French. In fact, the French are the yardstick by which others are constantly measured: as the Galicians were the closest, so the Navarrese are the farthest away from *nos gens gallica*, the usual way the author designates those he considers his compatriots.

The chapter dealing with relics and reliquaries, the eighth, is the longest of the *Guide*, and it is the one composed with the greatest thoughtfulness and an unusually deft hand in the handling of its subject. There is no hesitation here: St. Trophimus, St. Foy, St. Leonard, St. Hilary and many other saints are paraded here in style, their miracles told with relish, their relics and reliquaries described with minute detail and with a still early-medieval gusto for the costly and the precious. Three of the four French roads are thus amply treated in terms of the shrines to be visited. Concerning the *via podense*, on the other hand, all is centered around the story of that marvelous maiden-martyr St. Foy. She tiptoes in and out of the *Guide* as an apparition in a dream. Quite apart from the above, two further saints receive unusually extensive treatment, each several pages long, which actually exceeds all sense of proportion within the *Guide*: St. Giles's bejeweled reliquary casket is accorded a particularly detailed description, while the martyrdom of St. Eutropius of Saintes, southwest of Poitiers, is allotted a never-ending account of his conversion and martyrdom. All these saints, then, repose in good French saintly odor. The emphasis is placed unabashedly and explicitly on the famous Gallic relics and reliquary churches: no matter where you go, so we read between the lines, these are the relics to be visited, *ad visitandam*, as the text so often reports.

Once we come to the Pyrenees, on the other hand, all of a sudden the author's ink dries up in the inkhorn: the five Spanish saints that manage to be mentioned at all are hardly assigned a three-line-long text each. Among these is St. James too, of whom the *Guide* says: "Finally, one must visit, with deference and devotion, the remains of the blessed Apostle James in the city of Compostela." This, however, may be well justified: the next chapter, the ninth, is entirely devoted to Santiago de Compostela. The city itself is dealt with in the briefest possible terms: therefore, the correlation with city descriptions such as the *Mirabilia urbis Romae* is, if at all appropriate, imperfect.

But lavish attention is devoted to the cathedral. The imposing monument dominates today the city no less than it did in times past, and with its magnificent portals and surprisingly ample inner spaces it conjures up in the imagination of the faithful, no less than in that of the casual visitor, visions of glory and fulfillment. Armed with no despicable know-how and considerable technical interest in the subject, the author of the *Guide* takes stock of the architectural organization and the sculptural layout and iconography of the cathedral as well as of the church furniture and *Kleinkunst* located in it. He speaks to us of windows and portals, of bell-towers and altars, of the reliquary of St. James and of its silver altar-front, of its ciborium and of the oil lamps hanging over it. One has, in fact, the feeling that the author is neither a mere casual visitor nor an all self-absorbed intellectual, but indeed a pilgrim, alert and intelligent, a pilgrim of flesh and blood, of skin and sweat, who after weeks and months of marching now under the parching sun, now under a drenching rain, finally makes it to the Cathedral of Santiago of Compostela. The evident Francophilia so outspokenly present throughout the *Liber* as a whole no less than in the *Guide* itself, now vanishes; in its place we find neither elation nor deprecation, but a solid account of what the cathedral and the reliquary shrine of St. James must have looked like sometime around the middle of the twelfth century: a lasting contribution indeed to the form-culture of Western art.[70]

PILGRIMAGE WITHOUT IDEOLOGY

The pilgrimage to Santiago de Compostela is, as a matter of course, in itself a historical phenomenon, and thus it is subject to the diachronic rise and decline of a multitude of historical coordinates. Little wonder, therefore, that conditions and situations effecting, underlying or affecting the pilgrimage in the eleventh and twelfth centuries underwent considerable changes in the thirteenth and in many ways became outdated by the fourteenth and the fifteenth centuries. It will do well to remember that the *Codex Calixtinus* and in particular the *Guide to the Pilgrim* reflect, in the main, that earlier period of the eleventh and twelfth centuries – the era of Romanesque culture – in which the pilgrimage to Santiago de Compostela outgrew already its narrow national boundaries, within which it had been born before the turn of the millennium, and consolidated itself into a veritable international movement – we may think of it as animated by a collective psychosis – of vast numbers, proportions, and boundaries. Concurrently, in those years the pilgrimage to St. James still harbored a certain freshness, genuineness, and idealization that the wear and tear of later centuries was destined, in part at least, to erode. With a structure, life modalities, rights and duties, legislation, and in a way a

35

folklore and a culture of their own, the pilgrims to Santiago constituted a genuine society, the society of pilgrims.[71]

The Society of Pilgrims

Such a society of pilgrims consisted of a floating population living, for as long as the pilgrimage lasted, on the margin of society at large, escaping its rules by the very mobility and the relative blending of its component social layers. That is perhaps also one of the reasons, quite apart from the inherent abuses that the pilgrimage system with the passing of time endured, that after a while, certainly by the later thirteenth and more sharply from the fourteenth century on, sedentary society at large became so suspicious of these vast masses roaming freely, unchecked and unrestrained, in and out of provincial, regional and even national boundaries. The medieval establishment was well justified in its uneasy feelings: the society of pilgrims ran headlong against the medieval fixed ordering and societal segmentation. Even a comparison with the military, though often drawn, is less than congruous: the latter, though also on the move, were so only temporarily; and furthermore, the life of arms merely translated the rigid sedentary structures into equally rigid military ones – the peasant infantry and the knightly nobility. All told, to go on pilgrimage, apart from other loftier goals, was a way of escaping societal restrictions and regimentation.[72]

At the same time, escaping the regimentation of any one given sedentary structure exposed the pilgrims to the hazards of all. Hence, at various junctures, local, regional, and even royal authorities felt that it was appropriate and even necessary to protect their frail existence with a particular legislation of their own. The length of the route and its inter-regional and even international character made, however, all such legislation little coordinated, at times contradictory, at best fragmentary, and on the whole eminently inefficient. The frequency of the repetitive enactments in some quarters seemed only to confirm the rudimentary implementation of the regulations. Some monarchs felt obliged to protect the person and the belongings of foreign pilgrims to an even further extent than those of their own citizens. One concern was the free and unburdened movement of the pilgrims; another, the observance, vis-à-vis the foreign pilgrims, of current prices, as well as the honest usage of weights and measures.

Banditry, thievery, murder, rape, and all sorts of asocial phenomena on the route were considerably more difficult to control, let alone to eradicate. Papal indictments and even the declared sword of excommunication were more often than not ignored. In the last analysis, pilgrims had no better alternative than to rely on the meager protection offered by their costume and insignia and on the safeguard documents many of them were able to exhibit. That was mighty little; but then the pilgrimage to St. James was never thought of as a promenade, and the hazards of the road were discounted as part of the tribulations of the Christian soul on its way to salvation.[73]

Pilgrims belonged to all social stations of life, from the humblest, dispossessed, and miserable to the highest and most distinguished, but they did so in varying proportions. We know of kings and queens, princes of the world and of the Church, as well as of members of the nobility making their way to Santiago with large retinues preceded by fanfares and followed by a numerous entourage: servants too became, *nolens volens,* pilgrims of some kind while turning to their advantage the magnificence of the grand personage they were serving. Such high-ranking individuals made their way, as a rule, in carriage or horseback.

There were then pilgrims who belonged to the class of the merchants, the artisans, the free professions, and the learned, both ecclesiastical and lay, who issued for the most part from cities, towns, or prominent ecclesiastical establishments. The number of these, at first reduced, increased towards the end of the period that interests us here and by the fourteenth and fifteenth centuries turned into a substantial proportion of the total. These made the pilgrimage on horseback or on foot, depending on the case.

But the large masses, those that carried upon themselves the living tradition of the pilgrimage and that converted ideology and theology into the very substance of everyday culture, of a vigorous folklore, were, without any doubt, the penniless, the dispossessed, the indigent, the miserable peasants. In most of central and western Europe of the eleventh and twelfth centuries, socially speaking, they belonged to two main classes. On one end stood the manorial or seignorial serfs or semi-serfs regimented within an amazing variety of written and consuetudinary legislations and ordinances that greatly differed even from province to province – always attached to a village or hamlet and mainly to the land. Serfs were lifelong working machines who toiled from the time they were born until their death. This usually occurred, if no intervening disease, accident, or war unexpectedly shortened it even further, at a relatively early age: forty-five years were considered well beyond one's prime. Marginal living conditions, unbalanced and, more often than not, scarce food, intensive and hard labor starting in early childhood and stretching from before dawn till after dusk took, perforce, their toll. The seignorial serf, therefore, who resolved to set out on a pilgrimage, could only do so at a relatively advanced age, at the slipping end of life, when his service on the farm was no more desired or needed. In strictly economic terms this meant that he was released from the economic cogwheel before his output shrunk below his food consumption. It is in such rather depleted, worn out, and, on the whole, pathetic conditions that we must imagine the seignorial serf towards the end of his existence setting out, on foot, on the long road to Santiago.

There was, however, a second peasant class too, that of the freeholders. These were better off in theory only. The land they owned or leased was small and usually not of the best quality; implements were poor and farmhands scarce – only the close family and a few servants – and one had to work harder to make ends meet. Hence, paradoxically, freeholders were prevented to an even further degree than serfs from leaving their land for a protracted time and could do so, for similar economic reasons, at an equally or more advanced age or in even feebler physical conditions.[74]

The Motivations of the Pilgrimage

One may question the marchers of the past concerning the reasons for their pilgrimage – but the answers are not always reliable. As so often one usually tells what one thinks the other one wants to hear. And furthermore, one can only ask the very few who bear a name, a personality, a distinguishing feature – those who have turned to the inkhorn or those concerning whom writings were produced, that is to say, the few, either famous or aristocratic or both. Arnauld du Mont, the monk of Ripoll who in 1173 transcribed the *Codex Calixtinus*, expressly states that he went to Santiago in order to obtain the remission of his sins as well as to see a site venerated by everybody. Bona of Pisa, subsequent to a vision at the end of which St. James himself had comforted her, made the pilgrimage to Santiago several times – according to the tradition, no less than nine – before dying in 1207. Hers is a pilgrimage of gratefulness. But the large masses of the past, as those of the present, are nameless and they do not talk. They are neither famous saints nor notorious sinners, thus nobody takes notice of their existence much less of their pilgrimage. And yet, it is they who constituted the better part of the thousands and tens of thousands of pilgrims who year after year filled the hospices, the inns, the *matroneum* of the pilgrimage churches and who, above all, on those much traveled roads constituted a living stream moving to and from Santiago.

Observing events from the often misleading perspective of a considerable historical distance, we tend to see a homogeneous, single motivation animating the pilgrims on their way to Santiago. In fact, there was a great diversity of motivations. We must first differentiate between the more or less freely taken resolve to visit the tomb of St. James and an imposed obligation to do so. Within the first category, the devotion to St. James constituted, in the widest sense, the primary motivation for undertaking the pilgrimage. That freely-taken resolve was, subsequently, often enough formalized through a vow which, by the later Middle Ages, could only be made under severe restrictions: the would-be pilgrim had to be a free individual, no longer under paternal authority, a bachelor, and unbound by the obligations of religious life of any kind. Such restrictions, however, apart from regional variations, were imperfectly spelled out in the period of our interest, let alone appropriately observed.

Within the ranks of the devotional pilgrims there were those who went to Santiago simply *orandi causa*, in order to pray; but there were also those who made the pilgrimage to ask for forgiveness in a vague sense only for a generically perceived dissolute existence of which one usually became aware on the downhill side of life; and there were, of course, those who made the pilgrimage as a personal penance for a very particular sin committed, buried in the depth of one's conscience. In many cases, furthermore, pilgrimages were prompted by a vow made in circumstances of mortal danger. That is what occurred even as late as the voyages of Columbus, when a terrible hurricane caught the Niña and the Pinta on the return leg of the first voyage. Columbus indeed honored his vow and went thereafter in pilgrimage to the Virgin of Guadalupe before embarking on his next crossing.

Within the class of the devotional marchers though there was a further sub-category of pilgrims that went to Santiago not on account of a negative experience in their past that called for redress, but in the hope of some positive occurrence in the future. These were the pilgrims, no doubt a majority, who made their way with the express purpose to beg at the tomb of the apostle for the satisfaction of a particular material and physical desire. Such natural desire was, more often than not, the recovery of physical well-being. These pilgrims, therefore, went to St. James the Thaumaturge, the miracle-maker, and were hopeful that their particular prayer and desire would indeed find proper fulfillment. That is a further reason that the army of pilgrims was full of fellows in poor health or actually lame, blind, deaf, mutilated, partially paralyzed, or handicapped in some other way. Miracle was invoked from the Great Intercessor, and miracle was expected to occur, if not immediately at his tomb, certainly later, perhaps subsequent to the pilgrim's return home. And often the psychosomatic experiences were of such an intensity and of such a profoundly felt nature that some solace and even alleviation did indeed occur, or, at least, it was felt to have occurred. There were also numerous cases in which the miracle was beseeched not for oneself but for some close relative, on behalf of a paralyzed son or a bedridden wife. These kind of pilgrims were thus miracle-seekers, and the mortifications of the flesh on the long march were the physical proof of their unquestioned devotion to St. James who would, therefore, listen to them and grant them the longed-for miracle.[75]

The category of the pilgrimage to Santiago as an imposed obligation entails a complex set of juridical ordinances whose origin apparently harks back to an epoch anterior to the first flourishing of the Galician shrine. The imposition of juridically-sanctioned pilgrimages included two important variants – penitence and punishment. The distinction between the two was not always clearly defined and depended, in most cases, apart from great regional differences, on particular court rulings. In general it may be said that while pilgrimage as penitence was imposed in cases of moral misdemeanor and, on the whole, in cases of relatively light transgression, pilgrimage as punishment was reserved for grave crimes, and often as only a portion of the condemnatory sentence. Such sentences corresponded to appropriate canonical legislations and were controlled by regular ecclesiastical judiciary courts. There were rulings in which individuals condemned for homicide and who had undertaken the pilgrimage as part of their punishment were chained with iron rings around their chest or neck forged from the arms they had utilized to perpetrate their crime. In a rather amusing instance of juridical inventiveness, which combined the useful with the commonsensical, vagrants charged with social uselessness and ineptitude were at times sent on the Santiago pilgrimage simply to disembarrass the township from their presence. Elsewhere, witnessing to a great finesse in the legal-psychological conceptions at work, pilgrimages were also imposed in the course of a process of civil reconciliation: each of the quarreling parties was sent off to a different sanctuary – one being usually Santiago – to cool off during the route in a kind of a peripatetic meditation. The perspicacity of such legal measures throws light, on the whole, upon the deeper effects of the pilgrimage upon the pilgrim: by the time he or she attained Santiago de Compostela, a process of self-purification had taken place in the mind and the heart. Precisely, it is peripatetic meditation that was thought of, with good reason, as conducive to such purification.[76]

There were also largely profane – that is to say, non-sacred motivations feeding the pilgrimage to Santiago de Compostela. Apart from the marginal economic interests of merchants, entertainers, and artisans which will be considered in a moment, we should be able to better understand the mainstream of these profane motivations thinking for a moment of the nature of the large peasant masses of the early and central Middle Ages who, whether serfs, demi-serfs, or freeholders, were born, grew up, married, made children, and died within the limited confines of a single hamlet or village. Once every now and then there would be a Sunday fair in some not too distant town, perhaps once in a year a larger fair at a saintly shrine in a city one or two day's marches away – this was the horizon within which by far most medieval peasants worked away their life, literally, from cradle to coffin. Within such a disconsolate prospect the pilgrimage to Santiago de Compostela must have appeared as the one luminous exception, the one great adventure, the one almost-miraculous opening to distant lands, unheard-of customs, the marvels of the world – no matter how perilous the journey would turn out. It is only partly appropriate to associate such a motivation with the modern notion of tourism. It was much more than that. For the majority of the eleventh- and twelfth-century pilgrims to Santiago, those six to nine months spent on the road in strange lands and among strange people meant the only occasion to cast a glimpse upon broader existence, to measure for once the world and its wonders, to see, once in their lives, the mountains and the sea.

On the one hand, therefore, the pilgrimage to Santiago de Compostela represented different things to different people; on the other hand, and this is the particularly important point, it represented many things, though in various proportions, to one and the same individual. The above categorization of the motivations of pilgrimage is only that: the categorization of historians who in order to understand history try to reorder it. Such ordering of the historical happening, however, runs against the very holistic essence of life of which we all, in one way or another, partake. The devotional pilgrim might have looked for some miraculous intervention of St. James along the route; and the pilgrim in pursuit of a particular miracle at the sacred tomb was at the same time surely infused with a general devotion to the saint. The penitential pilgrim also, whether of the self-imposed type or not, but even the pilgrim cast upon the road by a juridically sanctioned punishment, must have felt something of the mystic aura hovering upon the pilgrimage route and, in particular, at the reliquary Church of St. James. They must have felt it because the mysticism of the Jacobean pilgrimage route was an integral part of the mentalities of the time,[77] because everybody else felt it, because that pilgrimage constituted for the centuries that interest us here a collective fascination of the first magnitude. Most significantly, no matter from where the pilgrims came and what the ultimate declared goal of their pilgrimage was to be, all of them, from saint to sinner, felt the invigorating air of a new world gradually unfolding before their incredulous and astonished eyes in all its unpredictable complexity and savagery, but also in its surprising beauty and magnificence. This was a lesson that none of them would henceforth forget.[78]

With time, however, a certain decline in the standards of pilgrimage set in. This was noticeable in the eleventh and twelfth centuries already. The order of the two-beat operation – pilgrimage first, miracle later – became often enough reversed: one beseeched the thaumaturgic intercession of St. James first, at home, surely in front of some image of the saint or perhaps some memorabilia brought back by somebody else from Santiago; one promised, at the same time, if indeed the miracle took place or even if the slightest improvement in the condition of some ailment occurred, to undertake the pilgrimage to the tomb of the saint. An appropriately formulated vow followed. Similarly, there was also the widespread usage of invoking in captivity, usually of the infidels, the miraculous help of the saint. Subsequently, upon eventual liberation conveniently facilitated by the required ransom payment, one made the pilgrimage to St. James, depositing dutifully at the reliquary tomb of the saint the unlocked shackles and chains.[79]

Also during the same centuries, and increasingly so afterwards, a further corruption of the original notion of the necessary suffering and mortification of the flesh during the pilgrimage set in. By degrees the notion of the vicarious pilgrimage came into being: somebody made the pilgrimage instead of, or commissioned by, somebody else. It goes without saying that appropriate financial arrangements were stipulated in return for the service. We have considered already the morally-speaking easily vindicable pilgrimage to St. James on behalf of a gravely ill family member evidently prevented from undertaking any journey. A more scurrilous, though admittedly still justifiable, case was that of the pilgrimage vow as well as testamentary disposition included in the last will and to be carried out vicariously postmortem. Such pilgrimage vows were recognized and validated early enough by canon law. From here, however, a further slippage occurred, apparently only from the thirteenth century onward, in the wake of which the right of enjoying the benefits of a vicarious pilgrimage became extended to the living. This was already tantamount to buying by weight of gold benefices that one was supposed to acquire by the unmediated personal contact with the relics of St. James only: the rich alone could afford it, and a kind of a professional pilgrim – by all standards a contradiction – made its appearance.[80]

We reach further levels of corruption when we come to meet the false pilgrims of various sorts who, as time went by, kept plaguing, in increasing numbers, the roads and the pilgrimage-supporting structures as a whole. Vagabonds of various persuasions; merchants offering dubiously-acquired, spurious goods; artisans surreptitiously exercising their trade at nightly stopovers[81]; professional mendicants begging their passage as far as Santiago; motley fools at large; charlatans posing as preachers; quack doctors and humbug lawyers hoodwinking gullible audiences; dissembling, sanctimonious priests selling blessings and dispensations at will; harlots cajoling their customers from the roadside – all these and more not merely infested the underlying supporting structure of the pilgrimage but, what was worse, undermined its moral soundness and drained its spiritual contents. By the end of the period of which the *Guide* is the mirror, the suspicious augmentation of regulatory ordinances and dispositions seems to suggest that these had little curative, let alone preventive, effect on the plague of the false pilgrims on the road.

Negative as the influence of the asocial elements on the structure, as well as on the loftier aims of the pilgrimage to Santiago, might have been, they lent the road a many-sidedness and a zest for life's lighter corners that greatly contributed to keep for so many centuries the pilgrimage to Compostela in the mainstream of the *comédie humaine* of the Middle Ages. Truants, simulators, jesters, fools, and vagrants were so much an integral part of the scenario as the topography and the weather, the pilgrims' constant fellow-travelers.[82]

The Geography of the Road

The mountains of Navarra and Galicia that seemed to touch the sky; long and sharp uphill climbs that lasted for hours and often enough for days; defective, at times muddy, at others rocky causeways on which the unevenness of the ground jerked and jolted the sole, the ankles, and the legs; the long stretches of desolate, treeless, sandy regions of the endless dunes of the Landes in which the trail got mapped out anew at each step; the disheartening roads without shade, water, or respite of any kind in Castilla; a savage and uncouth land in which the path dangerously skirted deep precipices or moved alongside forbidding rocky formations – this was the grand scenario of untamed or barely tamed nature that the pilgrim was called upon to master. The climatic conditions – heat, cold, storm, rain, snowdrifts, hail – and the natural eco-system that complemented it – flies, insects, and wild boars on the plains; bears and wolves in the mountains – contributed their share to the normal plagues and pains of the route. The four to five hours of marching, the hardly-ever-adequate let alone satisfying and tasty food, the often pathetic resting and overnight shelter conditions – these alone were sufficient, on a protracted itinerary, to wear out the bravest and the strongest among the pilgrims.[83]

In the lands and regions to be traversed for weeks and months in a row everything was at every step new, strange, uncommon, outlandish, never before seen, hardly ever heard of, never before practiced: food, drinks, language, landscape, human countenance, custom, behavior. Within so many new and strange things the foreign pilgrim himself must have looked, in the eyes of the local folks, by far the strangest. Barbarous – a strange foreigner, as the Romans knew so well – were always the others. The French author of the *Guide* does not conceal his preferences and shows little understanding for whatever lies beyond the Pyrenees.[84]

All depends however upon the mental attitude governing the body. The month-long exhausting marches on the route of St. James, the general duress on body, limbs, back, and particularly on legs and feet that such prolonged marching on uneven causeways entailed, let alone the more specific vexations that pilgrims occasionally imposed upon themselves, provided an appropriate frame to the ideology of the mortification of the flesh that the devotion to St. James and the concomitant discipline of penance and self-punishment elicited. In a sense, all this amounted to a longed-for reality that the pilgrim pursued in the very nature of the pilgrimage. At times portions of the route were made barefoot; at others, more rarely, on the knees; still at others, bearing stones or in chains. Stone-carrying had occasionally an eminently practical scope too: the transportation of cut or uncut pieces from a quarry to some nearby ecclesiastical construction site. The very pilgrimage road, both in ideological as well as in concrete, factual terms, provided the pilgrim with a striking parallel to the road to Calvary, the *via dolorosa*, that Christ Himself undertook on the way to His crucifixion. The pilgrim, as *homo viator*, felt himself enacting a particularly pregnant variant of the *imitatio Christi* imposed upon every Christian within the larger context of Christian sacred history.[85]

Among the hardships – and occasional blessings – encountered on the road, water commanded a place of particular significance. Potable water was a constant preoccupation for the pilgrim. While generally speaking, except for the Landes region between Bordeaux and Saint-Jean-Pied-de-Port, there was abundant water on the French side of the route, in Spain scarcity was endemic and the quality of the water a perennial worry. Telling the good from the harmful waters, the drinkable from the poisonous one, was no easy task for the pilgrim. The *Guide* devotes an entire short chapter to the subject. The proposed scenario of the Navarrese sharpening their knives ready to skin the miserably ensnared pilgrims who had just breathed their last from drinking the wrong water did not help morale.

If drinking water was hard to come by, the crossing of streams and rivers was no small headache either. In the springtime, insignificant brooks were liable to suddenly turn into impetuous torrents. Moreover, ferrymen, while practically controlling the passageways, had an infamous reputation for exacting exorbitant tolls for their services which, as the *Guide* notes, at times were no more than deadly traps. That is the reason why bridges were highly appreciated – even if a toll was exacted on the major ones, such as at Puente la Reina: pilgrims were all too happy to pay their dues for the sake of a speedy, safe, and orderly passage. On mountain passes too a toll was exacted, at times legally, at others underhandedly; the *Guide* bitterly indicts the exactors at Cize.[86]

Water or streams, however, were not merely a problem to overcome but also an occasional blessing to cherish. Water liturgy, otherwise also present in the life of the Christian, assumed for the Santiago de Compostela pilgrim a particular relevance. The *Guide* specifically mentions a stream only two miles from Santiago, Lavamentula, in the waters of which pilgrims used to immerse themselves stripped of all their clothing.[87] Such a liturgy of purification reminds one of the ablution rites in Mecca where, before entering the Ka'aba, the Muslim faithful disrobes, washes up, and puts on a seamless dress. The purification of the Christian pilgrim assumed a particular relevance at welcoming washing rites at monasteries and confraternities. In monasteries, following an age-old practice, the abbot or the prior himself, in confraternities the chapter-head, were supposed to wash the feet of the pilgrims. And more often than not they did wash them. This was a practice that harked back to a biblical usage deeply rooted in the prophylactic and hygienic practices of the Middle East. Christ, before the Last Supper, had washed the feet of the disciples, starting with Peter, and offered the injunction "ye also ought to wash one another's feet." The Lord's washing and drying the feet of Peter, found in many representations along the road to Santiago, carried with it connotations of purification and the remission of sins, and, on the whole, reflected upon Christian charity with the pilgrim as its greatest beneficiary.[88]

Companions on the Road

But the pilgrim hardly ever faced alone either the perils of the ferryboat or the blessings of the monastic feet-washing. Due to the dangers and incertitudes of the road, as well as common-sense practicality, pilgrims almost always traveled in a group. Under the uncertain conditions of the roads, companionship was a dire necessity. One set out, as a rule, with fellow travelers. The loosely conceived companies, at times veritable collective pilgrimage groups, were usually established on a close geographical and hence on a narrowly conceived *Landsmannschaft* basis: often its members belonged to a single village or township, or perhaps to two or three neighboring villages or the dispersed hamlets of a single county or parish. Such group-travel, though badly necessitated by the circumstances, required a discipline that few could hold steady and for long. Furthermore, the route was protracted, tempers unpredictable and fortune flimsy. Therefore, though setting out in a company, no matter how tightly composed, with the passing of time dissensions and strifes made their effect felt, and many a pilgrim soon saw himself parting company, changing group allegiance, trodding his way now with these now with those wayfarers, and often enough alone. On a road that was as long as that of St. James and on which so many splendid reliquaries or unheard of country fairs were enticing the pilgrims for more or less extended stays – let alone the more worldly niceties on the way – it seems only natural that one frequently parted and joined company. The mid-route transfers were also conditioned by fortuitous encounters on the road, whenever one group happened to overtake another or when in the late afternoon one chanced into some confraternity or met around a free meal in a monastery or even at night in the large bed of some run-down hospice.

Such new companionships and group-allegiances were also built within and around *Landsmannschaft* ties. These were felt to be stronger the farther removed the pilgrims were from home. It was through such *Landsmannschaften* that the momentarily lost fatherland became recreated on the route. German, northern, and eastern pilgrims, in particular, held such bonds in special awe, partly due perhaps to rather sharp language barriers and partly to innate sentiments of gregariousness anchored in their distant tribal past. Italian, Languedocian, or Catalonian pilgrims were considerably more at ease in the distant northern regions of Spain.[89]

Occasionally women also participated in the pilgrimage to Santiago de Compostela, but their numbers must have been exiguous, and we know next to nothing about them except, of course, whenever the pilgrimage concerned some important or saintly personage as the earlier mentioned Bona of Pisa. Fortunately, however, we have some visual representations which, though belonging to later times, may serve at least as an approximate indication of their role. These representations always show the female pilgrim together with her husband, never alone and never in the company of other women, let alone other men. Evidently, at least concerning the peasantry and the artisan class, for single women, whether young maids or widows, it was inappropriate to set out on the road, as it was for married women without their husbands. There were, of course, some objective problems: hospices, often with a single large straw mattress as a collective bed, were hardly equipped to offer separate quarters for women or for married couples. Ordinances trying to control prostitution on the route point to the central preoccupation of the ecclesiastical authorities: women on the road are a devilish temptation that could only be shunned by eliminating altogether their presence from the route – with the single exception of women with their husbands. But since it must have seemed little fun setting out for months with one's own wife, they were nearly always left at home. On the rare occasion, indeed, that a couple went on a pilgrimage, husband and wife marched, as everybody else, together with this or that company of pilgrims. It is unrealistic to expect that rampant medieval misogyny would have spared the otherwise predominantly male organization of the pilgrimage.[90]

The Hazards of the Road

The logistics of the pilgrims' safety depended in various ways on the social categories to which they belonged. As a general rule, the higher the social strata they belonged to, the better organized and protected they were; at the same time, having more to lose, their persons and belongings were more coveted and hence more at risk. Concerning the large masses, marching in company afforded them with a reasonable security against the smaller evils of the road – vagrants, thieves, asocial characters of various kinds, and individually operating bandits.[91]

While the pilgrims' insignia and garments were both practical and helpful to identify their bearers and hence to ensure their being granted the privileges to which they were entitled, these same insignia became also the object of much abuse and often enough served to mask as pilgrims those who were not. Vagrants, scoundrels, and bandits, while scheming as foxes, appeared in them as lambs. Chanting at times "Deus, adiuva, Sancte Jakobe," they turned, on the first occasion, into highway robbers. Legislation and ordinances had ever since the early days of the pilgrimage tried to clean the roads from such unwanted guests. In practice, however, it turned hardly possible to translate paper into reality. Ordinances of the Spanish crown of a later period reserved the pilgrimage outfit, upon presentation of the appropriate episcopal documents, for foreign pilgrims only.[92] The multiplication of such and similar documents invariably points to their inherent inefficaciousness. The regimentation into companies, for its part, proved of only limited value against the major virus of organized banditry on the road, which the *Guide* too expressly mentions concerning the Basque country and Navarra. Against these nothing turned out to be helpful except here and there some company of soldiers that chanced to find itself in the vicinity and that agreed to enter into an unpleasant melee. This occurred but with the greatest rarity.[93]

Such were then the roads to St. James that the eleventh- and twelfth-century pilgrim had to face: dangerous, unpredictable, and long – 1,000 to 1,200 km long, if he departed from somewhere in southwestern France, 1,600 to 2,000 km, if he set out from the eastern provinces or the north, and from 2,000 to 2,500 and even close to 3,000 km, if he departed from somewhere in Germany or the northern countries. Pilgrims from Poland, Hungary, Slovenia, Croatia, the eastern Austrian domains, and Slovakia had to cover an even longer route. Irregular and changing as the pilgrim companies were, so too was the daily distance covered. For the large masses of pilgrims who walked their way – the only ones we are concerned with here – 20 to perhaps 25 km represented, for the most part, a reasonable average daily march; but there were certainly mountainous stretches in which no more than 15 km were made, or perhaps even less, while there were others, on the easier flat lands and with good weather, in which 30 km or perhaps a little bit more were covered.[94]

Two considerations though must be kept in mind in order to justly evaluate this daily output: first, the social state of the peasant-pilgrims, their general worn-out and declining physical condition, the relatively advanced age of most at the time of the pilgrimage, and the ailments and often handicaps that many were suffering and which were the primary cause of their setting out on the road to Santiago in the first place. With such rather disheartening picture in mind, the daily 20 to 25 km, sustained over weeks and months in a row, represented no mean effort.[95]

Second, the pilgrimage to Santiago hardly ever meant an uninterrupted day after day march along the route stopping only for the mandatory nightly rest. Quite to the contrary: the most common pattern, which is also apparent from the *Guide*, was that of making longer halts at reliquary churches of particular prominence and fame, modulated probably by personal taste and preference. In contradistinction to the pilgrimage to Jerusalem, but even in a way to that to Rome, the embarking upon the pilgrimage road to Santiago meant at one and the same time nearly mandatory visits at many or most of the great relics on the way. The French portion of the *Guide*, in fact, heavily promotes such a perception of the pilgrimage. It seems appropriate to infer though – and indeed we know this from other accounts as well as from the Romanesque and Gothic monuments on the way – that what the *Guide* suggests for France was operational in Germany, Austria, Italy, England, and the rest of the countries in central and northern Europe as well, and particularly so on the Spanish portion of the route – in Aragón, the Basque land, Navarra, Castilla, and Galicia. Quite apart from such essentially devotional stations,[96] however, other more worldly motivations were also at play in dictating the pace of the journey: advantageous food and lodging opportunities would not be lightly dismissed; wealthy country fairs, not bypassed; celebrated preachers whose fame ran ahead of their words would not be missed; even the slightest material gains would not be scorned; occasional personal adventures, not neglected. All told, one had to reach the faraway relics of St. James; but one lived only once.

Irrespective of the question of the more or less prolonged stays at chosen stopovers, the long march was divided by stations on the route. The *Guide* provides us with a list that comprises stations, corresponding to days' journeys, between Somport and Puente la Reina. Even a cursory examination of this chart against the actual distances will show that many of the days' journeys on the route offered by the *Guide* are illusory and optimistic. In no way could the pilgrims have made the stretch from Borce to Jaca, or from Jaca to Monreale in one day's march. The same applies to other portions of the route. It seems safe to assume thus that the stations quoted by the *Guide* are, at best, the result of a willfully manipulated calculation, fundamentally unrealistic, meant to attract pilgrims by shortening the road; at worst, the illusory reckoning responds to a gaping lacuna in the actual survey of the terrain or perhaps to an inappropriate intermingling of distances covered partly on horseback and partly on foot. Had the motivations for the optimistic reckoning been a propagandistic move towards would-be pilgrims, it would be hard to justify the accounts of banditry and water-related calamities that the *Guide* provides with a nearly malicious gusto and a gory luxury of details.[97]

On such inordinately long marches, tall tales, adventurous stories, mouth-to-mouth pieces of news and information were passed along, sometimes on the route itself, at other times in the hospice or over the inn-counter. No matter how questionable, flimsy, or braggart, these accounts and reports were always welcome. They were the very stuff of which the dreams and realities of the pilgrimage folklore were made. It may, indeed, be said that the route to Santiago de Compostela constituted, apart from the great Romanesque spatial and visual culture of its ecclesiastical monuments, an essentially mobile oral tradition in which, next to the spirit and the legs, it was the *mouth* that kept the pilgrimage movement alive. Such an oral culture, quite naturally, was further conditioned and modulated by *Landsmannschaft* bonds; but there are good reasons to believe that it actually transcended narrowly conceived linguistic barriers. These, in fact, did not run along barely defined national lines, but rather along regional and even provincial ones. Germans from the Rheinland had as much difficulty understanding their fellowmen from Saxony as the Catalan pilgrims their Galician innkeeper. Concurrently with such a colorful multilingual ambiance, and partly due to it, the floating population of these roads made sign language and sign communication a welcome ancillary necessity. Music, also an international language, in addition to actual pilgrimage songs, of which many have survived, came to complete the circle of oral culture so critically important for the society of pilgrims to keep alive and thriving a sense of belonging, purpose, sanity, and mutual encouragement.[98]

Money for the Journey

We know far too little of the economics of the pilgrimage road to Santiago de Compostela. The circulation of coinage was far from being unknown on the route. The *Guide* speaks of the money changers of the *via francigena* entering the city of St. James, and there must have certainly been money changers at other important centers along the route, such as at Estella or Burgos, as well as at regional and jurisdictional borders, such as Roncesvalles, Jaca, or Villafranca del Bierzo. The nobility as well as the wealthy travelers had, as a matter of course, larger sums at their disposal, at times in various currencies; the modest class of the artisans, the ecclesiastical and lay intelligentsia, the merchants and the members of the free professions also carried with them, without any doubt, certain sums of money in the form of coins, greatly varying in amount depending on the individual case. The latter classes, as well as the aforementioned nobility, enjoyed the additional advantage, not a mean one, of being at least somewhat familiarized with the exchange rates in current use. The peasant-pilgrims, on the other hand, whether serfs or freeholders, carried with them – concealed in their shoes, boots, socks, or the inside pockets of their breeches – considerably lesser amounts of coinage, the meager fruit of years of savings; and, what made their situation more precarious, they had mighty little inkling of exchange rates. The peasant-pilgrims were thus at the mercy of the merciless: toll-gatherers, money changers and, perhaps to lesser extent, innkeepers hardly ever hesitated to take shameless advantage of their ignorance.[99]

But coins could only do as much as their accepted value, and the purses of the peasant-pilgrims were as thin as their faces were emaciated. Supporting structures were needed if they were to make it to Santiago. Often enough the inclemencies of the weather or the accidents of the route prevented pilgrims from reaching their day's destination and forced them to seek haphazard shelter for the night just anywhere on the route. In such predicaments they felt lucky if they happened to stumble even on a haystack. Pilgrims soon learned that to be choosy was the surest way of remaining in the cold. In the twelfth century by far most of the Continent was nothing but untamed nature and unreclaimed land – it is enough to think, even for a much later time, of Shake-speare's green comedies – in which one speaks here and there of islands of cultivated soil, patches of grassland and occasional hamlets or villages. In these the state of existence was more often than not marginal for their own inhabitants too who thus could spare less than a pittance for the poor pilgrim begging at the door. It is under such conditions that the network of hospices and hospitals that dotted the route to Santiago must be particularly appreciated – and pilgrims ever since the earliest times did appreciate it.

Hospitals, Hospices, and Monasteries

Hospices and hospitals – not always clearly differentiated – were numerous and variously maintained by a host of ecclesiastical and lay institutions, some of them strictly welfare-oriented, others less so. The services they provided – if one may so call them – varied a great deal in nature and quality. There were those standing under royal or high ecclesiastical patronage or even under some privileged lay institutional patronage, and these were few. The *Guide* mentions in the highest laudatory terms the famous hospice of Santa Cristina on the Somport Pass; in the royal hospice of Burgos food was said to have been abundant, at least at times. Most of the hospices, however, were of the humblest nature supported by low-ranking ecclesiastical institutions, municipalities, or confraternities of St. James. These provided only the most rudimentary facilities for the marchers: often a single sleeping quarter consisting of one large straw mattress, a kind of a communal bed on which ten, fifteen, or even twenty pilgrims accommodated themselves as well as they could, lumped closely together, warming each other with the compound body heat of their tired limbs. In such conditions, it was little wonder that more than once one found oneself next morning in the company of strange bedfellows. Among these, lice and flees never failed the appointment. Clearly, the dependence upon hospices alone would not have done. Fortunately though there were also monasteries.[100]

The virtue of charity, prominent otherwise too in the economy of Christian life, found on the pilgrimage roads – often at some affordable distance from it – a particularly fertile ground for its unhampered exercise. Welcoming the pilgrim, feeding, and occasionally clothing him, and most importantly providing him with shelter for the night constituted primary Christian obligations variously fostered by collateral traditions and practiced with particular integrity and fervor in various monastic establishments. It had been customary, quite independent of pilgrimages, to welcome in the community, especially in remote areas of difficult access, the casual traveler. The needy pilgrim was no exception to such welcoming. On these occasions feet-washing, feeding, and shelter were more often than not observed.[101] Next, there were a number of independent narrative traditions, some of which are quoted in the *Guide*, that hinged on the divine retribution allotted to those who failed in their obligation vis-à-vis needy pilgrims in search of shelter. Lastly, there was a deeply running perception rooted in the evangelical texts – the episode of the Disciples at Emmaus – according to which one could never be sure whether the anonymous wayfarer or pilgrim knocking at the door was not himself Christ.[102]

But there were also confraternities. Those of St. James, particularly important in the northern regions of Europe and in Germany, made their entrance into the pilgrimage system towards the end of our period. They were predominantly an urban phenomenon with roots in towns and cities, whose declared aim was two-fold: on the one hand, to extend, as far as possible, the beneficial effects of the pilgrimage and of the contact with the sacred beyond the actual experience itself. On the other hand, and quite apart from such lofty moral and spiritual aims, the confraternities were also a point of social rally with elaborate constitutions and by-laws concerning membership, authorities, functions, and activities, some of which concerned, precisely, the pilgrims. In fact, many confraternities of St. James sponsored or partially supported hospices for the pilgrims on their way to and from Santiago. While such confraternities or *Brüderschaften*, as they came to be called in German, provided a solid home-base for the pilgrimage as a whole – this constituted the welfare aspect of their program – they did not neglect some more festive and epicurean appurtenances either. In particular they celebrated the festivities of St. James on July 25 with elaborate pageantry and juicy banqueting.[103]

In terms of welfare considerations only, inns and innkeepers were at the bottom of the supporting system alongside the road to Santiago. Otherwise, they were quite efficient and reliable: little wonder, for they quenched the thirst, filled the belly, and provided shelter, all for good money at costly exchange rates. Wayside inns were always notorious for compounding the pleasures of libation with those of the flesh. A pilgrim in an inn would never know which of the local maidservants would slip in the dead of the night under his cover. And since in three out of the four seasons nights were cold, rooms chilly, and the straw mattress hardly more than an ice box that the fully dressed pilgrim could not hope of warming up, the unexpected bonanza was quite welcomed. There was, of course, a fee to be paid for such extra services quite apart from the concomitant spiritual perils. That not all innkeepers were honest, some only marginally so, lies somewhat in the nature of the profession. Some took assuredly more advantage of foreign pilgrims than others: witness the episode, so sprightly alive on the road, of the pilgrim at Santo Domingo de la Calzada double-crossed by his innkeeper's daughter or maid and hanged on the gallows from which St. James would eventually rescue him.[104]

Pilgrims' Outfit

The long road to Santiago demanded an appropriate outfit. Never for a moment could the pilgrim forget that whatever he owned at this stage of life, as a pilgrim he would have to carry along at all times. Nomad as he became for as long as the pilgrimage lasted, he was tightly and indissolubly bound to his belongings. The suitable outfit for the long march of months was a matter of considerable concern for him. The shoes had to be both well-made and solid, but at the same time sufficiently light and practical. Shoemakers and shoe repairmen stationed in the major pilgrimage centers and working out of workshops at times made up of their lap only, had a busy time mending the out-trodden shoes of the marchers. Quite naturally, those among the pilgrims who were themselves shoemakers, worked on the side during the entire pilgrimage. Soles and heels, as always, were the most affected parts of the footwear.

As to the garments, these had to be sufficiently short and light not to encumber the limbs on the long march, but at the same time sufficiently protecting against the inclemencies of the weather. A short cloak reinforced with leather, the *pèlerine*, as well as a surcoat, became by the later Middle Ages nearly mandatory pieces of the outfit, as did also a wide-brimmed felt hat for protection from both sun and rain. Many of the French roads were lined with trees at least on one side, offering the traveler a welcome shade; but the Spanish roads on the plains were as a rule bare, open to the inclemencies of a weather tending to extremes. Some pieces of the outfit were, however, even more important than shoes and garments: those that carried a symbolic value.[105]

In part because medieval society provided each of its constituent classes with distinctive signs, in part because of juridical requirements, and in part because the marchers themselves, out of pride but also convenience, wished to be duly recognized, the pilgrims to Compostela displayed at all times some visible attributes of their own. These in the twelfth century were three: the *bordón* or *bourdon*, the *escarcela* or *besace*, and the scallop shell. To the above in subsequent centuries the *patenôtre* – a chapelet or hood, the box of documents on the waist belt, and the *calabaza* – gourd or *calebasse*, were added, though the latter had probably been in use already earlier without any particular symbolism attached to it. The *calabaza* was a common bottle gourd for wine or water, made usually from the hard globose shell of a herbaceous fruit and hung either on the belt or on the hook of the *bordón*. This was a more or less long staff that terminated in an iron point at the lower end and in an enlarged button or *pommeau* and often in a hook on the upper end. While in the twelfth century it was normally shorter than the pilgrim, in the following centuries it gradually increased in length. The *bordón* proved most useful as an aid in the march and particularly on the uphill stretches and as a reasonable defense weapon mainly against vagrants of various sorts, stray dogs, and other minor nuisances. It was also of some value against wolves, provided they did not roam in a pack. But the *bordón* had also its symbolic significance: it was credited with chasing the devil away, and it stood for the *lignum crucis*, the Wood of the Cross.

As to the *escarcela*, it was a medium-size sack or bag made usually of deer leather, surprisingly flat and hence of questionable usefulness for holding food or anything else; normally of trapezoid shape, it was narrower at the mouth than at the base and, thrown across the shoulder, it was secured with a leather strap. Though of limited practical value, deep were its symbolic reverberations: the *escarcela* had to be narrow and flat to remind the pilgrim to rely on the Great Provider alone instead of on his own provisions, it had to be always open in order to give and receive, and it had to be made of an animal skin to evoke the mortifications of the flesh.[106]

An integral part of the pilgrimage outfit was, and still is, the famous scallop shell that since at least the eleventh century constitutes the distinctive symbol of the Jacobean pilgrimage. Nearly all twelfth-century representations of St. James display it: the sculptures at Mimizan, Bayonne, Estella, and Santa Marta de Tera. This *concha venera* – the *pecten jacobeus* according to some or the *pecten maximus* according to others – is found, of course, in great abundance on the Galician beaches near Santiago. Various medieval legends speak of a prince who, having fallen into the ocean waves, was rescued, covered with shells, by St. James; another legend speaks of a horse emerging from the waves of the ocean wrapped in shells. The various accounts belong to a beloved medieval *topos* whose stories are all patterned upon the Jonas legend. The delightful episode of the mother finding her child safe in the submarine grotto of St. Clement in the Sea of Azov, represented in the lower church of San Clemente in Rome, also belongs to the same cycle.

The importance of the shell, however, apart from its handiness and innocent beauty, which children know intuitively when they gather them on the sea shore, lies in the symbolism attached to it. The sermon *Veneranda dies* explains why the scallop shell is symbolic of the good works the pilgrim is expected to perform: it reminds him of the spread out fingers of the back of the hand. Little wonder, therefore, that even whenever some components of the Jacobean pilgrim's outfit were missing, the shell was always there as the *signum peregrinationis* par excellence. The scallop shell finds its secure place on the *escarcela*, the hat, or the jacket of the pilgrim and, with great preference, it is carried into the pilgrim's very tomb too. In fact, many pilgrim tombs contain one or more shells. At Eunate, in the pilgrims' graves immediately adjacent to the octagonal open porch of the Templars' church many shells were found. The shells were also, and still are, imitated in metals of various sorts and sold at the Portal de las Platerias of the Cathedral of Santiago. Though ordinances regulated both the fabrication and the sale of such and similar souvenir objects, with time their exclusive Compostelan production was much impugned by interested competition.[107]

We gather an indication of the extraordinary significance that the Jacobean outfit had for the pilgrims if we follow its fortune subsequent to the successful completion of the pilgrimage. At times confraternities and sanctuaries that had aided the pilgrims on the route became the beneficiaries of the pilgrimage trappings and garments after the return of the marchers. More often than not, however, the pilgrimage paraphernalia remained, subsequent to the return to the village, a cherished personal memento of that great, unique, once-in-a-lifetime adventure. Here and there, during festivities and solemnities, it was paraded around and, once death had called at the door, it became the proper outfit for the exequies.

A judicial problem of particular relevance and constant preoccupation concerned the ownership of the personal belongings of the pilgrims who had died on the route. The fact that this was considered a problem of such magnitude is indicative of the high number of pilgrims who must have ended their days on the pilgrimage road. This, in turn, is a pointer at the relatively advanced age at which they must have set out on the long march, at their oftentimes poor health, and at the common perils of the route. Royal ordinances established that the earthly remains of a pilgrim were to be buried by his companions. This presupposed, therefore, the common knowledge that pilgrims, as a rule, traveled in groups.[108]

The real problem, however, concerned not so much the burial as the fate of the meager belongings: these were supposed to be carried back to the legal inheritors of the defunct by his pilgrimage companions coming from his own village, township, hamlet area, or from nearby. But the route was long, memories short, and good intentions, in the face of possible benefits, volatile: the personal belongings seldom reached their destination. Since often enough severe illness on the way might force a pilgrim to take refuge in some private inn on the roadside while his companions had perforce to continue their march, innkeepers played a prominent role, in case of defunction, in their burial and, more often than not, in sharing the benefits of the personal belongings left over. Royal ordinances established that, in any event, if a pilgrim happened to die in an inn or close by, the innkeeper was allowed to keep the best pieces of his garments while the lesser items were to be sent back – God knows how – to his family. No doubt such regulations were issued in order to provide an incentive to the innkeeper charged with the pious duties of the burial.

Departure, Arrival, and Return

Since all pilgrimages, and hence that of Santiago de Compostela too, are circular – one sets out in order to come back – particular rites marked the departure and the return of the pilgrims, rites that harked back, though on an infinitely humbler level, to the imperial *profectio* and *adventus* of classical culture. The would-be pilgrims first confessed and took Holy Communion and then underwent the rites of the blessing of the pilgrimage insignia. As the arms of the Christian knight were blessed at the moment of the knighting ceremonies, so were also the *insignia peregrinorum*, the spiritual marching arms of the pilgrims – *escarcela* and *bordón* – at the moment of departing: in fact, pilgrims were also thought of as a kind of a Christian militia, and their marching implements, as their arms. Concerning the particularities of the blessing rite, on the whole there were no absolute and overall practices set and much less observed. Things depended to a large extent upon social standing and group dynamics. A rather common procedure consisted in the following: the would-be pilgrims kneeled down before the altar, with the *bordón* and the *escarcela* placed in front of them; these were blessed by a priest with a formula that varied from place to place but which almost always, concerning the *bordón*, evoked the insidious perils of the devil and, concerning the *escarcela*, the mortifications of the flesh. The ritual ended with the blessing of the pilgrims themselves, upon which the departure followed. Whenever a

larger company assembled for the march or a collective pilgrimage proper was drummed up, more elaborate liturgical
procedures were set in motion: having administered the various blessings in the church, as usual, psalms were chanted
to infuse courage into the heart of the new pilgrims, and at
the sound of litanies the local assembly set out with the
marchers on the first few miles of the journey.[109]

The liturgy upon the actual arrival at Santiago de
Compostela became, as time went by, gradually more elaborate. In earlier times, the visit to the tomb of the apostle took
place upon arrival, quite indifferently before or after attending mass in the cathedral: also, appropriate offerings for
candles and oil were expected to be forthcoming spontane-
ously. With the passing of a few generations, however, more
elaborate practices were devised to ensure a more efficient
and uniform flow of cash: an all-night wake in the cathedral
followed by confession and Holy Communion became practically required preparatory steps for the subsequent tour of
the cathedral and the veneration of the reliquary tomb of St.
James. Between the two the offerings were expected to be
left in the appropriately placed chest, and officials were
around to remind the pilgrim forgetful of his duties.

The visit of the vast cathedral together with its many chapels, sacristies, altars, and sundry dependencies in which images *ad adorationem,* didactic cycles of various kinds, and,
more than anything else, relics were appropriately ordered,
displayed, and highlighted – a glittering chest of astonishing marvels – took at least a day or two. Within such a mandatory itinerary the veneration of the remains of St. James in
the vaulted tomb and the worshipping at his altar in the chancel constituted moments of the highest reverberation for the
pilgrim, moments that he would henceforth cherish and, jealously guarded, take back with him to his village or town
and actually down into his grave. In the vaulted tomb – the
crypt – kneeling in front of the reliquary that treasured the
remains of St. James and with their hands placed upon its
lid or against its front, the pilgrims sank in thought and
prayer that more often than not included some long-guarded
personal wish for a miraculous intervention of the saint. In
the chancel, on the other hand, under the stupendous
ciborium, they admired the magnificent high altar of St.
James, its silver antependium and, in the rare occasions that

this was removed, the modest small altar that the first disciples of St. James had erected over his tomb.[110]

Having stayed for a few days in town, at times even for a week or two, and having received from the appropriate ecclesiastical authorities the pilgrimage certificate attesting to their having indeed been in Santiago, many pilgrims chose to push still a bit farther towards the west and to reach the shores of the immense ocean at Padrón where, as it was told, the boat bearing the body of St. James had put in, or even to venture as far as Finisterre where they could gather as many scallop shells as their hearts desired. It was only after all this that the pilgrims set out upon their homeward trail.[111]

The returning from Santiago did not always follow the same itinerary as the coming: turning off from the main road for asides such as Oviedo in Asturias or Santo Domingo de Silos in Castilla la Vieja or San Millán de la Cogolla in La Rioja – not to speak of the many collateral attractions in France – meant a choice treat for pilgrims relieved already from the pressures of their main preoccupation or perhaps intent upon some off-the-program sightseeing. The route of the Salvador took them to the fabulous *Camera sancta* in Oviedo; a two-day-long southern road from Burgos, to the famed monastery of Silos; and a collateral route from Santo Domingo de la Calzada or from Nájera, to some of the most preciously bejeweled ivory reliquaries in Christendom in San Millán de la Cogolla. Once all that was also over, the Pyrenees left behind and more often than not the well-irrigated plains of France too, and the tired but rather content pilgrim company re-entered, in Burgundy or Flanders or Saxony or the Hungarian lowlands, the village or town of its *Landsmannschaft*, the *bordón* and the *escarcela* were finally laid to rest. By then for most pilgrims who had set out from France close to six months must have gone by, and for those coming from central, southern, or northern Europe, close to one year.

As the returning wayfarer crossed the threshold of his lowly hamlet, as must have been the case for the large masses of the peasant-pilgrims, some celebration might have followed, stories must have been told, and the local confraternity of St. James, if there were one, might have won a new member. But other than this, life in most cases would henceforth be bound to follow its habitual course. And it would be a downward course, for most who undertook the pilgrimage to Santiago de Compostela did so in the later part of their life, once their strength was waning. That is the reason why so many of the pilgrims of peasant extraction, worn out by the effort, had died on the way; and that is also the reason why so many of them would go to their final resting place not long after their return from Santiago. At that point though the *bordón*, the *escarcela*, and the scallop shell, which had guided them to the tomb of St. James, would now take their place side by side with the pilgrims' own earthly remains. Not unlike the *miles christianus* buried with the arms with which he had fought for Christ, the pilgrim to Santiago too was buried with the pilgrimage arms he bore on the way. The memory of St. James was thus destined to remain with him forever.

THE ICONOGRAPHY OF ST. JAMES

Byzantine form-culture recognizes two typologies in the representation of St. James the Greater: in the first, St. James figures as a member of the College of the Apostles. This might occur either in generic scenes in which the disciples appear flanking the enthroned Christ in heaven, or in specific episodes of the Christological cycle proper. James is present in these cases anonymously, without bearing any specific attribute or ascertainable sign of differentiation by which we could tell him apart from the rest of his companions. Most of these too go undifferentiated, except for Peter who often enough is recognizable by his characteristic strait haircut, and for John and Judas Iscariot, who are distinguished by their respective position within the groupings: the former, bent upon the chest of Christ in representations of the Last Supper, and the latter in his evident role in the same episode as well as in the Kiss and the Detention of Christ. The presence of St. James in such groupings is manifest by the total number of participants only – twelve, the symbolic-canonical number that evokes the Twelve Tribes of Israel. Since all apostles are present here, we infer that St. James the Greater is also present.

Such representations include some of the best-known scenes of the Christological cycle, and in particular, of the

Passion and the Resurrection cycles: the Washing of the Feet, and especially the Last Supper and the Ascension of Christ. It is only on rare occasions that the Kiss of Judas and the Detention of Christ sequence, as well as the Entry in Jerusalem, may be counted on, for in these the number of the apostles greatly fluctuates. In the Last Supper, on the other hand, the number twelve is traditionally observed with great rigor. Equally rigorous is the presence of the entire College of the Apostles in the Pentecost, already outside the Passion cycle, as well as, more rarely, in the so-called Koimesis or the Death of the Virgin. In all the above cases then the presence of St. James is axiomatic but undifferentiated. The great Byzantine mosaic cycles of Monreale in Sicily or St. Mark in Venice may be cited here as appropriate instances of such a first iconographic orientation.

There is a second typology too in Byzantine culture that calls for an *obbligato* presence of James: the Transfiguration. The famous theophany on Mount Tabor is witnessed, albeit in a kind of a psychologically fortifying mental torpor, only by the inner circle of the apostles, Peter, John, and James. In these representations Peter usually turns up on the left of the mountain top. He is the most composed of the three: having just offered the tabernacles, the familiar activity has helped him to recover his confidence. John, in the center, the closest to Christ, is in a deep *proskynesis*; and finally James, on the right, is usually shown in an awkward pose, halfway between genuflection and standing. In the Transfiguration, therefore, James is recognizable by both his pose and position. A bronze panel of St. Paul outside the Walls in Rome and an illumination from a Tetraevangelistary of the Bibliothèque Nationale in Paris, both of the eleventh century, may serve us as appropriate examples.

Romanesque form-culture adopts the ready-made Byzantine traditions with the usual Western formal energy and iconographic reinterpretation: we find James in the College of the Apostles on the tympanum of the abbey church of Carennac and on the Porte de Miègeville of Saint-Sernin in Toulouse, in order to remain close to the pilgrimage roads, and in any number of further Last Supper and Ascension scenes – so on an early eleventh-century illumination in the Evangelistary of Bishop Bernward of Hildesheim or on the late twelfth-century bronze door of Bonannus of Pisa in the cathedral of the same city. The

INTRODUCTION: ICONOGRAPHY OF ST. JAMES

iconography of the Transfiguration is also appropriated by Romanesque form-culture, though not without considerable jerks and jolts in the figural arrangements and in the space relationships: often both John and James appear now in *proskynesis* and hence there is some ambivalence in their identifcation. Moreover, and most significantly, it is the Romanesque centuries that are destined to lend a powerful and decisive turn to the iconography of James. This seems only natural for, all told, tenth- and eleventh-century Romanesque culture is responsible for the revival of the cult of St. James and for the development of the pilgrimage road to his tomb in far off Galicia. Within the parameters of such a renewed interest, two distinct iconographies were developed, one military in character and national in orientation, though not without some international reverberations, and the other devotional in character and decidedly western European in scope and orientation. We do not know which of the two iconographic trends antedates the other, for the instances that have come down to us from each hark back, at the earliest, to the first half of the twelfth century.[112]

The first of these, developing along national lines, is rooted in the historical necessity of the *Reconquista*. It plays upon the notion of active, engaged military leadership provided by St. James to the exiguous and hard-pressed Christian forces pushed back into the recesses of the northernmost tier of the peninsula. Victorious on all fronts, unchallenged within the domains of el-Andalus, the ultimate glory of Islam in Spain lay in its ability to provide a viable socio-cultural alternative to ample sectors of the Jewish but mainly of the Christian masses: these were quite naturally and effortlessly integrated into the superior Islamic el-Andalusian society, economy, way of life, and culture. It is upon such a complex global scenario that the linguistic transmutation of *Sanctus Iacobus* into *Santiago* was effected and the creation of a broad-shouldered folkloric figure was made in the conscience of the masses a reality of ponderous historic weight. Henceforth Santiago would ride upon a white horse ahead of the Christian hosts, leading them to victory.

The iconographic sedimentation that ensued faithfully preserved the above traits. Santiago is represented on a galloping horse, usually in profile, entering from left to right, at times in armor, at others with a billowing cape, sword in the right hand and the banner of victory in the left. Behind him the defeated infidels, crushed to the ground, helplessly moan; in front of him the powerless enemy surrenders. It is thus that the brave saint is said to have appeared in the battle of Clavijo, a first, largely mythical turning point in the military fortunes of the Christians in 844, and later, in 1212, in the doubtlessly decisive battle of Las Navas de Tolosa, no less than in the rest of the victorious confrontations. He is said, on the other hand, to have stayed prudently at home in moments of clamorous defeats. Appropriately enough for the historical reality and the temper of the times, such an iconography of Santiago has received the designation of *Matamoros*, that is to say, the slayer of the moors. It does not seem fortuitous that a mid-twelfth century stone relief of *Matamoros* should greet the visitor on the inside of the Portal de las Platerías of the Cathedral of Santiago. Later instances of the *Matamoros* iconography are found, though in surprisingly scant numbers, in scattered locations throughout the Hispanic meseta and the northern tier of the peninsula. Outside Spain, the iconography of the riding saint is little known.

The second iconography of Santiago, on the other hand, is eminently international in character, scope, and diffusion, and it stems directly from the early pilgrimage folklore of the eleventh and twelfth centuries: it shows St. James as a pilgrim on his way to or from Santiago. Now, to be sure, from the twelfth century onward there are also a considerable number of wall paintings, reliefs, and sculptures representing *pilgrims*, always anonymous, sometime in company and at others alone. Each of the two groups of images – Santiago as a pilgrim and pilgrims in general – is characterized by a set of three iconographic attributes that appear now together, now individually, now in sundry combination: the *bordón*, the *escarcela*, and finally the ever present scallop shell – the *pecten maximus* – appended at times onto the hat, at others to the lapel or to the *escarcela* or in various combination thereof. Apparelled in such a manner, James was differentiated from pilgrims at large by the saint's occasional halo, or by his visible membership in the College of the Apostles, or by some other rather evident programmatic position. We find twelfth-century instances of such an iconography on the Romanesque portal of Mimizan, on the portal of the remains of the old cathedral of Bayonne, on a remarkable sculpture in the round in front of the church of the Holy Sepulcher in Estella, and in the very center of the Portal de la Gloria in Santiago de Compostela.

The community of attributes shared by James and his pilgrims is only the expression of a fundamental ideological perception: to leave as slim a margin as possible between the saint and his pilgrims, to represent Santiago as a pilgrim directed to or coming from the saint's tomb. Herein lies, precisely, an inherent theological problem and the relative anomaly of its iconographic resolution. Within the pyramidal structure of Christian hierarchical organization, the principles of Christocentrism and sacred Christian history reign supreme. Deriving from them is the notion of *imitatio Christi* which, subsequently, is endlessly reproposed for each of the disciples no less than for the entire host of the faithful: the Lord is followed and imitated by the apostles; the apostles are followed and imitated each by his own disciples; each saint is followed by a throng of his or her own devotees, and so on. Within such ideological parameters, Santiago too is followed by his devotees, and his tomb is visited by his pilgrims. It is perfectly appropriate therefore that the followers of Santiago be characterized as pilgrims who walk to or return from the saint's tomb: hence the *bordón* and the *escarcela* – the implements of the protracted journey on foot; and hence the scallop shell, the very symbol of the pilgrimage to the much longed-for saintly relic in the vicinity of the Galician shores.

But why would Santiago himself be characterized and actually described as a pilgrim? The only plausible answer to the query seems to rest on the notion of the saint's unusual and essentially altruistic and self-effacing identification with his devotees, with pilgrims making their way to his own tomb. Such a resolution, however, constitutes an ideological and iconographic orientation that no other saint ever undertakes: St. Nicholas of Bari, St. Foy of Conques, St. Isidore of León, to name a few, each is represented with his or her particular and idiosyncratic iconography, and none of them is shown with the specific iconography, if any, of his or her devotees. The anomalous representation of Santiago, therefore, must be ascribed to the extraordinary mass devotion that has surrounded the apostle for centuries and which had grown, during the critical era of the central and later

Middle Ages, to a level of overwhelming fascination that knew no frontiers and no ideological limitations.

This overbearing mass-phenomenon is responsible for a still further development that the iconography of Santiago undergoes, a turn directly connected with his pilgrim attributes. The case in point constitutes a clamorous aberration of the Christocentric principles that govern Christian sacred history: the scene of the Disciples at Emmaus in some twelfth-century representations is made coetaneous to, and hence overlapping with, the medieval devotion to Santiago. In the cloister of Saint-Trophime in Arles one of the two disciples of the episode is shown with a scallop shell on his conic headgear; and in a clamorous instance that concerns one of the most sublime reliefs of the entire repertory of Romanesque art, in Santo Domingo de Silos, Christ himself is represented as a pilgrim to Santiago. *Bordón* in hand and *escarcela* thrown across His shoulder, Christ turns back towards the two disciples who have just asked Him to go with them (Luke 24.28–30). The cruciform halo leaves no doubt concerning the identity of the Lord. That Christ is not merely a wayfarer, hence entitled to a staff and a pouch, but a pilgrim to Santiago, is unmistakably determined by the scallop shell on his *escarcela*; a large shell is adorning its flap, and several smaller ones are on two loose strips flanking the pouch. The iconographic attributes of Santiago the pilgrim are thus lent to Christ who, incredible as this might seem, is signaled as a devotee of one of His three preferred disciples. The theological anomaly encountered earlier concerning St. James and his devotees has come now to a full circle: it is Christ Himself who turns into a pilgrim of Santiago.

Our saint's identification with his devotees lies at the root of the theologically anomalous iconography which, precisely because of its extraordinary character, had captured the minds and hearts of generations of Jacobean pilgrims. This same identification is responsible for a group iconography in which James often enough appears. We find the saint, otherwise armed with his usual attributes, in the company of his pilgrims who are also variously signaled as such – more often than not by the *bordón*. Such an iconography belongs to the later Middle Ages and it constitutes an evolution of the earlier notion of identification: at this point, it seems not quite sufficient to represent Santiago *qua* pilgrim anymore; the saint must engage now in concrete and hence visible acts of protection vis-à-vis his followers. It is thus that we find him in Linz-am-Rhein in the company of pilgrims who take refuge under his cape; and it is thus that he appears on many a *Kleinkunst* carving in the act of receiving the devotion of his pilgrims. This last iconographic resolution is invariably built around a centrally placed, frontally seated or standing figure of Santiago with one pilgrim flanking him on each side, quite often husband and wife. The pilgrims are represented kneeling, some in profile, others frontally, and they are modeled on a considerably diminished scale if compared to the saint. At times Santiago places crowns on their heads in what is known as *coronatio peregrinorum*. The old Byzantine principle of size as an indicator of theological relevance is apparent here. The *Kleinkunst* quality of these statuettes, as well as the material many of them are made of – *azabache*, that is to say, jet – make of them eminently portable objects of devotion. *Azabache* is mined in Asturias, but, apart from Spain, most such statuettes come to us from central-European countries – an indication that they were carried by German, Hungarian, or Austrian pilgrims on their journey home. A precious exemplar of such a statuette is in the Instituto de Valencia de Don Juan in Madrid.

Within the broader perspective of the traditions connected to James the Greater, a number of further episodes have entered the standard iconographic repertory. In these representations Santiago appears now with some of his pilgrimage attributes, now without them. One of the most famous thaumaturgical interventions of James concerns the magician Hermogenes, an episode patterned upon the better-known one of Peter and Simon the Magician. An early twelfth-century instance of the scene is found on the Porte Miègeville of Saint-Sernin in Toulouse. More important for Hispanic sensitivities and for the gradually evolving Marian cult in Spain is the mystical story involving both Santiago and the Virgin Mary. Weary and disheartened by the labors imposed upon him, Santiago is comforted by the Virgin who appears to him standing on a jasper column planted in the Ebro River. This episode constitutes the ideological foundation of Nuestra Señora del Pilar in Zaragoza, the most famous Marian shrine of the peninsula. The overall significance of this mystic encounter and of the iconographic representations ensuing from it cannot be underrated, for the episode constitutes the critical meeting point of the two most important Hispanic traditions, that of Santiago and that of the *Virgen del Pilar.*

On other occasions the story of James's passion is connected to that of his subsequent Galician destiny: at times he is represented at the moment of his beheading; at others, as on a fourteenth-century panel painting in the Prado, in the episode of the embarkation of his body and head in the miraculous boat; at others, at the arrival of the boat at Padrón on the Galician shores; and still at others, in the fanciful story of Queen Lupa and of his burial in what would become Compostela. Often enough partial cycles are developed around one or another of the above episodes: this occurs, for instance, on a rather late folkloric and rustic wood relief sequence in the Cathedral Museum of León. More significant and also widespread is the colorful episode of the pilgrim who, condemned on the strength of a false accusation, is hanged on the gallows only to be rescued subsequently by Santiago. A follow-up to this incident is the even more fanciful one of the cock or hen that, witnessing the veracity of Santiago's aforementioned miracle, stood up in the frying pan and started to crow. Both of these episodes are said to have occurred in the vicinity of Santo Domingo de la Calzada on the Castilian meseta; but since the pilgrim in question was a young French lad, the stories have attained a particularly wide currency in France too. The twelfth-century capitals of the cloister of the Colegiada Church of Tudela and the late twelfth-century cloister capitals today in Tarbes, depict these episodes with characteristic expressive naiveté.

The single, most ample treatment of the various episodes of the passion, of the Galician tradition, and of the subsequent miracles of Santiago occurs in a splendid fifteenth-century panel painting cycle from Szentjákobfalva in Hungary, preserved in the Christian Museum of Esztergom, also in Hungary. The original site and the present location of this cycle remind us once again of the particular strength of the central-European devotion to Santiago: no doubt, large throngs of pilgrims must have arrived at Santiago de Compostela from the regions of the Rhine, the Danube, and the Elbe. Strenuous marchers as these central-Europeans might have been, they would not have been able to cover the distance of three to four months of tireless walk were they not bearing Santiago in their hearts.

🐚

NOTES

1. On the notion of the sacred and on spirituality in general, see Oursel-*Pèlerins*, Labande-*Spiritualité*, Sigal-*marcheurs*, Delaruelle-*Piété populaire*, Vauchez-*spiritualité*, Labande-*pèlerins*, Dupront-*Sacré*, and the collective volume *Jacques Quête sacré-Dupront*. For its particular application to the pilgrimage to Santiago de Compostela, see the bibliographic items of n. 10 below.

2. On the medieval cult of saints and relics, see Delehaye-*martyrs*, Fichtenau-*Reliquienwesen*, Töpfer-*Reliquien Pilger*, Kötting-*Reliquienverehrung*, Schreiner-*Discrimen*, Schreiner-*Reliquienwesen*, HermannMascard-*reliques*, Constable-*Opposition Pilgrimage*, Constable-*Monachisme pèlerinage*, Brown-*Saints*, Geary-*Saint Shrine*.

3. On miracles and, in particular, on the attitudes and expectations of pilgrims vis-à-vis the miraculous happening, see Finucane-*Miracles Pilgrims*, Geary-*coercition saints*, Geary-*humiliation saints*, Sigal-*Miracle Gaule*, Ward-*Miracles*, Sigal-*miracle*.

4. On the *translatio* of relics, see Hotzelt-*Translationen Bayern*, Hotzelt-*Translationen Elsass*, HermannMascard-*reliques*, and Heinzelmann-*Translationsberichte*. On the immobility of relics, see Fichtenau-*Reliquienwesen* and Schreiner-*Reliquienwesen*. On the traffic and theft of relics, see Silvestre-*reliques*; Fichtenau-*Reliquienwesen*; Hermann Mascard-*reliques*, pp. 339–63; and the comprehensive monograph Geary-*Furta Sacra*.

5. On works emphasizing the theory of pilgrimage, see Dünninger-*Wallfahrt*, Brückner-*Wallfahrtswesen*, and Sumption-*Pilgrimage*, as well as four articles in the collective work, *Wallfahrt-Grenzen*: Kriss-*viator*, Baumer-*Wallfahrt Metapher*, Boglioni-*Pèlerinage religion populaire*, and Geary-*Saint Shrine*. Cf. also Constable-*Opposition Pilgrimage*. On the relationship between pilgrimage, monasticism, solitude, and the hermit's life, see Kötting-*Peregrinatio*, Leclercq-*Mönchtum Peregrinatio*, Constable-*Monachisme pèlerinage*, and Löwe-*Peregrinatio*. Also, on a topic overlapping this one, see Plötz-*Peregrini Palmieri*.

6. On the differentiation between full-fledged *corpora* relics and marginal, "touching" relics, see Kötting-*Reliquienverehrung*, Hermann-Mascard-*reliques*, McCulloh-*Cult Relics*, and Heinzelmann-*Translationsberichte*. On the official, and particularly papal, position concerning relics and their worship, see Fichtenau-*Reliquienwesen* and McCulloh-*Papal Relic*. For a particular case in point, see Hefele/Leclercq-*Conciles*, 3/2, p. 781 ff.

7. On the relative standing of Jerusalem, Rome, and Santiago de Compostela, see Sánchez/Barreiro-*Santiago*, Oursel-*Pèlerins*, Sigal-*marcheurs*, and Plötz-*Santiago-peregrinatio*. On the relationship

71

between the crusading drive to Jerusalem on the one hand and pilgrimages on the other – considered mainly from the former's point of view, see Erdmann-*Kreuzzugsgedankens*, Mayer-*Kreuzzüge*, and Labande-*Pellegrini crociati*.

8. On pilgrimages in classical and biblical times, see JoinLambert-*Pèlerinages Israël*, Abecassis-*hébraique juif*, and Simon-*antiquité chrétienne*, as well as *Pèlerinage biblique classique*. On pilgrimages in general, see Schreiber-*Wallfahrt*, Kötting-*Peregrinatio*, Venece-*Pèlerinages chrétiens*, Roussel-*pèlerinages*, Labande-*pèlerins*, Oursel-*Pèlerins*, Labande-*limina*, Spicq-*pérégrination NouvTest*, Sigalmarcheurs, Sumption-*Pilgrimage*, Turner-*Image Pilgrimage*, Plötz-*Peregrini Palmieri*, Chélini/Branthomme-*chemins Dieu*, Löwe-*Peregrinatio*, Baumer-*Wallfahrt Metapher*, and Maraval-*Lieux saints*. See also the two volumes of Stopani on the Italian peninsula, Stopani-*strade Roma*, and Stopani-*vie pellegrinaggio Medioevo*. Some of the collective works, such as *Pellegrinaggi culto santi-Todi*, *Pèlerinage-Fanjeaux*, *Wallfahrt-Grenzen*, and *Pellegrinaggio Europa-Padova*, should not be neglected either.

9. On the theory of the three apostolic sees (Peter in Rome, John in Ephesus, and James in Santiago de Compostela), see Vones-*Compostellana*, pp. 394 ff. and 520; as well as Herbers-*Jakobsweg*, p. 21. On the differentiation between the Compostela pilgrimage and the other great pilgrimage goals, see Plötz-*Strukturwandel peregrinatio*. On the significance of the apostolic relic in the raising of Santiago de Compostela to archiepiscopal dignity, see *Historia compostelana* 2:1–3 and 15–19, in Flórez-*Sagrada*, 20:251-59 and 285-97. Cf. also Vones-*Compostellana*, pp. 271–473.

10. On the pilgrimage to Santiago de Compostela, see the still refreshingly important VázquezParga-*pereg* and LaCosteMess-*Europe Jacques*; and further, King-*way James*, Lambert-*pèlerinage*, Bottineau-*Jacques*, Mullins-*Santiago*, Layton-*Santiago*, Davies-*Compostela*, and Oursel-*Route Saints*. See also the collective works *Pellegrinaggi culto santi-Todi*, *Pèlerins chemins Jacques-LaCoste Messelière*, *Santiago-Madrid*, *Saint-Jacques-dossiers*, *Pellegrinaggio Letteratura Jacopea-Perugia*, *Santiago-Europalia*, and *Santiago Routes-Bamberg*. On the great popularity enjoyed by the pilgrimage to Santiago de Compostela in the twelfth century, cf. *Historia Compostelana* 2:50, in Flórez-*Sagrada*, 20:350–51; and further, Schmugge-*Kirche Gesellschaft*, Schmugge-*Pilgerfahrt Frei*, and Dupront-*Puissances pèlerinage*. General works on the pilgrimage to Santiago, many of them in the genre of travel guides and surely some more popular than others, include the following: Fita-*Recuerdos*, Huidobro-*peregrinaciones*, Secret-*Jacques*, Starkie-*Santiago pilgrims*, Hell-*Wallfahrt*, Bennassar-*Saint Jacques*, Goicoechea-*Rutas*, Arrondo-*Rutas jacobeas*, PortelaSandoval-*Santiago*, Domke-*Spaniens Santiago*, Gruber-*Tagebuch Pilgers*, Barret/Gurgand-*Priez*

INTRODUCTION: NOTES

Compostelle, Stokstad-*Santiago Pilgrimages*, Bonet Correa-*Santiago*, Davies-*Compostela*, Barret/Gurgand-*Jakobspilger*, Domke-*Frankreichs Santiago*, Chocheyras-*Jacques*, Passini-*Camino*, Pardo-*Camino*, and Enríquez-Salamanca-*Camino*.

11. On the origin and development of the cult of St. James, see the following: Stone-*cult Santiago*, PérezUrbel-*Orígenes culto*, Sánchez Albornoz-*culto jacobeo*, PérezUrbel-*culto Santiago X*, Hohler-*Jacobus*, PérezUrbel-*Santiago*, Herwaarden-*Origins Cult*, Díaz Díaz-*litt. jacobite*, Plötz-*Traditiones*, and PrecedoLafuente-*Santiago Patrón*.

12. For the scriptural passages, see Matthew 4.21–22, 17.1–13, 20.20–28, 26.36–46; Mark 1.19–20, 3.17, 5.37, 9.2–13, 10.35–45, 14.32–42; and Luke 5.10, 8.51, 9.28–36, 22.39–46.

13. Acts 12.2.

14. Through apocryphal accounts: cf. Lipsius-*apokryphen Apostel*, 2:201–08.

15. Cf. DíazDíaz-*literatura jacobea anterior*, pp. 640–42.

16. See below, p. 170, nn. 201 and 202; and p. 180, n. 269.

17. On Clement of Alexandria, see Lipsius-*apokryphen Apostel*, 1:177–78; on Eusebius of Caesarea, H. J. Lawson, and Olten J. E. L. (trans. and ed.), *Eusebius Pamphili, Bishop of Caesarea* (Ecclesiastical History, 1), London, 1928.

18. On the Gospel of the Twelve Holy Apostles, see Haase-*Apostel Evangelisten*, p. 26.

19. Romans 15.24–29. On Paul's letter, see Dvornik-*Apostolicity Andrew*, pp. 35–36.

20. On the position of Innocent I, see Haase-*Apostel Evangelisten*, pp. 35, 51, 53–55.

21. On the *Breviarium apostolorum*, see GarcíaVillada-*Historia eccl Esp*, 1:26 ff.; VázquezParga-*pereg*, 1:27; and DíazDíaz-*Jakobus Legende Isidor*, p. 472.

22. Subsequent to the *translatio* of his relics. The Hispanic legend of Santiago may be traced back in Whitehill-*Liber*, 1:48–61, 94–103, 294–99; and in Hämel-*Überlieferung*. On the legend itself, see VázquezParga-*pereg* 1:9–36, PérezUrbel-*culto Santiago X*, Hohler-*Jakobus*, Herwaarden-*Origins Cult*, Plötz-*Jacobus*, Herbers-*Jakobus-kult*, Herwaarden-*James*, and PrecedoLafuente-*Santiago Patrón*. Cf. also Delisle-*Jacobi*, PérezUrbel-*Orígenes culto*, and Herwaarden-*Jacobus*.

23. Ehwald, R., *Aldhelmi opera*. MG-*Auctorum Antiquissimorum* 15, Berlin, 1919, p. 23.

24. DíazDíaz-*Jakobus Legende Isidor*, p. 469; Gaiffier-*Breviarium Apostolorum*, pp. 108–11.

25. Sanders-*Beati*, p. 116.

THE PILGRIM'S GUIDE TO SANTIAGO

26. See PérezUrbel-*himnos mozárabes*, pp. 125–27; Vázquez Parga-*pereg* 1:27–28; PérezUrbel-*Orígenes culto*, pp. 16-19 etc.; and Díaz Díaz-*antigua literatura*, p. 642.

27. For the text, see DíazDíaz-*antigua literatura*, pp. 623–26.

28. On the great complexities involved in the hymn *O dei verbum patris*, see Herwaarden-*Origins Cult*, pp. 7–17. On Ephrem the Syrian's position, see Haase-*Apostel Evangelisten*, p. 44; for Ado of Vienne, see Migne-*PL* 123:80.

29. "The sacred bones of the blessed Apostle having been translated to Spain and buried in its farthest region, that is to say, against the British sea, are splendorously kept in veneration by the people." On Ado's revision of Florus of Lyon's *Martyrologium*, see Quentin-*martyrologues*, pp. 385–408.

30. On Usuard, see Dubois-*martyrologe Usuard*, p. 135; and on Notker, Quentin-*martyrologues*, p. 466, n. 1 and p. 679. On the problem of the *translatio* of the remains of Santiago, see Hell-*Wallfahrt*, Kirschbaum-*Grab Jakobus*, and Herwaarden-*Origins Cult*. On the theory of a Mérida *translatio*, see PérezUrbel-*Orígenes culto* and PérezUrbel-*Santiago*; and on that of a Braga *translatio*, Costa-*cabeça Santiago*.

31. On Alphonso II and Bishop Theodemir, see VázquezParga-*pereg* 1:31–32; and below, p. 216, n. 515. On the usurper king Mauregatus, see MenéndezPelayo-*Heterodoxos*, p. 292; and Pérez Urbel-*comienzos Reconquista*, pp. 38–39.

32. On the corruption of the toponym *Marmarikes* into an architectural description, see Duchesne-*Jacques Galice*, p. 159 ff.; VázquezParga-*pereg* 1:30, and Bottineau-*Jacques*, pp. 28–29. On the intermediate stops in the *translatio*, see Hell-*Wallfahrt*, pp. 35–38; but also Herwaarden-*Origins Cult*, pp. 25–27.

33. On the Islamic invasion and the creation of the cultural space of al-Andalus, see, among many others, the classical works Castro-*España historia* (chaps. 2 and 3, "Islam e Iberia" and "Tradición islámica y vida española," pp. 47–81 and 82–103), Lévy Provençal-*España Musulmana*, and Arié-*España musulmana* (mainly chap. 1, "Evolución política," pp. 13–47).

34. On Asturias, its kingdom, and its place in the *Reconquista*, see FernándezConde-*Iglesia Asturias*, SánchezAlbornoz-*Orígenes Asturias*, FernándezConde-*medievo asturiano* and Sánchez Albornoz-*reino astur-leonés*. On the wider perspectives of the *Reconquista*, considered though under various ideological coordinates, see MenéndezPidal-*Cid*, PérezUrbel-*comienzos Reconquista*, Sánchez-Albornoz-*España enigma*, and GarcíaCortazar-*medieval* (particularly chap. 3, pp. 127–52, "La creación de los núcleos de resistencia hispanocristianos," and pp. 153–76, "La Recon-

INTRODUCTION: NOTES

quista...". On the *Reconquista* ideology of a Visigothic Renaissance, see VicensVives-*España*.

35. On Toledo, the Visigothic and ecclesiastic epicenter of the peninsula, see Gibert-*reino visigótico*, TorresLópez-*España Visigoda*, Thompson-*godos España*, and GarcíaCortazar-*medieval* (chap. 1, pp. 7–48, "El epigonismo visigodo").

36. On the gradual predominance of Castilla, see Gibert-*Libertades urbanas rurales León Castilla*, and Lacarra-*predominio Castilla*. On the decisive role of Alphonso VI, see O'Callaghan-*Alfonso VI*.

37. On French military assistance and the gradual socio-economic penetration, see Boissonade-*croisades françaises Espagne*; Defourneaux-*Français Espagne*; Reilly-*Santiago Saint Denis*; as well as Herbers-*Jakobskult*, p. 130, nn. 143–45; and Herbers-*Jakobsweg*, p. 17, n. 19.

38. On the repopulation and resettlement of the reconquered territories and in particular the areas adjacent to the pilgrimage routes, see González-*Reconquista repoblación*, Moxó-*Repoblación España*, and Barbero/Vigil-*orígenes sociales Reconquista*. On the resettlement and revitalization of towns and cities as a consequence of the pilgrimage activities on the routes, see Vázquez Parga-*pereg*, passim; Lacarra-*Jacques économique*; Passini-*Compostelle*; and Lacarra-*burguesía*. On particular problems of resettlement, including the assignation of special quarters to the newcomers, see Higounet-*chemins Jacques*, Ennen-*Stadt Wallfahrt*, Bishko-*Frontier*, Valiña-*Camino*, López Alsina-*ciudad*, and Valiña-*Camino Compostela*.

39. On the role of Cluny within the French interests in Spain and along the route to Compostela, as well as on the penetration of Cluniac spirit into the peninsula, see Valous-*pénétration française*, Valous-*cluniens*, Defourneaux-*Français Espagne*, Bischko-*Cluniac Priories Galicia*, Bischko-*Fernando I Cluny*, Gaillard-*clunisienne*, Gaillard-*Cluny Espagne*, Bischko-*Frontier*, Bischko-*Monastic*, and Williams-*Cluny*. Pacaut-*Cluny* provides a good overview of the Order. For a partial revision of Cluny's role in Spain, see Segl-*Cluniazenser*, Segl-*Cluny Spanien*, Werckmeister-*Cluny*, and Lyman-*Eclecticism*.

40. On San Juan de la Peña, its preeminent position among the Aragonese monasteries and its role in the introduction of the Roman rite, see UbietoArteta-*rito romano Aragón Navarra*; and Durliat-*Jacques*, p. 22.

41. For the constant French preoccupation of offsetting or at least counterbalancing the Roman apostolic predominance, see below, p. 174, n. 228; p. 179, n. 264; and p. 184, n. 310; as well as pp. 233–34.

42. On Charlemagne, the Roland tradition, and the *chansons de gestes,* see Bédier-*épiques* 3, Burger-*rolandienne,* Burger-*Roland Turpin Guide,* MenéndezPidal-*Roland,* Mandach-*chanson geste,* Owen-*Roland,* and the *Festschrift Louis-geste carolingien.*

43. On Charlemagne's Spanish campaign, see Bautier-*Charlemagne Espagne.*

44. On the discovery of the tomb of St. James and his identification, see Engels-*Jakobusgrabes,* GuerraCampos-*sepulcro,* and DíazDíaz-*litt. iacobite.* On the archeological diggings under the cathedral, see Kirschbaum-*Grabungen Santiago,* and Kirschbaum-*Grab Jakobus.* On Bishop Theodemir's own tomb, see Kirschbaum-*Grabungen Santiago,* p. 253 ff.

45. On Diego Peláez, see UbietoArteta-*destierro Peláez.*

46. On the powerful personality of Gelmírez, see Murguía-*Gelmírez,* Biggs-*Gelmírez,* Reilly-*Church Reform Santiago,* Pastor Togneri-*Gelmírez,* Fletcher-*Gelmírez,* and Barreiro Somoza-*Gelmírez;* also, Servatius-*Paschalis II,* and Vones-*Compostellana.*

47. On Pope Calixtus II, see Pellegrini-*curia Callisto II.*

48. On diocesan and metropolitan disputations with Braga, Mérida, and Toledo, see RodríguezAmaya-*metropolitana Emeritense Compostela,* MansillaReoyo-*Disputas Toledo Braga Compostela,* and MansillaReoyo-*metrópoli Compostela.*

49. On the relative notion of the pilgrimage route and on the metaphoric value of the term, see Oursel-*Pèlerins;* LaCosteMess-*routes;* Georges-*pèlerinage Belgique iconographie,* pp. 167–70; Cohen-*Pilgrimage;* Cohen-*Roads Pilgrimage;* and Herbers-*Jakobuskult,* p. 174. On the pilgrimage routes in France and Spain in general, see Lambert-*routes pèlerinage,* Jugnot-*chemins pèlerinage France,* Oursel-*Pèlerins,* Oursel-*route saints,* Oursel-*routes solitudes,* LaCosteMess-*Voies compostellanes,* Enríquez-*Pirineo aragonés,* and Viñayo-*Caminos.* Goicoechea-*Rutas,* pp. 699–707, provides a bibliography for the Spanish portion of the route. For the Portuguese route, see Aurora-*Caminho portugues;* and for the Via de la Plata, Sendin Blazquez-*Via Plata.* On the geography and the cartography of the Hispanic portion of the route, see Goicoechea-*Cartografía,* Valiña-*Camino,* Valdeón-*camino Santiago,* Enríquez Salamanca-*Camino Santiago,* Passini-*Camino,* Valiña-*Camino Compostela* and the recent and important SoriaPuig-*camino Santiago,* whose first volume deals with the road and the second with stopovers and signs. On northern European pilgrims and ship travel to Santiago, see Georges-*pèlerinage Belgique iconographie,* Heyne-*Hansestädten Santiago,* and Stalley-*Pèlerinage maritime.* On British pilgrims visiting Compostela on their way to the Holy Land, see VázquezParga-*pereg* 1:73–74; otherwise on British pilgrims, Storrs-*Pilgrims England,* and Storrs/ CorderoCarrete-*Peregrinos ingleses.*

50. For the literature of the pilgrimage routes in general, see Richard-*pèlerinages* and Richard-*relations pèlerinage*. On some early accounts of pilgrims, see Mieck-*témoignages*, Howard-*Writers Pilgrims*, Löwe-*Peregrinatio*, and Caucci-*Testi italiani Santiago*. On the possible journey of St. Francis to Santiago, see López-*San Francisco*. On some of the later pilgrimages, see Damonte-*Firenze Santiago*, Gruber-*Tagebuch Pilgers*, Mieck-*Wallfahrt Santiago*, Laffi-*Viaggio*, and Bonnault-*Compostelle*.

51. On German pilgrims and on the devotion to Santiago in Germany, see Hüffer-*Jacobus Deutschland*, Hüffer-*Sant'Jago Deutschen*, Hell-*Wallfahrt*, and Plötz-*Santiago-peregrinatio*.

52. On the via turonense in the Poitou, see LaCosteMess-*chemin Poitou*.

53. See pp. 186–88, nn. 345–52; and p. 293.

54. On the *via podense*, see Jugnot-*via Podensis*.

55. On the Italian routes leading towards southern France and thence to Compostela, see Caucci-*chemin italien*, Stopani-*francigena*, Caucci-*itinerari italiani*, and the collective work *Pistoia cammino Santiago*.

56. On Roncesvalles and the Pass of Cize, see Lambert-*Roncevaux Cize*.

57. On the routes of the Pyrenees in general and on Roncesvalles, see Lambert-*Roncevaux*, Lambert-*Roncevaux Roland*, Lambert-*Pyrénées*, EnríquezSalamanca-*Pirineo aragonés*, and Urrutibéhéty-*Voies Navarre*.

58. On the ancient hospitals on the Pyrenees, that of Santa Cristina on the Somport Pass and that of the Pass of Cize or Ibañeta at Roncesvalles, see UbietoArteta-*Santa Cristina* and Durliat-*Jacques*, p. 27.

59. On the supporting service institutions alongside the route, and in particular on hospices, hospitals, and the like, see Vázquez Parga-*pereg*, 1:281–99, LaCosteMess-*hospitaliers*, Jetter-*Hospitals*, La CosteMess-*Accueil Pèlerins Toulouse*, Schmugge-*Verpflegung Pilgern*, and Schmugge-*Pilgerverkehrs*.

60. On the motif of the unjustly hanged pilgrim, see Gaiffier-*pendu sauvé*.

61. The portal was only executed in 1188.

62. On the extant manuscripts of the *Liber*, see David-*Jacques*, X (I); Hämel-*Überlieferung*; and Mandach-*chanson geste*, pp. 364–99.

63. The term *Liber Sancti Jacobi* goes back to Bédier-*épiques* 3:73–75.

64. On the *Liber Sancti Jacobi* in general, on its genesis and on its various parts of different weight and importance, see Whitehill-*Liber*, David-*Jacques*, Defourneaux-*Français Espagne*, Hämel-*Über-*

THE PILGRIM'S GUIDE TO SANTIAGO

lieferung, FilgueiraValverde-*Calixtino*, Herbers-*Jakobuskult*, Díaz Díaz-*calixtino*, and Mandach-*Pilgrim's Guide*.

65. On the two yearly celebrations of James – July 25 for the *passio* and December 30 for the *translatio* – see Herbers-*Jakobuskult*, pp. 102–5; and Herbers-*Jakobsweg*, p. 21, n. 7.

66. For the possible influences of Cluny in the generation of the *Liber* itself, see Herbers-*Jakobsweg*, p. 162, n. 387; as well as nn. 37 and 39 above.

67. On the pseudo-Turpin, see MeredithJones-*Karoli*, Lambert-*pseudo Turpin*, David-*Jacques*, *XII (III)*, and Burger-*Roland Turpin Guide*.

68. On the French interests and on Charlemagne, see above nn. 37 and 42.

69. On the elaboration, modifications and amplifications of the *Guide*, as well as on its authorship and the identity of its author, see below pp. 140–41, n. 31; Le Clerq-*Aimeric*, David-*Jacques*, X and XII (I and III); Louis-*Aiméri*; Defourneaux-*Français Espagne*; Lambert-*Aymeric*; Herbers-*Jakobuskult*; Herbers-*Jakobsweg*; Herwaarden-*James*; and DíazDíaz-*litt. jacobite*.

70. On the national and regional prejudices of the author of the *Guide*, and in particular on his anti-Navarrese attitude, see VázquezParga-*Navarra* and Schmugge-*nationale Vorurteile*.

71. On the society of pilgrims, see Daux-*Pèlerinage confrérie*, Schreiber-*Gemeinschaften*, and Sigal-*société Pèlerins*.

72. On the essential mobility of the pilgrimage and on the sense of freedom it provided, see Bosl-*Mobilität*, Schmugge-*Pilgerfahrt frei*, and Plötz-*Strukturwandel peregrinatio*. On the essential change of status that the pilgrimage provided, cf. Ladner-*Viator*.

73. On the immunities granted, in principle, to pilgrims, see PochGutiérrez-*inmunidad Peregrino*.

74. On various economic and social aspects of the pilgrimage, see the studies of J. M. Lacarra and of E. Cohen: Lacarra-*arancel*, Cohen-*signa*, Cohen-*Pilgrimage*, Cohen-*Roads Pilgrimage*, Lacarra-*burguesía*, and Lacarra-*Jacques économique*.

75. For miracles and miraculous expectations, see above, nn. 2 and 3; on supplications in particular, MariñoFerro-*Peregrinaciones símbolos*.

76. On penitential pilgrimages in general, see Schmugge-*Pilgerfahrt frei*, and Plötz-*Strukturwandel peregrinatio*. More specific works on the same subject include Schmitz-*Bussbücher*, Berlière-*pèlerinages iudiciaires*, LeBras-*Pénitentiels*, Cauwenbergh-*Pèlerinages expiatoires judiciaires*, Maes-*pèlerinages expiatoires*, Maes-*Strafwallfahrten*,

Vogel-*pèlerinage pénitentiel*, Sigal-*marcheurs*, Herwaarden-*Opgelegde Bedevaarten*, and Jugnot-*pèlerinage droit pénal*.

77. On mystic and hermetic interpretations of various aspects of the pilgrimage, not always sound, see Charpentier-*Jacques mystère* and Morín/Cobreros-*camino iniciático*.

78. On the categorization of pilgrimages, whether executed individually or in a procession-like formation (*Pilgerfahrt / Wallfahrt*), see Brückner-*Wallfahrtswesens*. On the various kinds of pilgrims and an attempt at their categorization, see Vázquez Parga-*pereg* 1:119, Georges-*pèlerinage Belgique iconographie*, Mieck-*Wallfahrt Santiago*, Dossat-*Types Pèlerins*, Sigal-*types pèlerinage*, and Sigal-*société Pèlerins*.

79. The *Guide* (see below p. 172–73, nn. 219 and 220) speaks of the shackles and chains hanging at the pilgrimage church of Saint-Léonard of Noblat. The same is true elsewhere too: Santo Domingo de Silos, San Juan de los Reyes Católicos in Toledo, etc.

80. On the pilgrimage by proxy, see MariñoFerro-*Peregrinaciones símbolos*, pp. 259–62.

81. On lawful and unlawful exercise of trades, see the *Historia compostelana*, III, xxxiii, in Flórez-*Sagrada* 20:534 ff., Herbers-*Jakobuskult*; and RemuñánFerro-*Gremios compostelanos*.

82. On asocial characters on the road, see CorderoCarrete-*Peregrinos mendicantes*, LaCosteMess-*abus pèlerinages*, Carro Celada-*Picaresca via*, Dossat-*Types Pèlerins*, and FernándezAlbor-*delincuencia Camino*.

83. For the day's marches, see below pp. 137–38, n. 16.

84. On the prejudices of the author of the *Guide*, see below p. 143, n. 40; p. 146, n. 63; p. 150, n. 86; and p. 154, n. 106.

85. For the concept of *homo viator*, see Ladner-*Viator*, and Kriss/Illich-*viator*.

86. Chapter VI of the *Guide* is entirely devoted to problems concerning water, rivers and their fording or crossing. See below, p. 146, n. 62; and p. 148, n. 69.

87. See below, p. 144, n. 49.

88. See below, p. 180, n. 268.

89. On the change of status, mobility, and the new social consolidation entered upon at the moment of setting out for the pilgrimage, see Bosl-*Mobilität*; and Kriss/Illich-*viator*, p. 14 ff.

90. The participation of women in pilgrimages, and the status of women on the road in general, has been little researched. A promising field in this respect is constituted by mainly pictorial representations of pilgrims which often include female pilgrims too. [The author was preparing a study on the subject at the time of his death. (Ed.)]

91. See above, n. 9.

92. On identification documents of pilgrims, see Sigal-*marcheurs*, p. 85; Schmugge-*Pilgerfahrt frei*, p. 29; and Köster-*Pilgerzeichen*.

93. On juridical aspects of the pilgrimage in general, see Vázquez Parga-*pereg* 1:255–79, Garrison-*Pèlerins juridique*, Valiña-*camino jurídico*, and Gilles-*lex peregrinorum*.

94. On the speed of the pilgrims' progression and on the days' marches, see Ludwig-*Marschgeschwindigkeit*, Renquard-*étapes vitesse*, and Labande-*déplacement pèlerin*.

95. On medical subjects and problems on the route, see Baltar-Domíguez-*médicos peregr* and Campo-*medicina Santiago*.

96. Chapter VIII of the *Guide*, one of the two longest chapters, is entirely dedicated to such devotional stations on the route, and to the saints (mainly French) to be visited on the pilgrimage to Santiago. See below, pp. 229–71.

97. See n. 86 above.

98. On the vast song literature on the route, see Daux-*chansons Pèlerins*, LópezCalo-*música peregrinaciones*, and EchevarríaBravo-*Cancionero Peregrinos*.

99. On coinage, the circulation of currency, and related matters, see Lacarra-*Jacques économique*, as well as n. 74 above.

100. On the pilgrims' spending the night in a pilgrimage church, see Labande-*Limina*; and Herbers-*Jakobuskult*, p. 178. On the galleries or *triforia* as pilgrimage lodging, see below pp. 199–200, n. 409.

101. On hospices and hospitals on the route, see Villaamil-*establecimientos beneficencia*, Masson-*architecture hospices*, Aubert-*Hospice Pons*, LaCosteMess-*hospitaliers Pèlerins*, FernándezCatón-*hospital Reyes Cat*, Boshof-*Armenfürsorge*, Jugnot-*assistance Navarre*, and Schmugge-*Verpflegung Pilgern*.

102. On religious orders in general along the route, see Lambert-*Ordres confréries*, Jugnot-*fondations augustiniennes*, and Bishko-*Monastic*. On military orders, see Cocheril-*ordres militaires*. On the competition of religious orders in their zeal to fulfill the charitable mandate vis-à-vis the pilgrims, cf. Defourneaux-*Français Espagne*, p. 110 and passim; and Durliat-*Jacques*, pp. 26–27.

103. On the confraternities on the road and elsewhere, see Daux-*Pèlerinage confrérie*, Lambert-*Ordres confréries*, Labande-*Pèlerins*, and Schreiber-*Gemeinschaften*.

104. On everyday life on the route and elsewhere, see Sánchez Cantón-*vida Galicia*, and Rowling-*Everyday Life Travellers*.

105. On the pilgrim's clothing and general outfit, see Thorel-*equipement pèlerin*, Georges-*pèlerinage Belgique iconographie*, Brück-

ner-*Pilger*, and Wilckens-*Kleidung*. See also the bibliography for the iconography of St. James in n. 112 below.

106. On signs, symbols, and badges of pilgrims and of the pilgrimage to Santiago, see Cohen-*signa*, Cohen-*Pilgrimage*, Köster-*Pilgerzeichenmuscheln*, Cannata-*insigne*, and MariñoFerro-*Peregrinaciones símbolos*. Consider also the entries concerning the scallop shell in n. 107 below.

107. On the famous scallop shell, see Locard-*coquille Pèlerins*, CorderoCarrete-*Veneras cruces Santiago*, LacosteMess-*Coquille*, Treuille-*Coquille*, LaCosteMess-*Fleurs lys coquilles*, and Köster-*coquilles*. See also the entries in n. 106 above.

108. On pilgrim tombs and pilgrimage mementos in it, see Gavelle-*Tombes Pèlerins*.

109. On the rites of departure and the rites of return, see Plötz-*Ikonographie Jacobus*.

110. On the pilgrim's attaining Santiago de Compostela, see Labande-*Limina*.

111. On the pilgrim's reaching Finisterra, see Maes-*Finisterra*.

112. On matters pertaining to the iconography of Santiago, but also of the pilgrims en route to and from Santiago de Compostela, apart from general works of generous amplitude [such as Mâle-*XII* (especially "Les pèlerinages: Les routes d'Italie," pp. 245–79; and "Les pèlerinages: Les routes de France et d'Espagne," pp. 281–313); Mâle-*XIII*; Mâle-*fin Moyen Age*; and KingsleyPorter-*Pilgrimage*, I, IV, VI], the following should be consulted: Osma-*Azabaches Compostelanos*, Apraiz-*representación caballero*, Gaiffier-*pendu sauvé*, FilgueiraValverde-*iconografía Santiago*, Vázquez Parga *pereg* 1:541–73, MáizEleizegui-*urte jacobeo*, Bottineau-*Jacques*, pp. 107–13, VázquezParga-*peregrinacion iconografía*, Goyheneche-*Iconographie Jacques Basque*, Gaiffier-*hagiographie iconologie*, Goicoechea-*Rutas*, pp. 88–97; Crozet-*cavalier victorieux pèlerinage*, Georges-*pèlerinage Belgique iconographie*, Brückner-*Pilger*, Kimpel-*Jakobus Ikon*, Martinez-*camino jacobeo*, pp. 231–36; Ahlsell-*peintures Rabastens*, SicartGiménez-*Santiago ecuestre*, Oursel-*route saints*, LaCoste Mess-*signe coquille*, Plötz-*Imago Iacobi*, Steppe-*iconographie Jacques*, Babelon–*Violence*, Rodríguez/Ríos-*iconografía Jacobea*, Piccat-*pellegrino impiccato*, Sicart Giménez-*figura Santiago*, and Plötz-*Iconographie Iacobus*. In addition, see the articles in *Les dossiers de l'archéologie* 20.

Castilla. Ancient Roman causeway alongside the
pilgrimage route to Santiago.

PART II

THE PILGRIM'S GUIDE TO SANTIAGO DE COMPOSTELA

An English translation of Book Five of the *Codex Calixtinus*
in the archival library of the Cathedral of
Santiago de Compostela

HERE BEGINS THE FIFTH BOOK[1] OF THE APOSTLE ST. JAMES[2]

Summary of the Blessed Pope Calixtus[3]

If the knowledgeable reader seeks the truth in this work of ours, he will surely find it, without hesitation or embarrassment, in this codex; for many people still in life witness to the truth of what is written in it.

CHAPTER I

OF THE ROUTES OF ST. JAMES[6]

There are four roads[7] which, leading to Santiago, converge to form a single road at Puente la Reina,[8] in Spanish territory. One crosses Saint-Gilles, Montpellier, Toulouse, and the pass of Somport[9]; another goes through Notre-Dame of Le Puy, Sainte-Foy of Conques and Saint-Pierre of Moissac; another traverses Sainte-Marie-Madeleine of Vézelay, Saint-Léonard in the Limousin as well as the city of Périgueux; still another cuts through Saint-Martin of Tours, Saint-Hilaire of Poitiers, Saint-Jean-d'Angély, Saint-Eutrope of Saintes and the city of Bordeaux.[10]

The road that traverses Sainte-Foy,[11] the one that proceeds through Saint-Léonard, and the one that does so through Saint-Martin[12] meet at Ostabat and, having gained the pass of Cize, join at Puente la Reina the road that comes from the Somport; thence a single road leads as far as Santiago.[13]

CHAPTER II

THE DAYS' JOURNEY[14]
ON THE APOSTLE'S ROAD
— POPE CALIXTUS[15] —

From the Somport to Puente la Reina there are three short days' journeys: the first goes from Borce, a village at the foot of the Somport on the Gascon side, as far as Jaca; the second, from Jaca to Monreal; the third, from Monreal to Puente la Reina.

From the pass of Cize as far as Santiago there are thirteen days' journeys: the first proceeds from the village of Saint Michel, which is located at the foot of the pass of Cize, to be sure on the Gascon side, to Viscarret – this is a short journey; the second leads from Viscarret to Pamplona – and this is also a short one; the third goes from the city of Pamplona to Estella; the fourth, from Estella to the city of Nájera is to be made, to be sure, on horseback; the fifth, from Nájera to the city called Burgos is to be made equally on horseback; the sixth proceeds from Burgos to Frómista; the seventh, from Frómista to Sahagún; the eight, from Sahagún to the city of León; the ninth, from León to Rabanal; the tenth continues from Rabanal to Villafranca, that is to say, after having cleared the passes of Mount Irago, to the mouth of the Valcarce; the eleventh goes from Villafranca to Triacastela; the twelfth goes from Triacastela to Palas; the thirteenth, finally, goes from Palas as far as Santiago – and this is a short journey.[16]

CHAPTER III

OF THE NAMES OF TOWNS ON THIS ROAD

These are the towns[17] that are located on the road to Santiago from the Somport to Puente la Reina: first, at the foot of the mountain on the Gascon side, there is Borce; next, having climbed over the summit of the mountain, there is the hospice of Santa Cristina[18]; then, Canfranc; then, Jaca; next, Osturit; and then, Tiermas[19] where there are continuously running hot royal baths; next, there is Monreal; and finally one reaches Puente la Reina.

From the Cize Pass onwards and as far as the basilica in Galicia these are the most important towns one finds on the route of St. James: first, at the foot of the very Mount Cize, to be sure on the Gascon side, there is the village of Saint-Michel; at that point, having cleared the summit of the same mountain, one reaches the hospice of Roland[20] and then the town of Roncesvalles; next comes Viscarret; then, Larrasoaña; then, the city of Pamplona; next, Puente la Reina; and then, Estella, where bread is good, wine excellent, meat and fish are abundant, and which overflows with all delights. Next comes Los Arcos, then Logroño, then Villaroya, and then the city of Nájera. Then follow Santo Domingo, Redecilla, Belorado, Villafranca, the forest of Oca, Atapuerca, the city of Burgos, Tardajos, Hornillos, Castrogeriz, the bridge of Itero, Frómista and then Carrión, which is a well-managed and industrious town, abundant in bread, wine, meat, and all kinds of produce. Next comes

Sahagún, prosperous in all sorts of goods: a meadow is there in which, as it is reported, the sparkling spears of victorious warriors, planted for the glory of God, were once blooming. Next comes Mansilla, and then León, a royal and courtly city, packed with plentiful riches.

Follow Orbigo, the city of Astorga, Rabanal called the captive, [21]the pass of Mount Irago, Molinaseca, Ponferrada, Cacabelos, Villafranca at the mouth of Valcarce, Castro Sarracín, Villaus,[22] the pass of Mount Cebrero and then the hospice on the summit of the same mountain. Then comes Linares del Rey and shortly after Triacastela, already in Galicia to be sure, at the foot of the above-mentioned mountain.[23] There pilgrims are given a stone which they carry with them to Castañeda in order to make lime for the construction of the apostolic basilica.[24] Next come the towns of San Miguel, Barbadelo, the bridge over the Miño, Sala de la Reina, Palas de Rey, Libureiro, Santiago de Boente, Castañeda, Villanova, Ferreiros, and at long last Compostela, the most excellent city of the Apostle, filled to the brim with plentiful delights. The city guards the precious body of the Blessed James, for which it is recognized as the happiest and the most splendid of all cities in Spain.

If I have sparingly enumerated the above towns and days' journey, it was in order that the pilgrims who depart for Santiago, having listened to all this, may try to anticipate the expenses necessary for their travel.[25]

CHAPTER IV

THE THREE HOSPICES OF THE WORLD[26]

God has, in a most particular fashion, instituted in this world three columns greatly necessary for the support of his poor, that is to say, the hospice of Jerusalem,[27] the hospice of Mount-Joux,[28] and the hospice of Santa Cristina[29] on the Somport Pass. These hospices, established in places they were very much needed, are holy sites, the house of God for the restoring of saintly pilgrims, the resting of the needy, the consolation of the sick, the salvation of the dead, and the assistance lent to the living.[30] Therefore, he who had built those holy places, no matter who he may be, will partake, without any doubt, of the kingdom of God.

CHAPTER V

THE NAMES OF THOSE WHO RESTORED THE ROAD TO ST. JAMES
— AIMERY[31] —

Here are the names of some roadmen[32] who in the times of Diego,[33] archbishop of Santiago, of Alphonso,[34] emperor of Spain and Galicia, and of Pope Calixtus, before the year 1120, under the reign of Alphonso,[35] king of Aragón and of Louis the Fat,[36] king of France, for the love of God and of the Apostle, rebuilt the road of St. James from Rabanal as far as the bridge over the Miño: Andrew, Roger, Alvito, Fortus, Arnold, Stephen and Peter[37] who reconstructed the bridge over the Miño demolished by Queen Urraca.[38]

May the souls of these and of their assistants rest in eternal peace.

CHAPTER VI

THE BITTER AND SWEET WATERS FOUND ALONG THIS ROAD
— POPE CALIXTUS[39] —

These are the rivers one finds from the mountain passes of Cize and Somport as far as St. James: from the Somport descends a salubrious river called the Aragón which waters Spain; from the pass of Cize, to be sure, a healthy river issues called by many the Runa. This stream crosses Pamplona. At Puente la Reina both the Arga and the Runa flow by.

In a place called Lorca, towards the east, runs a river called Rio Salado. Beware from drinking its waters or from watering your horse in its stream, for this river is deadly. While we were proceeding towards Santiago, we found two Navarrese seated on its banks and sharpening their knives: they make a habit of skinning the mounts of the pilgrims that drink from that water and die. To our questions they answered with a lie saying that the water was indeed healthy and drinkable. Accordingly, we watered our horses in the stream, and had no sooner done so, than two of them died: these the men skinned on the spot.[40]

At Estella flows the Ega: its water is sweet, healthy and excellent. By the town called Los Arcos flows, on the other hand, a deadly stream; and beyond Los Arcos, next to the first hospice, that is to say between Los Arcos and the same hospice, flows a stream deadly for the horses no less then for the men that drink from it.[41] By the town called Torres, to be sure in Navarrese territory, there is a river that is fatal to horses and men that drink from it. Thence and as far as a town called Cuevas runs an equally deadly stream. By Logroño,[42] in contrast, there is a large river called Ebro which is healthy and abounds in fish.

The water of all rivers one encounters between Estella and Logroño has been recognized as deadly for the men and the horses that drink from it, and their fish is no less dangerous to eat.[43] Should you anywhere in Spain or in Galicia eat either the fish vulgarly called *barbo,* or the one those of Poitou call *alose* and the Italians *clipia,* or even the eel or the tenca, you will no doubt die shortly thereafter or at least fall sick.[44] And if somebody by chance ate them without falling sick, this is either because he was healthier than most, or because he had stayed in that country for a long time.[45] All fish and the meat of beef and pork from all of Spain and Galicia cause sickness to foreigners.[46]

Concerning the rivers whose waters are sweet and healthy to drink, these are the names by which they are ordinarily known: the Pisuerga, a stream that flows, to be sure, under the bridge of Itero; the Carrión that runs by Carrión; the Cea, at Sahagún; the Esla, at Mansilla; the Porma, under a certain large bridge[47] between Mansilla and León; the Torio which flows by León underneath the encampment of the Jews[48]; the Bernesga which flows by the same city, but on the other side, that is to say, towards Astorga; the Sil that waters Ponferrada in Valverde; the Cua that flows by Cacabelos; the Burbia that runs by the bridge of Villafranca; the Valcarce that flows in its own valley; the Miño that runs by Puertomarín. There is furthermore a certain river located at a distance of two miles from the city of Santiago, in a wooded place, and which is called Lavamentula, because there the French pilgrims that go to St.

James, for the love of the Apostle, use to wash not merely their virile member but, having taken off their clothes, wash off the dirt from their entire body.[49] The river Sar which flows between Monte del Gozo and the city of Santiago is considered healthy; similarly, the river Sarela which runs from the other side of the city towards the west is also reported as healthy.[50]

If I have thus described these rivers, it was in order that the pilgrims that proceed to Santiago may strive to avoid unhealthy waters and may choose to drink those that are good for them and for their mounts.

CHAPTER VII

THE QUALITY OF THE LANDS
AND THE PEOPLE[51] ALONG THIS ROAD

On the road of the Blessed James by the route of Toulouse, having crossed the river Garonne, one enters first the land of Gascon; thereafter, having cleared the pass of Somport, one finds the country of Aragón and then, as far as the bridge on the Arga[52] and beyond, the land of Navarra. If one takes the route of the pass of Cize, on the other hand, one finds, after Tours, the country of Poitou, a land well-managed, excellent and full of all blessing. The inhabitants of Poitou are vigorous and warlike; extraordinarily able users of bows, arrows and lances in times of war, they are daring on the battle-front, fast in running, comely in dressing, of noble features, of clever language, generous in the rewards they bestow and prodigal in the hospitality they offer.[53] Then comes the country of Saintonge. Having crossed somehow a sea-sound and the river Garonne,[54] one arrives to the region of the Bordelais, excellent in wine, abundant in fishes, but of rustic language.[55] Those of Saintonge have already a rustic language, but those of Bordelais prove to have an even more rustic one. Thence one needs three more days of march, for people already tired, to traverse the Landes of the Bordelais.

This is a desolate region deprived of all good: there is here no bread, wine, meat, fish, water or springs; villages are rare here. The sandy and flat land abounds none the less in honey, millet, panic-grass, and wild boars.[56] If perchance you cross it in summertime, guard your face diligently from the enormous flies that greatly abound there and which are called in the vulgar wasps or horseflies[57]; and if you do not watch your feet carefully, you will rapidly sink up to the knees in the sea-sand copiously found all over.

Having traversed this region, one comes to the land of Gascon rich in white bread and excellent red wine, and covered by forests and meadows, streams and healthy springs.[58] The Gascons are fast in words, loquacious,[59] given to mockery, libidinous, drunkards, prodigal in food, ill-dressed, and rather careless in the ornaments they wear. However, they are well-trained in combat and generous in the hospitality they provide for the poor.

Seated around the fire, they have the habit of eating without a table and of drinking all of them out of one single cup.[60] In fact, they eat and drink a lot, wear rather poor clothes, and lie down shamelessly on a thin and rotten straw litter, the servants together with the master and the mistress.[61]

On leaving that country, to be sure on the road of St. James, there are two rivers that flow near the village of Saint-Jean-de-Sorde, one to the right and one to the left, and of which one is called brook and the other river. There is no way of crossing them without a raft. May their ferrymen be damned! Though each of the streams is indeed quite narrow, they have the habit of demanding one coin from each man, whether poor or rich, whom they ferry over, and for a horse they ignominiously extort by force four. Now, their boat is small, made of a single tree, hardly capable of holding horses. Also, when boarding it one must be most careful not to fall by chance into the water. You will do well in pulling your horse by the reins behind yourself in the water, outside the boat, and to embark but with few passengers, for if it is overloaded it will soon become endangered.

Also, many times the ferryman, having received his money, has such a large troop of pilgrims enter the boat that it capsizes and the pilgrims drown in the waves. Upon which the boatmen, having laid their hands upon the spoils of the dead, wickedly rejoice.[62]

Then, already near the pass of Cize, one reaches the Basque country,[63] on the seashore of which, towards the north, lies the city of Bayonne. This land, whose language is barbarous,[64] is wooded, mountainous, devoid of bread, wine, and all sorts of food for the body, except that, in compensation, it abounds in apples, cider,[65] and milk.

In this land, that is to say near Port-de-Cize in the town called Ostabat and in those of Saint-Jean and Saint-Michel-Pied-de-Port, there are evil toll-gatherers[66] who will certainly be damned through and through. In point of fact, they actually advance towards the pilgrims with two or three sticks, extorting by force an unjust tribute. And if some traveler refuses to hand over the money at their request, they beat him with the sticks and snatch away the toll-money while cursing him and searching even through his breeches. These are ferocious people; and the land in which they dwell is savage, wooded and barbarous. The ferociousness of their faces and likewise of their barbarous speech scares the wits out of those who see them. Though according to the rules and regulations they should not demand a tribute from anybody but merchants, they unjustly cash in from pilgrims and all sorts of travelers. Whenever they ought to receive, according to the usage, four or six coins for a certain service, they cash in eight or twelve, that is to say, double.

Wherefore we admonish and entreat that these toll-gatherers as well as the king of Aragón[67] and the other powers that be who receive from them the tribute money, as well as all those who are in agreement with them, that is to say, Raymond de Soule, Vivien d'Aigremont, and the viscount of Saint-Michel with all their future progeny, together with the said ferrymen as well as Arnaud de la Guigne with all his future progeny,[68] no less than the other lords of the said streams who unjustly cash in from the ferrymen the toll-money for the crossing, and also the priests who, knowingly, confer upon them the penitence and the Eucharist and celebrate for them the divine office or admit them into the church – all these, until such a time that they expiate their sins through a long and public penance, and further introduce moderation in their tributes, be they diligently excommunicated not merely in the episcopal sees of their lands but also in the basilica of St. James in the presence of pilgrims. And if a prelate, no matter who, would wish, out of charity or interest, to pardon them, may he be stricken with the sword of anathema.[69]

It ought to be known that these toll-gatherers should by no means collect tribute from pilgrims, and that the said ferrymen should demand for the crossing of two men, provided they are rich, but one *obolum*,[70] and for a horse, according to the regulations, one coin only. But from the poor they should ask nothing at all. And furthermore, they must have large enough boats in which men and mounts can easily fit in.

In the Basque country there is on the road of St. James a very high mountain, which is called Port-de-Cize, either because that is the gate of Spain, or because it is by that mountain that the necessary goods are transported from one country to the other.[71] Its ascent is eight miles long, and its descent, equally eight. In fact, its height is such that it seems to touch the sky: to him who climbs it, it seems as if he was able to touch the sky with his hand. From its summit one can see the sea of Bretagne and that of the west,[72] as well as the boundaries of three regions, that is to say, Castilla, Aragón, and France.[73] On the summit of this mountain there is a place called the Cross of Charles,[74] because it was here that Charles, setting out with his armies for Spain, opened up once a passageway with axes, hatchets, pickaxes and other implements, and that he first erected the sign of the cross of the Lord and, falling on his knees and turning towards Galicia, addressed a prayer to God and St. James.[75] Wherefore the pilgrims, falling on their knees and turning towards the land of St. James, use to offer there a prayer while each planted his own cross of the Lord like a standard. Indeed, one can find there up to a thousand crosses; and that is why that place is the first station of prayer of St. James.

On that mountain, before Christianity had spread out on Spanish lands,[76] the impious Navarrese and the Basques used not merely to rob the pilgrims going to St. James, but also to ride them as if they were asses[77] and before long to slay them. Near this mountain, to be sure, towards the north, there is a valley called Valcarlos where Charles himself encamped together with his armies after his warriors had been slain at Roncesvalles. Many pilgrims proceeding to Santiago who do not want to climb the mountain go that way.

Afterwards, in descending from the summit, one finds the hospice and the church with the rock that Roland, the formidable hero, split with his sword in the middle, from top to bottom, in a triple stroke. Next, one comes to Roncesvalles, the site where, to be sure, once took place the big battle in which King Marsile, Roland, Olivier as well as forty thousand Christian and Saracen soldiers were slain.[78]

After this valley lies the land of the Navarrese which abounds in bread, wine, milk, and livestock. The Navarrese and the Basques are very similar and show much the same characteristics in their food, garments, and language,[79] though the Basques are easily recognized by their complexion, which is whiter than that of the Navarrese.[80] The Navarrese wear black and short garments, only knee-long, in the Scottish fashion, and use a footwear which they call *lavarcas*[81] made of uncured, hairy leather, attached around the foot with leather straps, which cover the bottom of the foot only, leaving the rest bare. They wear dark, elbow-long, wool cloaks, fringed in the manner of a cape[82] and which they call *sayas*.[83] They dress most poorly[84] and eat and drink disgustingly. The whole household of a Navarrese, to be sure, the servant no less than the master, the maid no less than the mistress, eat from a single dish all the food mixed together; and they eat not with spoons but with their own hands and furthermore drink from a single cup.[85] If you saw them eating, you would take them for dogs or pigs in the very act of devouring; if you heard them speaking, you would be reminded of the barking of dogs.[86] Their language is, in fact, completely barbarous. They call God *Urcia*; the Mother of God, *Andrea Maria*; bread, *orgui*; wine, *ardum*; meat, *aragui*; fish, *araign*; house, *echea*; the master of the house, *iaona*; the mistress, *andrea*; the church, *elicera*; the priest, *belaterra*, which means beautiful land; grain, *gari*; water, *uric*; king, *ereguia*; St. James, *Iaona domne Jacue*.[87]

This is a barbarous nation, distinct from all other nations in habits and way of being, full of all kind of malice, and of black color.[88] Their face is ugly, and they are debauched, perverse, perfidious, disloyal and corrupt, libidinous, drunkard, given to all kind of violence, ferocious and savage, impudent and false, impious and uncouth, cruel and quarrelsome, incapable of anything virtuous, well-informed of all vices and iniquities.[89]

In malice they resemble the Getae and the Saracens,[90] and are in everything inimical to our Gallic nation.[91] If they could, the Navarrese or the Basque would kill a Frenchman for no more than a coin.[92] In certain of their regions, namely in Vizcaya and Alava, when the Navarrese warm up, the man shows to the woman and the woman to the man their respective shame. The Navarrese also make use of animals for incestuous fornication. It is told that the Navarrese affixes a lock to the behind of his mule or horse, so that no one else but he may have access to them. Also, he kisses lasciviously the vulva of women and mules.[93]

That is the reason why the Navarrese are rebuked by all who are prudent. Notwithstanding the above, they are valorous on the battlefield, inept in the assault of fortresses,[94] reliable in the payment of the tithe, and assiduous in making offerings on the altar. Every day, in effect, when the Navarrese goes to church, he makes an offering to God of bread or wine or wheat or some other substance.[95]

Wherever the Navarrese or the Basque may go, he shows a horn hanging from his neck, as hunters do, and he carries in his hands, as customary, two or three javelins which he calls *auconas*.[96] And when he enters his house or returns to it, he whistles with his mouth as a kite; and when in secret places or hidden in solitude on the look-out he wishes to call his companions while remaining undetected, either he sings in the manner of an owl or he howls as a wolf.[97]

It is usually told that they descend from the race of the Scots, because they resemble them in their habits and general countenance.[98] Julius Caesar, as it is told, sent to Spain three nations,[99] namely the Nubians,[100] the Scots, and the tailed ones from Cornwall,[101] in order to wage war on the Spanish people, for these refused to pay him tribute. He ordered them to pass all males by the sword, sparing only the life of women. Having entered that land from the sea and having destroyed their ships, the invaders devastated everything by sword and fire, from the city of Barcelona to Zaragoza and from the city of Bayonne[102] as far as the mountains of Oca.[103] They could not however proceed beyond these limits because the Castilians, assembled together, took them by storm and threw them out of their territories. While escaping thus, they reached the maritime mountains which lie between Nájera, Pamplona and Bayonne, that is to say, towards the sea, in the land of Vizcaya and Alava.[104] Having settled down there, they built many fortresses and, having slain all males, seized their wives by force.[105] With these they begot children who subsequently were called Navarrese by their successors.

Whence, Navarrese should be glossed as *non verus*,[106] that is to say, not generated from a true lineage or a legitimate stock. Furthermore, the Navarrese first took their name from a certain city called Naddaver,[107] which is in the lands from which they came at the beginning. To be sure, the Blessed Matthew,[108] apostle and evangelist, by means of his preaching, in early times converted this city to the Lord.

After this land, one traverses the forest of Oca, to be sure in the direction of Burgos. There follows the land of the Spaniards, that is to say, Castilla and Campos.[109] This country is full of treasures, of gold and silver[110]; it abounds in fodder[111] and in vigorous horses, and it has plenty of bread, wine, meat, fish, milk, and honey. On the other hand, it is poor in wood[112] and full of evil and vicious people.[113]

Thence, having crossed the territory of León and cleared the passes of Mount Irago and Mount Cebrero, one arrives to the land of the Galicians. This country is wooded, provided with excellent rivers, meadows and orchards, and with plenty of good fruits and clear springs; on the other hand, it is poor in cities, towns, and cultivated fields.[114] Bread, wheat, and wine are scarce, but rye bread and cider[115] abound, as do livestock and beasts of burden, milk, and honey. The sea fish is either enormously large or small.[116] The land abounds in gold and silver, fabrics,[117] the fur of wild animals and many other goods, as well as in Saracen treasures.[118]

The Galicians, ahead of the other uncouth nations of Spain, are those who best agree in their habits with our French people; but they are irascible and contentious.[119]

CHAPTER VIII

THE SAINTLY REMAINS ON THIS ROAD[120] AND THE PASSION OF ST. EUTROPIUS

St. Trophimus and St. Caesarius

First of all, those who go to Santiago by way of Saint-Gilles must visit in Arles the remains of the Blessed Trophimus the confessor.[121] It is he whom the Blessed Paul, writing to Timothy,[122] remembers, and it is he who was ordained bishop by the same Apostle[123] and was the first one to be directed to the said city to preach the Gospel of Christ.[124] It is out of this most lucid spring, as Pope Zosimus[125] writes, that the whole of France has received the stream of faith.[126] His feast is celebrated on December 29.[127]

In like manner, one must visit too the remains of the Blessed Caesarius, bishop and martyr, who established in the same city the monastic rule and whose feast is celebrated on November 1.[128]

St. Honoratus and St. Genesius

In like manner, in the cemetery of the said city,[129] the assistance of the Blessed Honoratus, bishop, should be invoked, whose solemn feast is celebrated on January 16, and in whose venerable and magnificent basilica the remains of the most illustrious martyr, the Blessed Genesius, are resting. There is, in fact, between the two branches of the Rhône, a village next to Arles called Trinquetaille where there is a certain magnificent and very high marble column,[130] erected upon the ground, to be sure behind his church. It is to this column, as it is told, that the perfidious populace tied the Blessed Genesius before beheading him. Even today it appears reddish from his rosy blood. No sooner had he been beheaded, than the saint himself, taking the head into his hands, cast it into the Rhône. As to his body, it was carried by the river as far as the basilica of the Blessed Honoratus where it honorably rests.[131] The head, on the other hand, floating down the Rhône to the sea, lead by an angel, reached Cartagena, a Spanish city, where now it splendidly rests and performs many a miracle. His feast is celebrated on August 25.[132]

The Alyscamps

Subsequently, one should visit the cemetery next to the city of Arles, in a place called Alyscamps, and intercede there, as is customary, for the deceased with prayers, psalms, and alms.[133] Its length and width are one mile each. In no cemetery anywhere, except in this one, can one find so many and so large marble tombs set upon the ground.[134] They are of various workmanship and bear antique engravings in

Latin letters but in an unintelligible language.[135] The farther into the distance one looks, the lengthier the rows of sarcophagi become.[136]

In the same cemetery there are seven churches.[137] If in any of them a priest celebrates the Eucharist for the defunct, or if a layman has a priest celebrate it devoutly, or if a cleric recites the Psalter, he may be certain to have those pious deceased lying there intercede[138] for his salvation in the presence of God at the final Resurrection. In effect, the remains of numerous holy martyrs and confessors[139] are resting there, while their souls rejoice already in the paradisiacal realm.[140] Their commemoration is celebrated, according to the usage, on Monday after the octave of Easter.[141]

St. Giles

Likewise, one must pay a visit with particular attentiveness to the most dignified remains of the most pious and Blessed Giles, confessor and abbot. Because the most Blessed Giles, extraordinarily famous in all latitudes of the world, must indeed be venerated by all, celebrated with dignity by all, by all esteemed, invoked and beseeched.[142] After the prophets and the apostles,[143] nobody among the other saints is more worthy, nobody more holy, nobody more glorious, nobody more prompt to lend help. In effect, it is he who, ahead of all other saints, is accustomed to come most rapidly to the assistance of the needy, the afflicted and the anguished who invoke him. Oh, what a beautiful and valuable labor it is to visit his tomb! The very day that one invokes him with all one's heart, no doubt one will be happily assisted.[144]

I myself have verified what I am saying. I have once seen somebody in the town of the saint who, the day he had invoked him, escaped, under the protection of the blessed confessor, from the house of a certain shoemaker Peyrot[145]; this house, old and decrepit, soon after collapsed. Who, then, shall look at his dwelling the longest? Who shall worship God in his most sacred basilica? Who shall embrace most fervently his sarcophagus? Who shall kiss his altar ever to be venerated, or who shall tell the story of his most pious life?[146]

Thus, a sick man wears his tunic and is restored to health; another man is bitten by a snake and, by his inexhaustible virtue, is healed; still another one, deranged in his mind, is delivered from the devil; a storm in the sea abates; the daughter of Theocritus is returned to her father restored to long-desired health; a sick man, wanting health in his whole body, regains his long-wished-for sanity[147]; a hind, previously untamed, is domesticated by his command and becomes his servant[148]; the monastic order, under the patronage of this abbot, flourishes[149]; a possessed is delivered from the devil[150]; a sin of Charles, revealed to him by an angel, is remitted to the king[151]; a dead man is returned to life; a crippled man is restored to health[152]; and furthermore, two door leaves of cypress engraved with the images of the princes of the apostles make their journey on the waves of the sea from the city of Rome as far as the port of the Rhône with no other guidance but his sovereign power.[153]

I regret, indeed, having to die before being able to report all his feats worthy of veneration[154]: these are truly so many and so great. This most brilliant Greek star,[155] having illuminated with his rays the people of Provence, reclined magnificently among them without ever declining but increasing, without letting his light go but offering it, redoubled, to everybody, without descending towards the abyss but ascending to the summit of Olympus. While setting, his light did not darken but, through his starry signs, it became only more brilliant than the other holy stars in the four parts of the earth.[156]

It was at midnight, a Sunday, the first of September, that this star declined,[157] that a choir of angels set him in their midst on an elevated throne,[158] and that the Gothic people[159] together with a monastic order offered him hospitality with an honorable tomb on their free territory, that is to say, between the city of Nîmes and the river Rhône.

The large golden casket which is behind his altar,[160] above his venerable remains, is engraved on the left side of the first register with the images of six apostles; on the first place of this register a fitting representation of the Blessed Mary is sculpted.[161] On the second register above there are the twelve zodiacal signs in the following order: ram, bull, twins, crab, lion, virgin, scales, scorpion, a centaur shooting an arrow, goat, a man pouring water, fishes.[162] And among them there are golden flowers in the form of vine.[163] On the third and highest register there are the images of twelve of the twenty-four elders with these verses written above their heads:

This is the splendid choir of twice twelve elders
who sing sweet canticles on their sonorous citharae.[164]

On the right side of the first register there are likewise seven other images, six of which are apostles and the seventh, any one you will of the disciples of Christ.[165] Furthermore, above the heads of the apostles there are sculpted on either side of the casket, in the image of women, the virtues that resided in them: namely, Benignancy, Meekness, Faith, Hope, Charity, etc.[166]

On the second register to the right there are flowers sculpted in the form of vine scrolls. On the third register, above, as on the left side, there are sculpted the images of twelve of the twenty-four elders with these verses written above their heads:

This extraordinary urn, ornate with precious stones and
    gold,
Contains the relics of St. Giles.
Whoever breaks it, may he be cursed eternally by God,
And likewise by Giles and by the whole sacred court.[167]

The lid of the casket, on the top and on either side, is worked out in the manner of fish scales.[168] On its summit there are indeed thirteen rich crystals inlaid, some in chequered manner, others in the form of apples or pomegranates.[169] There is a large crystal in the form of a big fish, namely of a trout, erect, with its tail turned upwards.[170] The first crystal, cut in the manner of a large pot, is enormous; above it a precious and all-glittering golden cross is placed.[171] In the middle of the front of the casket, that is to say, on the anterior face, the Lord is seated in a golden circle[172] making the sign of benediction with His right hand and holding in the left[173] a book on which it is written: "Love peace and truth."[174] Under His footstool, actually at His feet, there is a golden star,[175] and on the flanks there are two letters inscribed, one to the right and one to the left, in this way: A Ω.[176] And above His throne two precious stones glitter in an indescribable manner.[177]

Next to the throne, on the outside, are the four evangelists provided with wings. Each is holding at his feet a scroll on which it is written, in order, the beginning of the respective Gospel: Matthew, to the right and above, appears in the figure of a man, and Luke, underneath, looks like an ox; John, to the left and above, is modeled in the image of an eagle, and Mark, underneath, in the form of a lion.[178] Next to the throne of the Lord there are two angels sculpted with admirable workmanship: namely, a cherub to the right, with his feet above Luke, and a seraph to the left, with his feet likewise above Mark.[179]

Two sets of precious stones of all sorts, one around the throne on which the Lord is seated and the other, likewise, around the rim of the casket, and further three stones joined together, to be sure in order to represent the figure of the Trinity of God – are set in admirable workmanship.

But somebody much celebrated,[180] for the love of the blessed confessor, has affixed with golden nails at the foot of the casket, towards the altar, his image[181] worked in gold; one can appreciate it there even today, for the greater glory of God.

On the other end of the casket, that is to say, on the back, the Ascension of the Lord is sculpted. On the first register there are six apostles, with their faces turned upwards, in the act of beholding the Lord as he rises to heaven.[182] Above their heads these words are written: "Oh men of Galilee! This Jesus who has been assumed to heaven from among your midst shall come back in the way you have seen him depart."[183]

On the second register, standing in the same way, six additional apostles are sculpted; but here there are also, on either side, golden columns between the apostles.[184] On the third register, the Lord appears erect on a golden throne and two angels are standing beside the throne, one to His right and one to His left. The angels point out the Lord to the apostles with raised hands, one of them directed upward and the other one downward.[185]

And above the divine head, to be sure outside of the throne, there is a dove nearly fluttering above Him.[186] On the fourth and top register, the Lord is sculpted on another golden throne, and next to him there are the four evangelists: Luke, towards the south and below, in the form of an ox, and Matthew, above, in the image of a man; on the other side, towards the north, is Mark in the image of a lion, below, and John, above, in the form of an eagle. One should notice though that the Divine Majesty on the throne is not seated but is standing, with His back towards the south and His head raised as if staring towards heaven; His right hand is raised upwards and in His left He holds a small cross. Thus He ascends towards the Father who receives Him on the summit of the casket.[187]

Such is then the tomb of the Blessed Giles the confessor, in which his venerated body honorably rests. May therefore the Hungarians who claim to possess his body blush [188]; may those of Chamalières, who vainly imagine having the whole of his body, be thrown into confusion[189]; may those of Saint-Seine, who pride themselves in having his head, waste away[190]; may the Normans of Cotentin,[191] who boast of having the whole of his body, stand likewise in fear, because in no way could his most sacred bones, as this was proven by many, be removed from his place. Some people have in effect tried once to snatch away quite fraudulently the venerable arm of the blessed confessor and to carry it out of the country of Giles towards far-away shores,[192] but in no manner could they get off with it.

There are four bodies of saints which, as it is told and as it has been proven by many, could never be removed by anybody and by any means from their sarcophagi: namely, those of the Blessed James the Zebedee, of the Blessed Martin of Tours, of Saint Leonard of Limoges, and of the Blessed Giles the confessor of Christ.[193] It is told that Philip, king of France, attempted once to carry off their bodies to France, but he could in no way remove them from their sarcophagi.[194]

St. William

Those who go to Santiago by the route of Toulouse ought to visit the remains of the Blessed Confessor William. For the most saintly William was an eminent standard-bearer as well as count of no small stature of King Charles the Great, a most valiant soldier and a great expert in war. It was he who by his firm valor, as it is told, brought under Christian subjection the cities of Nîmes, Orange and many others, and furthermore carried the wood of the Lord into the valley of

Gellone[195]; it was in that valley, to be sure, that the confessor of Christ led a hermit's life and, after a blessed death, found his honorable resting place. His sacred feast is celebrated on May 28.

St. Tiberius, St. Modestus, and St. Florence

Similarly, on the same route one ought to pay a visit to the remains of the blessed martyrs Tiberius, Modestus, and Florence who, in the time of Diocletian, underwent for the faith of Christ a variety of torments and suffered martyrdom. They rest on the banks of the river Hérault in a most beautiful tomb. Their feast is celebrated on November 10.[196]

St. Saturninus

In similar manner, on the same route one ought to visit also the most worthy remains of the Blessed Saturninus, bishop and martyr, who, detained by the pagans on the capitol of the city of Toulouse, was tied to some furious and wild bulls and then precipitated from the height of the citadel of the capitol over a flight of stone stairs on a mile-long course. His head crushed, his brains knocked out, his whole body torn to pieces, he rendered his worthy soul to Christ. He is buried in an excellent location[197] close to the city of Toulouse where a large basilica was erected by the faithful in his honor, where the canonical rule of the Blessed Augustine is, as a matter of course, observed and where many benefices are accorded by the Lord to those who request them. His feast is celebrated on November 29.

St. Foy

Similarly, the Burgundians and the Teutons who proceed to Santiago by the route of Le Puy[198] must visit the most saintly remains of the Blessed Foy, virgin and martyr, whose most saintly soul, after the body had been beheaded by her executioners on the mountain[199] of the city of Agen, was taken to heaven in the form of a dove[200] by a choir of angels and was adorned by the laurel of immortality. When the Blessed Caprasius, bishop of the city of Agen, who in order to eschew the fury of persecution was hiding in a certain cave, saw this, he himself found the necessary courage to bear his martyrdom.[201] He hurried to the place where the blessed maiden had suffered and, having deserved the palm of martyrdom in a brave combat, he even went so far as to reproach his executioners for their sluggishness.[202]

At last, the most precious body of the Blessed Foy, virgin and martyr, was honorably buried by the Christians in a valley commonly called Conques. Above the tomb a magnificent basilica was erected by the faithful in which, for the glory of the Lord, the rule of the Blessed Benedict has until this very day been observed with great punctiliousness. Many benefits have been granted there to the healthy no less than to the sick.[203] In front of the portals of the basilica there is an excellent stream, more marvelous than what one is able to tell.[204] Her feast is celebrated on October 6.

St. Mary Magdalene

Thereupon, on the route that through Saint-Léonard[205] stretches towards Santiago, the most worthy remains of the Blessed Mary Magdalene must first of all be rightly worshipped by the pilgrims. She is, in fact, that glorious Mary who, in the house of Simon the Leprous, watered with her tears the feet of the Savior, wiped them off with her hair, and anointed them with a precious ointment while kissing them most fervently.[206] Accordingly, she was remitted of her many sins because she had much loved Him who loves the universe,[207] that is to say, Jesus Christ, her Redeemer. It is she who, arriving after the Ascension of the Lord from the region of Jerusalem together with the Blessed Maximinus, the disciple of Christ, as well as other disciples of the Lord, went by sea as far as the country of Provence, namely the port of Marseille.

In that area she led for some years, to be sure, a celibate life and, at the end, was given burial in the city of Aix by the same Maximinus, bishop of that city.[208] But, after a long time, a distinguished man called Badilon, beatified in monastic life, transported her most precious earthly remains from that city to Vézelay where they rest up to this day in a much honored tomb.[209] In this place a large and most beautiful basilica as well as an abbey of monks were established.[210] Thanks to her love, the faults of the sinners are here remitted by God, vision is restored to the blind, the tongue of the mute is untied, the lame stand erect, the possessed are delivered, and unspeakable benefices are accorded to many.[211] Her sacred feast is celebrated on July 22.

St. Leonard

One must equally visit the sacred remains of the Blessed Leonard the confessor who, born into a most noble Frankish family and brought up at the royal court, renounced the wicked world for the love of the supreme Numen[212] and led for a long time in the land of Limousin, in a place commonly called Noblat,[213] a celibate and hermit-like life with frequent fasts and plentiful of vigils amid cold, nudity and unspeakable labors. Finally, in his own free land, having passed away in a saintly manner, he took his rest. One is told that his sacred earthly remains are unmovable.

May therefore the monks of Corbigny blush for saying that they possess the body of the Blessed Leonard: for in no way can the smallest bone of his bones, or for that matter his ashes, as stated above, be removed. Those of Corbigny, no less than many others, are enriched by his benefices and his miracles, but they delude themselves concerning his corporeal presence. Not having been able to obtain his body, they worship, in lieu of the remains of Saint Leonard of Limoges, the remains of a certain man by the name Léotard who, so they say, was brought to them placed in a silver casket from the country of Anjou. They have even changed his proper name after death, as if he would have been baptized a second time, and imposed upon him the name of Saint Leonard in order that by the fame of a name so great and celebrated, that is to say of Saint Leonard of Limousin, pilgrims would flock there and enrich them with their offerings.[214] His feast is commemorated on October 15.

Thus, first they make Saint Leonard of Limousin the patron of their basilica; subsequently they put somebody else in his place, in the manner of envious serfs who forcefully rob their master of his own inheritance and offer it, unworthily, to somebody else. They are similar, also, to a bad father who snatches his daughter away from her legitimate spouse and offers her to another.[215] "They have exchanged – says the psalmist – his glory for the image of a

105

calf."[216] A certain man of wisdom has once reproached those who act in such way by saying: "Do not give your honor to others."[217] The devout, whether foreigner or from the land, who come there with the idea of finding the body of Saint Leonard of Limousin whom they honor, find, unawares, another one in his place.[218] Whosoever he may be that performs the miracles at Corbigny, it is the Blessed Leonard of Limousin, removed from the patronage of that church, who delivers the captives and takes them there. That is the reason why those of Corbigny are liable of a double fault: they do not recognize him who with his miracles enriches his worshippers; nor do they celebrate his feast, but venerate, inappropriately, somebody else in his stead.[219]

Thus, divine clemency has already spread to the length and breadth of the whole world the fame of the Blessed Leonard the confessor from Limousin. His extraordinarily powerful virtues have delivered from prison countless thousands of captives; their iron chains, more barbarous than what one can possibly recount, joined together by the thousands, have been appended in testimony of such great miracles all around his basilica, to the right and to the left, inside and outside. One remains astonished more than one can tell in seeing the masts loaded with so many and so large barbarous ironworks. There are indeed hanging there iron handcuffs, collars, chains, fetters, snares, levers, yokes, helmets, scythes, as well as sundry ironware from which the most powerful confessor of Christ, by his mighty virtue, has freed the captives.[220]

What is particularly admirable in him is that he used to appear under a visible human form to those enchained in penitentiaries even beyond the sea, as witnessed by those whom he set free by the power of God. Through him it has been marvelously fulfilled what the divine prophet had once prophesied, saying: "Often he has delivered those sitting in the darkness and the shadow of death, as well as those enchained in mendicity and irons. And they have invoked him in their tribulations, and he delivered them from their anguish. He has removed them from the road of their iniquities, for he has crushed the bronze doors, broken the iron bolts; he has delivered those bound in fetters as well as many noble ones in iron manacles."[221] Often, also, Christians were given over, enchained, into the hands of gentiles – such is the case of Bohemund[222] – and were subsequently enslaved by those who hated them; their enemies made them suffer tribulations and humbled them under their hands. And more often than not he delivered them and led them out of the darkness and the shadow of death, and broke their chains.[223] To the enchained he said "come forth," and to those in the shadows, "come to light."[224] His sacred feast is celebrated on November 6.

St. Fronto

After the Blessed Leonard, one must visit in the city of Périgueux the remains of the Blessed Fronto, bishop and confessor who, ordained as bishop in Rome by Peter, the blessed apostle in pontifical dignity, was sent with a certain presbyter by the name George to preach in that city.[225] They had departed together. But George having died on the way and having been buried, the Blessed Fronto returned to the apostle and announced to him the death of his companion. At which the Blessed Peter handed over to him his staff saying: "Once you have placed this staff of mine over the body of your companion, you should say: 'In virtue of the mission you have received from the apostle,[226] in the name of Christ, rise and accomplish it.'"[227] And so it was done. Thanks to the staff of the apostle, the Blessed Fronto restored his companion from death[228] and converted the above-mentioned city, by his preaching, to Christ. Also, he rendered it illustrious through many miracles and died in it in all dignity.

The Blessed Fronto was buried there, that is to say, in the basilica[229] erected in his name where, by God's generosity, many benefices are accorded to those who solicit them. It is even told by some that he belonged to the college of the disciples of Christ.[230] His tomb does not resemble the tomb of any other saint: indeed, it was built with the greatest care in a round form as the sepulcher of the Lord, and it surpasses in beauty and its admirable workmanship the sepulchers of all other saints.[231] His sacred feast is celebrated on October 25.

St. Euverte

Turning to those who go to Santiago by way of Tours,[232] these must visit in the Church of the Holy Cross in Orléans the wood of the Lord as well as the chalice of the Blessed Euverte, bishop and confessor.[233] As the Blessed Euverte was one day celebrating mass there appeared to the eyes of the attendants high above the altar the hand of God in human form[234] doing whatever the priest was doing at the altar. When the priest made the sign of the cross over the bread and the chalice,[235] the hand did it in like manner; and when he raised the bread and the chalice, the very hand of God raised in like manner the true bread and the chalice. Once the sacrifice was over, the most pious hand of the Savior vanished. Whence it is given to understand that whoever might sing the mass, it is Christ himself[236] that sings it.

That is the reason why the Blessed Doctor Fulgentius[237] says: "It is not man that offers the sacrifice of the body and the blood of Christ, but he who was crucified for us, Christ himself." And the Blessed Isidore declares: "Neither does one better by virtue of the goodness of the good priest, nor does one worse by virtue of the evil of the bad one."[238] The said chalice is, according to the usage, always at the disposition[239] of the faithful, whether countrymen or foreigners, who request it for communion.

In the same city one must equally visit the remains of the Blessed Euverte, bishop and confessor[240]; and still in the same city, in the Church of Saint-Samson,[241] one ought to render visit to the knife[242] which has veritably been present at the supper of the Lord.

St. Martin

One must equally visit on this route, on the banks of the Loire, the venerable remains of the Blessed Martin, bishop and confessor. It is asserted, indeed, that he is the magnificent one who has resuscitated three dead,[243] and further that he rendered much-desired health to the leprous, the possessed, the insane, the lunatics, the demoniacs, as well as to others who were sick and ill.[244]

The sarcophagus[245] in which his most sacred remains rest in a place adjoining the city of Tours glitters with an immense display of silver and gold as well as precious stones and shines forth through its frequent miracles. Above this, an immense and venerable basilica has been erected in his honor, similar to the Church of the Blessed James and executed in admirable workmanship.[246] The sick come here and are healed, the possessed are delivered, the blind are restored to their vision, the lame rise, all sort of illnesses are cured, and upon all those who ask for it a complete relief is conferred.[247] That is the reason why its glorious fame has, for the honor of Christ, spread such worthy praises everywhere. His feast is celebrated on November 11.

St. Hilary

Afterwards one ought to visit the most holy remains of the Blessed Hilary, bishop and confessor,[248] in the city of Poitiers. Among other miracles, infused by the grace of God, he has vanquished the Arian heresy and has taught us how to advance the unity of the faith. But Leo the heretic,[249] unwilling to accept his sacred teachings, having left the council, died abominably in the latrines afflicted by a corruption of the belly.[250] Wishing Saint Hilary, on the other hand, to participate in the council, the earth rose under him providing him with a seat.[251] It is he who, with his mere voice, shattered the door locks of the council[252]; it is he who, for the sake of the Catholic faith, was kept for four years in exile on a certain island of Frisia[253]; it is he who put to flight, by virtue of his power, a great many serpents; and it is he who, in the city of Poitiers, restored to a weeping mother her child struck prematurely with a double death.[254]

The tomb where his venerable and most sacred bones are resting is decorated with abundant gold, silver, and extraordinarily precious stones,[255] and its large and splendid basilica is venerated by virtue of its many miracles. His sacred feast is celebrated on January 13.[256]

St. John the Baptist

One should also visit the venerable head of the Blessed John the Baptist, brought by some ecclesiastics from the lands of Jerusalem to a place called Angély,[257] to be sure in the land of Poitou. There, a large basilica was erected under his patronage, executed with admirable workmanship,[258] and in which the most holy head is worshipped day and night by a choir of one hundred monks[259] and extolled by virtue of his innumerable miracles. While this head was being transported on sea and land, it already gave indications of countless prodigies. On sea, it drove away many a maritime danger, and on land, as it is reported in the codex of its translation,[260] it restored many dead to life. That is the reason why one believes that this one is truly the head of the venerable Precursor.[261] Its discovery took place on February 24 in the times of Emperor Marcianus, when the Precursor himself had first revealed to two monks the place where his head was lying hidden.[262]

St. Eutropius

On the way of Saint James, in the city of Saintes, pilgrims must render a devote visit to the remains of the Blessed Eutropius, bishop and martyr. His most saintly passion was written in Greek[263] by his companion, the Blessed Dionysius, bishop of Paris, and sent, by the mediation of the Blessed Pope Clement,[264] to his parents in Greece where people were already believing in Christ.[265] One day I had found this passion in a Greek school of Constantinople, in a certain codex concerning the passions of many saintly martyrs and, for the glory of our Lord Jesus Christ and of his glorious martyr Eutropius, I translated it the best I could from Greek into Latin.[266] And it began in the following way:

> Dionysius, bishop of the Franks, of Greek stock, to the most reverend Pope Clement, greetings in Christ. We notify you that Eutropius, whom you had sent with me to these lands in order to preach the name of Christ,[267] has attained in the city of Saintes, at the hand of gentiles, for the faith of the Lord, the crown of martyrdom. That is the reason why I humbly entreat your paternity to send with no delay and as soon as you possibly can this manuscript of his passion to my relatives, acquaintances and faithful friends in the land of Greece, and particularly in Athens, in order that they themselves as well as others who had, together with me, accepted from the Blessed Paul the baptism of a new regeneration,[268] upon hearing that a glorious martyr has submitted to a cruel death for the faith of Christ, they themselves rejoice to undergo tribulations

and anguishes for the name of Christ.[269] And if by chance some form of martyrdom should be inflicted upon them by the fury of the gentiles, may they learn to suffer it patiently for Christ and not to dread it in any way any more. In effect, all who wish to live piously in Christ must suffer the opprobrium of the impious and the heretics and must be despised as insane and stupid.[270] For it behooves us to enter into the kingdom of God through many tribulations.

Far in body
But close in soul and good wishes,
I say you now farewell;
May it be forever with you.[271]

The Passion of the Blessed Eutropius of Saintes, bishop and martyr

Eutropius,[272] a glorious martyr of Christ, the gentle bishop of Saintes, the offspring of a noble Persian family, descended, to be sure, from the most excellent lineage of the whole world: the emir[273] of Babylon, by the name Xerxes, begot him of Queen Guiva in the flesh.[274] Nobody could have been of a more sublime stock nor, after his conversion, more humble in faith and deeds.[275] Already in his childhood he was taught Chaldean[276] and Greek letters and, once he became equal in discretion and thirst of knowledge to the highest personages of the entire realm,[277] he wished to ascertain whether per chance there were at the court somebody more eager to learn than himself or whether there were there things strange enough to elicit his curiosity, and so he went to King Herod in Galilee.[278] While he stayed in that court for several days, having heard about the fame of the Savior's miracles, he searched for Him from city to city; and since this one had gone to the other shore of the sea of Galilee, that is to say Tiberias,[279] followed by a large throng of people amazed at the miracles the Savior was performing, he too went after Him.

Now, by a disposition of divine grace, the day came in which the Savior, in His ineffable generosity, with five loafs of bread and two fishes satiated five thousand people that were with Him.[280] Seeing this miracle, having heard about the fame of His other miracles and furthermore believing already somewhat in Him, the young Eutropius developed a strong desire to speak to the Savior: but he did

111

not dare to do so, dreading the severity of Nicanor, his tutor,[281] whom the emir, his father, had entrusted with his own custody. Satiated, anyhow, with the bread of divine grace, he set out for Jerusalem and, having worshipped the Creator in the temple, according to heathen customs,[282] returned to the house of his father.

And he began telling him everything that he had diligently seen in the country where he had come from. "I have seen, he said, a man called Christ; no one like Him can one find in the whole world. He renders life to the dead, tidiness to the leprous, sight to the blind, hearing to the deaf, to the lame their former vigor, and good health to all sorts of sick people.[283] What more? Before my eyes he fed five thousand men with five loafs of bread and two fishes; and His companions in fact filled up twelve baskets with the rest.[284] There can be no room for hunger, storm or mortality in the places where he dwells. If ever the Creator of heaven and earth condescended to send Him to our country, may your goodwill show Him due honor!"

The emir, hearing such and similar things from the boy, kept wondering diligently and quietly how he could see Him. After a while, wishing to see the Lord once again and having secured an authorization from the king, the lad went to Jerusalem in order to worship in the temple. And there were with him Warradac,[285] the chief of the army, and Nicanor, steward to the king and tutor of the lad as well as many other noblemen whom the emir had sent for his safekeeping.

One day, as he was returning from the temple and the Lord was coming back from Bethany where He had just resuscitated Lazarus,[286] the young prince run into an enormous crowd rushing from everywhere to the gates of Jerusalem. When he saw the Hebrew boys as well as the multitudes of other nations that were going out to meet the Lord scattering flowers and twigs of palms, olives and other trees on the road the Lord was about to take, among exclamations of "Hosanna to the son of David,"[287] Eutropius rejoiced more than one can say and he too started to scatter flowers before Him. Then he was told by some that the Lord had resuscitated Lazarus[288] who had been dead for four days,[289] and he rejoiced even more. But since at the time he could not fully see the Savior due to the great multitude of people streaming all around, he began to feel once again greatly saddened.

He was, indeed, among those of whom John bears testimony in his gospel[290] by saying: "Now, there were some gentiles[291] among those who had come to adore Him on the day of the festivity. These approached Philip who was from the city of Bethsaida and said to him: 'Sir, we want to see Jesus.' At which Philip, together with Andrew, relayed this to the Lord." And soon the Blessed Eutropius together with his companions saw Him face to face and, greatly rejoicing, started secretly to believe in Him. At last, he fully joined the Lord, though he was still afraid of the recriminations of his associates[292] whom his father had instructed, above all, to guard him strictly and to bring him home.

Then he was told by some that the Jews were soon to slay the Savior.[293] Unwilling to see the death of such a great man, the next day he left Jerusalem.[294] Having returned to his father, he told everybody in his country, in an orderly fashion, all he had seen in the land of Jerusalem concerning the Savior. Then, after a short stay in Babylon, desiring to join the Savior in everything and believing Him still alive in the flesh, accompanied by a certain squire and without the knowledge of his father, forty five days later he returned once again to Jerusalem.[295]

Soon he heard that the Lord, Whom he secretly loved, had been crucified and put to death by the Jews, and he was greatly afflicted. But when he was told that He had risen from among the dead, that He had appeared to His disciples and that He had triumphantly ascended to heaven, he began once again to greatly rejoice.

Finally, on the day of Pentecost,[296] having joined the disciples of the Lord, he was told in what manner the Holy Spirit had descended upon them in the form of tongues of fire, how It had filled their heart and taught them all the languages.[297] Filled with the Holy Spirit[298] he returned to Babylon and, burning with the zeal of love for Christ, slew by the sword the Jews he found in that country on account of those who, by putting the Lord to death, had execrated Jerusalem.[299]

At that point, after a short time, while the disciples of the Lord betook themselves to the various latitudes of the world,[300] two golden candelabra glittering of faith by disposition of the divine grace, that is to say, Simon and Thaddeus, apostles of the Lord, set out for Persia.[301] When they entered Babylon, having thrown out from that land the magicians Zaroen and Arfaxat who by their vain speeches and prodigies had deflected the masses from their faith,[302] the apostles distributed to everybody the seeds of eternal life and distinguished themselves in all sort of miracles.

The holy child Eutropius, rejoicing in their coming, kept urging the king to abandon the error of the gentiles and of their idols and to embrace the Christian faith by which he would certainly deserve the reign of heaven. What more could I say? Soon after, upon the predication of the apostles, the king and his son,[303] together with a large number of citizens of Babylon, were regenerated through the grace of baptism administered to them by the same apostles. Finally, once the whole city had been converted to the faith of the Lord, the apostles established in it a church with all its hierarchies.[304] Furthermore, they ordained the most faithful Abdias,[305] an individual imbued with evangelical doctrine whom they had brought along from Jerusalem, as bishop over the Christians, and Eutropius as archdeacon.[306] It is only then that they[307] set out to other cities preaching the word of God. And when, not many days later, they were to consume elsewhere[308] their present life in the triumph of martyrdom, the Blessed Eutropius celebrated their passion in Chaldean[309] and Greek.

At that point, having heard the fame of the miracles and virtues of the Blessed Peter,[310] the prince of the apostles, who at that time was discharging in Rome the office of his apostolate, Eutropius wholly renounced the world and, provided with the authorization of his bishop but without his father's knowledge,[311] went to Rome. He was received with great amiableness by the Blessed Peter and was instructed by him in the precepts of the Lord. Having stayed with him for a while, he set out with other brothers,[312] under his order and advise, to the regions of Gaul.

And as he was entering a city called Saintes, he saw it well-enclosed from each side by ancient walls,[313] decorated with high towers, located on an excellent site, well proportioned in extension and width, prosperous in all goods and provisions, abounding in excellent meadows and clear springs,[314] protected by a large river,[315] most fertile all around in gardens, groves and vineyards, engulfed in a salutary air, provided with handsome squares and streets, and beautiful in many ways.[316] Upon which this fine disciple of the Lord started to think that God would indeed condescend to have this beautiful and remarkable city convert from the error of the gentiles and the cult of idols and submit to Christian laws.

Thus, walking around on its squares and streets, he started to preach ardently the word of God. But no sooner did the citizens realize that he was a foreigner[317] and hear him once preaching the words concerning the Holy Trinity and the baptism previously ignored by them[318] that, all excited, they expelled him from the city, burning him with torches and hitting him with large sticks. But he, bearing patiently this persecution, built himself a wooden hut on a nearby hillside where he stayed for a long time. By day he would preach in the city while by night he would spend his time in that hut in vigils, prayers, and tears.[319] And since in a very long time he was able to convert to Christ by his preaching only a few, he used to recall the precept of the Lord: "If somebody would not welcome you and would not listen to your words, in leaving that house or that city, shake off the dust of your feet."[320]

Then he went again to Rome where, since the Blessed Peter had in the meanwhile been crucified, he was ordered by Saint Clement, who was pope at the time,[321] to return to the said city and, while preaching the precepts of the Lord, to look forward there to gaining the crown of martyrdom.[322] Finally, having received the episcopal consecration from the pope himself, together with the Blessed Dionysius who had come from the land of Greece to Rome as well as other friars whom Clement had sent to preach in France, he went as far as Auxerre. There, parting among embraces of divine affection and weeping farewells, Dionysius together with his companions proceeded to the city of Paris and the Blessed Eutropius returned to Saintes. Valiantly animated by the will to undergo martyrdom, full of zeal for Christ, he encouraged himself by saying: "The Lord is my sustenance: I shall not fear what man may perpetrate to me.[323] Even if the persecutors kill the body, they cannot kill the soul.[324] Man ought to give for his soul everything he possesses, even his skin."[325]

Thus, entering courageously the city, he preached, as one possessed, the faith of the Lord, insisting at times opportunely, at others inopportunely,[326] and teaching everybody concerning the Incarnation of Christ, His Passion, Resurrection, Ascension and the rest which the Lord had decided to suffer for the salvation of the human race[327]; furthermore, he instilled publicly into all the notion that nobody could enter into the realm of God if he was not newly born[328] through water and the Holy Spirit. At night, on the other hand, he would dwell in the said hut as before. While he was thus preaching, soon the divine grace

115

descended from heaven and many people turned out in the city to be baptized by him.[329]

Among these was the daughter of the king of the city, by the name Eustella,[330] who too was regenerated by baptismal water. When her father learned this, he cursed her and expelled her from the city.[331] She, on her part, seeing herself driven out due to her love for Christ, settled down to live next to the hut of the holy man. In the meanwhile her father, impelled by the love he felt for his daughter, repeatedly sent emissaries to her in order to have her return home.[332] But she answered that she preferred to dwell outside the city for the faith of Christ rather than return to the city and be contaminated by idols.[333] At that the father, burning with wrath and having summoned the butchers of the city – one hundred fifty in all[334] – ordered them to kill Saint Eutropius and to return the young girl to the paternal home.[335] These, on April 30,[336] having gathered a multitude of gentiles, came to the said hut and, firstly, stoned the saintly man of God; then they battered him, all naked, with sticks and leather belts studded with lead; and finally they slew him by beating his head to pieces with hatchets and axes.[337]

With the assistance of some other Christians,[338] the young girl buried him at night in his hut[339] and, as long as she lived, never ceased to hold vigils for him by candlelight while reciting divine offices. And when, in saintly death, she departed from this life, she asked to be buried in a free plot of hers next to the sepulcher of her master.[340] Later on the Christians erected in his honor over the saintly body of the Blessed Eutropius[341] a large basilica executed with admirable workmanship and dedicated to the name of the holy and undivided Trinity, in which those afflicted by various kinds of illness are often liberated, the lame stand up, the blind recover their sight, hearing is returned to the deaf, the possessed are freed, and all those who with a sincere heart ask for it are accorded a salutary assistance. Iron chains, handcuffs, and various other iron instruments from which the Blessed Eutropius had freed those enchained in them are hanging there.[342] May he, therefore, by his worthy merits and prayers obtain indulgence for us before God,[343] may he wash clean our vices, quicken in us the virtues, lend direction to our life, extradite us from the gates of hell in the perils of death,[344] appease at the Last Judgment the great wrath of the Eternal Judge in our regards, and lead us into the highest realm of heaven with the help of our Lord Jesus Christ who, together with the Father and the Holy Spirit, is the living and reigning God for the infinite centuries to come. Amen.

St. Romanus and St. Roland

Next to Blaye, on the seashore, one must ask for the protection of the Blessed Romanus in whose basilica[345] the remains of the Blessed Roland the martyr rest.[346] Issue of a noble family, count of King Charlemagne and one of his twelve paladins, prompted by the zeal of faith, he[347] entered Spain in order to expel the infidels. Such was his strength that at Roncesvalles, as one is told, with three strokes of his sword he parted a rock in the middle from top to bottom and, sounding his horn, he similarly broke it in the middle by the power of his mouth. His ivory horn parted thus in the middle is found in the basilica of the Blessed Seurin in the city of Bordeaux; and over the rock in Roncesvalles a church has been built.[348]

Having thus vanquished kings and nations in many wars, exhausted by hunger, cold and excessive heat, struck by mighty blows and frequent whippings due to his love of the divine Numen, wounded by arrows and spears, Roland, the valorous martyr of Christ, died of thirst, as it is reported, in the said valley.[349] His most holy body was buried by his companions with respectful veneration in the basilica of the Blessed Romanus in Blaye.[350]

St. Seurin

Afterwards, in the city of Bordeaux one should visit the remains of the Blessed Seurin,[351] bishop and confessor; his feast is celebrated on October 23.

The Paladins of Charlemagne

Similarly, in the Landes of Bordeaux, in the town called Belin, one must visit the remains of the holy martyrs Olivier; Gondebaud, king of Frisia; Ogier, king of Dacia; Arastain, king of Bretagne; Garin, duke of Lorraine[352]; and of many other paladins of Charlemagne who, having defeated the pagan armies, died by the sword in Spain for the faith of Christ.[353] Their companions carried their precious remains as

117

far as Belin and buried them with the greatest care. All of them lie together in a single grave from which emanates an extremely soft scent that heals the sick.[354]

St. Domingo

Subsequently, one ought to visit in Spain the remains of the Blessed Domingo the confessor who built the pavement of the road that stretches between the city of Nájera and Redecilla, at the place where he rests.[355]

St. Facundo and St. Primitivo

In the same way, one ought to pay a visit to the remains of the Blessed Martyrs Facundo and Primitivo whose basilica was erected by Charlemagne. Next to their town there are wooded meadows in which, as one is told, the planted poles of the warriors' lances bloom.[356] Their feast is celebrated on November 27.

St. Isidore

Hereafter, in the city of León, one ought to pay a visit to the venerable remains of the Blessed Isidore,[357] bishop, confessor and doctor, who established a most pious rule for ecclesiastical clerics,[358] infused the Hispanic nation with his doctrines, and decorated the entire holy Church with the flower of his writings.[359]

St. James

Finally, one must visit in the city of Compostela, with the greatest care and attention, the most worthy remains of the Blessed Apostle James.[360]

May the saints hitherto spoken of together with all the other saints of God assist us with their virtues and prayers before our Lord Jesus Christ who lives and reigns with the Father and the Holy Spirit, God for the infinite centuries to come. Amen.[361]

CHAPTER IX

THE CHARACTERISTICS OF THE CITY AND THE CHURCH OF ST. JAMES — POPE CALIXTUS AND AIMERY THE CHANCELLOR[362] —

The city of Compostela lies between two rivers of which the one is called the Sar and the other, the Sarela.[363] The Sar flows to the east, between Monte del Gozo[364] and the city; the Sarela, to the west. There are seven[365] entrances and gates to the city: the first is known as the Puerta Francesca[366]; the second, the Puerta de la Peña[367]; the third, the Puerta de Subfratribus[368]; the fourth, the Puerto de Santo Peregrino[369]; the fifth, the Puerta Fajera[370], which leads to Padrón[371]; the sixth, the Puerta de Susannis[372]; the seventh, the Puerta de Mazarelos[373] through which the precious liquor of Bacchus[374] enters the city.

The Churches of the City

In this city one counts usually ten churches[375] of which the first is that of the most glorious Apostle James, the son of Zebedee[376]: this church, in the middle of the city,[377] shines gloriously; the second is that of the Blessed Apostle San Pedro, a monastic abbey church near the French road[378]; the third, that of San Miguel, is called of the Cistern[379]; the fourth, that of San Martín the bishop, also a monastic church, is called of the Pinario[380]; the fifth, that of the Santa Trinidad, serves as burial ground for pilgrims[381]; the sixth, that of Santa Susana virgin,[382] is next to the road leading to Padrón[383]; the seventh is that of San Félix martyr[384]; the eight is that of San Benito[385]; the ninth, that of San Pelayo martyr,[386] is behind the basilica of the Blessed James; the tenth, dedicated to the Santa Maria Virgen[387] is behind the Church of Saint James and is provided with an entry into this basilica between the altar of San Nicolás and that of the Santa Cruz.

The Measurements of the Church

The basilica of Saint James[388] measures in length fifty-three times a man's stature, that is to say, from the west portal to the altar of the San Salvador; and in width, thirty-nine times, that is to say, from the French to the south portal.[389] Its elevation on the inside is fourteen times a man's stature.[390] Nobody is really able to tell its length and height on the outside.[391]

The church has nine aisles on the lower level and six on the upper,[392] as well as a head, plainly a major one, in which the altar of the San Salvador is located,[393] a laurel crown, a body, two members, and further eight small heads in each of which there is an altar.[394]

Of the nine naves, six are considered of moderate size and three large. The first, the principal nave, runs from the west portal as far as the middle piers[395] which, four in number to be sure, dominate the whole of the church. This nave is flanked by an aisle to the right and another to the left. Two other large naves are located in the two transepts, the first of which runs from the French portal[396] to the four piers of the crossing, and the second one, from those same piers to the south portal. Each of these naves has two lateral aisles.

The three principal naves rise as far as the vault[397] of the church, while the six aisles ascend only as far as the middle of the arch reinforcements.[398]

Each of the large naves[399] has a width of eleven and a half times[400] a man's stature. We evaluate the height of a man, properly speaking, as eight palms.

In the largest nave there are twenty-nine piers, fourteen to the right and as many to the left,[401] and one is on the inside between the two portals against the north,[402] separating the vaulted bays.[403] In the naves of the transepts[404] of this church, that is to say from the French to the south portal, there are twenty-six piers, twelve on the right and as many on the left,[405] as well as two more placed before the doors on the inside, separating the entrance arches and the portals.[406]

In the crown[407] of the church there are eight single columns around the altar of the Blessed James.[408] The six small naves which are above in the palace[409] of the church are equal in length and width to the corresponding aisles below. They are supported on the one side by walls,[410] and

on the other by the piers which from the large naves below ascend to the top, as well as by the double pillars
stonecutters call middle arch supports.[411]

There are as many piers in the lower part of the church as
there are in the naves above,[412] and there are as many principal transverse ribs[413] in the lower part below as there are
above in the triforia; but in the aisles of the triforia there are
furthermore, between the single pillars, two twin shafts
which stonecutters call reinforced columns.[414]

In this church, in truth, one cannot find a single crack or
defect: it is admirably built, large, spacious, luminous, of
becoming dimensions, well proportioned in width, length
and height, of incredibly marvelous workmanship and even
built on two levels as a royal palace.[415]

He who walks through the aisles of the triforium above, if
he ascended in a sad mood, having seen the superior beauty
of this temple, will leave happy and contented.[416]

The Windows

There are sixty-three glass windows proper in this basilica,
and above each of the altars that surround the ambulatory
there are three. On the upper level of the basilica,[417] around
the altar of the Blessed James, there are five windows through
which the apostolic altar is well illuminated. In the triforium
above there are forty-three windows.[418]

The Portals

This church counts three main portals[419] and seven small
ones[420]: one opens to the west, that is to say, the main one;
another, to the south, and still another, to the north. And in
each of the main portals there are two entrances, and in each
entrance, two doors.[421] The first of the seven small portals is
called the Portal of Santa Maria[422]; the second, of the Via
Sacra[423]; the third, of San Pelayo[424]; the fourth, of the
Cañonica[425]; the fifth, of the Pedrera[426]; the sixth, similarly, of
the Pedrera[427]; the seventh, of the Grammar School,[428] which
also gives access to the archbishop's palace.

The Fountain of Saint James

When we Frenchmen[429] wish to enter the basilica of the Apostle, we do so from the northern side.[430] In front of this entrance, next to the road, is the hospice[431] of the poor pilgrims of Saint James, and further, beyond the road, there is a parvis with nine descending steps.[432] At the bottom of the stairs of this parvis there is a marvelous fountain,[433] the like of which is not to be found in the whole world. This fountain, in fact, rests on a base of three stone steps which support a most beautiful stone basin, round and hollowed out in the form of a bowl[434] or a saucer, and which is so large that it seems that fifteen men can easily bathe in it.[435] In the middle of it a bronze column of well-proportioned height rises, thick at its base and fashioned of seven square panels fitted together.[436] Four lions[437] jut out of its summit, through whose mouths four water spurts spout to quench the thirst of the pilgrims of the Blessed Saint James and of the inhabitants at large. The water that issues from the mouth of the lions pours directly into the basin underneath, and from there, through a hole in the basin, escapes and gets lost in the ground. As one cannot see whence the water comes, so one cannot tell where it goes.[438] Moreover, this water[439] is sweet, nourishing, healthy, clear, excellent, warm in winter and fresh in summer. All around the above-mentioned column, under the lions' feet, the following two-line inscription is engraved:

> I, Bernard,[440] treasurer of the Blessed James, brought this water hither[441] and erected this monument for the salvation of my soul and of that of my parents, on the third ides of April of the year 1160 of the era.[442]

The Parvis of the City

Behind the fountain, as we have mentioned, there is the parvis,[443] all of it paved out with stones. It is there that scallop shells,[444] the insignia of Santiago, are sold to the pilgrims; and one sells there also wineskins,[445] shoes,[446] knapsacks of deer-skin,[447] side-bags, leather straps, belts, all sort of medicinal herbs[448] no less than sundry drugs and many more things. On the Camino Francés on the other

hand, one finds money changers, innkeepers and merchants of all sorts.[449] The dimensions of the parvis in both
length and width are those of a single stone throw.[450]

The North Portal

Beyond this parvis we have the north portal of the basilica
of Santiago, called the French.[451] It has two entrances and
there is beautiful ornamentation carved on both. On the outside each entrance has six columns, some of marble, some of
stone, three to the right and three to the left, that is to say, six
to one entrance and six to the other, which makes a total of
twelve. On a column erected between the two portals, on
the outside walls,[452] the Lord is seated in majesty giving the
blessing with his right hand while holding a book in the left.[453]
The four Evangelists are all around his throne, as if sustaining it.[454] To the right, Paradise is represented, within which
the figure of the Lord appears once again, upbraiding Adam
and Eve on account of their sin[455]; and, similarly, to the left
He reappears in yet another image[456] expelling them from
Paradise.

In the same place there are sculpted all around many images of saints, beasts, men, angels, women, flowers, and other
creatures whose aspect and characteristics we cannot provide here due to their great number. We should mention,
however, that, as one enters into the basilica, above the left
door, that is to say, on its tympanum,[457] the Annunciation to
the Blessed Virgin Mary is represented with the angel Gabriel
speaking to her.[458] And still to the left, on the lateral entrance
above the doors, there appear sculpted the months of the
year[459] and many other beautiful works. Two large and ferocious lions are placed against the exterior walls, one to the
right and the other to the left, as if staring at the doors while
continuously watching them.[460] Above the jambs four
apostles are represented, each holding a book in the left and
with the raised right blessing those who enter into the basilica. In the left entrance Peter is standing to the right and
Paul to the left[461]; and in the right entrance it is the Apostle
John who is standing to the right and the Blessed James to
the left. Above the head of each apostle, ox heads[462] in high
relief are carved on the uprights.

The South Portal

On the south portal[463] of the apostolic basilica there are, as we have said, two entrances and four door-leaves. On the first register of the right entrance, above the doors, on the outside, the Betrayal of the Lord is represented in an admirable fashion.[464] Here the Lord appears tied to a column by the hand of the Jews[465]; there He is whipped with leather straps[466]; and farther on Pilate is seated on his throne, as if judging Him.[467] Above, on another register, the Blessed Mary, the Mother of the Lord, is represented with her Son in Bethlehem, as well as the Three Kings who come to visit the Child with His Mother while offering Him presents; and furthermore the star and the angel admonishing them not to return by way of Herod.[468]

On the jambs of that same entrance, as if guarding the door-leaves, there are two apostles, one to the right and one to the left. Similarly, in the other entrance, to the left, that is to say on the door jambs, there are two further apostles[469]; and on the first register of that entrance, above the doors, the Temptation of the Lord[470] is sculpted. Before the Lord, in fact, there stand some repellent angels looking like monsters who set Him on the pinnacle of the Temple; others offer Him stones and urge Him to transmute them into bread; and still others display before Him the kingdoms of the world feigning to hand them over to Him if, on His knees, He adored them – may that never happen![471] There are, however, other angels – white, that is to say, good ones – some behind Him and some above, who are ministering to Him with censers.[472]

There are four lions on that same portal, one on either side of each entrance.[473] Above the pier rising between the two entrances there are two more ferocious lions, the ramp of the one pressed against that of the other.[474]

Eleven columns flank the portal: five at the right entrance, that is to say to the right, and the same number at the left entrance,[475] to the left. The eleventh column is placed between the two entrances dividing the portal arches. Some of these columns are of marble, others of stone, all of them admirably sculpted with figures, flowers, men, birds, and beasts. The marble of these columns is white. And one should not forget to mention that there is a woman next to the Temptation of the Lord, who holds in her hands the filthy head of her lover beheaded by her own husband; and this one forces her to kiss it twice a day. Oh, what a great and admirable punishment meted out to the adulterous woman, to be recounted to everybody![476]

On the upper register, above the four door-leaves and towards the triforium of the basilica,[477] a magnificent stone ornamentation of white marble glitters splendidly. The Lord is standing there, in fact, with Saint Peter to his left holding the keys in his hand, and the Blessed James to his right between two cypress trees and with Saint John, his brother, next to him. To the right and left, finally, the rest of the apostles are placed.[478] All told, above and below, to the right and to the left, the entire wall is richly adorned with flowers, men, saints, beasts, birds, fishes, and with other works that we cannot describe here in detail. One must notice, none the less, the four angels placed above the archivolts of the passageways, each with a single trumpet, announcing the Day of Judgment.[479]

Concerning the West Portal

The west portal,[480] with two entrances, surpasses the other portals in splendor, size and workmanship. It is larger, more beautiful and executed with further magnificence than the others. It is provided, on the exterior, with a large stairway and with diverse marble columns decorated in various ways with sundry figures: men, women, beasts, birds, saints, angels and flowers, all of which sculpted in a variety of ornamentation and manner. Its decoration, in fact, is so abundant that we cannot describe it in detail.[481] Notwithstanding, we should notice, on the top, the Transfiguration[482] of the Lord as it occurred on the Tabor Mountain, and which is sculpted in marvelous workmanship. The Lord appears there in a dazzling cloud, his face shining as the sun, his garments sparkling as snow, while the Father is speaking to Him from above[483]; and Moses[484] and Elias, who appeared together with Him, are there too conversing with Him of His ultimate destiny that was to be fulfilled in Jerusalem. Saint James is also there,[485] with Peter and John to whom, before anybody else, the Lord revealed His Transfiguration.

Concerning the Towers of the Basilica

There are nine towers[486] in this church, that is to say, two above the portal of the fountain,[487] two above the south portal,[488] two above the west portal,[489] two above each of the corkscrew staircases,[490] and another, the largest one,[491] above the crossing, in the middle of the basilica. By these and by the many other utmost precious works the basilica of the Blessed James shines in magnificent glory. All of it is built in massive bright and brown stone which is hard as marble.[492] The interior is decorated with various paintings[493] and the exterior is perfectly covered with tiles and lead.[494] Of all we have hitherto been speaking, some portions are entirely finished while others still remain to be completed.[495]

Concerning the Altars of the Basilica

The altars[496] of the basilica correspond to the following order: first of all, next to the French portal, which is on the left, we have the altar of San Nicolás[497]; then the altar of the Santa Cruz[498]; then, in the ambulatory, the altar of Santa Fe, virgin[499]; then the altar of San Juan,[500] apostle and evangelist, brother of Saint James; then the altar of San Salvador[501] in the large apsidal chapel; then the altar of San Pedro,[502] apostle; then the altar of San Andrés[503]; then the altar of San Martin,[504] bishop; and finally the altar of San Juan Bautista.[505] Between the altar of Santiago and that of the San Salvador, there is the altar of Santa Maria Magdalena[506] at which morning masses are sung for the pilgrims.[507] Above, in the triforium of the church, there are three further altars the principal of which is the altar of San Miguel Arcangel[508]; another, on the right side, is the altar of San Benito[509]; and still another, on the left side, the altar of San Pablo the apostle and San Nicolás[510] the bishop. It is there, too, that the chapel of the archbishop lies.[511]

Concerning the Body and the Altar of Saint James

Up to this point we have treated the characteristics of the church; now we ought to treat the venerable altar of the Apostle. In this revered basilica, under the high altar erected, with the greatest deference, in his honor[512] rests, as it is reported, the venerated body of the Blessed James. It is enclosed in a marble casket placed in a most precious vaulted tomb of admirable workmanship and harmonious dimensions.[513]

His body is immovable,[514] according to what is asserted and furthermore as it is witnessed by Saint Theodemir,[515] bishop of the city, who had discovered it a long time ago and in no way could remove it from its place.[516] May therefore the imitators from beyond the mountains blush who claim to possess some portion of him or even his entire relic.[517] In fact, the body of the Apostle is here in its entirety, divinely lit by paradisiacal carbuncles, incessantly honored with immaculate and soft perfumes, decorated with dazzling celestial candles,[518] and diligently worshipped by attentive angels.

Over his tomb there is a small altar which, as it is told, was made by his disciples and which, for the sake of the love for the Apostle and his disciples, nobody subsequently wanted to demolish.[519] And above this there is a large and most admirable altar which measures five palms in height, twelve in length, and seven in width.[520] So have I measured it with my own hands. The small altar is, consequently, enclosed under the large one on three sides[521] – on the right, the left, and the back; but it is open on the front in such a way that, once the silver antependium[522] has been removed, one is able to clearly see the old altar.

If somebody would want to donate, out of devotion for the Blessed James, an altar-ornament or a linen-cloth in order to cover the apostolic altar,[523] he must send it of nine palms in width and twenty-one palms in length. If, on the other hand, one would like to send, out of love for God and the Apostle, an ornamental linen-cloth to cover the front of the antependium,[524] one must see to it that its width be seven palms and its length, thirteen.

Concerning the Silver Antependium

The antependium which overlays the front of the altar is a magnificent work in gold and silver.[525] In its middle the throne of the Lord is sculpted, surrounded by the twenty-four elders[526] in the order as the Blessed John, the brother of Saint James, has seen them in his Apocalypse: there are twelve on the right and the same number on the left, in a circle,[527] holding in their hands zithers and gold phials full of perfumes.[528] In their midst the Lord is seated, as if on a throne of majesty, holding in His left the Book of Life and giving His blessing with the right. Around the throne, as if supporting it, there are the four evangelists.[529] The twelve apostles are placed on the right and on the left, three in a first row to the right, and three above. The same takes place on the left, three on the lower row below and three on the higher one.[530] Finally, magnificent flowers[531] are displayed all around and exquisite columns separate the apostles. The antependium, of splendid and superior workmanship, is inscribed on its top with the following verses:

Diego II,[532] bishop of Saint James, made this antependium in the fifth year of his bishopric.
He disbursed from the treasure of James eighty silver marks less five.[533]

And below there is this inscription:

Alphonso[534] was the king, Raymond, his son-in-law, the duke,
When the above-mentioned bishop completed this work.

Concerning the Ciborium of the Apostolic Altar

The ciborium[535] that covers this revered altar is magnificently decorated on the inside and outside with paintings, drawings[536] and various ornaments. It has a square form, it rests on four columns and, with regards to its height and width, it is most harmoniously executed.[537]

On the first register of the interior[538] there are eight principal virtues, those celebrated by Paul, in the form of female figures: in each corner there are two.[539] Above the heads of each of these there are angels standing erect and sustaining with their raised hands the throne placed on the summit of the ciborium.[540] In the middle of this throne is the Lamb of God, holding the cross with its foot.[541] There are as many angels as there are virtues.[542]

On the first register of the exterior four angels announce, by means of trumpet sound, the Resurrection on the Day of Judgment: two of these are on the front side and two on the back.[543] On the same register there are also four prophets, that is to say, Moses and Abraham on the left side and Isaac and Jacob on the right one,[544] each holding in the hand a roll with his own prophecies.[545]

The twelve apostles are seated on the upper register round about.[546] On the frontal side, as the first, the Blessed James is placed in the very middle: he holds a book in his left hand and is blessing with the right.[547] To his right there is another apostle, and to his left still another, all on the same register. Similarly, on the right side of the ciborium there are three other apostles, on the left also three, and in the back, in the same way, three more. On the roofing above four angels[548] are seated as if guarding the altar. Furthermore, in the four corners of the ciborium, at the base of the roofing, the four evangelists are represented,[549] each in his appropriate likeness.[550]

The interior of the ciborium is painted, while the exterior is both sculpted and painted.[551] On the exterior, at the top, an end-structure with a triple arcade has been erected within which the divine Trinity is represented: under the first arch, which faces the west, the person of the Father is situated; under the second one, which turns towards the south and the east, the person of the Son; and under the third arch, which faces the north, the person of the Holy Spirit.[552] Furthermore, above this end-structure there is still a shiny silver ball on which a precious cross is affixed.[553]

Concerning the Three Lamps

In front of the altar of the Blessed James, three large silver lamps are suspended honoring Christ and the Apostle. The one in the middle is very large and it is admirably fashioned in the shape of a big mortar; it contains seven alveoli that stand for the Seven Gifts of the Holy Spirit,[554] and in each of which a wick is set in. The alveoli are fed with nothing but oil of balsam, myrtle, benjamin,[555] or olive. The largest alveolus is in the middle of the others; and on each of those that are around, two images of apostles are sculpted on the outside.[556]

May the soul of King Alphonso of Aragón[557] who, as it is told, has donated them to Saint James,[558] rest in eternal peace.

The Dignity of the Church of Saint James and its Canons

At the altar of the Blessed James, as a rule, no one celebrates mass unless he is bishop, archbishop, pope, or cardinal of this church.[559] In fact, according to a long-established custom, there are in the basilica seven cardinals who celebrate the divine service on the altar.[560] Their constitution and privileges were established by many popes and were confirmed, in particular, by Pope Calixtus.[561] Such a dignity deriving from a venerated tradition that the basilica of the Blessed James possesses should, out of love for the Apostle, by no means be despoiled by anybody.

The Stonecutters of the Church and
The Beginning and Completion of their Work

The master stonecutters that first undertook the construction of the basilica of the Blessed James were called Master Bernard the elder[562] – a marvelously gifted craftsman – and Robert,[563] as well as other stonecutters, about fifty in number,[564] who worked assiduously under the most faithful administration of Don Wicart,[565] the head of the chapter Don Segeredo,[566] and the abbot Don Gundesindo,[567] during the reign of Alphonso[568] king of Spain and during the bishopric of Don Diego I,[569] a valiant soldier and a generous man.

The church was begun in the year 1116 of the era.[570] From the year it was started until the death of Alphonso, valiant and famous king of Aragón, there are fifty-nine years,[571] and until the murder of Henry, king of England, sixty-two years,[572] and until the death of Louis the Fat, king of France, sixty-three.[573] And from the year that the first stone of the foundations was laid down until such a time that the last one was put in place, forty-four years have elapsed.[574]

This church, furthermore, from the moment it was started until today, has shined by the refulgence of the miracles of the Blessed James: in fact, the sick have been restored to health in it, the blind have been rendered their eyesight, the tongue of the dumb has been untied, the ear of the deaf unplugged, movement has been restored to the lame, the possessed has been delivered and, what is more, the prayers of the faithful have been fulfilled, their wishes granted, the chains of sin have crumbled,[575] heaven has opened to those who have knocked at its door,[576] the afflicted have been given consolation,[577] and foreign people of all parts of the world have rushed in in large masses bringing in laudation their gifts to the Lord.[578]

The Dignity of the Church of Saint James

One should not forget that the Blessed Pope Calixtus,[579] worthy of good memory, out of love for the Apostle and in his honor, had transferred to the basilica of Saint James and to its city the archiepiscopal dignity formerly held by the city of Mérida, metropolitan in the land of the Saracen; because of this, he ordained and confirmed Diego, a man of high nobility, as the first archbishop of the apostolic see of Compostela. Indeed, this same Diego had previously been bishop of Saint James.[580]

CHAPTER X

THE DISTRIBUTION OF THE OFFERINGS AT THE ALTAR OF ST. JAMES

Seventy-two canons, corresponding to the number of the seventy-two Disciples of Christ,[581] are attached to this church; they follow the rule of the Blessed Doctor Isidore of Spain.[582] They divide among themselves, by successive weeks, the oblations of the altar of Saint James.[583] To the first canon correspond the oblations of the first week; to the second, those of the second; to the third, those of the third; and so they share the oblations to the last one.[584]

Each Sunday, tradition dictates that the oblations be shared out in three parts: the first is assigned to the hebdomadary[585] to whom it corresponds; the other two are first drawn together and are then divided in their turn into three parts; one of these is given to the canons for their communal meal; another, to the fabric of the basilica; and the third one, to the archbishop of the church.[586] But the oblations of the week which goes from Palm to Easter must be given, according to accepted custom, to the poor pilgrims of Saint James lodged in the hospice.[587] Furthermore, were the justice of God appropriately observed, one would be obliged to give at all times the tenth part of the oblations of the altar of Saint James to the poor who drop in at the hospice.[588]

Indeed, all poor pilgrims must, the first night that follows the day of their arrival to the altar of the Blessed James, receive at the hospice, for the love of God and the Apostle, full hospitality. Those who are sick, to be sure, must be charitably taken care of there either until their death or until their complete recovery. So it is done at Saint-Léonard[589]: no matter how many poor pilgrims make it there, all receive subsistence.[590] Furthermore, custom dictates that the leprous of the city be given the oblations that reach the altar each Sunday, from the beginning of the morning until the hour of terce.[591] And if a prelate of the same basilica committed fraud in this matter or changed in some way the destiny of the oblations, as we have just described it, may his sin stand between God and him.[592]

CHAPTER XI

THE PROPER WELCOMING OF THE PILGRIMS OF ST. JAMES

Pilgrims, whether poor or rich, who return from or proceed to Santiago, must be received charitably and respectfully by all.[593] For he who welcomes them and provides them diligently with lodging will have as his guest not merely the Blessed James, but the Lord himself, who in His Gospels said: "He who welcomes you, welcomes me."[594] Many are those who in the past brought upon themselves the wrath of God because they refused to receive the pilgrims of Saint James or the indigent.[595]

In Nantua,[596] which is a city between Genève and Lyon, a weaver refused to hand out some bread to a pilgrim who had asked for it: all of a sudden some linen of his dropped to the ground torn in its middle.[597] In Villeneuve,[598] a woman kept some bread under hot ashes. A needy pilgrim of Saint James asked her for alms by the love of God and the Blessed James. When she answered that she had no bread, the pilgrim exclaimed: "May the bread you have turn into stone!"[599] And when the pilgrim left her house and was already at a considerable distance, this vicious woman turned to the ashes with the idea of retrieving her bread, but found only a round stone instead. With contrite heart[600] she set out to look for the pilgrim, but could not find him anymore.

Two valiant Frenchmen, returning one day from Santiago destitute of all,[601] kept asking for lodging, by the love of God and Saint James, all about the city of Poitiers from the house of Jean Gautier and as far as Saint-Porchaire – and they could find none.[602] And having finally been put up by some poor man in the last house of that street next to the basilica of Saint-Porchaire,[603] by the effects of divine vengeance, a violent fire burned to the ground that very night the entire street, starting from the house where they first asked for lodging and up to the one which had welcomed them. And these were about one thousand houses in all.[604] But the one in which the servants of God[605] had been put up remained, by divine grace, untouched.

That is the reason why it should be known that the pilgrims of Saint James, whether poor or rich,[606] have the right to hospitality and to diligent respect.

Here ends the fourth book[607] of Saint James the Apostle; Glory to him who wrote it and glory to him who reads it.

This book has first been diligently received by the
Church of Rome[608]; it was written in various
places, that is to say, in Rome, in the
lands of Jerusalem, in France, in
Italy, in Germany, in Frisia
and mainly in
Cluny.[609]

NOTES

1. Though the Compostela manuscript reads "IIII^{us}," it is appropriate to translate "Book V," for until the seventeenth century this was indeed the fifth book. It was then that the *Pseudo-Turpin*, originally the fourth book, was detached from the *Codex* and the *Guide*, originally the fifth book, became the fourth. The present correction of the *incipit*, by a late hand, was indeed entered in the seventeenth century. The Ripoll manuscript reads: "Incipit liber V^{tus}." Cf. Vielliard-*guide*, n. a. on page facing p. l; Moralejo-*Calixtinus*, p. 495, n. l; and BravoLozano-*Guía*, n. 2.

2. The *Pilgrim's Guide to Compostela*, or briefly, the *Guide*, as it is usually known, had been first published by Father Fita in the *Revue de linguistique et de littératures comparées* and subsequently re-published in 1882 in Fita-*codex*. A Spanish version by F. J. Sánchez Cantón, *Guía del Viaje a Santiago: Libro V del Códice Calixtino* (Madrid, 1929), appeared before the important face-to-face French translation of Vielliard of the year 1938 (Vielliard-*guide*), which opened the door for a renewed interest in the text as well as in the road to Compostela in general. Whitehill's transcription of the Latin text of the entire *Liber Sancti Iacobi* of 1944 (Whitehill-*Liber*), and Moralejo, Torres, and Feo's translation into Spanish of the same of the year 1951 (Moralejo-*Calixtinus*), were important steps towards a diligent and accurate interpretation of a text which is not always simple and univocal. During this time there were also a number of partial translations of the *Guide* whose list may be consulted in n. 1 on p. 495 of Moralejo-*Calixtinus*. Important for us, among these, is the translation into English of the last chapters of the *Guide* that concern the description of the Cathedral of Compostela, Conant-*Santiago*, which had appeared a year earlier [in *Art Studies* 3 (1925), p. 143–63]. Lately a German translation has appeared, Herbers-*Jakobsweg*, a Spanish one, BravoLozano-*Guía*, and two Italian ones, Caucci-*Guida* and Oursel-*Compostella*. A Dutch version too saw the light in 1983 (J. van Herwaarden, *O Roemrijke Jakobus Bescherm uw volk*, Amsterdam).

3. The *Liber*, in toto, is set under the particularly benevolent tutelage of Calixtus II and actually is presented as written by him. Such an attribution is evidently spurious. The composition of the *Liber*, or at least of some of its portions, is determined on the one hand by the date of the last miracle inserted in the book, 1139, and on the other, by the date of its transcription by a monk of Ripoll, 1173. Pope Calixtus II, before ascending to the Pontifical See, had been Guy of Burgundy, abbot of Cluny. In fact, he was elected pope in 1119 by the cardinals gathered in Cluny and did not make his entry in Rome before the next year. The Abbey of Cluny, thus,

founded by Duke William of Acquitaine in 910, reached within a short span of time a power and an unquestioned magnificense second to none. Well over 1,000 monasteries obeyed the orders of the mother house. Little wonder thus that when Alphonso VI looked abroad for support for his expansionist national policies of *Reconquista*, he readily zeroed upon Burgundy and Cluny. Calixtus himself was closely connected with Hispanic and particularly Galician power circles: he was the brother of Count Raymond of Burgundy married to Doña Urraca, daughter of Alphonso VI. The latter's political openings towards Europe, France, and particularly Burgundy and Cluny was destined to receive thus, with the ascent of Abbot Guy to the papacy, an added momentum. Cluny, for its part, makes its influence felt both in Rome and in Compostela. Cf. DíazDíaz-*calixtino*, pp. 87-90, and pp. 18–19 above.

4. Folio numeration without indications of recto or verso, are also of a later date, probably corresponding to the time when the original Book IV, the *Pseudo-Turpin*, was detached. Cf. Vielliard-*guide*, p. 1, note b.

5. *Viator* (*viatorum*) in the text, which actually corresponds to traveler, wayfarer. The sense of the chapter, as well as its more extended title at its heading – Of the names of those who restored the road of Blessed James – confirm the reading given here of those engaged in public works as restorers of the road, in the sense of repairmen, repairers, maintenance men, road builders or roadmen, eventually engaging in works of construction, that is to say, public works. Vielliard-*guide* (especially p. 11, n. 5), Moralejo-*Calixtinus*, Caucci-*Guida*, Oursel-*Compostella*, Herbers-*Jakobsweg*, and BravoLozano-*Guía* interpret *viator* in the same way.

6. The title, present in the table of contents of the *incipit* appears neither in the text of the manuscript of Santiago de Compostela nor in that of Ripoll (Archivos de la Corona de Aragón, Barcelona). Except for Moralejo-*Calixtinus*, all other translations do convey it.

7. See pp. 23–28 above. There is no reason to take such an opening as proof for the French authorship of the *Guide*: cf. BravoLozano-*Guía*, p. 90, n. 3.

8. In order to avoid confusion, Spanish and French geographical toponyms will be given henceforth in their respective original language. In the case of Galician toponyms, whenever warranted, they will be given in both Spanish and Gallego.

9. The southernmost route, in reality, departs from Arles, some 30 km from Saint-Gilles. The *via tolosana* connected thus one of the most famous cemeteries of antiquity, Alyscamps, with the most important city of the Languedoc, Toulouse. The *via tolosana* and

the pass of Somport were mostly used by Italian, Provençal, and Languedocian pilgrims.

10. The other three routes – the *via podense* for originating in Le Puy, the *via lemovicense* for passing through Limoges, and the *via turonense* for crossing Tours – joined at Ostabat by Saint-Jean-Pied-de-Port and crossed the Pyrenees at Roncesvalles. The first of these was used by – aside from the French – Hungarian, Austrian, and South-German pilgrims; the second, by Polish, East-European, and German pilgrims in general; and the third, by North-German, Scandinavian, Flemish, and British pilgrims. The latter often joined the northernmost route at Bordeaux or Mimizan in the Landes.

11. Of Conques in the Rouergue (Aveyron).

12. Of Tours. As noted by Vielliard-*guide*, p. 3, n. 4, the French cities are mostly designated by their saints. For the pilgrims, the city is recognizable and actually significant on the strength of the saintly relic it holds. Joseph Bédier had already noticed the close connection between pilgrimages, in particular the one to Compostela, and medieval epic literature (Bédier-*épiques* 3:39–166). Such connection must be extended now to include the reliquary churches on the route. The undertaking of the pilgrimage to Compostela meant to visit most of the famous relics on the way. It must also be noted that most of the great reliquary churches mentioned are abbey churches, at the time belonging to the reformed Benedictine order of Cluny: so Saint-Gilles-du-Gard, Saint-Pierre of Moissac, Sainte-Marie-Madeleine of Vézelay, Saint-Jean-d'Angély, Saint-Eutrope of Saintes. The same is true on the other side of the Pyrenees: San Zoilo of Carrión de los Condes and San Facundo of Sahagún were the central Cluniac bastions in Spain that included in their network of possessions and dependencies many other of the most important monastic settlements: San Juan de la Peña near Jaca, Santa Colomba of Burgos, etc.

13. That is to say, the *via francigena*, the French road, a denomination that can hardly be read without ironic overtones. Originally this road ran farther to the north, in the valleys of the Cantabrian mountains, in order to avoid possible Islamic incursions from the south. Such an itinerary though was terribly wearisome. Sancho el Mayor of Navarra, at the beginning of the eleventh century, transferred the road to the plains farther south making it coincide, more often than not, with the old Roman road passing through Logroño, Nájera and Carrión. Later, Santo Domingo de la Calzada pushed the western portion of the road still further to the south, running it through Burgos. Today, from Puente la Reina to Santiago 623 km must be traveled. Cf. Moralejo-*Calixtinus*, p. 498,

n. 4. For the cartography of the *via francigena*, see Goicoechea-*Cartografía*, Valiña-*Camino*, and Passini-*Camino*.

14. I have translated *dietis*, as further down in the paragraph *diete*, as "days' journey" and "day's journey," respectively. It is conceivable, however, to translate the term also as "day's travel," or even as the more neutral "stage," roughly corresponding to the French *étape*, Spanish *etapa*, Italian *tappa*, or German *Etappe*: as does Viellard-*guide*, and following her, everyone else.

15. To Pope Calixtus are ascribed, in a specific way, the table of contents and chaps. 2 and 6. Chap. 9 is attributed in joint authorship to Callixtus and to the chancellor-scribe Aymeric (Aymery). It seems evident that such haphazard allocations are nothing but arbitrary. See also below, n. 31.

16. On the problem of the day's journey, in general far too long, and on that of the total number of days needed, much underestimated, see above, pp. 50–52. Goicoechea-*Cartografía*, Valiña-*Camino*, and Passini-*camino* compute the distances of the three days' journey of the Borce to Puente la Reina branch of the route, as well as the thirteen days' journey of the Saint-Michel to Santiago main itinerary. BravoLozano-*Guía* (p. 92, n. 11) sums up the distances: Borce to Jaca 36 km; Jaca to Monreal 97 km; Monreal to Puente la Reina 27 km. The middle portion of 97 km constitutes at least a three days' journey, not to speak of possible attractive side visits to San Juan de la Peña or Sanguesa. On the thirteen sections of the main itinerary, matters are no less unrealistic. The 693-km distance between Saint-Michel and Compostela are divided in the following way: Sain-Michel to Viscarret 21 km; Viscarret to Pamplona 28 km; Pamplona to Estella 43 km; Estella to Nájera 69 km; Nájera to Burgos 85 km; Burgos to Frómista 59 km; Frómista to Sahagún 55 km; Sahagún to León 52 km; León to Rabanal 64 km; Rabanal to Villafranca 49 km; Villafranca to Triacastela 47 km; Triacastela to Palas de Rey 58 km; Palas de Rey to Santiago 63 km.

Various sections are over 60 or 70 km in length, which require at least two days' journey under favorable conditions. The author of the *Guide*, furthermore, qualifies as "short," sections of over 60 km, and quite haphazardly assigns a horse ride to some of the sections of the route but not to others. Apart from this, it is strange and out of common practice to have skipped Puente la Reina as a mandatory stopover. Even with moderately long stays at particularly significant sites on the way, it would require on the whole at least one month of travel to reach Santiago. Vázquez de Parga and Filgueira Valverde (VázquezParga-*pereg* 1:210–15; Romero/alia-*Calixtino*, p. 33) seek the answer for the unrealistic attitude of the *Guide's* author in his poeticizing and rhapsodic approach. It may be so. But it may be that overall carelessness in assembling the data joined to a post-factum reconstruction of the travel might have also been the reason for the above inaccuracies and unrealistic propositions. If, furthermore, "day's journey" is on the whole equated with "day's march," then the outcome is even more unrealistic.

17. *Villa* in the text is applied to towns and large villages. *Urbs* is reserved for large cities. Cf. Vielliard-*guide*, p. 7, n. 1.

18. See below, n. 29.

19. *Termas* in the *Codex*, toponymic allusion to the thermal water sources in the vicinity.

20. Hospital of ancient and venerable tradition linked to the name of the greatest hero of the medieval Carolingian legends. Known indirectly from before the end of the eleventh century, in 1110 it was attached to the monastery of Leyre which in turn sold it to the monks of Roncesvalles around 1280. There is considerable lack of clarity in the early history and in the dating of this hospital as well as of the monuments of Roncesvalles in general. Cf. Herbers-*Jakobsweg*, p. 88, n. 11; Moralejo-*Calixtinus*, p. 503, n. 1; Lambert-*Roncevaux Cize*; and Lambert-*Roncevaux*, passim. The latter argues for the priority of Somport based on the doubtful thesis that the monuments of Roncesvalles do not seem to be older than the twelfth century. See also Lambert, "Roncevaux" [*Bulletin Hispanique* 37 (1935): 417]; and Lambert-*peregrinación*. Together with the Silo of Charlemagne, the Hospital of Roland constituted the Santuario de San Salvador de Ibañeta later on dismantled and transferred to Roncesvalles (Bédier-*épiques* 3:316–20). Cf. also BravoLozano-*Guía*, p. 98, n. 25. See Gazetteer below for Roncesvalles.

21. "Qui captivus cognominatus est" in the Latin text. Vielliard-*guide* (p. 9), translates "surnommé le Captif"; and so do Caucci-*Guida*, p. 80, Oursel-*Compostella*, p. 40, and BravoLozano-*Guía*, p. 23; Moralejo-*Calixtinus* (p. 505, n. to line 1), on the other hand, makes *captivus* derive from the gallego-portuguese *cativo*, in the sense of "small."

22. *Villaus*, of various and uncertain interpretation: for Fita, *Villa Urz* (Fita-*codex*, p. 15); for Moralejo, *Vila Uz* (Moralejo-*Calixtinus*, p. 505, n. 3).

23. El Cebrero, O Cebreiro in Gallego, the *portus montis Februarii* of the *Codex*.

24. The image of the pilgrims carrying limestone for some 80 km (from Triacastela to Palas de Rey there are 59 km, and from there to Castañeda some 20 more) in order to feed the ovens of Castañeda and hence to provide lime for the construction of the Cathedral of Santiago is moving to say the least. Cf. BravoLozano-

Guía, p. 104, n. 40. As suggested by Caucci-*Guida* (p. 80, n. 12), apart from the evident economic utility deriving from the transportation of the limestone, the pilgrims too found benefits to harvest. They must have felt a direct and concrete participation in the construction of the Cathedral of Santiago, strengthening thereby their devotion to St. James.

25. On the economics of the pilgrimage and in particular on the pilgrim's financial preoccupations, see above, pp. 53–54.

26. Vielliard-*guide* (p. 11), Caucci-*Guida* (p. 80), and Oursel-*Compostella* (p. 42) add a magnifying adjective to *hospitalibus*. I do not see any reason for it. The evocation of Santiago de Compostela together with Jerusalem and Rome is geared towards the exaltation of the Galician shrine in the shadow of its ancient and by far more dignified companions.

27. It is not absolutely clear to which hospice in Jerusalem the reference is directed. Owing to the fact, however, that the Order of the Knights of St. John of Jerusalem was considerably active on the pilgrimage road to Santiago in sustaining hospitals and hospices on the way, it might well be that the *Codex* makes reference, precisely, to the hospital established by this order in Jerusalem subsequent to the conquest of the city in 1099. The hospital of the order, known also as that of the *Frères hospitaliers*, was the life work of one Gerard, known also as Tom. The original aim of the hospital was that of tending to the needs of the pilgrims, including medical treatment. The second great master of the order, Raymond du Puy or Dupuy as he is sometimes named, however, introduced the added notion of defending the pilgrims against the infidels. This military aspect of the operation ended up becoming the main preoccupation of the order, particularly after the reconquest of Jerusalem by Saladin in 1188 and the subsequent gradual retreat of the headquarters of the order to Acre first, and then to Cyprus, Rhodes, Sicily, and finally to Malta. See J. D. Le Roulx, *Les Hospitaliers en Terre Sainte et en Chypre* (Paris, 1904); also, F. Cardini, *Le Crociate tra il mito e la storia*, (Rome, 1984, p. 80).

28. Montis Jocci corresponds to the Mont-Joux hospital on the Great St. Bernard Pass, at the ancient Mons Jupiter of the Romans, along one of the most important communication lines between Central Europe and Italy. Hence, too, it became quite naturally a vital thoroughfare for the German pilgrims making their way towards Rome. The Mont-Joux hospice was established by Bernard, or better, Bernhard of Aosta, known also as Bernhard of Menthon, in the middle of the eleventh century. Bernhard died in 1081. He was canonized only in the seventeenth century. Cf. A.-M. Lovey, "Bernhard v. Aosta," in *LexMitt*; and L. Quaglia, "Les hospices du Grand et du Petit Saint-Bernard du Xe et XIIe siècle,"

in *Monasteri in Alta Italia. Dopo le invasioni saracene e magiare (sec. X–XII)* (Turin, 1966), pp. 427–41.

29. The Hospice of Santa Cristina was established on the Somport towards the end of the eleventh century. Owing to its strategic position, it enjoyed the special protection of the viscount of Béarne on the French side and of the kings of Aragón on the Spanish one. The hospice soon became a priory and by 1226, in accordance with a bull of Innocent III, it governed already some thirty churches in Aragón and about half as much in France. With time though, Santa Cristina became overshadowed by the hospice of Roncesvalles. Cf. n. 20 above, and the Gazetteer for "Somport" and "Roncesvalles" below; Caucci-*Guida*, p. 81, n. 13; and foremostly UbietoArteta-*Santa Cristina*.

30. In the manner of a litany recitation, in a free rendering, of the works of mercy and charity.

31. This Aimery is with all certainty identical with Aymery the Chancellor to whom chapter 9 is ascribed jointly with Pope Calixtus. The reference is to a remarkable Frenchman, a native of the region of Berry, who became the advisor of three popes – Calixtus II, Honorius II, and Innocent II – and, in that capacity, an indefatigable protector of Archbishop Gelmírez of Santiago. Aimery was elevated to the cardinalate by Calixtus II on or around 1120, and he appears as *cancellarius*, that is to say, scribe and epistolary correspondent, in 1123. The densely woven relations between Aimery and Gelmírez are attested to by the correspondence found in *Historia compostelana* vol. 2, chap. 83; and vol. 3 , chaps. 5, 27, and 50. See also Flórez-*Sagrada* 20.

Aymericus cancellarius appears also among the signatories of a document of authentication of a letter of Pope Innocent II (1130–43), located among the liturgical compositions that follow the *Guide*. The letter serves as an appropriate conclusion to the entire *Liber* and as its authentication. The papal letter, in its turn, is authenticated by eight signatories – Aimery the Chancellor, six cardinals, and a papal legate. The letter is, in all probability, spurious, and it has been added to the *Codex*, as the letter of Calixtus at the beginning, for purposes of evident dignification and authentication. Therefore, spurious is probably also the participation of the papal chancellor in the compilation of the *Guide*, and, by extension, of the *Liber*.

The letter of Innocent II mentions another individual, Aimery Picaud of Parthenay-le-Vieux, responsible for having donated the *Codex* to the Cathedral of Santiago. This same Aimery Picaud appears also as the author of the last hymn ("Ad honorem Regis summi") of the musical compositions following immediately the *Guide*. To these two textual references, a number of further considerations should be added: first, the native town of this

Aimery, Parthenay-le-Vieux, lies west of Poitiers, today in the department of Deux-Sèvres, but once belonging to the ancient region of Poitou; second, the author of the *Guide* makes a telling reference to *nos gens gallica* (see below, nn. 91 and 429), by which he identifies himself with Gaul or France in general; third, he offers us a particularly warm and engaging description of the Poitou; fourth, the very last instance of chap. 11, the last chapter of the *Guide*, concerning the welcome to be offered to the pilgrims of Santiago, takes place in a most typical street of Poitiers, the capital of Poitou; and fifth, in contradistinction to the accounts devoted to most saintly relics to be visited on the road to Santiago, the author of the *Guide* dedicates a particularly long, and elaborate narrative to St. Eutropius of Saintes, a city in the immediate vicinity of Poitou. This narrative reaches the dimensions of a small treatise. The inclusion of a text on a saint from Saintonge out of proportion to the texts devoted to the other saints on the route, and, furthermore, inserted close to the very end of the chapter as a sort of crowning hagiographic reference, raises specific questions concerning the identity of the author / compiler of the *Guide*. The temptation exists to consider Aimery as a viable candidate for the authorship of the *Guide* in no matter what loose context.

But things are not so simple. First, the text of Innocent's letter speaks of donation, and not of writing or authoring or even copying; second, it is not at all clear whether the donation was effected jointly by two or three individuals. The passage in question speaks also of one Oliverus de Iscani and of a woman, Girberga Flandrensis. If the donors of the *Codex* were indeed three, then Girberga is to be considered the wife of Oliverus; if, however, the donors were only two, then Aimery should be glossed as a family name and Oliverus as a monastic name attached to the Abbey of Asquins (Iscan) of one and the same person. In this case Girberga, the *sotia*, should be understood as a kind of travel companion of this resourceful talent from Parthenay who, as we learn from the text, was also a presbyter. All told, at the present state of our knowledge, Aimery and the question of authorship of the *Guide* remain largely in the air. Opinions continue to be divided on the subject. On the spurious authenticity of Innocent's letter, see Bédier-*épiques* 3:87, n. 1; David-*Jacques* 10:24; and Moralejo-*Calixtinus*, p. 587, nn. to lines 2 and 3. On the question of authorship, see LeClerc-*Aimeric*; David-*Jacques* 12:187–223 and passim; Louis-*Aimeri*; DíazDíaz-*Calixtino*, pp. 81–87; Lambert-*Aymeric*; and Hohler-*Jacobus*.

32. *Viatorum* in the text, see n. 5 above.

33. This is Diego Gelmírez, the great statesman, organizer, and executive manager operating in the background of the early twelfth-century developments in Santiago de Compostela. Bishop

in 1100 and archbishop in 1120, his special relationship with Calixtus II, through Calixtus's brother, Raymond, count of Galicia by his marriage with Doña Urraca, daughter of Alphonso VI of Castilla and León, won for Compostela in 1120 the coveted metropolitan title previously held by Mérida. See, for Gelmírez and his Burgundian connections, pp. 22–23 above.

34. There is considerable confusion both in the *Codex* as well as among the commentators, concerning the several kings by the name of Alphonso that pop up at each turn in the various kingdoms of medieval Spain (cf. Vielliard-*guide*, p. 13, n. 1; and BravoLozano-*Guía*, p. 106, nn. 45–46). This one must be Alphonso VII. Born in 1105 in Galicia, he becomes its king in 1111, king of León and Castilla in 1126, and emperor of Spain – a traditional title which went back to the Visigothic Roman imperial pretensions of the monarchs of León – in 1135. He dies in 1157 and is buried in Toledo.

35. This must be Alphonso I el Batallador, the Warlike, king of Aragón and Navarra, who was born around 1073 and died in 1134. See n. 67 below.

36. Louis VI, born on 1081 and king in 1108. He died in 1137.

37. Except for the last one, nothing is known about these seven men, perhaps the number seven is also symbolic here. *Fortun* in the text is abbreviated; it could stand for *Fortunius*. Cf. Moralejo-*Calixtinus*, p. 509, n. 10. The Peter mentioned at the end is probably that *Petrus peregrinus* who reconstructed the bridge on the Miño at Puertomarín. Alphonso VII reconfirmed to this Peter in 1126 the donation of the church of Santa María de Portomarín that he had already received from Alphonso's mother Queen Doña Urraca as reward for his reconstructing and subsequently maintaining the bridge and the nearby hospital. The donation must be understood perhaps in terms of the revenues deriving from the church. Cf. López Ferreiro-*Santiago* 4:75 and 306; VázquezParga-*pereg* 2:336, nn. 4–5; 4:75, n. 1; and Puertomarín in the Gazetteer.

38. A colorful and, in her time, controversial woman, born in 1077, daughter of Alphonso VI, and queen of Castilla and León from 1109 to 1126. Her first husband was Raymond of Burgundy, brother of Guy, the future Calixtus II. Upon Raymond's death, she married Alphonso I of Aragón and Navarra, but stood up in arms against the attempts of her husband to incorporate Castilla to his reign. She must not have been an easy character, for she led a military campaign against her son Alphonso VII too, once he had been recognized king by the Castilians. The bridge over the Mino was destroyed during her military operations against Alphonso I.

39. On the problem of attribution of the *Guide* and portions of the *Codex* in general, and particularly the attribution to Calixtus, see above, nn. 3, 15, and 31.

40. If the story told at this point is indeed veracious, then it goes a long way to explain the violent aversion of the *Guide's* author with regards to this particular stream. If, on the other hand, it is a construed story, it is in character with the general animadversion that characterizes the author's perception of things west of the Pyrenees and particularly in Navarra. His anti-Navarrism will soon reach levels of paroxism which carries the flavor of having been fed by hearsay. There must have been a rich, at times deadly rich, vein of oral communication on the road. On this oral culture, see above, p. 52; VázquezParga-*Navarra* hypothesizes on the author's having perhaps been in one of the French colonies settled in some Navarrese town. But such an immediate experience might conceivably have called, precisely, for a quite contrary reaction. I suspect that behind such and similar statements there is simply old-fashioned, parochial, gregarious prejudice and xenophobia that, to no mean extent, lives until our own days.

41. The text speaks of two streams here: one of these must be the Odrón that flows by Arcos; the other, a small brook, affluent of the former, that streams by at a short distance to the west of the town.

42. The rest of the chapter, from this point on, is missing in the manuscript of Ripoll of the *Codex* (ms. 99 of the Ripoll Collection, Archives of the Crown of Aragón in Barcelona). It is interesting to note that the Ripoll manuscript replaces all that follows with an eminently negative remark, making explicit that it will not deal with the good rivers at all: "Omnes fluvii qui a Stella usque ad Grugnum habentur, letiferi ad bibendum hominibus et jumentis et pisces eorum ad commedendum approbantur. De bonis fluminibus non curam habeo" – "All told, I shall not take care of the good rivers."

43. Essentially Navarrese territory has once again been selected for sweeping denigration. See above, n. 40.

44. In the translation I have left the terms in their original in order to keep the flavor of the multilingual ambiance that the *Codex* creates at this point and which is, I presume, a reflection of the international spirit of the pilgrimage that must have always existed on the road to Santiago. *Barbo* is the barbel; *alose* is what in English is called shad from the *genus alosa*; *clipia* must be the same, though I could not identify it; *tenca* is the tench.

45. The first portion of the reasoning here is spurious: of course, the healthier one is the more resistent one is to sickness; this should have been left inside the argument to start with, and not lifted out of it as an exception. The second part, on the other hand,

holds an important point of observation: human metabolism needs time to adjust to regional specificities and peculiarities.

46. For this sweeping negative generalization, see above, n. 40.

47. The medieval bridge referred to is at Villarente, already very close to León. A late fifteenth-century pilgrim, Küning, mentions it in 1495. There is a pilgrim's hospital near the bridge established by the archdeacon of Triacastela (VázquezParga-*pereg* 2:239–41).

48. The reference to the encampment of the Jews is attested by what is recorded as Castro de los Judíos, literally, the fort of the Jews (GomMor-*Cat León*, p. 7). It is situated some 3 km from the center of the city and it witnesses to an ancient community.

49. Lavamentula, from *mentula, -ae* (fallus), hence the washing of the viril member. LópezFerreiro-*Santiago* 5:92, reports *Lavacolla*, which corresponds to the present toponym. *Colla*, traced to Romance tongues, signifies scrotum. Of particular interest is the rhetorical construction of the sentence which is intentionally misleading. It is easy to realize the liturgical value of such total ablution which reminds us of the ablution rites at the Ka'aba in Mecca. LópezFerreiro-*Santiago* 5:92; and VázquezParga-*pereg* 1:415–24 insist variously on the prophylactic value of such ablution, no less than on that of the *botafumeiro*, a giant censer, set into operation from time to time in the Cathedral of Compostela. Due to misguided puritanism, Vielliard-*guide*, Caucci-*Guida*, BravoLozano-*Guía*, but even Moralejo-*Calixtinus* translate *mentula* with inappropriate euphemisms.

50. The Mons Gaudii, Monte del Gozo, the Joyous Mountain, is the height from which the pilgrims for the first time catch site of the city of Compostela, that is to say, of the belltowers of the cathedral; and it is there that they cry out, each *Landsmannschaft* in its own tongue, *Mont Joie, Monte del Gozo, Berg der Freude, Monxoy* in Galician, and so on. LópezFerreiro-*Santiago* (3:239) follows up the derivation of the vulgar *Manxoi* or *Monxoi* from *Mons Gaudii*. The tradition of declaring as king the first who is able to catch sight of the cathedral, has for long been alive. Bonnault-*Compostelle* reports an eighteenth-century witness. Caucci-*Guida* (pp. 83–84, n. 17) justly notes the parallels with other sanctuaries and/or holy cities: so the Montjoya of Oviedo and even the Monte Mario in Rome, also called Mons Gaudii. Such matters, furthermore, depended also on local topography: in Jerusalem or Monte Sant'Angelo in Southern Italy, being the sacred sites themselves on a mountain, such vantage point is not available. Actually, the Galician toponym probably derived, even if indirectly, from the Roman one (cf. Mâle-*XII*, p. 246; Vielliard-*guide*, pp. 83–84, n. 4; and Goicoechea-*Rutas*, pp. 618–20). On the

Galician Monte del Gozo there was once a chapel of Santa Cruz (Moralejo-*Calixtinus*, p. 345, n. to line 30).

51. It should not escape us that the author of the *Guide* is primarily interested in the quality of the people of the territories traversed, *qualitatibus gencium*. Throughout the whole of the document, the emphasis will be on people, their character, their way of life, their beliefs, their thinking. This will be the case too when we arrive to the lengthy hagiographic chapter, the eighth.

52. The bridge on the Arga is, of course, Puente la Reina, the bridge and the town.

53. This passage amounts to a *laudatio*, a formal laudatory discourse. That it is precisely the Poitou that is made object of such high praise – though couched in sensible, factual, well-poised language – is characteristic of the author of the *Guide*. We remember that Aimery, the *cancellarius* of Calixtus II as well as of Innocent II, is precisely from Parthenay-le-Vieux in the department of Deux-Sèvres in the region of Poitou. Cf. n. 31 above.

54. The crossing of the vast waterway occurred usually not on the level of the estuary of the Gironde, by far too vast, but on that of the Garonne, large too but manageable.

55. The emphasis on language and on its increasing rustic nature as one proceeds southward, is another indication for the author's propensities to take the Poitou as his yardstick. In matters of language, in particular, the Touraine and the Poitou are considered even today the epitome of the pure and unadulterated French.

56. *Grugnis*. Vielliard-*guide* translates "porcs," on the strength of the Fr. *grogner*, Sp. *gruñir*: to grunt, or growl; Fita-*codex* renders "Porcs a bois," that is to say, wild boars. This is the version I follow here. Cf. Vielliard-*guide*, p. 19, n. 2.

57. In the text *guespe* and *tavones* (in Pliny, *tabanus*), ancient French terms and graphia for *guêpe* and *taon*, respectively wasp and horsefly.

58. Here is meant the southern portion of Gascony, what now is called the Basses Pyrenées. See A. Lavergne, *Les chemins de Saint-Jacques en Gascogne* (Bordeaux, 1887).

59. In this case too, the first thing the author notices is the speech of the Gascons (cf. above, n. 55, on the emphasis the author places on language). The text reads *levilogi, verbosi*. The first term, from *leviloquus*, a neologism, signifies literally "light in speech." We could have also translated "light in speech and verbose."

60. The *cypho* of the text stands assuredly for *scyphus, –i*, cup.

61. There ought to be but little excitement about this. Half of Europe lived with such practice until considerably later. Furthermore, though some promiscuity was unavoidable, it had also, socially speaking, its brighter side: at least at night, class differentiations eased up a little.

62. The virulent invective launched against boatmen and ferrymen acquires yet further significance if we consider that the author of the *Guide* is not yet in Spain at this point, though admittedly already close to the Pyrenees. The crossing of streams of all sort was a continuous problem for the pilgrims. Such and similar stories were no doubt circulating in what we have called the oral culture of the pilgrimage road and, as all stories, they were hardly free of dramatic magnification and exaggerating elements. It is against such factual as well as mental realities that we must measure the extraordinary significance attached ever since the earliest times of the pilgrimage to bridges, a significance that the *Guide* underlines each time anew. Concerning the toll exacted, Caucci-*Guida* (p. 86, n. 21), takes note of the imprecise language of the author. This may be so. Caucci suggests a later and better witness of the year 1477: see Damonte-*Firenze Santiago*. We should not forget, however, that between our author and his Italian colleague no less than three centuries went by during which time, in the wake of the development of early bourgeois capitalism, a further degree of economic consciousness arose in Europe.

63. *Tellus Basclorum* in the text. Perhaps the letter "l" has slipped in inadvertently: better *Bascorum* (BravoLozano-*Guía*, p. 111, n. 72). The Basques are a tenacious, racy, and sagacious ethnic group that settled originally on a considerably larger area than the present Basque country in Spain and France (most of Navarra is, and considerable portions of Gascony were, once of Basque ethnic culture). Their history may be summed up by saying that dominated they have always been, but submitted hardly ever. The Basque knew how to eschew Romanization and kept their national identity, somewhat like the dispersed Jewish nation, under the Visigoths, the Muslims, the Franks, and beyond until our own days. The Basques might not have been the easiest folks with whom to get along, a fact to which the by-no-means easy geopolitical situation of their country must certainly have contributed; but the language used in their regard as well as in regard to the Navarrese by the author of the *Guide* is reminiscent of virulent xenophobic attitudes.

64. Once again the attention to language is paramount. Cf. n. 55. The "barbarous" quality of the language, on the other hand, in the sense of *foreign*, is partly a carryover from classical culture but partly it bears also overtones of rudeness, uncouthness, and savagery.

65. Cf. Vielliard-*guide*, p. 21, n. 2 and Moralejo-*Calixtinus*, p. 516, n. 17. The latter argues the pro and con of the reading of *sicera* as either cider or chickpea. The first reading seems dominant. It witnesses to agricultural practices, apple groves, and the derived process of fermentation that has lasted to our own days. See A. de Apráiz, "Notas sobre la cultura de las peregrinaciones...," *Bulletin Hispanique* 41 (1939): 60–64.

66. Toll-gatherers at the mountain passes are severely indicted here. It is not clear from the *Guide's* description whether the three checkpoints – Ostabat, Saint-Jean, and Saint-Michel – were complementary or supplementary to each other. From the description of the beating and the concomitant search the pilgrims were exposed to, we are reconfirmed in the assumption (see above, pp. 36 and 49) that money was more often than not hidden away, a common practice in our own days too. The speech of the toll-gatherers, barbarous, to be sure, is noted here again. The *Guide* makes here a distinction between merchants and pilgrims, a distinction among wayfarers not always easy to make. I suspect, also, that just as there were bandits and thieves in pilgrim's attire, so there were also merchants trying to cash in on the benefits due to pilgrims. See above, p. 79, nn. 81 and 82.

67. Moralejo-*Calixtinus*, p. 517, n. 5 and BravoLozano-*Guía*, p. 112, n. 76 identify this monarch as Alphonso I el Batallador, the Warlike, reigning between 1102 and 1134, close to the period of the composition of the *Guide* (see also n. 35 above.) But the reference could also be to some of the previous monarchs, back as far as Sancho Ramírez, though in any case during the period in which Navarra was united with Aragón and thus the Aragonese king had authority over Navarrese territory. The probability that the reference is to Alphonso I, however, only increases if we think of this monarch's continuous commitment to matters pertaining to the pilgrimage road.

68. Little certainty has been gathered concerning the identification of these individuals (Vielliard-*guide*, p. 23, nn. 1–4; Moralejo-*Calixtinus*, p. 517, n. 9; David-*Jacques* 3:125 and 194). Raymond de Soule may perhaps be Raymond-Guillaume de Soule from around the middle of the eleventh century; the name of Raymond, anyhow, was hereditary in the house of Soule from the middle of the eleventh century (Vielliard and Moralejo, above). On Vivien de Gramont or d'Aigremont hardly anything is known except that about 1130 there was somebody by that name. In the Second Romance of the Marqués de Mantua there is a character by this name: "el duque de Vibiano de Agramonte natural" (Moralejo, above). The viscount of Saint-Michel may have been the lord of Saint-Michel-Pied-de-Port (Vielliard, above). One Arnaud de la

Guigne or perhaps better, Arnaldo de La Guinge is recorded about the first third of the twelfth century (Moralejo and David, above).

69. The long and judiciously incisive indictment against toll-gatherers is remarkable in several respects. First, toll-gatherers and ferrymen are being considered together. Second, the responsibility is broadened to include both the temporal lords and the ecclesiastical authorities: the former set up the whole machinery of tolls and fares, are in connivance with exactors, and cash in on the benefits; the latter are also in connivance with the wrong-doers by exculpating and pardoning the exactors and those who send them. Third, excommunication is demanded for the wrong-doers until such time that the appropriately sanctioned tributes are reapplied. And fourth, the excommunication ought to be proclaimed not only in the local parish church but in the basilica of St. James in the presence of the pilgrims.

70. A monetary unit of small value.

71. Etymological play on words: *Portus Cisere – porta Yspanie*, the Pass of Cize – the gate of Spain, in which the mountain pass becomes the gate of the country. The metaphor is taken still farther for *transportantur* in the last phrase derives from the same etymological root: *porta*. This has nothing to do with Isidore of Seville, as BravoLozano-*Guía* (p. 113, n. 78), seems to suggest. Instead, we are facing here a rhetorical game of etymologies and conceptual analogies widespread in the Middle Ages.

72. Moralejo-*Calixtinus* (p. 518, n. 4) seems to be correct in assuming that the reference here is, more than anything else, directed to two cardinal points, north and west: the Sea of Bretagne lies indeed to the north; while the open ocean is to the west.

73. The three territorial overlords are seen here from the geopolitical perspective of the height of Cize and furthermore of the pilgrimage road to Santiago. From such a double viewpoint these are the three realms with which the pilgrim must be concerned. We must remember that Navarra had at the time been incorporated into Aragón: see above, n. 67.

74. The search for the archeological vestiges of the *Crux Caroli*, Charlemagne's Cross, has so far been unsuccessful (Bédier-*épiques* 3:320–23). Bédier suggests that the cross might have not been Carolingian and might have been set only later on as a celebrative monument. In the light of the general French trend for grand-scale post-factum Carolingian exaltation, it might well be that the famous cross was erected sometime in the eleventh century, about the time in which the *Chanson de Roland* and the other French Carolingian epics were consolidated and written down. Cf. Lambert-*Roncevaux*, pp. 16–17. In some documents the cross is indicated as a *mojón*, a milestone: so the one between the dioceses

of Bayonne and Pamplona (Caucci-*Guida*, p. 88, n. 23). On Charlemagne's Spanish campaign, see below, pp. 186–87, n. 347.

75. This is an important passage in the *Guide*, for it emphasizes the Carolingian tradition – better to call it myth – according to which Charlemagne was, among many other things, the first pilgrim at the tomb of St. James. The prayer he addresses, on his knees and turning towards Galicia, is, so to speak, the metaphoric journey that he would henceforth make good in flesh and blood. It is significant too that the exemplum of Charlemagne, in the account of the *Guide*, is immediately followed by the pilgrims. The heroic opening up of a passageway with axes, on the other hand, reminds us of other epic crossings and particularly of Hannibal's army traversing the Alps (Livy XXI, XXXVII). See the *Pseudo-Turpin*, chap. 19 in Whitehill-*Liber* and Moralejo-*Calixtinus*.

76. I believe detecting here a perception according to which Christianity was introduced into Spain later than into the rest of continental Europe, which really means France. Coming from French quarters – whether Aymeric or somebody else, there seems to be no doubt in the mind of anybody that the author of the *Guide* and indeed the compiler of the *Codex* as a whole was a Frenchman. There is little surprise in such a standing. It is enough to leaf through the *vita* of some of the French saints to realize the sagacious effort invested in the notion of the precocity of the Gallic church: the tradition of the direct apostolic connection of St. Dionysius, St. Saturninus, and others, not to speak of the Provençal tradition of Lazarus, Mary Magdalene, Maximin, and still others, amply confirm this. Cf. the articles on the above saints, below on pp. 233–34, 259 62, 265–68.

77. The author of the *Guide* differentiates the two ethnic groupings, Navarrese and Basque. As to "ride them as if they were asses," it bears probably sexual and actually phallic connotations.

78. See Bédier-*épiques* 3:185–385, Roncesvalles in the Gazetteer, and the article on Roland, pp. 268–70. The number "forty" has probably numerological connotations: it is a biblical notion of an indefinite but very large number of units. Unlike Fita-*codex*, Whitehill-*Liber*, and Caucci-*Guida*, who read "*C.XL milibus*," that is to say, one-hundred-forty-thousand warriors; Vielliard-*guide*, Moralejo-*Calixtinus*, BravoLozano-*Guía*, and Oursel-*Compostella* read "*cum XL milibus*" on the strength of the dot after C and the ablative of *milibus*. The above-mentioned numerological connotation reinforces the latter reading.

79. J. Caro Baroja, "Materiales para una historia de la lengua vasca..." [*Acta Salmanticensia, Filología y Letras* I, 3 (1945): 27], maintains that the distinction between Basque and Navarrese was understood until the seventeenth century in the following terms:

THE PILGRIM'S GUIDE TO SANTIAGO

the Basques were the French-Basques on the northwestern side of the Pyrenees, and the Navarrese were the Hispanic-Navarrese on the southwestern side of the mountain chain. Moralejo-*Calixtinus* (p. 519, n. to line 6), and BravoLozano-*Guía* (p. 114, n. 85) claim that the author of the *Guide* precisely follows such an interpretation. I remain somewhat skeptical about this point.

80. The remark concerning the color of the skin is somewhat puzzling. It certainly does not correspond to the reality of today: on both sides of the western Pyrenees, as far as I can tell from my own experience, an indistinct brownish complexion prevails. The alleged whiter complexion of the Basques, on the other hand, tends to strengthen the argument of Moralejo and of Bravo Lozano of the previous note: it plays into the hands of French susceptibilities concerning the Pyrenees as the western borderline of Christian Europe.

81. The 1956 edition of the *Diccionario de la Lengua Española* of the Real Academia Española makes *abarca* derive from the Basque voice of the same graphia, and *albarca* derive from the former. The voice *lavarca*, therefore, must have also derived from *abarca*. So Vielliard-*guide*, p. 27, n. 4. Moralejo-*Calixtinus*, p. 519, n. to line 10, argues for a different derivation. Cf. also BravoLozano-*Guía*, p. 114, n. 86.

82. *Penule* in the text, which derives from Latin *paenula*, a kind of a travel cape.

83. From Latin *sagum, -i,* from which the Spanish *saya*, also a kind of travel cape. For this clothing terminology, see the article of J. Caro Baroja quoted in n. 79 above.

84. *Turpiter* in the text; *puercamente* of Moralejo-*Calixtinus* (p. 519) does not seem justified.

85. As above, at n. 60.

86. Cf. the anti-Basque and, by extension, the anti-Navarrese attitude mentioned above in n. 63. VázquezParga-*pereg* (1:482–89) reports a similar blind incomprehension in the attitude of the chroniclers of Sahagún vis-à-vis the Aragonese. BravoLozano-*Guía*, p. 115, n. 89, speaks of a probable class tension existing in Navarra between the peasantry on the one hand and the bourgeoisie and the higher clergy on the other: the latter were, for the most part, of French extraction, while the former, of older Celtic stock. If this is indeed so, then we have here not merely an instance of xenophobic nationalism but, superimposed upon or parallel to it, also an expression of class-phobia, and actually of class struggle. The use of language is once again drawn into the comparison: cf. above, nn. 55 and 64.

87. Concerning this important early list of Basque words, the earliest according to some and not quite the earliest according to others, I refer the reader to the pertinent, specialized Basque philological studies: J. Vinson's article in *Revue de linguistique* [14 (1881): 120–45, 269–74]; R. M. de Azcue in Whitehill-*Liber* (3:xxxix–xli); J. Caro Baroja, "Materiales...," (see n. 79 above, p. 149); J. M. de Barandiarán, *El hombre primitivo en el país vasco* (San Sebastian, n. d., pp. 79–82, 86–87); as well as Moralejo-*Calixtinus* (p. 520, n. to line 7) and BravoLozano-*Guía* (p. 115–16, n. 91). I shall add here only a few comments of rather general interest: *Andre* = lady, hence *Andre Maria* = Lady Mary, and not *Andrea* as the text proposes; bread is *ogui* and not *orgui*; wine, *ardum,* may be a Latinization from *ardao* or *ardo*; "meat" and "house" bear the graphia of their respective pronunciation rather than that of their spelling. The case of *belaterra* is rather amusing: *priest* with its article is *beretera; belaterra* is a corruption of the above, according to Caro Baroja's often-mentioned article, possibly under the influence of *bela,* crow, in the sense of the priest's expertise in omens and augury; the interpretation proposed for it in the text, however, *pulcra terra,* derives from its formal parallel to one of the Romance tongues (Italian: *bella terra;* or French: *belle terre*). Much of the above has been borrowed from Moralejo-*Calixtinus,* p. 520, n. to line 7.

88. *Colore atra* in the text, of black or dark color. The reference echoes what the *Guide* has already proposed earlier: cf. n. 80. One is tempted to infer from it, apart from general xenophobia, also racial prejudice, though admittedly the evidence for it is quite slim.

89. The whole paragraph has the flavor of a rhetorical disparagement rather than of a factual description.

90. *Getis* in the text, from *Getae, -arum.* The Getae were a nation in Thrace living near the lower Danube, probably related to the Sarmatae, themselves, according to Herodotus, the progeny of Scythian men and Amazons. Ovid, who was ostracized in their land and died in their midst, speaks of them in his *Ex Ponto* and *Tristia* in rather negative terms. From here it comes that the Getae became for classical culture the epitome of savagery and barbarous inhumanity. The Saracens, on the other hand, were quite well known and concerning them no such notions of savagery could possibly be sustained in earnest. At this point, however, the unmediated association with the Getae is utterly detrimental to their Muslim colleagues. See also n. 91.

91. This is the famous passage in which the author of the *Guide* reveals, with the use of the possessive adjective, his own national background. The passage, however, coming as it does after the

pairing of the Getae and the Saracens, further reinforces the supposed equivalence of the two. In this case, however, it is the enmity between Saracens and Christians (and hence also the French) which spills over upon the Getae.

92. "Navarrese" and "Basque" are used pretty much interchangeably. The phrase underlines the precarious safety conditions of this part of the route. The passage belies to some extent the theory of Caro Baroja and others concerning a sharp division of the two ethnic groups: cf. above, n. 79

93. Not much novelty in all this, except for the amusing notion of affixing locks on the behind of mules and horses, an idea (the author's, almost certainly, and not of the Navarrese peasants) which probably was borrowed from the infamous chastity belts widely used in the Middle Ages and of which Boccaccio too is an eager witness. Mutually gratifying erotic liaison between master and his or her pets or domestic animals is quite well known and, even if not accepted, widely practiced to our own day. A considerable measure of promiscuity, on the other hand, and not merely among the economically lower classes, followed by fits of puritanic culpability, has been a commonplace in the European, and certainly not only European, history of social customs until our own times. The display of the erogenous zones as well as their mutual manipulation including their kissing belongs to practiced commonplaces of the sexual game prior to copulation. Cf. in this regard the testimony of Bishop Oliva in Flórez-*Sagrada* 28:281.

94. Rhetorically inappropriate after *tamen*.

95. Curiously, after much denigration of the Navarrese and the Basque on either French patriotic or simply ethical grounds, whenever the author of the *Guide* comes to a plain and straightforward account of some of the civic or devotional habits of the Navarrese, quite a positive picture emerges.

96. Of uncertain origin, with the significance of a small javelin or spear, the voice has been documented in late Latin in the form of *aucona*, and subsequently has entered all three Hispanic Romance languages, the *langue d'oc*, and the Basque. In the latter, it has been altered to *azcona*, under the influence of terms denoting instruments ending in *az* (cf. Corominas-*Br dicc*). Contrary to the opinion of BravoLozano-*Guía* (p. 116, n. 94) there is nothing strange in the author of the *Guide* using the non-Basque term, *aucona*, instead of the Basque *azcona*: Moralejo-*Calixtinus* (p. 521, n. to line 20) reports the voice in the *Poema de Fernán González*, couplet 630 (edition of Zamora Vicente, p. 17), in the *Libro de Aleixandre*, 1435, and in the *Libro de Buen Amor* of the Arcipreste de Hita, 1056.

97. One of the most noteworthy passages of the *Guide* attesting to a great sense of concrete veracity collected through first-hand observation. Together with what has been said above at n. 95, the passage goes a long way to rehabilitate the Navarrese by considering them in a light true to life: an ethnic group settled on a difficult terrain, within a nature with which it becomes fully identified. The mimetic skills of the Navarrese in imitating the natural sounds of the forest integrate them into their own natural habitat. In the light of the above, at the same time, the earlier comments of the *Guide* on fornication with animals becomes more plausible, though by no means reproachable.

98. This is a correlation both tenuous and fantasy-full, resting probably on still classical prejudices.

99. Hispania was, probably together with Sicily and portions of North Africa, for sheer economic reasons, one of the most important provinces of Rome. The numerous military campaigns recorded in the peninsula (the siege of Numancia, of Lérida, the Cantabrian wars: see BravoLozano-*Guía*, p. 117, n. 95), the divers emperors of Hispanic descent (Trajan, Hadrian, Marcus Aurelius), and some of the greatest Roman men of letters actually born in the peninsula (Seneca, Lucan, Martial), testify to the particularly close ties by which Hispania was felt to be an integral part of Rome. To the historicity of such connections, subsequent wishful desiderata were added to further tighten the relations with Rome. It is among such desiderata that the fantastic episode of Caesar's despatching three nations to Spain must be catalogued. Fita-*Recuerdos* (p. 60) suggests that the author of the *Guide* might refer to the emperor Magnus Maximus proclaimed Augustus by disaffected troops in 384 or 385, for Gaul, Hispania, and Britannia alone. During the turbulent years before and after his proclamation, Maximus might have initiated some troop movement from Britannia into Hispania which later could have been interpreted as the "tres gentes quae Caesar ad Yspaniam misit." See also MeredithJones-*Karoli*, pp. 248–51.

100. The Numians of Devonshire are confused here with the Nubians of Ethiopia. Cf. Fita-*Recuerdos*, p. 60.

101. *Cornubianos caudatos* in the text. The reference is to Cornwall, in the southwest of Britain. As to *caudatos*, from *cauda, -ae*, "tail," it is an epithet with the sense of pusillanimous often applied to the British by continental sources in the Middle Ages. The cowardliness associated to the tail might derive from the well-known fact that some domestic animals, and dogs in particular, when retreating curl their tails between the buttocks. Du Cange-*Glossarium*, s.v. "cauda," quotes Jacques de Vitry, "Anglicos potatores et caudatos," that is to say, drunkards and tailed. Cf.

Vielliard-*guide*, p. 31, n. 2; also, p. 30, n. g. It is not quite clear how the Scots made the list. Perhaps simply to complete the symbolic number three.

102. The three cities mentioned, though in inverted order, seem to point to the natural invasion routes by sea from the north. The Vikings used the same route.

103. The western limits of the supposed invasions of the three British nations are the mountains of Oca, a particularly rough and impenetrable territory at the time northeast of Burgos. It will be realized that this region overlaps with the pilgrimage road which, in turn, corresponds to the territory beyond the limits of the early Islamic domains in Spain. The mountains of Oca were also one of the scenes for the road building activities of Santo Domingo de la Calzada: see below, pp. 298–99.

104. The author of the *Guide* returns now to the geographical regions he had earlier mentioned concerning the sexual abuses of the Navarrese.

105. An established, even if forced, tribal and national settlement and resettlement procedure from the earliest Roman period: for example, the Rape of the Sabines.

106. "Navarrus interpretatur *non verus*" (italics mine) in the text. The tendentious gloss of the text making Navarrus derive from *non verus*, that is to say, "not true," is, one hardly needs to mention, spurious. Fita-*Recuerdos* (p. 60), Moralejo-*Calixtinus* (p. 522, n. to line 17), and BravoLozano-*Guía* (p. 117, n. 97) refer to the passage in terms of a popular etymology; Moralejo even calls it "mala." The Middle Ages was full of such etymologies always based on coarsely understood formal analogies which often enough are, of course, misleading, and always programmed to fit some preconceived notion, in this case that of a non-autochthonous origin. Such and similar tendentious readings, however, by no means originated in or were transmitted through popular quarters only: fifteenth-century encyclopaedias – for instance, that of Gregor Reisch – glossed *femina* as *fe* + *minus* = those who have little faith.

107. Naddaver seems to refer to Nadabar in Ethiopia (Moralejo-*Calixtinus*, p. 522, n. to line 19). From here derives a double prejudice: European-centered anti-African, as well as anti-black bias. The latter suits what had been said earlier concerning the darker complexion of the Navarrese.

108. The apostolate of St. Matthew is surrounded by uncertainty: Irenaeus, Clement of Alexandria, and Eusebius speak variously of the regions evangelized by Matthew. Whenever Ethiopia is mentioned though, this never refers to Ethiopia in East Africa, but

to a region south of the Caspian Sea, sometimes made equivalent to the Hebrew and Assyrian Kush.

109. The large central Spanish meseta which east-west extends from the Montes de Oca to the Pisuerga River, and north-south from roughly the line of the pilgrimage road to Santiago, to the Sierra Morena on the border with Andalucía. The size, centrality, fertility, and communication facilities of these areas, in spite of its limited water resources, has assured until our own days the ultimate political preeminence of this region over all others in Spain. As to the Tierra de Campos, between the Pisuerga and the Cea, see below, p. 292.

The text simply says "sequitur tellus Yspanorum, Castella videlicet et campos" (Vielliard-*guide*, p. 32). Moralejo-*Calixtinus* (p. 523), translates correctly. Caucci-*Guida* (p. 9), on the other hand, gives it a different turn: "continua la terra degli spagnoli e cioè Castiglia e Campos"; Oursel-*Compostella* (p. 51) reads "si incontra il paese degli Spagnoli, cioè la Castiglia e i suoi territori." The difference in the nuances of the verbs "to continue" or "to be found" carries implications concerning our understanding of the limits of the territory in question.

110. It is not clear whether the treasures to which the author of the *Guide* makes reference, as well as the gold and the silver, are to be taken metaphorically – perhaps in terms of abundance — or factually and concretely. In the second case we must think of churches, monasteries, as well as perhaps the dwellings of the nobility: so also Moralejo-*Calixtinus*, p. 523, n. to line 2.

111. *Palleis*, for *paleis*, that is to say, straw. On the strength of the context of what follows – horses – it should be read as fodder. So Vielllard-*guide*, p. 33 and Oursel-*Compostella*, p. 52; GómMor-mozárabes, p. 355, Moralejo-*Calixtinus*, p. 523, n. to line 523, and Caucci-*Guida*, p. 91 prefer the reading *palliis*, that is to say, fabrics, woven material.

112. An appropriate observation of the author of the *Guide*: notwithstanding the economic bounty of the region, it is poor in trees. For a Frenchman, then as today, it must have appeared a desolate landscape without trees. Such an early observation concerning the lack of trees in Castilla belies the notion often repeated that the trees had been abundant on the meseta up to the imperial expansion of the sixteenth and seventeenth centuries which converted the forests into ships. This might have applied to certain ship-building coastal regions, but not to the central meseta.

113. For the xenophobic remark, see above, nn. 55 and 64.

114. The description, or better characterization, of Galicia is fairly accurate; this is also the opinion of Moralejo-*Calixtinus*, p. 523, n. to line 17. The trees, conspicuously absent in Castilla la Vieja, are

the first thing noticed in Galicia. Accurate too is the scarsity of towns and large plough fields, a topographical situation evident also today. The author of the *Guide* seems to recognize the economic and social fragmentation of the region.

115. *Sicera* is surely "cider" here. Cf. Vielliard-*guide*, p. 33, n. 1. Bonnault-*Compostelle*, p. 173, translates it as "beer."

116. It is preferable to render *paucis* as small in size rather than as scarse in number. Vielliard-*guide*, p. 33, prefers the second solution, though in n. 2 of the same page she admits the first solution too, adopted already by Bonnault-*Compostelle*, p. 173, a reading which is followed then by Moralejo-*Caltixtinus*, p. 523 and n. to line 17 of the same page; BravoLozano-*Guía*, p. 38 and p. 118, n. 100; as well as Caucci-*Guida*, p. 91; and Oursel-*Compostella*, p. 52. Herbers-*Jakobsweg*, p. 105, opts for the second solution.

117. *Palleis*, for *palliis*, that is to say, fabrics, an interpretation that is appropriately inserted into the congenial context of gold and silver on the one hand, and the fur of animals, on the other. So also Moralejo-*Calixtinus*, p. 523 and BravoLozano-*Guía*, p. 38.

118. Whether one takes *gazis sarracenicis* as *valiosas mercancías sarracénicas*, as BravoLozano-*Guía*, p. 38, or as "treasures" – in our translation as well as that of Moralejo-*Calixtinus*, p. 523; Caucci-*Guida*, p. 91; and Oursel-*Compostella*, p. 52 – it remains a puzzle why the Islamic economic connection is brought in at the farthest removed and the most unlikely site.

119. *Iracundi et litigiosi* does not seem to be an unrealistic characterization of the Galician temperament. The author closes the chapter with a positive evaluation of the Galicians, though here too, as this is to be expected, in terms of the French.

120. Right in the heading of the chapter, by far the longest one in the *Guide*, the earthly remains of saints receive an appropriate emphasis: the visitation of these remains all along the route, the saintly relics, becomes the overriding purpose of the pilgrimage. To go on pilgrimage to Santiago de Compostela means therefore to visit – that is, to see and touch – each and all the relics on the way. As is to be expected from a Frenchman, the author of the *Guide* devotes an overwhelming portion of his attention to the French saints on the route. These nearly overshadow Santiago himself.

121. See the article on Trophimus on pp. 268–70. The cathedral of Arles bears presently St. Trophimus in its *titulus*; the earlier structures on the site were dedicated to St. Stephen who, appropriately, is also prominently represented on the actual twelfth-century facade. Otherwise, the present cathedral is an eleventh- to twelfth-century structure. Cf. E.-R. Labande, "Étude historique et archéologique sur Saint-Trophime d'Arles, IVe-XIIe

siècles" [*Bulletin Monumental* 67 (1903): 459–97 and 68 (104): 3–42]. "Confessoris," is left out in Moralejo-*Calixtinus*, p. 524. For the notion of confessor, see n. 139 below.

122. 2 Tim. 4.20, evoked also in Acts 20.4. This Trophimus, however, one of the twenty-two disciples of Christ and probably martyred in Rome together with St. Paul or shortly after the latter's death, cannot be identical with Trophimus the Confessor, bishop of Arles, for there are no indications that the episcopal see of Arles existed before the third century. Gregory of Tours, in *Historia Francorum*, 1.30, speaks of Trophimus's arrival in Gaul in the third century. The tradition that identifies him with the disciple of Paul, and that further antedates him to the first century, is from the fifth century only. St. Caesarius is the originator of this tradition. Cf. the article on Trophimus in the Hagiographical Register below; and L. Levillian, "Saint-Trophime..." in its bibliography. Moralejo-*Calixtinus* (p. 524, n. to line 7), gives erroneously the first century for Trophimus's bishopric.

123. Paul did not belong to the original group of the Twelve Apostles of Christ: he is considered apostle *sensu lato* only; at times he figures as the substitution for Judas Iscariot, at other times, independently from that necessary replacement.

124. There was a constant and insistent French preoccupation from the fifth century on to find, and actually to fabricate, a direct and unmediated line of discipleship between the apostles, mainly between Peter and the evangelizers of France.

125. Zosimus, of Greek extraction, saint and pope (417–18) was the author of various epistles on the primacy of the bishopric of Arles over the other bishoprics of Gaul. His *Epistola tractoria* is an anti-Pelagian tract.

126. Historically speaking, Arles has probably been the most important center for the diffusion of Christianity in the valley of the Rhône. The indiscriminate overlapping of Trophimus with Arles, and the expansion of the concept of Christianization to include the whole of Gaul, however, are ecclesiastical and political desiderata.

127. The calculation of the saints' days occurs throughout the text in accordance with the ecclesiastical calendar, which has carefully retained the classical Roman division of the month and the reckoning of the days of the month. The Roman calculation of the days of the month was cumbersome and embarrassingly complex. Romans divided the month by three fixed time frames: the Calends or Kalends which were the first day of each month; the Ides which fell either on the thirteenth or the fifteenth day of the month; and the Nones which were the ninth day before the Ides. The days of the month were counted backwards from each of the

three fixed time frames. Every month had invariably eight days named backwards from the Ides; in March, May, July, and October the Ides fell on the fifteenth day and the Nones on the seventh – consequently each of these months had six days named backwards from the Nones; in all the other months the Ides fell on the thirteenth day and the Nones on the fifth – hence there were only four days named backwards from the Nones. The days named from the Calends, necessarily of the next month, invariably backwards, depended on two variables: the number of days in the month and the day of the month (thirteenth or fifteenth) on which the Ides fell. All in all, a disarming complexity. Cf. Clavius, *Romani Calendarii a Gregorio XIII P. M. restituti. Explicatio* (Rome, 1603), and Perdrizet-*calendrier*.

128. There seems to be a considerable confusion here: St. Caesarius, bishop of Arles, was no martyr and furthermore died on August 27 and not on November 1. There was another Caesarius who died indeed a death of martydrom on November 1. He was St. Caesarius of Terracina who lived in the late third century. Confusion might have occurred with still another St. Caesarius of Damascus. Cf. Cottineau-*Repertoire*, s.v. "Arles"; Perdizet-*calendrier*, p. 250; and Croiset-*Année* 4:1324–27; and further, Vielliard-*guide*, p. 35, nn. 4 and 5; Moralejo-*Calixtinus*, p. 525, n. to line 3; Oursel-*Compostella*, p. 53, n. 48; and BravoLozano-*Guía*, p. 119, n. 105.

129. Alyscamps.

130. This column was in its place until 1806 and gave its name to the church of Saint-Genès-de-la-Colonne, that is to say, St. Genesius of the Column: cf. Benoît-*cimitières*, pp. 4–14; and Vielliard-*guide*, p. 37, n. 1. Gregory of Tours already mentions this column: cf. Herbers-*Jakobsweg*, p. 106, n. 117.

131. The river carrying the body and depositing it at the bend it forms at Alyscamps at Arles fits precisely the mythical but also the actual historical pattern at the source of the constitution of the famous cemetery. Trinquetaille, on the other hand, on the western shore of the descending river, is far too close to the bend – nearly opposite – to allow the current to take the body to Alyscamps. There is here an idealistic *amplificatio* of the given geographical conditions.

132. The author of the *Guide* proposes here an inappropriate overlapping between at least two saints of the same name: St. Genesius of Arles, the soldier-notary, and St. Genesius of Cartagena, in southern Spain. In this last location there is indeed a hermitage of San Ginés de la Xara or Jara. Cf. the article in the Hagiographical Register on St. Genesius; Croiset-Année 4:1277–81; Benoît-*cimitières*, p. 10; and *ActaSS*, Aug. 5:123–36. Also, cf.

Vielliard-*guide*, p. 37, n. 2; and Moralejo-*Calixtinus*, p. 25, n. to line 9. There is, however, a third St. Genesius, an actor, who suffered martyrdom under Diocletian in Rome and who became in consequence the protector-saint of actors. On the various homonymous saints, as well as on the phenomenon of the multiplication of homonymous saints, which must have occurred due to the early fame of our saint, see the above bibliography. On an Italian San Genesio, whose site is located at the confluence of the Elsa and the Arno on the *via francigena* in Tuscany, see Stopani-*francigena*, p. 29 and Oursel-*Compostella*, p. 93, n. 32.

133. The efficacy of the intervention on behalf of the deceased was for the mentality of the masses and in the current practice, until the French Revolution, an unquestioned reality. It was supposed to have worked through appropriately placed *materialia* (alms) and suitably directed *spiritualia* (prayers and invocations). A particular tradition held that prayers became eventually decanted and condensed in the flasks of the Twenty-Four Elders of the Apocalypse.

134. The remarkable extension of the cemetery and the large number of tombs gave rise to two different legendary interpretations: according to the first, the warriors of Charlemagne would be resting in Alyscamps (*Historia Turpini* of the *Codex Calixtinus*, Book 4, end of chap. 21); according to the second, the tombs would pertain to Christian soldiers slain in a bloody confrontation with the Saracens. The latter legend has been picked up by the *Chanson des Alyscans*, which is a part of the William of Orange cycle (cf. Bédier-*épiques* 1:365–85, 393–98; and Moralejo-*Calixtinus*, p. 526, n. to line 4). The size of the tombs, on the other hand, seems to point at the dignity and hierarchy of the deceased personages.

135. *Dictatu intelligibili* of the Latin text has been amended by Vielliard-*guide* (p. 36) to *dictatu inintelligibili*, followed subsequently by everybody else. It is hard to see though why a recognizably Latin text would be inintelligible: perhaps the intention is only, as suggested by Moralejo-*Calixtinus* (p. 526, n. to line 10), to signal the difficulty of the language.

136. A notably acute and altogether remarkable observation. Translation variants of "quanto magis longe...tanto magis longe" abound: cf. Vielliard-*guide*, p. 37; Caucci-*Guida*, p. 93; Oursel-*Compostella*, p. 54; BravoLozano-*Guía*, p 41; Moralejo-*Calixtinus*, p. 526. I have never encountered anything similar in any early medieval text. It cannot be dismissed that the author of the *Guide* refers here to one of the following two visual phenomena: either to atmospheric perspective; or to the angle of vision which, the more elevated it is, the more visual space it embraces.

137. Benoît-*cimitières*, pp. 32–61 and Vielliard-*guide*, p. 37, n. 4.

THE PILGRIM'S GUIDE TO SANTIAGO

138. The notion of intercession is deeply rooted in the Judeo-Christian and particularly in the Christian consciousness. We may define it by the following: the benevolent interest that some long-deceased saintly figure takes in the destiny in this world or the next of a mortal. In a sense intercession supplements the intervention on behalf of a deceased described above, at n. 133.

139. From *confiteor,* that is to say, those who declare and manifest their adherence to Christ and Christianity in the face of mortal danger. The confessor thus effects a declaration of faith. Confessors are not necessarily martyrs, though martyrs are almost always confessors. both categories, on the other hand, pertain to sainthood.

140. Theologically somewhat unorthodox: "in heaven" would be better.

141. That is to say, on the Monday following an eight-day period of observances starting with Easter Sunday. This is a collective commemoration and hence there is no single *dies natalis.*

142. There is hardly any exaggeration in the unbridled celebrative tone and content of the opening passage to this particularly long section devoted to St. Giles. Without any doubt he was one of the most popular and widely revered saints of the central Middle Ages, and particularly so from the eleventh century on. Two undisputed reasons for such popularity, apart from colateral factors, were the connection of the traditions of St. Giles with those of Charlemagne, and the strategic location of Saint-Gilles on the Petit Rhône and at the same time on the *via tolosana* leading to Santiago de Compostela. The southernmost route to Santiago, in effect, was known also as *via egidiana,* and the magnificent sanctuary of the saint in Saint-Gilles was one of the major pilgrimage sites on the route. Caucci-*Guida* (p. 94, n. 34), qualifies Saint-Gilles as *pellegrinaggio maggiore* vying with Rome and Santiago. This might be a slight overstatement in terms of recognized category, though not in terms of sheer popularity and number of visitors. That there was a mutually beneficial traffic of interests between the famous sanctuary on the Petit Rhône and the southern route to Santiago remains beyond any reasonable doubt. The episode, mythical or otherwise, of the Visigothic King Wamba's hunting party in Provence served to pave the way for the Hispanic connection which, ultimately, benefitted the integration of Saint-Gilles into the pilgrimage road to Santiago. Apart from the bibliography in the article on St. Gilles on p. 250 below, see J. Charles-Roux, *Saint-Gilles, sa légende, son abbaye, ses coutumes* (Paris, 1911); Gaston Paris, *Vie de saint Gilles par Guillaume de Berneville, poème du XIIe siècle* (Société des anciens textes français, Paris, 1881, pp. i–lxxxix); *ActaSS,* Sept. 1:284; and

David-*Jacques*, 2:70. Apart from the two connections mentioned above, Giles was considered one of the fourteen protecting saints of the needy (BravoLozano-*Guía*, p. 120, n. 111).

143. The strict hierarchical order is at all times observed. St. Giles comes immediately after the apostles. Whether he shares such high ranking with others or not remains unclear. It is interesting, and somewhat unusual, that the prophets are mentioned in the same breath as the apostles.

144. The promptness in the lending of assistance is considered of the utmost importance in the ranking of the saints. No less than three times within a few lines the text returns to the notion of the necessary time element.

145. Nothing further is known of this shoemaker. It is characteristic though that the instance evoked concerns a manual worker or a tradesman.

146. Series of rhetorical questions that enhance the discourse. Probably borrowed from a *vita* of a saint, perhaps of St. Giles.

147. The list of miracles is standard procedure in the accounts concerning saints. Five of the first quoted six miracles have to do with the passage from infirmity to health; of these one case concerns mental health – the possessed delivered. Of Theocritus we know nothing more. The one miracle outside of the circle of physical or mental condition concerns the storm at sea: this too is found quite often – for instance, in the life of St. Nicholas of Bari.

148. This most idiosyncratic of the miracles of Giles caught the imagination of the masses and singles him out with a kind of a miracle-attribute. See, for the details of the miraculous operation, the article of St. Giles below, pp. 247–50. It is also the episode that ties together Spain and Visigothic culture on the one hand with the saint on the other, and that serves therefore to establish the place of Saint-Gilles on the route to Santiago. The episode has a particular ecological interest. The psychological traits of the fearful and trembling hind who takes refuge with the saint are transposed to humans: St. Giles will specialize in curing the paranoid and those suffering from the psychological aftermath of persecutions.

149. Rhetorical incongruence: one of the two cases in which it is not a negative happening that calls for redress. See below the instance of the door leaves.

150. *Energuminus* in the text: possessed, possibly an epileptic. To be added to the above list of infirmities. See n 147 above. It is the second instance of exorcism.

151. The *peccatum Karoli* (Veillard-*Guide*, p. 38) is an allusion to the incestuous relationship of Charlemagne with his sister Bertha, a liaison from which Roland is said to have been born. There is,

however, another version of the story, according to which the great paladin of Charlemagne is the offspring of the love of the emperor's sister with Milon. In this case, though, there is no place for the emperor's *peccatum*. Cf. Bédier-*épiques* 2:212; Moralejo-*Calixtinus*, p 418, n. to line 8. Milon appears as a knight in the Franco-Italian poem of the thirteenth century, *Berta e Milone*. Of particular interest in the story is the double benefit that Charlemagne is made to enjoy: that of the dispensation from having to confess his sin, and that of the sin's remission altogether. The first of these dispensations effects the sequel of the story: the revelation of the sin to the saint by an angel (Bédier-*épiques* 3:354–61). Both benefits must be understood in terms of the particular semidivine status of the emperor for medieval sensitivities. The miraculous revelation of the emperor's sin to St. Giles is the subject of several medieval art works.

152. Two further classical miracles to be added to those commented upon in nn. 147 and 150. The miracle of raising the dead to life is patterned after perhaps the most famous of the miracles of Christ, the Raising of Lazarus. Such miraculous happenings, however, are not resurrections but rather resuscitations: while the latter bears the connotation of returning to this life, the former – a mystery, rather than a miracle – refers to participation in eternal life. As to the second miracle, *contractus* in the text, may also be rendered as paralytic.

153. The interest of the passage is twofold: one aspect concerns the door; the other, navigation. As to the first, we must remember that a certain number of wooden doors of the eleventh and twelfth centuries came down to us in entire or fragmentary states. The most famous of these are the eleventh-century door in St. Maria im Kapitol in Cologne, and the early thirteenth-century door in the converted palace of Diocletian in Split, Croatia. Cypress wood makes us think of the Middle East, perhaps of Lebanon, but it is also possible that the wooden planks were imported to Rome where their actual carving was executed. The program of the doors ("prelatorum imaginibus apostolorum") might well refer to Peter and Paul, quite a natural subject for Roman iconographers. One door with precisely such a subject – to be sure of bronze and executed only in the fifteenth century by Filarete – has come down to our own days decorating the central portal of St. Peter's Basilica; it was already in place on the portal of Old St. Peter's.

Concerning the navigation, on the other hand, miraculous navigation without pilot of the kind described in the text constitutes a much diffused typology in hagiographic literature. Its most famous instance is probably that of the decapitated remains of St. James the Greater that made their way in an unmanned boat from Jaffa in Judea, in the eastern Mediterranean, to the Atlantic shores of Galicia. The boat episode might have been mentioned as a parallel to Santiago's.

154. The text of Whitehill-*Liber* 1:362 reads: "Tedet memori quia narrare nequeo"; Vielliard-*Guide*, p. 40, interprets: "Tedet me mori,..." that is to say, "je regrette de devoir mourir avant d'avoir pu raconter" (p. 41), followed also by Caucci-*Guida*, p. 95; Oursel-*Compostella*, p. 56; and our own version. Moralejo-*Calixtinus* (p. 527 and n. to line 29 of the same page), on the other hand, following Fita-*codex*, prefers the original reading of Whitehill and hence he translates "Me duele no recordar..."; so also Herbers-*Jakobsweg*, p. 109 and n. 129, as well as BravoLozano-*Guía*, p. 43, and p. 120, n. 113.

155. On the Athenian origin of St. Giles, cf. *ActaSS* Sept. 1:303. The Olympus mentioned further down refers to both, the geographical site of Giles's birthplace, as well as the Platonic or Neoplatonic mythological implications of the mountain of the muses.

156. The reference is probably to the four cardinal points. "Non moriendo eius lux atra efficitur" (Vielliard-*guide*, p. 40) must be rendered in a conceptual affirmative phrase – "While setting, his light did not darken" – otherwise it makes no sense with the notion of the declining of the star of the following paragraph. Only Vielliard-*guide*, p. 41, reads the passage in such way.

157. The saintly virtues are conveyed in terms of light symbolism. The midnight eclipse of the star further emphasizes the light-dark contrast.

158. This must be interpreted in terms of an ascension or an apotheosis that culminates in an enthronement.

159. That is to say, in generic terms, the Christianized barbarians that settled in Provence.

160. On the history of the abbey of Saint-Gilles and on its famous reliquary casket, see A. Fliche, *Aigues-Mortes et Saint-Gilles* (Paris, n. d.); and C. Nicolas, "Peintures murales et châsse de Saint-Gilles au XIIᵉ siècle" [*Bulletin du comité de l'art chrétien* (Nîmes) 22 (1908): 108–14]. It is not certain when this splendid reliquary casket did disappear – during the iconoclastic upheavals of the twelfth and thirteenth centuries or during the Wars of Religion of the sixteenth century (cf. Vielliard-*guide*, p. 41, n. 3). According to Canon Cantaloube, reported in the *Addenda et corrigenda* of Vielliard-*guide*, (p. 147, n. to p. 41) an inventory of the treasury of Saint-Gilles of the year 1362 still carried the casket as extant in its entirety. Later inventories, on the other hand, speak only of fragments, the last of which disappeared during the Wars of Religion.

161. That is to say, on the left side of the first register seven figures appear: the Virgin Mary and six apostles.

162. The given order of the zodiacal signs is standard. It starts with Ram, Taurus, and Twins, that is to say, the zodiacal signs of Spring. The centaur shooting an arrow is Sagittarius, the goat stands for Capricorn, and the man pouring water, for Aquarius. The zodiacal signs figure quite often within medieval sacred programs, variously integrated into the iconological ensemble. Their ultimate reference is probably cosmic: placing the particular sacred monument or object in relationship to the cosmic coordinates of the universe and thereby effecting its definition in terms of space and time.

163. That is to say, vine-scrolls.

164. Two hexameters. The Twenty-Four Elders of Apocalypse 4.4 are standard Romanesque programmatic features. Their iconography usually emphasizes both of their attributes: musical instruments of various sorts and flasks. The latter are supposed to contain the condensed prayers of the faithful (Apocalypsis 5.3: "each one of them was holding a harp and had a golden bowl full of incense made of the prayers of the saints").

165. To the seven figures on the left – six apostles and the Virgin – seven more are set on the right: the other six apostles and *cujuslibet Christi discipuli.* There is no way of telling from the details at our disposal who these thirteen apostles were. The canonical number of the original Twelve Disciples underwent a rearrangement subsequent to the betrayal of Judas Iscariot. The latter became variously replaced, at times by Paul. On the casket, in all probability, there was no differentiation among the apostles according to physiognomy or attribute, except perhaps for Peter, and conceivably for John and Paul, if the latter was even present. As to the supernumerary apostle, this might be Paul, if he is not already replacing Judas; or he might be St. John the Baptist. This last iconological solution seems particularly in keeping with the structure of a balanced program: in fact, the Virgin and the Baptist often appear in commensurate roles. So, for instance, in the Byzantine iconography of the deesis – showing Christ enthroned between Mary and John the Baptist.

166. It seems as if these virtues, that is to say, their personifications, were located immediately above the apostles, on either side of the front of the reliquary casket. If so, then their total number should be twelve, or perhaps fourteen, considering the Virgin and possibly St. John the Baptist added to the Twelve Apostles (cf. above, nn. 161 and 165). The somewhat haphazard way in which the five virtues are identified here by their names gives us little cue as to the identification of the rest. Faith, Hope,

and Charity constitute, of course, the famous Theological Virtues which, complemented by an additional variable virtue, are often set in contrast with the Four Cardinal Virtues – Prudence, Justice, Temperance, and Fortitude. So it occurs, for instance, on the early fourteenth-century bronze door of Andrea Pisano in Florence. Beyond this, there is no way of telling the identity of the rest of the virtues most of which might have responded to the dictates of poetic fantasy. It may be said though that such an enlarged series of twelve or fourteen virtues is quite rare.

167. Two elegiac distichs of leonine and imperfect rhymes. The permanence and unmovable quality of relics constitutes a basic principle of Christian theological thought as well as a solid frame of reference for the medieval mind. Its necessary counterpart is nothing but the pilgrimage. See pp. 2–3 above.

168. As it occurs on the lid of many late-classical sarcophagi.

169. In Middle Eastern and Mediterranean cultures, one of the widespread symbols of fertility and, by extension, of abundance. The Phoenician goddess Astarte (Ashtoreth), the Greek goddesses Demeter, Persephone, Aphrodite, as well as their Roman colleagues were all associated in one way or another with the pomegranate. In medieval Christian culture the hard shell of the pomegranate containing the many seeds was often interpreted symbolically as the ecclesiastical community, the Mystic Church, and the red juice of the seeds, as the blood of the martyrs. Cf. Du Cange-*Glossarium*, s.v. "milgrana, migrana."

170. The *trostee* of the text is the genitive of *trostea*, interpreted as *tructa* and translated as *trout* by Vielliard-*guide* (p. 13) and Moralejo-*Calixtinus* (p. 529 and n. to line 14 of the same page). We follow the same interpretation. The representation of a large fish in Romanesque form-culture usually had socio-economic connotations expressed in a popular-folkloric language, for instance, in cycles representing trades and crafts as on the portal of the church of Sainte-Marie in Oloron. The early Christian mystic-symbolic representation of the fish (ΙΧΘΥΣ) so prominent in the catacombs, had by the central Middle Ages lost much of its currency.

171. Reliquaries belong to the most preciously, magnificently, and expensively decorated *Kleinkunst* of medieval culture. The transposition of economic values into theological ones, and specifically of court values and practices into religious-devotional ones, had been a steady feature of Byzantine culture and thereafter of medieval culture in general. Some of the great treasure collections along the Compostela road or in its vicinity contain such precious reliquary caskets (Conques, San Millán de la Cogolla, Santo Domingo de Silos, San Isidoro in León).

172. That is to say, in a mandorla.

173. Erroneously, *in dextera* in the text: it should say *sinistra* or *leva*.

174. Zechariah 8.19.

175. This star seems to be of decorative significance only. See below, n. 177.

176. After Isaiah 44.6, "I am the first and the last; there is no other God besides me," as well as Apocalypse 1.8 "'I am the Alpha and the Omega,' says the Lord God, who is, who was, and who is to come, the Almighty." Alpha and omega, on a different level, are the first and last letters of the Greek alphabet in which the Septuagint version of the life of Christ had been written: such a perception corresponds to a Hebrew tradition according to which the first element of a series stands for all that follows.

177. As above n. 175. It is not to be ignored, however, that these two precious stones might be connected to the one under Christ's footstool, forming a triangle – symbol of the Trinity.

178. The winged-animal symbols of the Evangelists may be traced back on the one hand to the Tetramorph in the vision of the chariot of Yahweh (Ezekiel 1.4–12) and on the other hand to the four animals of Apocalypse 4.7. The ultimate source of these symbols rests in the ancient eastern conception of the four bearers of heaven or guardians of the corners of the world. The order in which the Evangelists are placed around Christ does not correspond to the canonical disposition which, from the upper right corner (Christ's right), counterclockwise, runs as follows: Matthew, Mark, Luke, John. There are many Romanesque instances though in which the normal order is altered: as, on the famous facade relief of the church of Santiago in Carrión de los Condes on the pilgrimage route.

179. Cherubs and seraphs constitute the highest of the nine angelic hierarchies. The cherubs are assigned as guardians to the gates of Paradise (Genesis 3.24) and to the Throne of Mercy of the Ark of the Tabernacle (Exodus 25.18–22). The cherubs of the Throne of Mercy are made of gold: from here might derive the iconography of the enthroned Christ guarded by cherubs. Their representation follows that of the four-winged Tetramorphs of the vision of Ezekiel 1.4–12. The seraphs, on the other hand, appear in the vision of Isaiah above the throne of Yahweh. They are described as six-winged angels, of which two serve for flying.

180. No clues are given for the identification of this person.

181. That is to say, an image of St. Giles.

182. Together with the six further apostles of the next paragraph, a standard frame for the Ascension. The Virgin too is often present at the Ascension.

183. Acts 1.11.

184. Such columns between the apostles could be an indication that each of the apostles is standing under an archivolt sustained by two columns.

185. There is a problem here. The text reads: "Dominus stat erectus in trono." Of the various typologies for the representation of the Ascension there is one in which the enthroned, and hence seated, Christ is born heavenward, in a mandorla, by angels; and there is another in which a standing Christ, also in a mandorla, is similarly carried towards heaven. The seated and the standing poses are kept apart: either Christ is enthroned (so on a Monza ampulla, on the Chludoff Psalter, on the Monreale mosaics, etc.), or He is standing erect (so on the Rabula Codex, the Poussay Evangelistary from Reichenau, the Carolingian Evangelistary of St. Médard, etc.). In our text the two notions are made to overlap and there is no way of telling which one was meant. Matters become further complicated by another representation of Christ on the fourth register. See below, n. 187.

186. Another unorthodox iconographic resolution: the dove, that is to say the Holy Spirit, is never represented above the ascending Christ. Instead, more often than not, the hand of God the Father appears at that point.

187. This additional representation of the ascending Christ is both incongruous in itself and ill-fitted to the Christ representation of the third register. First, the enthroned Christ surrounded by the Four Evangelists constitutes a *Maiestas Domini*: such a representation never appears in an Ascension scene. Second, the angels variously bearing Christ heavenward are missing here. Third, the text of the *Guide* seems to amend itself when it describes the standing Christ with His raised head (probably in profile) and cross in hand ascending towards God the Father. This indeed constitutes a third Ascension typology in addition to those described in n. 185, but there is no way of harmonizing it with the *Maiestas Domini* representation, nor with the missing angels. Furthermore, whatever the Christ representation on the fourth register, it cannot be conformed with that of the third register. A possible solution to the problems prompted by the Christological representations on the third and fourth registers may be stated in the following terms: the author of the *Guide* has partly inverted the third and fourth registers and partly mixed up their elements: the standing Christ with the cross as He is ascending towards the Father of the fourth register together with the angels of the third register constitute the original third register of the casket; the *Maiestas Domini* representation of an enthroned Christ of the fourth register, on the other hand, together with the Holy Spirit

above it, constitute the original highest register of the casket. Such an arrangement is programmatically and iconologically cogent, and particularly so in terms of the vertical sequence of the scenes and their elements: first comes the *Ascension*; and once in Heaven, the *Maiestas Domini*. The absence of the Virgin though remains inexplicable. Cf. C. Nicolas, "Peintures murales...," quoted in n. 160 above; and the article of Ch. Pétourad quoted in Vielliard-*guide, Addenda et corrigenda* to p. 46; in *Albums du Crocodile*, 2 vols. (Lyon, 1950–63, pp. 8–10), which, unfortunately, I could not consult.

188. The *ActaSS* Sept. 1:286 speaks of the attachment and devotion of the Hungarians to St. Giles (cf. Vielliard-*guide*, p. 46, n. 1). Herbers-*Jakobsweg* (p. 112, n. 140) notes that the abbey of Sirmich in Hungary, established in 1078, depended on Saint-Gilles. The case of the Hungarians, as well as that of the others reported subsequently – all of which vie with Saint-Gilles for the actual physical possession of the full or partial earthly remains of the saint – is typical of the fierce competition that went on in the Middle Ages concerning relics. The *furta sacra* (see p. 71, n. 4 above) constitutes a particular aspect of the same phenomenon.

189. *Cammelarii* in the text is a reference to the monks of Chamalières-sur-Loire in the department of Haute-Loire, devoted to St. Giles. Cf. Vielliard-*guide*, p 46 n. 2, who cites Ch. Pétouraud's article quoted above in n. 187. Earlier translations in terms of "camel drivers" should, therefore, be discarded.

190. *Sancti Sequanici*, that is to say, those of Saint-Seine. There are various toponyms so designated, and it is not clear to which the *Guide* refers here. Vielliard-*guide, Addenda et corrigenda* to p. 47, n. 3, proposes a Saint-Seine in the diocese of Langres, Dijon. There was in place a church dedicated to St. Giles, destroyed in 1803, and of which some capitals remain extant. Cf. the note of J. Vallery-Radot in *Congrès archéologique de Dijon* (1928): 153 and 179; and further, Moralejo-*Calixtinus*, pp. 530–31, n. to line 36. C. Nicolas, "Peintures murales,..." quoted in n. 187 above, translates "Bourguignons."

191. *Constanciani Normanni* of the text are the Normans of the diocese of Coutances in the department of Manche. Their collegiate church of Saint-Gilles had pretensions of possessing the relics of St. Giles. Cf. Vielliard-*guide*, p. 47, n. 4; Gaston Paris, *Vie de saint Gilles*, quoted in n. 142 above, p. xvi, n. 4.

192. According to the *ActaSS* Sept. 1:289, an arm of St. Giles was venerated in the church of Saint-Sépulcre of Cambrai. Cf. Vielliard-*guide*, p. 47, n. 5, and BravoLozano-*Guía*, p. 121, n. 120. Arms as relics, as well as the corresponding reliquary-arms, were particularly beloved in the Middle Ages. The Treasure of Conques possesses more than one of these.

193. These are some of the great pilgrimage churches on the route to Santiago with their respective relics, headed by the Cathedral of Santiago de Compostela itself. The abbey church of Conques and Saint-Sernin of Toulouse shine by their absence.

194. The identity of this Philip is questionable. Chronologically speaking, the reference seems to point to Philip I who died in 1108, but we have no indication that he ever made the pilgrimage to Santiago de Compostela (cf. Vielliard-*guide*, p. 47, n. 6). Even if he did, it is most doubtful that he would have embarked upon such an unheard-of wholesale *furta sacra* which, apart from practical difficulties, would have been politically disastrous. Le Clerc-*Aimeric* (p. 283) proposes an identification with Philip Auguste, that is to say, Philip II (1165–1223), who was king of France from 1180 on. His dates, however, are far too late for the author of the *Guide*.

195. Grandson of Charles Martel, William was closely related to the royal Carolingian house. This became with time the monastic community of Gellone founded by William on a remote site of difficult access, next to the Hérault stream, today in the department of Hérault, to which William retired in 806 and which, in the twelfth century, was renamed after its founder as Saint-Guilhem-le-Desert. *Lignum dominicum* refers to a fragment of the True Cross.

196. Tiberius, or Thibéry, Modestus, and Florence were natives of Agde — the ancient Agatha, on the River Hérault not far from its mouth on the Mediterranean – or at least came from there. The three saints suffered martyrdom on November 10, 304. They are known, collectively, as the Martyrs of Agde. Their remains were eventually buried upstream in the Benedictine abbey of Saint-Thibéry founded in the eighth century and destroyed during the Revolution. (cf. Croiset-*Année* 6:231; Vielliard-*guide*, p. 49, n. 3.

197. Concerning the first burial place of Saturninus and the subsequent *translatio*, see the article below on pp. 265–68. On the magnificent five-naved Romanesque basilica, see Bouillet-*Conques*, Aubert-*Sernin*, Cetto-*Miègeville*, Lambert-*cathèdrale Toulouse*, Durliat-*construction Sernin*, Cabanot-*décor Sernin*, Lyman-*style Miègeville*, Durliat-*Sernin*, Cabanot-*débuts romane*, and Durliat-*Jacques*. The pilgrimage church of Saint-Sernin constituted probably the single richest collection of relics and reliquaries on the road to Compostela: cf. Douais-*Trésor Sernin*. The proverbial abundance of relics at Saint-Sernin generated at times wishful expectations: an anonymous Italian pilgrim who made the journey to Santiago de Compostela in 1477 speaks of the body of St. James the Major as well as of the head and body of St. James the Less in

Saint-Sernin (see Caucci-*Guida*, p. 99, n. 37; and Damonte-*Firenze Santiago*, p. 1057).

198. The *via podense*, the second southernmost road to Santiago, originates in Le Puy and, in its time, channelled many of the Austrian, Hungarian, and southern German pilgrims. Marchers from the central German regions as well as from Bourgogne, on the other hand, mostly utilized the *via lemovicense* originating in Vézelay. See p. 25 above.

199. *Supra montem* must be understood in a metaphoric sense only: perhaps the esplanade of a temple or the like.

200. The accepted iconographic form that the soul takes in its ascensional flight is that of an *animula*, that is to say, of a newborn babe. The variation from common practice is probably due to the specific notion of purity and innocence attached to the figure of the young girl-martyr: hence the dove.

201. In traditional early Christian terms, martyrdom generates further martyrdom. This is the ultimate sense of the notion of "confessor": one who manifests publicly his or her faith in Christ, and therefore effectively propagates it by personal *exemplum*. See above, p. 160, n. 139; and below, n. 202.

202. An ironic turn of the hagiographic narrative at the crucial point preceding immediately the martyrdom: in a characteristic Christian paradoxical attitude, martyrdom must at the same time be both eschewed and sought after.

203. A striking and unusual remark: the traditionally preeminent position of the sick and the handicapped as the great beneficiaries of saintly miracles is displaced here in favor of the healthy who appear here in the position of *primus inter pares* – first among equals. Such an uncommon turn too must be understood as a consequence of the specific and uncommon personality of St. Foy. Cf. above, n. 200, and below pp. 241–44.

204. Most of the significant Christian sanctuaries rise on locations in which previous, often prehistoric cult-sites existed. Such cults, more often than not, were water-cults: proof of it is the living water we find in most of such sanctuaries. Monte Sant'Angelo, in Southern Italy, is a particularly striking instance; on the pilgrimage road examples abound: San Juan de la Peña, Conques, the Cathedral of Santiago itself.

205. That is to say, Saint-Léonard-de-Noblat, on the *via lemovicense*. See above, p. 25.

206. See pp. 259–61 regarding Mary Magdalene and the overlapping of her identity with the two other Marys.

207. Actually, because she had done one of the "good works" (Matthew 26.10), and because she had "prepared [the body of

Christ, while in life] for burial" (Matthew 26.13). Cf. also Luke 7.36–50 and John 12.1–8.

208. *Celibem vitam* probably meant as an understatement for a pure and chaste life. Subsequent to her apostolate in Provence, the sources speak variously of her being buried in the basilica of Saint-Maximin in the homonymous town, and by Bishop Maximinus, perhaps in Aix. On the various versions concerning the later destiny of the remains of Mary Magdalene, and on the many pretensions concerning the possession of her relics as well as those of St. Maximin, see the articles on Mary Magdalene and Maximin, pp. 259–62.

209. The *translatio* was probably a *furta sacra* of which one of the texts gives us as date the year 749. This, however, is by far too early, unless the precious relic was at first housed in some previous structure, for the magnificent basilica of Sainte-Madeleine in Vézelay was consecrated in the year 868 only. The historical parameters of the *translatio* were determined, according to the tradition but probably also in the reality of the events, by the general disarray caused by the Muslim invasions in the first half of the eighth century. On Badilon not much is known. He might have been a monk to start with, perhaps of Vézelay, or he might have been a nobleman, perhaps of Autun, who later on turned to monastic life. Cf. Herbers-*Jakobsweg*, p. 116, n. 163; and Oursel-*Compostella*, p. 61, n. 63. One Bedelon appears in a *chanson de geste*, *Girart de Roussillon* (Bédier-*épiques*, 2:76, 79–80, and 4: 350, 386).

210. In 684. On the famous abbey, first dependent on Cluny and later independent, and mainly its abbey church, see Ch. Porée, *L'ubbaye de Vézelay* (Paris, n. d.); F. Salet, "La Madeleine de Vézelay et ses dates de construction," [*Bulletin monumental*, 95 (1936): 5–25)]; F. Salet and J. Adhémar, *La Madeleine de Vézelay* (Melun, 1948). It was in Vézelay that St. Bernard preached in 1146 the Second Crusade.

211. The usual list of miracles whose beneficiaries are the sick and the underprivileged. It is telling though that heading the list we find the faults of sinners: this is probably an allusion to the career of Mary Magdalene herself.

212. *Summi Numinis amore* in the text. Such a classical designation (Latin *nuto, -are*; Greek *neuein*) is strange and uncommon for the Christian Godhead. In its original meaning, it refers to a spirit believed to inhabit a natural object.

213. Later on renamed as Saint-Léonard-de-Noblat.

214. There is considerable confusion at this point: we know nothing of a *viri nomine Leotardi*, Léotard or Saint-Léotard originally from Anjou. There must have been two homonymous

individuals, one Leonard of Noblat, as we known him (see pp. 255–57); and another one, Leonard of Corbigny, who lived somewhat later than the former, died perhaps around 570 (cf. BravoLozano-*Guía*, p. 123, n. 136; and Herbers-*Jakobsweg*, p 118, n. 168; as well as Cottineau-*Répertoire*, pp. 870–71), and who was considerably less important than his famous namesake. The festivities of the two fall on different days too: that of Leonard of Corbigny, on October 15; that of Leonard of Noblat, on November 6. As this happens so often – and not merely between homonymous saints: witness Santiago and St. Roch – a fierce competition developed between the two unequal saints and actually between the two ecclesiastical institutions that represented them, in the course of which the attributes, characteristics, and, most importantly the thaumaturgic powers of the more famous of the two saints were absorbed by and assigned to the less-known one.

There is no way of telling whether it is indeed the author of the *Guide* who, in his endeavours to tell the two apart, lends to the saint of Corbigny a similar, though different, name than that borne by the saint of Noblat, or whether the name change he speaks of corresponds indeed to a historical reality.

215. Both instances of economic nature: the envious serf and the bad father appropriate whatever or whomever does not belong to them anymore. In the case of the father, a monetary compensation must have accompanied the deal.

216. Psalm 106(105).20.

217. Proverbs 5.9.

218. So they are defrauded in their expectations. We are not told, however, how the devout find out the inappropriate impersonation.

219. An important passage for various reasons: first, because it is not being denied that somebody at Corbigny performs miracles; second, because miracles, in general terms, are here carefully differentiated from the deliverance of captives, which is considered the most popular of all miracles, entraining in its wake the pilgrimage of the freed prisoners. The deliverance of captives is the jealously guarded special prerogative of St. Leonard of Limousin, and it is this aspect of the thaumaturgic activities of the local saint that accrues economic benefits to Corbigny: *ibi adducit*, takes them there, is a euphemism for the donations that the delivered captives leave at Corbigny. Third, there is an evident contradiction here with all that has been argued heretofore: if somebody at Corbigny was impersonating the saint of Noblat, that is to say, if the relics of somebody else were being held as those of Leonard of Noblat, why should the latter answer the invocations directed to the former and free the prisoners? If, on the other

hand, the relics of Leonard of Noblat were actually, *in toto* or partially at Corbigny, than the latter's claim to fame is indeed justified. The first of the two faults laid at Corbigny's doorsteps by the author of the *Guide* seems to indicate that Corbigny did indeed possess at least a portion of the much-disputed remains of the saint.

220. The taking of prisoners and their freeing for ransom constituted a lucrative business in which both sides of the Christian-Muslim confrontation engaged for centuries. As late as the end of the sixteenth century Cervantes himself was a prisoner in Algiers. The writing to family and friends for ransom money went hand in hand with invocations to a protector saint. Many of these specialized in this kind of miracles: Santiago himself, Santo Domingo de Silos, and, more than anybody else, St. Leonard of Noblat. Once freed, the shackles and other ironware were customarily taken to the reliquary church of the invoked saint and there displayed to the furtherance of his glory. The ironware, on the other hand, was no doubt joined by more tangible benefactions too for the profit of the particular church. On the route to Santiago de Compostela, the above-mentioned monastic or pilgrimage churches all have shackles and chains prominently displayed on their walls. Such ironware is found elsewhere too: so, for instance, at San Juan de los Reyes in Toledo. Nowadays all ironware is affixed to the walls; in the past, though, many chains were hanging from masts variously placed in the church.

221. A somewhat liberal arrangement of Psalms 106 (105).43; 107 (106).10, 13, 16; and 149.8.

222. This Bohemund I is the son of the famous Robert Guiscard, a Norman duke of Apulia. Having joined the Crusaders, Bohemund conquered Antioch in 1095 establishing in it a principality that would last for nearly two hundred years. Prisoner of the Turks between 1100 and 1103, he regained his liberty through a large ransom. The phrase, "traduntur etiam Christiani vincti," of the text is obscure.

223. Evocation of the Anastasis, Christ's Harrowing of Hell after His Resurrection, and the ensuing liberation of Adam and Eve.

224. Isaiah 49.9.

225. Périgueux. The case of Fronto is parallel to that of many of the most illustrious early evangelizers of various regions of Gaul: so Dionysius, Trophimus, Saturninus, and others. Early French efforts tried hard to create for these saints a tightly-knit apostolic connection. The story of St. Front pretends that St. Peter himself had sent him from Rome to Périgueux (cf. pp. 244–46 below, as well as Herbers-*Jakobsweg*, p. 120, n. 178). As to the presbiter George, he is a secondary character whose like we find from time

to time in hagiographic accounts. His archetypal significance is probably legal or juridical: he is a witness to the events. In this particular case he is also the subject-witness of a miracle of which he will be the beneficiary.

226. So in the text: *ab apostolo accepisti.* However, since it is a direct speech, it would make more sense if it said *ab apostolo accepi.*

227. *Comple illam* in the text, that is to say, do it, accomplish it, facilitate the happening of the miracle.

228. There is a relief that once adorned the facade of the eleventh-century church and which now is kept in the local museum: it shows Peter handing over his pastoral staff to Front (M. Aubert, "L'église Saint-Front," in *Congrès archéologique de Périgueux*, 1927, reported in Vielliard-*guide*, p. 57, n. 4). The apostolic connection of Front is not conveyed on the level of the first sending of Fronto by Peter, but rather on the level of the handing over of the miraculous staff. Indeed, it is this staff that bears the symbolic thaumaturgic power to raise the dead, a power that, embedded in the *mandatum* itself, had been transmitted by Christ to the Apostles, and hence to Peter, and by Peter to Front.

229. A splendid basilica erected on an equal-armed ground plan and crowned by Byzantine-type domes constitutes the twelfth-century structure. Cf. C. Roux, *La basilique Saint-Front de Périgueux* (Périgueux, 1920); and M. Aubert, "L'église Saint-Front" (see n. 228 above).

230. This is probably not the College of the Apostles, but rather the College of the Seventy-Two Disciples of Christ.

231. We know that this remarkable funerary monument was completed in 1077 by one Guinamond, a monk of La Chaise-Dieu, while another individual, who either commissioned the work or otherwise facilitated its execution was one Itier, a canon of the basilica. The remains of St. Front were translated to this monument only later (1463: BravoLozano-*Guía*, p. 124, n. 145). The tomb was unfortunately destroyed in 1575 during the Wars of Religion. Some fragments of it are in the local museum. Vielliard-*guide*, p. 59, n. 1, quotes a description of the tomb from M. Aubert, "L'église Saint-Front," (see n. 228), who in his turn had transcribed it from a "red book" of the Municipal Archives of Périgueux (no date was provided: I could not see the document): "this edifice was round, covered by a vault in pyramidal shape, and on its exterior there were sculpted figures from antiquity as well as monsters, savage animals, and divers figures, so that there was hardly a stone which was not enriched with some beautiful sculpture, well executed, and particularly appealing due to its antique style." The text of the *Guide* tells us that the monument was "rotundum tamen ut dominicum sepulcrum." The reference

is to the interior of the Constantinian church of the Holy Sepulcher in Jerusalem, and conceivably to the Constantinian monument of the Holy Sepulcher itself, long destroyed and with no archeological trace, but of which the memory has survived in two ways: in the tradition of the round or octagonal churches such as Santo Stefano Rotondo in Rome or the octagonal Templar's church of Eunate and that of Torres del Río, both in Navarra, or even the architectural evocation of the Holy Sepulcher in the basilica of St. Cyriacus in Gernrode, in Saxen-Anhalt; and still more significantly, in early representations of the Holy Sepulchre on a few *Kleinkunst* pieces that fortunately withstood the vicissitudes of time: such are a famous wooden reliquary casket in the Museo Sacro in the Vatican (Grabar-*Iconography*, ill. 260) and some Palestinian ampullae in the Treasure of the Collegiale in Monza (ibid., ills. 317–18), all of them from about the sixth century. On the above *Kleinkunst* we are able to catch a glimpse, no matter how tentative and how rudimentary, of the interior of the Constantinian church of the Holy Sepulcher as well as of the Holy Sepulcher itself. The pyramidal vault of the interior, quoted in the archival document of Périgueux, is well visible on the above artifacts.

232. This is the *via turonense*, the northernmost of the four French roads that converge towards the Pyrenees and Santiago. Starting in Paris, it proceeds via Orleans, Tours, and Poitiers towards Roncesvalles.

233. The Church of the Holy Cross, as was the practice all across Europe, contained as its main relic a fragment of the True Cross, the *lignum dominicum* of the text. The church also kept a second relic of the greatest relevance for the local ecclesiastical history of Orleans, the miraculous chalice of Euverte that played a central role in the miracle-vision of the saint (see next note). On Euverte, cf. the short article on p. 238.

234. *Dominica dextera humanitus* in the text. There is a slight problem here: on the one hand *dominica dextera* refers to the hand of the Lord, but specifically of Yahweh, who has traditionally been represented, ever since Early Christian times (and perhaps even before that: witness the tradition of the *IAD*, hand, marking the lines in the reading of the *Torah*), precisely, in a metaphorical statement, as a human hand (see n. 235 below). On the other hand, *humanitus* conveys the idea of the human form in which the hand appears (Moralejo-*Calixtinus*, p. 538 justly translates *en carne y hueso*). But the Lord's specific manifestation or appearance in human form, *stricto sensu*, has been, from Christian perspectives, a jealously guarded prerogative reserved for Christ. One of the central tenets of the Christological mystery is Christ's human theophany. The whole point of the beautiful mimetic miracle (or

perhaps mystery) of which St. Euverte is made a part, as this becomes apparent at the very end of the episode, is that He who visibly appears is precisely Christ. Without facing a contradiction, we are witnessing here a shift in terms, perhaps best defined as an ideological overlapping. To suppose that such a subtle overlapping of the concepts of the visible hand of Yahweh with that of the visible and manifested Christ was intentional (that is to say, as a Trinitarian conception) on the part of the author of the *Guide* is possible but not probable.

235. *Ipsa Dei manus* reads the text, confirming what has been suggested in the previous note. This cannot be but the hand of Yahweh raising up *verum panem et calicem,* the consecrated Holy Host, that is to say, Christ.

236. *Ipse Christus* in the text. See above n. 234.

237. The reference is probably to Fabius Claudius Fulgentius, bishop of Ruspina or Ruspe in Africa who died in 532 or 533. His allegorical interpretations are justly famous. The quotation of the text could not be localized, except to note its general similarity with a passage from *De Fide ad Petrum,* chap. 19.60 (Migne-*PL* 65:699). Cf. Moralejo-*Calixtinus,* p. 538, nn. to lines 9 and 11. BravoLozano-*Guía* (p. 125, n. 147) suggests a possible confusion with one Panciade Fulgentius, bishop of Ecija, brother of Leandro and Isidore of Seville. Vázquez-Parga-*pereg* (2:480, n. 57) points out a similar confusion between the two Fulgentii.

238. This quotation could not be identified.

239. *Semper poscentibus* in the text. There might be a possible connection here with the notion of the permanently exposed consecrated Holy Host as this is practiced in very few chosen churches: so in San Isidoro of León.

240. Guarded outside the limits of the city in the abbey of Saint-Euverte: cf. C. Bernois, *Histoire de l'Abbaye royale de Saint-Euverte d'Orléans* (Orléans, 1918); and the article of G. Chenesseau in *Congrès archéologique d'Orléans,* 1930 – neither of which I could see (following Vielliard-*guide,* p. 50, n. 1).

241. On St. Samson, bishop and confessor, the information is scant. On the collegiate church of Saint-Samson, see Gallia-*christ,* 8:1516; and Croiset-*Année* 4:677.

242. *Cultrum* in the text. Vielliard-*guide,* p. 60, n. 3, follows DuCange-*Glossarium,* s.v. "cultrum," 2. patella, and translates *patène;* so does Oursel-*Compostella,* p. 66. Moralejo-*Calixtinus,* p. 538; BravoLozano-*Guía,* p. 53, and Caucci-*Guida,* p. 104, on the other hand, all opt for "knife," as we do.

243. The number three is probably of symbolic value.

244. This is a nearly customary list of infirmities that benefit from miraculous interventions, except that there is here a preponderance of mental disorders.

245. Nothing has remained of what must have been a magnificent monumental reliquary, which was dismantled and disappeared during the French Revolution.

246. A central monument for its significance among the pilgrimage churches along the route to Santiago, Saint-Martin of Tours was a magnificent five-naved basilica whose total width, at the level of the main nave, surpassed that of Saint-Sernin. Demolished in 1793, only its two belltowers, that of St. Martin and that of Charlemagne, remain today. The remarkably unified and stable typology observed in the great pilgrimage churches along the route to Santiago – Saint-Martin of Tours, Saint-Martial of Limoges, Sante-Foy of Conques, Saint-Sernin of Toulouse, and Santiago of Compostela – is readily recognized by the author of the *Guide*: "ad similitudinem scilicet ecclesie beati Jacobi miro opere fabricatur." Whether it was the Cathedral of Santiago de Compostela that served as prototype for the others, whether there was altogether a single paradigm to be followed, or whether one of the French pilgrimage churches served as model for the others continues to be a much-debated question (Cf. *Durliat*-Jacques, pp. 8–14). All the above pilgrimage churches were characterized by the amplitude of their nave and transept, the ambulatory at the chancel with the radiating chapels issuing from it, and the ample *matroneum* above the aisles. The latter served also as night shelter for the pilgrims. As to the ambulatory, always directly connected and in the same line with the aisles of the nave, it responded to a specific need: to ensure the flow of pilgrims and thus grant them access to the relics displayed in the radiating chapels and mainly in the crypt without disturbing the mass going on simultaneously on the main altar and in the central nave.

247. Unlike above (cf. n. 244), here we find a rather balanced listing of mental and physical disorders and pathological conditions.

248. See the article with bibliography on Hilary of Poitiers, pp. 256–58, and further, Voragine-*légende*, pp. 79–81; Perdizet-*calendrier*, p. 77; and Mâle-*XII*, pp. 204–7; also M. Meslin, "Hilaire et son temps," in *Actes du Colloque de Poitiers*, 1968 (Paris, 1969).

249. In the text *Arrius* is expunged and *Leo* is written above, between the lines. Fita-*codex* writes *Arrius* (Ariuo, 262–336, the principal promoter of the Arian heresy which denied the divinity of Christ), and so translates Moralejo-*Calixtinus*, p. 539, though in n. to line 12 of the same page he attempts to reorder the historical and the legendary facts. Voragine-*légende*, p. 79, already claims an

apocryphal status to the story of Leo: a pontiff of that name, swept away by the Arian heresy, is said to have called together a church council in the course of which he died while Hilary is supposed to have led the remainder of the confused bishops back to Catholicism (Vielliard-*Guide*, p. 63, n. 1; also Herbers-*Jakobsweg*, p. 143, n. 191).

250. According to the text, the "latrines" and the "corruption of the belly" are the ambiance-related and physiological correlatives of the Arian heresy.

251. A famous miraculous episode which refers either to the apocraphal event connected with Pope Leo (n. 249 above), or better, to the Council of Milan of 355. In the council a fourth condemnation of Athanasius, the Father of Orthodoxy, as well as of others was issued by Emperor Constantius II; in the wake of the condemnation Hilary too was exiled to the East from which, however, he soon returned to preside over further church councils of his anti-Arian crusade (cf. Moralejo-*Calixtinus*, p. 539, n. to line 12). Another tradition wants this and other miracles to have occurred at the Council of Seleucia in Cilicia (cf. Oursel-*Compostella*, p. 67, n. 75).

252. Referring to his conciliar activities in general, or perhaps to the one of Milan mentioned in the previous note.

253. *Frisiam* in the text, corrected by Fita-*codex*: *Phrygiam*. It is Phrygia, the great central plateau of Anatolia, where St. Hilary arrived in 356 after having been exiled at the Council of Milan of 355. So Vielliard-*Guide*, p. 63, n. 2; Moralejo-*Calixtinus*, p. 124, n. to line 2; and Herbers-*Jakobsweg*, p. 124, n. 193. Though a landlocked region of Anatolia, at times its southern limits are made to reach the Mediterranea. Wyzewa, in Voragine-*légende*, p. 79, speaks of the island of Gallibaria in the Mediterranean close to Alassio.

254. Having died without baptism, the child lost the life of his soul and his body.

255. This precious reliquary tomb too was long ago dismantled.

256. Since January 13 falls on the octave of Epiphany, Hilary's festivity is celebrated nowadays on the 14th.

257. The *Prodromos*, the Forerunner of Christ, perhaps the most significant figure of the Christian hierarchy after Christ himself and the Virgin. Amply reported in Luke, and to lesser extent in the other gospels and in the Acts of the Apostles, John's self-purification in the desert, his Baptism of Christ, his imprisonment at Machaerus, the episode of the banquet of Herod and Salome's dance, and his beheading at the instigation of Herodias constitute one of the best known string of events of the Sacred Scriptures that

have, ever since the earliest times, fuled the imagination of Christians.

We are facing here the tradition of a *translatio* that occurred in 1010, but upon which doubt had been cast shortly after by the monk Ademar of Chabannes (988–1034). The *ActaSS* for June 4:745–80 refers to it as an invention [Moralejo-*Calixtinus*, p. 540, n. to line 12, who relies on Castro-*España Historia*, pp. 141–42; and on E. Sackur, *Die Cluniacenser*...Halle, 1892–94) 2:68; see also Migne-*PL* 141:67; and Gallia-*christ* 2:1096]. The announcement by Abbot Alduin of the discovery of the precious relic – rendered particularly significant by the memory of the saint's beheading – brought to Saint-Jean-d'Angély a host of notables, among them Robert the Pious of France and Sancho el Mayor of Navarra. No doubt, the position of Saint-Jean-d'Angély on the *via turonense* created the conditions for a major relic to be associated with the place; and similarly and conversely, it is the pilgrimage road that conferred upon the place and its relic its subsequent historic importance. The baffling complexities of the various contradictory traditions concerning the relics of St. John the Baptist promise no easy solution: apart from Saint-Jean-d'Angély – Amiens, Nemours, and San Silvestro in Capite in Rome also claim his relics. Until a few years ago the famous treasure of San Isidoro in León displayed a lower jaw designated as of St. John the Baptist. Lately the identification tag has been removed.

258. One of the splendid Romanesque monuments on the route: particularly important are its lavishly decorated portals.

259. This is linked to the concept of *oratio perennis*, a continual, twenty-four hour, round-the-clock hymnody and prayer sequence which characterized also, in the larger churches, the functions of the later Gothic choirs.

260. In the sense of the *translatio* of a relic. It is not clear to which document the *Guide* refers.

261. The proof of authenticity of the relic rests on its efficaciousness.

262. February 24 corresponds to the celebration of the *prima inventio capitis*. There are other dates also asociated with the celebration of St. John the Baptist. The Marcianus in question is the Byzantine emperor who reigned 450–57. Croiset-*Année* 4:1395, sets the event in the times of Emperor Constantine, 306–37. Miraculous revelations accompanying the finding of relics are a hagiographic commomplace; so is the *campus stellae* of the Santiago tradition.

263. Nothing is known of this "passionem...litteris grecis." The *ActaSS* April 3:735, considers it a fabulous fabrication.

264. On Clement, the second, the third, or the fourth bishop of Rome, see the homonymous article, pp. 231–33, with bibliography.

The connection of Eutropius with Dionysius and through him with Clement is part of the ambitious eighth-century tradition that tried to antedate the early evangelizers of France to apostolic times: cf. the *passio* of Dionysius, the *Gloriosae,* in the article on Dionysius, pp. 233–34.

265. This corresponds to the ninth-century tradition that identifies Dionysius with the Athenian disciple of St. Paul. Cf. the article on pp. 233–34. The eighth- and ninth-century traditions continuously overlap.

266. Cf. above n. 263. With all certainty a spurious fabrication of the author of the *Guide* relying, probably, on earlier spurious accounts.

267. This is the eighth-century tradition concerning Clement.

268. "Nove regenerationis lavacrum" in the text. Matthew 19.28 reads: "quod vos,…in regeneratione cum sederit Filius…sedebitis"; and Paul, in Titus 3.5: "salvos nos fecit per lavacrum regenerationis," that is to say, "he saved us by means of the cleansing water of rebirth." It denotes the beginning of a Christian life which involves a mutation through grace from carnal to spiritual state. It is a formula much used by present-day fundamentalist Christians.

269. As is the case of St. Foy, martyrdom elicits more martyrdom. The *propagatio fides* finds in martyrdom, *passio,* its highest but also its most efficacious ally. The phenomenon of martyrdom, to be sure, transcends by far the parameters of Christian religious experience: it has been well known to all revolutionary movements, political or otherwise.

270. On the paradoxical character of martyrdom, a self-sacrificial act rejected by the body but sought after by the spirit, see above, p. 170, nn. 201 and 202.

271. Leonine hexameters in the text.

272. This is the beginning of the very long section on the conversion and martyrdom of St. Eutropius. See above, n. 31, for the predilection of the author of the *Guide* for the Saintonge and the Poitou.

273. *Admirandus* in the text, from late Latin *amiratus,* which in turn falls back on Arabic *amir,* that is to say, *emir,* in the sense of chief, commander.

274. I could not find in the pertinent literature any trace of the above oriental and even exotic account. It is hard to say whether the reference is to Xerxes I, king of Media and Persia (485–472 BC), the son of Darius I, or to any number of his homonyms. The empire of Babylonia – not to speak of the city of Babylon, close to Bagdad – in the lower plains of Mesopotamia, does not correspond to Persia either, nor to ancient Assyria. I could not identify

Guiva either. It seems that the eastern scenario made to coincide with the times of Christ is a colorful medieval pastiche in which Babylonia is a metaphor for the East in general, not otherwise as *baldachin*, a corruption of Bagdad, stands for any kind of oriental fabric. Neither Vielliard-*guide* nor the later commentators advance any hypothesis in this regard. For the many chronological, historical, and geographic incongruencies of the episode, see below, nn. 278–79, 282, 287, and 302.

275. In the opening sentence already Eutropius was given the adjective *venustus*, that is to say, graceful, kind; and now again, *humilior*. In his character description, gentleness and meakness prevail.

276. Probably standing for Hebrew or Aramaic. The Chaldeans, a Semitic nation, inhabited the southern alluvial plain of the Tigris and the Euphrates.

277. Parallel to the position of Christ among the Doctors.

278. Probably Herod Antipas, tetrarch of Galilee, who examines Christ (Luke 23.6–12). The examination, however, as that of Pilate too, took place in Jerusalem and not in Galilee (Luke 23.7). It is Christ who had come from Galilee to Jerusalem.

279. Tiberias, built by Herod Antipas in honor of Emperor Tiberius. Though Christ was very active in Galilee (the Galilean ministry), there is no record of his having stayed in Tiberias.

280. Matthew 14.13-21. This is the Five Loaves miracle. There is also a second miracle of Multiplication of the Loaves and Fishes, the Seven Loaves miracle (Matthew 15.32–39 and Mark 8.1–10).

281. Perhaps the tutor, a negative character in the story, is given this name in evocation of Nicanor, the general of the Syrian King Antiochus Epiphanes, who twice confronted Judas Maccabaeus only to be slain the second time.

282. There is a problem here: this *gentili more* of the text, if referring to what came before, makes little sense: it is not the usage of gentiles to worship the Creator in the Temple, but rather it is that of the Hebrews. *Creatore*, capitalized, must refer to Yahweh.

283. The usual list of infirmities and physical deficiencies.

284. This is the first miracle, that of the Five Loaves: cf. above, n. 280.

285. Moralejo-*Calixtinus*, p. 543, n. to line 15, following Croiset-*Année* 5:1425–26, suggests Baradach, borrowed from the lives of the apostles Simon and Judas Thaddaeus, venerated together in the West. Judas Thaddaeus will soon be mentioned in the text (cf. n. 301).

286. John 11.1–44 and especially 38–44.

287. John 12.12–13; also Matthew 21.1–11; Mark 11.1–11; and Luke 19.28–40. But John's is the only gospel that reports the Raising of Lazarus, an episode that here is given the impression as immediately preceding the Entry into Jerusalem, while in John two further episodes are intercalated, the meeting of the chief priests and the Pharisees (11.45–54) and mainly the Anointing in Bethany (12.1–11). Perhaps the "ubi Lazarum resuscitaverat" of the previous sentence should be simply understood as a qualifier of Bethany wherefrom Christ was coming subsequent to the anointment episode, rather than as an indication of the Raising which took took place immediately before.

288. John 12.17.

289. John 11.17.

290. John 12.20–22.

291. *Gentiles* in the text, that is to say, Greeks.

292. The dramatic crescendo is built with considerable psychological finesse in a sequence of bold advances and faint withdrawals.

293. Not in the Gospels.

294. "Tanti viri necem videre renuens" in the text. Not quite clear why this reluctance to stay with Christ when He would most have needed companionship: unless it is a further instance of the psychological finesse mentioned above in n. 292. This must have been the day after Palm Sunday.

295. We are not told how long the journey to Babylonia, or whatever stands for it, took; nor the length of the return trip: I assume at least a few days in each direction which, added to the forty-five days stay in Babylonia, brings the figure to just about fifty days. This is the lapse of time necessary to reach Pentecost; see n. 296 below.

296. The fiftieth day from the second day of *Pesach*, Passover, the Feast of Unleavened Bread; the first day of the feast falls on the 14th of Nisan; and the second day, on the 15th.

297. Acts 2.1–13.

298. As the Apostles themselves in Acts 2.4.

299. The justification of anti-Jewish sentiment in general and of pogroms in particular – the seed of what later was bound to become anti-Semitism. In fact, first, the collective responsibility of the Jews for the death of Christ is advocated; second, all Jews, without distinction of rank, position, sex, and age are exterminated: "quos... Judeos repperit"; and third, the special relationship of Jews to Jerusalem is now felt to be undermined: the death of Christ brings damnation upon Jerusalem. The position has been repudiated by the Church under John XXIII.

300. "Diversa cosmi climata aduentibus" in the text. This corresponds to the apostolic notion of the necessary evangelization of the whole world, hence of all its climates, that is to say, latitudes.

301. These are Simon Kananaios or Kananites or Zelotes (Matthew 10.4, Mark 3.18, Luke 6.15, Acts 1.13), to distinguish him from Simon Peter; and Judas Thaddaeus, to distinguish him from Judas Iscariot. According to the "Passio Simonis et Judae," both apostles evangelized in Persia and suffered martyrdom there, an account adopted by Venantius Fortunatus: "Hinc Symonem ac Iudam lumen Persida gemellum / Lata relaxato mittit ad astra sinu" (Migne-*PL*, 88:270).

302. Such and similar magicians, of demoniac powers but who are ultimately unmasked and soundly defeated by some Christian saint, are an *obbligato* phenomenon in early hagiography: so Simon Magus in the stories of Philip and Peter; and so Hermogenes in the story of Santiago (cf. p. 69 above; and Croiset-*Année*, 5:555. *Stricto sensu*, the text *a fide avertebant* is less than coherent, for the people could not have been deviated from their faith since up to that point they had none.

303. The latter, Eutropius himself, who is set thus in direct discipleship to the apostles.

304. "Ecclesiam cum omnibus gradibus suis...instituerunt" in the text. The general conversion is followed by the establishment of a structured Christian community with its recognized authorities.

305. We know nothing concerning this Abdias or Abadias or Obadia except what the text tells us: that he had come with the two apostles from Jerusalem already as a faithful convert. Hence he must have belonged, within the logic of the story, to the earliest disciples of the apostles or perhaps even to the group of the Seventy-Two Disciples of Christ (Luke 10.1–17). A namesake of his is one of the twelve minor prophets.

306. Once episcopal authority is established, a deacon is appointed as assistant in the work of ecclesiastical administration. The term *archidiaconus*, however, does not appear before the fourth century; earlier, *diaconus episcopi* was used.

307. Refers to Simon and Judas Thaddaeus.

308. At Suanir in Persia, according to some sources; and in Colchis, a region east of the Black Sea, according to others.

309. Nothing is known of this writing. Its mention in the text is probably a further attempt to align Eutropius with the Apostles: cf. n. 310. In the context of our text, the denomination might have conceivably referred to a popular, spoken, koine Hebrew.

310. This is once again the French apostolic syndrome that endeavours to link French saints to Peter, the Prince of the Apostles, and to Rome. Such a linkage is in this case particularly remarkable, for Eutropius, according to the text, had been exposed to the direct influence of Christ himself and furthermore had been baptized by two of His apostles. Even so, it was felt, the hierarchic stand of Peter necessitated his inclusion in the story. Cf. the cases of Trophimus and Saturninus, pp. 265–70.

311. Surely a symptomatic differentiation rooted in the Christian notion of the preeminence of the spiritual and ecclesiastical affinities over blood kinship. St. Francis will do the same when renouncing, in the presence of the bishop, his father's wealth and hence authority.

312. *Cum aliis fratribus* in the text. So the disciples, among themselves, called each other brethren, believers, disciples, saints (Acts 5.14, 9.26, 11.29, 15.1 and 23; 1 Corinthians 7.12; Romans 8.27 and 15.25). The outer world, on the other hand, knew them as Nazarenes or Galileans. *Christian* was, at the earliest times, a contemptuous expression.

313. *Muris antiquis* in the text is a probable reference to the city's classical past: Roman walls. Otherwise too Saintes preserves ancient monuments: so the so-called triumphal arch *de Germanicus*.

314. *Fontibusque lucidis:* emendation of Fita-*codex* signalled by Vielliard-*guide*, p. 73, n. c.

315. Of probably strategic importance.

316. A celebrative passage which only reinforces what has been said above, at n. 313.

317. A refined psychological perception: xenophobia, the fear and therefore the hatred of strangers and foreigners, is the first cause of the population's animosity.

318. "Verba olim sibi inaudita": as in the previous note – fear of the unheard and the unknown.

319. A confirmation of the haphazard nature of the popular hostility: after spending the night outside the walls, Eutropius was able to return in daytime to the city.

320. Matthew 10.14: an ironic remark by Christ concerning the recalcitrant hosts who chose to turn a deaf ear to the apostles. The passage reaffirms the parallel between Eutropius and the disciples of Christ.

321. See above, n. 264.

322. For the notion of martyrdom, see above, p. 160, n. 139; and p. 174, nn. 201 and 202. The discourse is conducted in a paradoxical vein: the evangelization itself is considered a means towards an

end, which is nothing but martyrdom; but martyrdom, at its turn, is the surest channel for the evangelization of the people.

323. Psalm 118 (117).6.

324. Matthew 10.28.

325. Job 2.4.

326. Fine psychological insight into the mind of a desperado whose fate is sealed.

327. Evident overstatement: not everything in the orbit of Christ is sufferance.

328. *Renatus fuerit* in the text. Vielliard-*guide* (p. 75) and Oursel-*Compostella* (p. 73) translate, erroneously, "regenerated."

329. The terms of the equation are now inverted: the previous "water and Holy Spirit" turns into "grace" and "baptism." Grace, in effect, whether deriving from the Holy Spirit or otherwise, is both the cause of rebirth as well as its consequence.

330. Nothing is known concerning Eustella. The name is probably a pun upon that of the saint, Eutropius. Her story has romantic and novelistic qualities which turn up quite frequently in hagiography: the young girl martyr, necessarily a virgin, who exudes faith and innocence, is on the whole a much-beloved figure of these stories.

331. An often-found pattern in hagiographic accounts: the younger generation rebels against the older one and turns to Christ. We have seen the same with Eutropius himself (cf. n. 311 above). Such a pattern, which runs against the Biblical tradition, is ultimately rooted in the notion of the son's supplanting the father by reason of the former's superior excellence.

332. The father's love for his daughter is evidently selfish love, ultimately a possession drive.

333. To which the fatherly image also belongs.

334. No way of telling why this figure: perhaps only a random designation of a large quantity.

335. *Ad patris thalamum* in the text: *thalamus* is, of course, also the nuptial bed.

336. BravoLozano-*Guía*, p. 128, n. 174.

337. The repeated attempts at bringing about his death, all of it conveyed with a wealth of gory details, corresponds to the usual hagiographic martyrdom. A late twelfth- or early thirteenth-century vivid representation of one such sequential slaying occurs on the reliquary monument of St. Vincent in the homonymous church in Avila.

338. Here *Christianis* in the text. Cf. above, n. 222.

339. The prompt burial of the relic assures its preservation. See above p. 2.

340. This too is a customary trait. The lying *ad sanctum*, whether permanently after death or temporarily in life, was and still is a widely practiced tradition.

341. On Saint-Eutrope of Saintes, see R. Crozet, "Saint-Eutrope de Saintes," *Congrès archéologique de France. La Rochelle* (Orléans, 1956, pp. 97–105).

342. The list of miracles, past and those to be expected in the future, is the usual one: cf. *BHL* 1:2787. For the ironware witnessing to the liberation of prisoners, cf. above, n. 220.

343. The notion of intercession, fundamental in the Christian hierarchical structure.

344. Possibly, patterned after the Christological episode of the Anastasis or the Harrowing of Hell, one of the surrogate scenes of the Resurrection.

345. Towards the end of the sixth century an Augustinian abbey was established in Blaye with Romanus as its titular saint. Two further building programs followed: one in the Romanesque period (eleventh and twelfth centuries) and another in the fourteenth century. All but destroyed by the English in 1441, the church was finally demolished by Louis XIV in 1676. I follow here Vielliard-*guide* (pp. 78–79, n. 1) and Herbers-*Jakobsweg* (p. 130, n. 220), who rely on Cottineau-*Repertoire* (1:393); and J. Lacoste, "La résurrection de Saint-Romain de Blaye," *Les dossiers de l'archéologie* 20 (1977): 50–57.

346. The Carolingian tradition in Blaye is, of course, on the strength of the presence of Roland, fundamental. Pseudo-Turpin, chap. 21, (see in Whitehill-*Liber*, 1:337; and Moralejo-*Calixtinus*, p. 475) speaks of Charlemagne's erecting a church in Blaye to house the remains of Roland – a church for which solid documentation is known from the year 1135 only (cf. Herbers-*Jakobsweg*, p. 130, n. 220; the bibliography of the previous note; Hämel-*Überlieferung*; and farther, Moralejo-*Calixtinus*, p. 430, n. to line 3. Though Roland was never canonized, the text reads at this point: "requiescit corpus beati Rotolandi martiris," a formula used exclusively for saints and martyrs. Unfortunately, no description of the tomb of Roland at Blaye came down to us and the medieval monument has long ago disappeared: cf. C. Jullian, "La tombe de Roland a Blaye," *Romania* 25 (1896): 161–73, and in general, Vielliard-*guide*, p. 79, n. 2.

347. That is to say, Roland; but this is, of course, part of the famous campaign of Charlemagne in Spain of the year 778. The controversy over this campaign is far from having subsided; we can only

point out here some of the pertinent bibliography: Bédier-*épiques* 3; MenéndezPidal-*Cid*, chaps. 3 and 18; VázquezParga-*pereg* 1:488 and passim; R. H. Bautier, "La campagne de Charlemagne en Espagne (778). La réalité historique" Actes du Colloque de Saint-Jean-Pied-de-Port, 1978, *Bulletin de la Société des Sciences, Lettres et Arts de Bayonne* 135 (1979): 1–51; B. Sholod, *Charlemagne in Spain. The Cultural Legacy of Roncesvalles* (Geneva, 1966); and M. de Menaca, *Histoire de Saint Jacques et de ses miracles au Moyen-Age (VIIIème–XIIème siècle)* (Nantes, 1987).

348. It is Charlemagne himself, according to the *Chanson de Roland* (vv. 3685–86), who deposited Roland's Oliphant in the basilica of St.-Seurin: "Dessus l'alter seint Sevrin le barun, / Met l'oliphant plein d'or et de manguns." The *Pseudo-Turpin* (Whitehill-*Liber*, p. 337; and Moralejo-*Calixtinus*, p. 475) gives a different version of the story: when the emperor buried Roland in Blaye, he placed his paladin's sword, Durendal, at the head, and his horn, Oliphant, at the feet of the slain hero. Subsequently, impious hands took the horn to Bordeaux. The ancient church of St.-Seurin in Bordeaux was built within a famous cemetery which is mentioned by the *Pseudo-Turpin* together with that of Alyscamps. The church became eventually incorporated into a Benedictine abbey. Cf. Ch. Higounet, *Bordeaux pendant le Haut Moyen Âge* (Bordeaux, 1963). As to Roncesvalles, cf. Lambert-*Roncevaux* and Lambert-*Roncevaux Roland*. In the latter, (pp. 170–75), it is maintained that in the years between 1130 and 1150 both a church and a hospital were in construction in Roncesvalles. So also Vielliard-*guide*, p. 79, n. 4 and Herbers-*Jakobsweg*, p. 130, n. 224.

349. The death of Roland is conveyed in quite different terms in the *Pseudo-Turpin*, chap. xxi (Hämel-*Überlieferung*, pp. 76–81; Moralejo-*Calixtinus*, pp. 465–70): the rhetorical chronicling sustained in protracted monologues does speak of tiredness and exhaustion, but not of thirst.

350. See above, n. 346. The text of the *Chanson de Roland*, vv. 3689–91, wants Olivier and Turpin too buried at Blaye. Cf. also C. Jullian, "La tombe...," p. 170, quoted in n. 346 above.

351. Little is known of Severinus or Seurin. According to Gregory of Tours, *Gloria confessorum* 45 (Migne-*PL* 71:862), he had come to Bordeaux *de Orientis partibus*, and his sudden appearance in the city had stirred so much excitement that Bishop Amand, in 410, abdicated his episcopal see in favor of Severinus and, upon the death of the newcomer in 420, assumed it once again. A different tradition whose spokesman is Venantius Fortunatus, has him come from Trier. Such a supposed German connection is responsible for a frequent overlapping with a homonymous saint from Cologne (BravoLozano-*Guía*, p. 130, n. 181; and É. Brouette,

"Severinus," in *LTK3*, s.v.). Irrespective of its origin, sources agree that the fame of Severinus was such that he soon became the patron of the city. The cloister church with the relics of St. Severinus, once manned by Benedictines and later by regular canons, was at the time located outside the city walls with a pilgrims' hospice attached to it [Higounet, *Bordeaux...*, (see n. 348 above), pp. 115–24].

352. The paladins of Charlemagne. Olivier is the famous friend and companion of arms of Roland, the brother of "la belle Aude," Roland's betrothed. He appears in many *chansons*, and is the central hero in Fierabras (cf. Moralejo-*Calixtinus*, p. 430, n. to line 6). While the *Chanson de Roland* speaks of Olivier and Turpin as buried in Blaye, vv. 3689–91 of the *Pseudo-Turpin* (Whitehill-*Liber*, p. 337; and Meredith-Jones-*Karoli*, pp. 214–15) and the *Guide* have Olivier and others rest in Belin. Since there was never an ancient necropolis in Belin, Jullian ("La tombe...," p. 171, see n. 346 above), thinks that a *tumulus*, of the kind that is frequent in the Landes, was taken as the tomb of Olivier. So with the other paladins too (Vielliard-*guide*, p. 81, n. 13).

Gondebaud is known only in the heroic epics of the Middle Ages (Herbers-*Jakobsweg*, p. 131, n. 228). Ogier or Oger is well known in the French heroic epic – *La Chevalerie Ogier de Danemarche* – and the chivalric novels, as well as in the *Karlamagnús saga ok kappa hans* of the Icelandic manuscripts. Cf. Moralejo-*Calixtinus*, p. 433, n. to line 4. "Dacie," in the text, stands for Denmark.

Arastain or Arastagnus is only known from the *Chanson d'Agolant* (Bédier-*épique* 3:136) and the *Pseudo-Turpin* (Meredith Jones-*Karoli*, pp. 214–15 and Whitehill-*Liber*, p. 337). Cf. Vielliard-*guide*, p. 81, n. 5. Garin – *Garini ducis Lotharingie* in the text – is the hero of a twelfth-century fierce and sanguinary *chanson de geste*, the *Garin le Loherain*, reflecting on the bloody feudal warfare in the region of Lorraine. The list of paladins corresponds to that conveyed in chap. xxi of the *Pseudo-Turpin* (Moralejo-*Calixtinus*, p. 475).

353. This is once again the somewhat brazen French syndrome that makes of France the defender par excellence of western Christendom from the onslaught of the infidels. At the same time, the paladins of Charlemagne have their cake and eat it too: first they defeat the infidels and thus become heroes, and then they themselves are slain turning into martyrs of the Faith. Cf. above, p. 160, n. 139; and p. 170, nn. 201 and 202. on the paradoxical nature of martyrdom.

354. The notion of the communal grave for the Carolingian heroes is present elsewhere too on the road to Santiago: at the Silo of Charlemagne in Roncesvalles and the forest of spears in Sahagún

(see below, pp. 296–97). Apart from the thaumaturgic component which is the theological proof of the sanctity of the slain paladins, the notion of the *suavissimus odor* makes us think of the flasks held by the Elders of the Apocalypse, in which the prayers of the faithful are condensed.

355. The *ubi* of the text should not refer to Redecilla: hence the translation "at the place where." In fact, the Saint is buried in the homonymous town that took the name from him.

356. This is part of the Carolingian tradition linking Charlemagne's exploits with Spanish campaigns in general and with Sahagún in particular. See pp. 296–97 below and further the *Pseudo-Turpin*, chap. 8 (Moralejo-*Calixtinus*, p. 422). There was a church already dedicated to the two saints in Sahagún in Visigothic times. Subsequently, the structure was at least twice renovated by Alphonso III, king of Asturias, after 866 and before 910, the year of his forced abdication in favor of his son García. The subsequent splendor of Sahagún is closely conditioned by the Cluniac connections insistently fostered by Alphonso VI. Cf. pp. 17–19 above; and Herbers-*Jakobsweg*, p. 132, n. 233, who relies on Segl-*Cluniazenser*, pp. 93–102. VázquezParga-*pereg* (2:223) reports of a pilgrim's hospice at place in the year 1195. But that must rely on a late documentation: it stands to reason to conceive of supporting services at such an important stopover already at an earlier date. Cf. also Moralejo-*Calixtinus*, p. 421, n. to line 10.

357. For the collegiate church of San Isidoro and the attached Pantheon of Leonese Kings, see GómMor-*Cat León*, GómMor-*románico*, Gaillard-*commencements*, Gaillard-*romane espagnol*, Whitehill-*Romanesque*, Durliat-*Espagne* (pp. 17-18), Williams-*León*, Williams-*Reconquest*, Moralejo-*Agneau-León*, Williams-*Camino*, and Durliat-*Jacques* (pp. 183–86 and 358–90).

358. *Stricto sensu*, inexact; as inexact is a similar assertion in chap. 10 of the the *Guide* above (cf. n. 582 below): a monastic rule of Isidore did come down to us, but not a canonical rule. Cf. Herbers-*Jakobuskult*, p. 162; and Herbers-*Jakobsweg*, p. 132, n. 237 and p. 159, n. 376.

359. On Isidore's writings, see the bibliography in the article on Isidore below, pp. 253–55. Further, see the introduction by M. C. Díaz y Díaz in *San Isidoro de Sevilla, Etimologías* (ed. J. Oroz Reta and M. Casquero, Biblioteca de autores cristianos, 433–34, 2 vols. Madrid, 1982-83, pp. 1–257). The author of the *Guide* displays here a measured enthusiasm for the literary-cultural contributions of Isidore. On the whole, however, it must be said that the three or four Spanish saints at the end of the chapter fare quite poorly if compared to the ample space and luxury of details with which the saints on the French side of the Pyrenees are handled, let alone the

monographic treatment that Eutropius enjoys. This alone is sufficient proof, were others unavailable, of the French propensities of
our author. Cf. above, n. 31.

360. To this the entire chap. 9 will be dedicated

361. The notion of intercession, several times already encountered:
cf. above, n. 138. The end paragraph gradually and imperceptibly
turns into a liturgical prayer-like phrase.

362. See above n. 3 for Calixtus, and n. 31 for Aimery the Chancellor.

363. Popular folklore has generated the saying "entre el Sar y el
Sarela está Compostela," which reflects well on the closely knit
geographical situation of the two streams.

364. For this famous height, today Monte San Marcos, some 5 km
from Compostela, see above, n. 50.

365. The number seven probably bears numerologico-symboli-
cal connotations: it might have originated as a further parallel
with the Eternal City which counts seven hills, though it has
many more. In the identification of the gates and in their description, I follow LópezFerreiro-*Santiago* 2:47 and 399, 3:43 and
passim, as well as appendices, pp. 8–24, 5:101 and 164, n. 3;
Vielliard-*guide*, pp. 84–85, nn. 1–7; Moralejo-*Calixtinus*, p. 550, n.
13; Herbers-*Jakobsweg*, p. 133, nn. 241–48.

366. The *Puerta Francesa*, the *Porta Francigena*, the French Gate,
is today the *Puerta del Camino*. It is situated to the northeast of
the city, at the end of the *camino francés* and at the point of the
present intersection of the Rua das Casas Reais, the Rua das
Ruedas, and the Rua de Aller Ulloa. Of the gate, or door, or
archway nothing remains today. According to the description
of Laffi in the seventeenth century, there was once a bridge in
front of it (Laffi-*Viaggio*, p. 196; following Caucci-*Guida*, p. 115,
n. 45). All French pilgrims, that is to say, all those coming from
France, most of which were French, German, and Central-European, entered the city this way.

367. The *Puerta de la Peña*, the Gate of the Rock, has kept its
etymology: *penna*, in medieval Latin, has transmitted to the
Hispanic regions its denotation of rock or mountain: *peña* in
Castilian, *penya* in Catalán. Thence, Puerta de la Peña, probably due to the topographic gradient in place even today:
the Cuesta Vieja that takes to the Monastery of San Francisco.
This gate was situated on the north side of the city, in direction of La Coruña. Of the gate nothing is left today except a
homonymous street between the Calle de la Fuente de San
Miguel and the Calle de los Laureles. Cf. Vielliard-*guide*, p.
84, n. 2.

368. The third gate, the *Puerta de Subfratribus,* the Gate below the Friars, is called today *Puerta de San Martín* for it is located on the eastern edge of the city, at the end of the Calle de San Francisco, in proximity to the Monastery of San Martín Pinario. López Ferreiro-*Santiago* (5:101) interprets *subfratribus* as referring to the friars of an old pilgrims' hospice, which was once in that area, rather than to the monks of San Martín Pinario. Moralejo-*Calixtinus,* pp. 550–51, n. to line 13 and p. 335, n. to line 3, notes that a fourteenth-century version in Gallego language of portions of the *Codex* refers to this gate as *a porta de San Francisco* (cf. LópezAydillo-*Santiago*): the homonymous monastery was already established at the time outside the gate.

369. The *Puerta del Santo Peregrino,* the Gate of the Holy Pilgrim, today *Puerta de la Trinidad,* on the west side of the city, was located at the end of the ramp that descends by the Great Hospice towards the Calle de las Huertas (I follow in this Moralejo-*Calixtinus,* pp. 550–51, n. to line 13). At the corner of Huertas and Carretas was the Chapel of the Trinity. In the fourteenth century Gallego version (see n. 368), it is called *do Santo Romeu,* an expression that carries connotations of pilgrimage. Pilgrims who continued their journey to Finisterre, on the shore of the ocean, passed by this gate (Caucci-*Guida,* p. 116, n. 48).

370. The fifth gate, the Gate of Fajera, on the southwest side of the city, is today too the *Puerta Fajera* or *Fajeira* leading out towards the Alameda and the gardens of the Herradura, and ultimately to Padrón (Moralejo-*Calixtinus,* pp. 550–51, n. to line 13). Vielliard-*guide* (p. 85, n. 5) derives the toponym from the Latin *falgueria,* from which the Provençal *fulgueira* and the Catalan *falguera* derive with the meaning of "fern," or better "fern-patch" or "fernery." There are, however, problems concerning the etymology: DuCange-*Glossarium* ignores the term; Moralejo-*Calixtinus* suspects a false latinization; and LópezFerreiro-*Santiago* (5:164, n. 3), proposes the form *faiariis,* deriving from *fagus,* beech-tree. Today there is nothing in place but the homonymous Avenida de Fajeira. The *Viaje de Cosme de Médicis por España, 1668-69* (ed. A. Sánchez Rivero, Madrid, 1933), shows a panoramic drawing by Pier Maria Baldi of Santiago de Compostela in which this gate with its pointed arch and two flanking fortified towers are visible. These towers were demolished in the early ninteenth century. The Gallego version of LópezAydillo-*Santiago* defines this gate as *de Fageiras.*

371. *Petronum,* pile of stones, possibly as boundary marker, at ancient Iria Flavia, the seat of the diocese, today El Padrón.

372. The sixth gate, the Gate of Susannis, is located along the Calle de las Huérfanas at the intersection with the Rúa da Seura and the

THE PILGRIM'S GUIDE TO SANTIAGO

Rúa da Fonte de Santo Antonio (formerly, Calvo Sotelo), which run alongside the present Plaza de Galicia. Nothing remains of the old gate except the memory of its changed name, *Puerta de la Mámoa*. The original etymology remains obscure: proposed readings include the Castilian *susano* deriving from the Low Latin *susannus*, (waste or fallow land) (these offered timorously by Vielliard-*guide*, p. 85, n. 6); and *sousan* or better *shoshana* in Arabic and Hebrew, from which the Castilian *azucena* (white lily), and the name *Susanna* or *Susan* derive (Vielliard-*guide*, *Addenda et corrigenda*, to p. 85). The version in Gallego of LópezAydillo-*Santiago* lends it already the reading of *Mámoa*: the reference seems to be to a heap of earth or mound covering perhaps a dolmen (Moralejo-*Calixtinus*, pp. 550–51, n. to line 13).

373. The Gate of Mazarelos, formerly the *Porta de Macerellis*, today the *Puerta de Mazarelos* or *del Mercado*, is also of difficult etymological reading. The term is absent in Du Cange-*Glossarium*. Vielliard-*guide* (p. 85, n. 7) ponders concerning *macellarius* "butcher," and farther, concerning some derivation from the Arabic *mazari*, that is to say, "brick," from which the Low Latin *maceria*, "wall of unburnt brick," and the French *moellon*, "rubble," "roughstone" derive (Mortet-*architecture* 2:496). Within the parameters of such a reading, the *macerelli* could be "bricklayers." The Gallego version of LópezAydillo-*Santiago* reads *de Macarelas*. It is the only gate extant today in the form of an entrance arch, the Arco de Mazarelos, located between the Calle de Mazarelos and the Plaza de la Universidad.

374. *Preciosus Baccus* of the text refers, of course, to the wine, probably from the valleys of the Ulla, the Avia, and the Miño.

375. I suspect that the number 10 here bears also, as the number 7 for the gates, numerologico-symbolic connotations: hence *solent esse* in the text.

376. That is to say, Jacobus the son of Zebedee, James the Elder, to be distinguished from Jacobus the son of Alpheus, James the Younger or the Less. For the description of the basilica-cathedral, see above, pp. 120–31.

377. *In medio sita*, that is to say, of the city. For the churches that follow, cf. also VázquezParga-*pereg* 2:377–78.

378. That is to say, San Pedro de Fora, or d'Afora, in the Rúa de San Pedro, outside of the Puerta del Camino, in order to distinguish it from San Pedro de Antealtares, inside the city walls. In the early nineteenth century the state of decay of the monastic structure was so advanced that it was demolished and its stones served as quarry for the Quintana and for the causeway from the Puerta Fajera to the Alameda (following Moralejo-*Calixtinus*, pp. 551–52, n. to line 4, who in turn relies on SánchezBarreiro-*Santiago*

1:200–201 and on Neira-*Santiago*, pp. 77–82. A marginal note of the fourteenth century in the text, reported by Vielliard-*guide* (p. 85, n. 8) speaks erroneously of San Pelayo, "Pelagius."

379. The parochial church of San Miguel dos Agros, northwest of the cathedral, belongs to the oldest ones in the city. It was rebuilt by Diego Gelmírez in the early twelfth century (see n. 380, as well as LópezFerreiro-*Santiago* 4:65; Vielliard-*guide*, p. 85, n. 9; and Moralejo-*Calixtinus*, p. 552, n. to line 2), an ogival chapel was added to it in the fifteenth century and it was radically renovated in the nienteenth. The attribute of *Agros* in its present name, as that of *Cisterna* earlier, must refer to some agricultural exploitation in place (so, for instance, the large water cistern just outside the cloister in Santo Domingo de Silos).

380. Pinario or Pignario (no way of telling whether from the Latin *pinna* in the sense of the merlon of a battlement, from which the Castilian *pina*, "stone landmark"; or from *pineus*, "pine," from which *pinar*, "pine grove") ended up qualifying the saintly *titulus*. The monumental ensemble, second in size in the city, is one of the many signals along the road to Santiago pointing to the great saint of the Loire Valley. The earliest Benedictine structures were erected in the ninth century in close proximity to, and to the north of, the cathedral. Its first church used by the monks, the so-called *Corticela*, is presently enclosed in the cathedral (see below, n. 387). The entire monastic complex was subsequently rebuilt by Diego Gelmírez within the vast campaign of restoration that he undertook in the city: apart from San Martín Pinario – San Miguel, San Benito, the monastery of Antealtares, San Felix, and others were rebuilt in the early twelfth century. The new construction of San Martín took place in 1105. Much later the structure underwent a profound renovation in the early and high baroque styles (cf. LópezFerreiro-*Santiago*, 2:47, 399 and passim, 3:43; Sánchez/ Barreiro-*Santiago*, 1:278; Otero-*Guía*, pp. 515–19; and Moralejo-*Calixtinus*, p. 552, n. to line 4).

381. See Moralejo-*Calixtinus*, p. 552, n. to line 4, for the complex topographic and historic situation that the Capilla de la Trinidad presented in the course of centuries, cf. also n. 369 above. The chapel, situated at the Porta de Sancto Peregrino, was demolished around 1930. Sánchez/Barreiro-*Santiago* (1:231) claims that it was also called *de Peregrinos*, which seems to fit a specific donation or grant of a terrain by Diego Gelmírez in 1128, "ad construendam ibi ecclesiam in pauperum et peregrinorum sepulturam" (*Historia compostelana* 2, chap. 94, in Flórez-*Sagrula* 20:472; LópezFerreiro-*Santiago*, 4:145). There are, however, questions concerning the location of the above terrain which might have been also, or perhaps mainly, a contiguous cemetery.

382. Diego Gelmírez had built a church at the height surrounded by the Paseo de la Herradura, and consecrated it in 1105 with the *titulus* of Santo Sepulcro. Sometimes later the relics of St. Susana – the object of a clamorous *furta sacra* perpetrated in 1102 in Braga, Portugal – were deposited in the church, a fact which subsequently determined also its specific *titulus* (cf. *Historia compostelana* 1, chap. 15, in Flórez-*Sagrada* 20:36–41; Sánchez/Barreiro-*Santiago* 1:220–21; and Vones-*Compostellana*, pp. 219–70. See also Herbers-*Jakobsweg*, p. 135, n. 254.) The Romanesque facade of this first church is still extant in spite of the vast baroque interventions of the seventeenth and eighteenth centuries (cf. Sánchez/Barreiro-*Santiago* 1:220–21; and Moralejo-*Calixtinus*, p. 552. n. to line 5).

383. *Juxta viam Petroni* in the text. This must be El Padrón, quoted earlier in connection with the fifth gate (cf. above, nn. 371 and 372), rather than simply a heap of stones: so Vielliard-*guide*, p. 86, n. 3.

384. The church of San Félix or San Fiz, on the western side of the once-walled city, constitutes a microcosm of Santiago de Compostela and of its monuments. Apparently, a church of San Félix was already in place prior to the eighth century, that is to say, prior to the *inventio* of the tomb of Santiago (cf. Moralejo-*Calixtinus*, p. 552, n. to line 6 and Herbers-*Jakobsweg*, p. 136, n. 256). If so, it is the oldest church of the city. Razed to the ground in 997 by Al-Mansur, it was totally rebuilt by Diego Gelmírez in the early twelfth century. San Félix did not escape either the eighteenth-century obligatory baroque renovation retaining, however, its lovely Romanesque portal with some remarkable sculptural reliefs (Adoration of the Magi). Cf. Sánchez/Barreiro-*Santiago* 1:189–91; and LópezFerreiro-*Santiago* 4:65. Presently the parish church is known as San Félix de Solovio.

385. The parish church of San Benito del Campo was originally a pre-Romanesque structure subsequently restored and rebuilt by Diego Gelmírez. Of its Romanesque legacy an Adoration of the Magi has withstood the wear and tear of the centuries. Neoclassical remodeling took place in the nineteenth century. Cf. López Ferreiro-*Santiago*, 4:65 and Moralejo-*Calixtinus*, p. 552, n. to line 7.

386. San Pelayo or San Payo is an abbey church for Benedictine nuns located east of, and in close vicinity to, the Cathedral of St. James. It boasts a venerable history that harks back to Alphonso II the Chaste (791–842) who established it in 813 under the *titulus* of St. Peter for Benedictine monks. Its ancient name, San Pedro de Antealtares, refers both to its topographic relationship with the cathedral, as well as to its role in fostering the pilgrimage to the shrine of St. James. The early twelfth-century building programs effected this monastery too, and its *titulus* was changed for that of

San Pelayo, the martyr child of Tuy. The monastic complex was totally rebuilt in the seventeenth and eighteenth centuries; a number of important Romanesque sculptures, previously part of the structure, have been preserved: so, among others, an early altar of the cathedral (cf. Sánchez/Barreiro-*Santiago* 1:269–72; Otero-*Guía*, pp. 514–15; LópezFerreiro-*Santiago* 3:43–44 and 4:65; and Moralejo-*Calixtinus*, p. 553, n. to line 1).

387. The ancient church of Santa María Virgen is known today as the chapel of Santa María de la Corticela, enclosed within the structure of the cathedral. The church is documented already in the ninth century as used by the Benedictine monks of what would become San Martín Pinario (cf. above, n. 380). The closeness of the cathedral generated a particular topographic relationship: communication was assured through one of the chapels of the cathedral, which one it is not quite clear: LópezFerreiro-*Santiago* (3, appendix, p. 9, n. 3) proposes the chapel of the Espíritu Santo in which there was indeed an entrance; Moralejo-*Calixtinus* (p. 553, n. to line 2), on the other hand, suggests that the communication was established through the chapel of San Nicolás, today considerably restructured, as restructured is also the chapel of the Holy Cross mentioned in the text. Cf. further Sánchez/Barreiro-*Santiago* 1:93–95 and Otero-*Guía*, pp. 503–4. The Corticela has a beautiful Romanesque portal with an Adoration of the Magi. The chapel has been the parish church of foreigners and the military (BravoLozano-*Guía*, p. 133, n. 192/10). As to the chapels of San Nicolás and Santa Cruz, see below, nn. 497 and 498.

388. The Cathedral of Santiago de Compostela constitutes one of the most significant monuments of Romanesque form-culture. Its importance, both in itself as well as in relation to the pilgrimage road to which in some way, at least, it constitutes the fountainhead, cannot be overstated. The architectural history of the cathedral, the successive interventions to which it was subjected in the course of the centuries, including the vast baroque program of two of its facades, has been the subject of great interest among art, architectural, as well as cultural and ecclesiastical historians. What follows is an abbreviated bibliography only of the subject.

A number of the earlier contributions have by now been largely superseded: Tormo-*Galicia*; Mayer-*románico*; CastilloLópez-*Galicia*; Camps-*románico*; Alcolea-*Santiago*. A few of the earlier works, on the other hand, continue to hold their seminal interest: so, in the first line, LópezFerreiro-*Santiago* 3·47–150 (with a 1975 re-edition in which only some of the subjects are treated: López Ferreiro-*Pórtico*); Mâle-*XII*, passim, always illuminating; Kingsley Porter-*Pilgrimage*, controversial but valuable; and GórMor-*románico*, often still sound. Conant-*Santiago*, and Moralejo-*Notas-*

Conant, a revision of the former, are essential instruments on the architectural history of the cathedral. Gaillard-*romane espagnole*, Durliat-*Pèlerinages*, Lyman-*Pilgrimage*, and Durliat-*Jacques* constitute instances of the new sound historic orientation that reaches to our own day. Finally, a large number of works treat particular aspects of the monumental ensemble: KingsleyPorter-*Leonesque*; Whitehill-*Date Santiago*; Deschamps-*Conques-Sernin*; Naesgaard-*Compostelle*; Moralejo-*fachada norte*; Durliat-*porte France*; Williams-*Spain Toulouse*; Moralejo-*portails cathédrale*; Moralejo-*Ars sacra*; BonetCorrea-*Jacques baroque*. There is also an unpublished dissertation, Ward-*Pórtico Gloria*.

389. It is not the Porta Francigena, the city gate, that is meant here (cf. above, n. 366), but rather the north portal of the transept.

390. Carré-*Coruña*, p. 965, gives the following dimensions: 94 m from the western facade, that of the *Obradoiro*, to the easternmost centerpoint of the Chapel of San Salvador, at the head of the chevet; 63 m from the facade of the *Azabachería* (north) to that of the Platerías (south); 24 m, the height from the pavement to the centerpoint of the vault of the main nave; and 32 m from the pavement to the summit of the dome of the crossing. The corresponding measurements of LópezFerreiro-*Santiago* (3:62–65) are slightly at variance with the above: 97 m, 65 m, and 22 m ("hasta unos 22 m.). Conant-*Santiago* (p. 50, nn. 2 and 3) on his part, measures 296 feet for the length, 218 feet for the width (the length of the transept) "from valve to valve," with 212 feet 10 inches for the net width. The variations in the above measurements are conditioned by the various reference points taken as base. Now, the *Guide* gives its measurements in *status hominis*, that is to say, in "height of man." To reckon this height I have calculated the proportional relations of the interior length of the main nave and of the transept, arriving for the figures in Carré-*Coruña* to a mean of 1.694 m, and for those in LópezFerreiro-*Santiago* to a mean of 1.748. Conant's cross nave measurements (p. 26 and p. 50, n. 4) give for the *status hominis* a value of 5.59 feet, that is to say, 1.7038 m. The variation in the figures must also be ascribed, apart from different reference points, to the elevation of the floor level and to the sagging vault.

391. Evidently, outside measurements are much more cumbersome to take. Conant-*Santiago* (p. 50, n. 5) provides outside length and width, but not height.

392. That is to say, one main nave, two transept naves, and six aisles below; and galleries or triforia above.

393. At the easternmost portion of the chevet, it is the largest of the radiating chapels of the ambulatory. It takes its name, San Salvador, the Holy Savior, from its altar. From the mid-fifteenth

century on, it also carried the title of its benefactor, Louis XI (1461–83), and it is called the Chapel del Rey de Francia. In 1447, while still a dauphin, the future Louis made the chapel the object of a large donation.

394. Moralejo-*imagen* (p. 41, n. 9, and passim) comments on the anthropomorphic terms used by the author of the *Guide* in his description of the cathedral: body, arms, laurel crowned head, members of the body, let alone the measurements given in human heights – all this suggests that the structure is conceived in anthropomorphic and anthropometric terms. Caucci-*Guida* (p. 118, n. 54) suggests, furthermore, a reading of the structure in terms of the Mystic Body of Christ. To these interpretative notions we may add still another concept, the relationship between micro- and macrocosm. Although such a metaphoric view of universal relationships attained a particularly forceful formulation only in the later Middle Ages and the Renaissance, their seed must have been already planted in the Romanesque age. The concept of hell in terms of an anthropoid complexion is part of such a view. *Laurea* is the name given to the ambulatory, for it surrounds the chancel as a laurel wreath (cf. Vielliard-*guide*, p. 87, n. 13). The term, apparently, is not found elsewhere (cf. Mortet-*architecture*, p. 399, n. 1).

395. The crossing.

396. Cf. n. 389 above.

397. *Ad ecclesie celum*, up to the "heaven" of the church, that is to say, the vault.

398. It is the most controversial *terminus technicus* in the entire text: it occurs several times, and twice in the particular combination *mediae cindriae*. Vielliard-*guide* (pp. 88–89, n. 3) proposes the relationship with a number of terms in romance languages – *cintre* in French, *cindria* in Catalan, *cimbra* in Castilian – and suggests the basic connotation of *arch*, from which the subsidiary meanings of supporting arch and hence support, prop, stanchion, reinforcement derive. This last term had been already proposed by É. Lambert (although it is not clear where) as the one that best fits the various passages in which the term occurs. To the historiography of the interpretations, the following must be said: the word does not figure in Du Cange-*Glossarium*. Bonnault-*Compostelle* (pp. 199-200) witnesses to *cindria* in a document of 1462 related to the construction of the cathedral of Rodez and interprets it as *moyens cintres* or *arcs*. Mortet-*architecture* (p. 399, n. 4) claims for the term an exclusive meaning. "...colonnes engagées dans les piliers, lesquelles supportent les arcs doubleaux sectionnant la voûte de forme cintrée." Conant-*Santiago* translates the term variously as "middle of the piers," "semi-cylindrical shafts," "cylindrical

shafts." M. Puig I Cadafalch proposes *demi-berceaux* (Vielliard-*guide, Addenda et corrigenda*, to p. 89). Her first five editions translate the term at this point as "renforts médians ou plutôt demi-berceaux." We ourselves have interpreted it here as "arch reinforcements." Vielliard-*guide*'s reasoning (p. 89, n. 3), looking for a single denotation for the term, is not necessarily correct.

In fact, *cindria* may refer to at least two architectural notions occasionally, but not always, overlapping: arch and support, variously employed by stonecutters and master masons. Two final points must be made in this regard: the author of the *Guide* is evidently not too familiar with the *termini technici* used in architecture; even more importantly, architectural terms were, during the Romanesque Middle Ages, greatly fluctuating and far from well established in both time and space. Such imprecision and lack of uniformity, however, should not be understood necessarily in negative terms: it was part of the framework of the jealously guarded secrets of the building crews, secrets that were rigorously handed down from father to son or from master to apprentice.

399. *Utreque magne naves* of the text is grossly misleading: what is meant here is the total width of the nave together with its two aisles, that is to say, the width from wall to wall.

400. Caucci-*Guida*, p. 119, translates erroneously *dodici e mezza*. LópezFerreiro-*Santiago* (3:62–65) executed quite precise measurements of the interior of the naves. The figures he has arrived at concerning the width of the main nave as well as that of the triple nave, that is to say, nave and two aisles, are the following: main nave – 9.74 m at the level of the long arm (*trascoro*) and 9.65 m in the transepts; triple nave – 19.64 m throughout; for the latter, Conant-*Santiago* (p. 50, n. 7) reckons an average of 64 feet 3 inches. Now, the measurements given by the *Guide* concerning the width of the *utreque magne naves* (see above, n. 399) as eleven and a half times a man's stature evidently correspond to the width of the triple nave (so, also, Moralejo-*Calixtinus* (p. 555, n. 4). The height of man, calculated upon the width of the triple nave – 19.64 : 11.5 = 1.7078 m (cf. n. 390 above), which roughly corresponds to the breakdown of the height of a man in palms: 1 palm = approximately 0.21 m, which gives 8 × 21 = 1.68 m (BravoLozano-*Guía*, p. 134, n. 197).

401. The fourteen piers on each side of the main nave do not seem to correspond to the reality of the present groundplan, nor to the "Plan in the Romanesque period" of Conant-*Santiago* (plate VIII); and it is questionable whether it ever did correspond to reality in the mid-twelfth century. From the west end of the nave, that is to say, the inner facade of what later became the Pórtico de la Gloria (completed in 1188), to the crossing, there are eleven piers. To this

figure one could add still the two of the crossing, or the two of the presbyterium which, due to the heavy baroque reconstruction, are not visible today but whose corresponding vault ribs are apparent: this would bring up the total to thirteen. Also, to the eleven of the long nave one could conceivably add both the piers of the crossing and those of the presbyterium: then we would come to a total of fifteen. (See, however, a possible objection in n. 405 below.) No solution though corresponds to the fourteen piers that the *Guide* proposes. The discrepancy has hitherto been little noticed.

402. *Adversus aquilonem* means towards the north; but it should be the west. Conant-*Santiago* (p. 50 and n. 8) of the same page, translates "designed as protection against the weather," which is far-fetched.

403. Neither is the word *ciborius* exempt from problems. Du Cange-*Glossarium*, s. v., and Mortet-*architecture*, p. 400 and passim, recognize the term as *baldachin*. Bonnault-*Compostelle* (pp. 199 and 204) translates it as *tympanon*, and Conant-*Santiago* (p. 50) as "arch." Vielliard-*guide* (pp. 89–90, n. 5) and Moralejo-*Calixtinus* (p. 555, n. to line 6) justly interpret the term as a vaulted passage-way, actually in our text two passage ways, that lead to the exterior double portal. Rather than to passage ways, the reference here is perhaps to the two inner vaulted bays on the short end of the north transept.

404. *In navibus...crucis* in the text: literally, in the naves of the cross, and perhaps, by extension, of the crossing.

405. The figure of twelve piers on each side comprises ten in the transept itself and two in the crossing. That is the reason why the piers of the crossing should not be taken into account when speaking of the piers of the main nave (see above, n. 401).

406. See n. 401 above. Vielliard-*guide* (pp. 90-91, n. 1) appropriately sees here an intended differentiation between *ciborius* and *portallus*. In point of fact though, the end-pier of each transept separates between the two bays and not between the two outer portals.

407. Above (cf. n. 394) the ambulatory was termed, in a language at once poetic and antropomorphic, a laurel wreath; now, that same ambulatory, or perhaps the ambulatory together with the chancel it surrounds (cf. Vielliard-*guide*, p. 91, n. 2; and Du Cange-*Glossarium*, s.v., "corona ecclesiae") is called a crown.

408. So, also, with some differentiation, at Saint-Sernin in Toulouse.

409. Or galleries. The denomination of the upper portion of the church as *palatium* (from Palatinum, the imperial hill in Rome) derives from the differentiation between *domus* or *villa* (a single

level dwelling), and *palatium* (a high-rise structure). One of the technological wonders offered by the large pilgrimage churches consisted precisely in the galleries or triforia running high above pavement level and all around the interior; these galleries are found in all five large pilgrimage churches on the way to Santiago (cf. above, n. 246), and they had, to be sure, a precisely-defined function: whenever the flow of pilgrims exceeded the capacity of the local welcoming infrastructures (hospices and hospitals), the tired wayfarers were given overnight facilities in the galleries.

410. The vaulting is of the half-barrel type.

411. Or middle arch reinforcement. See above, n. 399. The *duplices pilares*, double pillars but actually double columns, do not correspond to a pier below.

412. That is to say, in the galleries or triforia.

413. Or cross springers. *Cingule* in the text constitutes, though to lesser extent, another of the *termini technici* for architectural historians to wrestle with. Strap or belt in its first domestic meaning, the term came to signify a stone-belt or rib whose function was to reinforce the vault (Vielliard-*guide*, p. 91, n. 4, following Mortet-*architecture*, p. 400, n. 7). Both Bonnault-*Compostelle* (p. 199) and Conant-*Santiago* (p. 51) translate it simply, and inaccurately, as "arch"; É. Lambert (Vielliard-*guide*, p. 91, n. 4) reads *cingule* as an erroneous spelling for *singule* and translates it as "isolated columns"; Vielliard-*guide* (p. 91), appropriately, as *arcs doubleaux*; as Moralejo-*Calixtinus*, (p. 556) too with the Spanish equivalent *fajones*.

414. As in n. 413 above. *Columpne cindrie* is a variant of the former *medie cindrie*.

415. Cf. above, n. 409; and Vielliard-*guide*, pp. 92–93, n. 1: *dupliciter*, in the sense of two-storied or two-level structure. *Doblemente* in Moralejo-*Calixtinus* (p. 556) is not convincing.

416. In fact, a splendid view opens up from above: one may say indeed that any spatial appreciation of such and similar pilgrimage churches, any feeling for the exhilarating sense of space, volume, and massiveness, must necessarily include a view of the central naves from the height of the galleries. Cf. Kriss-*viator*, passim.

417. *In celum* in the text, that is to say, "in heaven": the macro-microcosmic relationship couched in a mystic language. Cf. above, n. 394.

418. Moralejo-*Calixtinus* (p. 556, n. to line 12) following the *Guide*, counts forty-three windows in the triforia, five all around the vault above the altar, and a total of fifteen in the five apsidal chapels. This makes indeed a grand total of sixty-three. LópezFerreiro-

Santiago (3:125) arrives at a total of 111 windows by considering the sixty-three given in the *Guide* as pertaining to the ground level only, and by adding to these the five around the vault above the altar and the forty-three of the galleries. His reasoning is questionable. I have checked myself the windows in the galleries and found the following: in the galleries of the main nave, eight on each side (many today blind), for a total of sixteen; in the galleries of the north transept, a total of thirteen (of which today four are blind); and in the galleries of the south transept, a total of eleven (of which five are blind). In the cul-de-four portion of the galleries (ovenshaped vault above and around the altar), furthermore, I have counted eight windows of which two are smaller ones. The grand total thus obtained, forty-eight, corresponds to the forty-three of the galleries plus the five around the altar for the forty-eight given by the *Guide*, though, to be sure, according to a different breakdown.

419. The three main portals will be described farther down with a luxury of details. See nn. 422–27.

420. Actually, door leaves.

421. Here too, the number of portals probably reflects numerological and symbolical concerns. Cf. above, n. 365.

422. At the northeastern corner of the north transept, the portal of Santa Maria once opened from the chapel of San Nicolás, through an intermediate passageway, into the church or chapel of Santa Maria de la Corticela (see above, n. 387). The chapel of San Nicolás has long been absorbed by the passage that leads to the Corticela, an ingress flanked presently by the Renaissance chapel of San Andrés and the Gothic chapel of the Espíritu Santo. Cf. for the seven minor portals, LópezFerreiro-*Santiago* 3:124–25 quoted in Caucci-*Guida*, pp. 101–21, n. 58. Herbers-Jakobsweg, p. 140, n. 285, has the portal of Santa Maria open between the two chapels of the eastern wall of the north transept, that is to say, the chapel of San Nicolás and the chapel of Santa Cruz, the Holy Cross (for the chapels, see nn. 497-98 below). The large number of chapels in the cathedral and the numerous transformations, as well as change of *titulus*, that many of them underwent at various periods subsequent to the Romanesque, makes the identification of the chapels as well as of the passageways and portals often hazardous and insecure.

423. The portal of the Via Sacra, or Holy Road, was, according to LópezFerreiro-*Santiago* 3:124–25, in the ambulatory, to the left of the chapel del Salvador, of the Saviour. In Gothic times it was replaced by the portal giving access to the chapel of Nuestra Señora la Blanca, Our Lady of White, known also as "de las Españas." Moralejo-*Calixtinus* (p. 557, n. to line 5) proposes a

different location identified with the walled-in doorway discovered by A. Kingsly Porter in 1934 between the apsidal chapels of San Juan Evangelista and San Bartolomé, formerly of Santa Fé, of the Holy Faith. Herbers-*Jakobsweg* (p. 140, n. 286) speaks of a still different location to be sought between the chapels of San Nicolás and Santa Fé. These, however, were not contiguous.

424. *De Sancto Pelagio.* According to LópezFerreiro-*Santiago* (3:124–25) this passage was used by the monks of San Pelayo or San Payo, formerly San Pedro de Antealtares (see above, n. 386). It corresponds to the present Puerta Santa, the Holy Door, to the right of the Chapel del Salvador. This is denied by Moralejo-*Calixtinus* (p. 557, n. to line 5) who, relying on J. Carro García, "La construcción de la actual Basílica," *Galicia* 4/19 (1935): 29, conjectures that this portal opened actually from what eventually became the Gothic chapel of Mondragón, to the right of the Puerta Santa.

425. That is to say, of the Chapter of Canons, for this portal provided a convenient access to and from their residence. The nearby Calle de la Conga, in a Gallego corruption, conserves the memory of such a functional relationship. The portal of the Canónica was in the south transept [given erroneously as north in LópezFerreiro-*Santiago* (3:124–25) and in Herbers-*Jakobsweg* (p. 141, n. 288)] opening from the actual baroque chapel of Nuestra Señora del Pilar. Moralejo-*Calixtinus* (p. 557, n. to line 5) places it, with further precision, between the two chapels on the east side of the south transept, those of San Martín and San Juan Bautista.

426. *De petraria,* that is to say, de la Pedrera, of the Stoneyard, is today the Puerta del Claustro, opening to the cloister, on the southwestern side of the cathedral. The name probably remembers the stonecutters working on the cloister, whose stoneyard was, at the time, precisely there (cf. LópezFerreiro-*Santiago* 3:124–25).

427. See previous note. This portal, cut in the fourth bay from the crossing on the south side of the main nave, opened also to the cloister (cf. LópezFerreiro-*Santiago* 3:124–25).

428. *De Gramaticorum scola.* Vielliard-*guide* (p. 95, n. 11) appropriately remarks concerning its name that there was probably a grammar school in the episcopal palace, as was frequent in the Middle Ages (cf. DíazDíaz-*escuela*). LópezFerreiro-*Santiago* (3:124–25) reports that this was the portal used by the prelates, and it was situated exactly vis-á-vis the former doorway (cf. n. 427 above), that is to say, on the north wall of the long nave.

429. A reference to the author's country. Cf. above, n. 31.

430. The Porta Francigena of the cathedral mentioned earlier (n. 389), at the very end of the Camino Francés.

431. We ignore the origin of this hospice for poor pilgrims at the north portal, or de la Azabachería (see below, n. 451), but we know that it was supported and perhaps restored by Diego Gelmírez (LópezFerreiro-*Santiago* 3:193, 4:145; Moralejo-*Calixtinus*, p. 379, n. to line 8; Jetter-*Hospitals*, p. 88). The shops of the *azabacheros* must have been included somehow in its courtyard. The importance of this hospice continued unabated until the time the Catholic Monarchs built the Gran Hospital Real to the north of the facade (1501–11 and subsequently). For the later history and final demolition of this hospice, cf. Moralejo-*Calixtinus*, p. 379, n. to line 8.

432. *Paradisus* in the text: cf. above and below nn. 380 and 443. Even today there is a sharp drop in the levels of the esplanade facing San Martín Pinario. In the eighteenth century the whole parvis as well as the portal were restructured and restyled in the baroque.

433. On this fountain, cf. LópezFerreiro-*Santiago*, 4:65-67, and Fletcher-*Gelmírez*, p. 177. It was meant as an important piece of urban development for which the old aqueduct had to be revamped. Demolished in the fifteenth century, a new fountain was erected at the south entrance facing the Portal de las Platerías. This still exists today.

434. *Parapsidis*, better *paropsis* (a dish or plate).

435. Probably a wild overstatement. There is a large vat or conch preserved in the cloister which Herbers-*Jakobsweg* (p. 142, n. 296) claims is the original from the north side. There are doubts concerning this attribution. At any rate, there is no place in it for such a bathing party.

436. That is to say, the base of the column was heptagonal and on each side of the heptagon, in vertical elevation, there was a square panel (cf. Vielliard-*guide*, p. 95 and n. 2 of the same page; López Ferreiro-*Santiago* 4:65–67; and Moralejo-*Calixtinus*, p. 558, n. 7). Conant-*Santiago* (p. 52) interprets the passage differently: "a bronze column of seven pieces fitted together." We find a similar columnar disposition on some Byzantine monuments, such as the celebrative columns on the central square in Ravenna.

437. Apart from their functional purposes, the lions might have responded to an eminently symbolic role: the four rivers of Paradise mystically transmuted into the Four Gospels that water the Ecclesia. Cf. Moralejo-*imagen*, p. 58.

438. There must have certainly been an outflow that led to an underground canal.

439. On prehistoric water cult and sanctuaries erected on the site of living water, see above, n. 204.

440. Bernard, perhaps the son of Bernard the Elder (see below, n. 562), treasurer of the Cathedral of Santiago at probably the most pregnant moment of its history, a multi-talented architect, sculptor, painter, expert in the mechanical arts as well as in calligraphy, must have been an exiting and powerful figure in the entourage of Diego Gelmírez. Apart from his concrete talents, Bernard was a great organizer and directly responsible, at least at given time periods, for the vast cathedral works. Bernard authored *Tumbo A*, the oldest and the most important collection of archival documents of the cathedral initiated in 1129. Bernard was also chancellor of Alphonso VII of León, the "Emperor" (1126–57). Cf. Vones-*Compostellana*, p. 497–99; and Herbers-*Jakobsweg*, p. 142, n. 298, for further bibliograhy on Alphonso VII. See also S. Portela Payos, "Anotaciones al Tumbo A de la Catedral de Santiago," *Biblioteca y Archivos Eclesiásticos (Santiago)* 2 (1949): 87–97; and further LópezFerreiro-*Santiago*, 4:172–74.

441. There was no natural water source at the site.

442. The reference is to the era of the Roman province of Hispania, which was reckoned from the year 38 BC and was in vigor until the later Middle Ages. The date corresponds to April 11, 1122.

443. *De paradiso* in the text: *parvis* in French and English derives from it (cf. above, n. 432). The term is applied at times to the porch, but more appropriately to the open space before the church, the *domus Dei*, in evocation of *gan eden*, the Garden of Eden, where Adam and Eve sinned and from which they were expelled. From such a mystic-ideological perspective, the access into the church was regarded as a concession granted only to the baptized. The topographic analogy is even more striking in cases where the parvis extends between the church and the baptistry (Parma, Pisa, etc.). Cf. also Caucci-*Guida*, p. 123, n. 62.

444. *Crusille piscium* in the text, a term which appears elsewhere too in the *Codex Calixtinus* [Whitehill-*Liber*, pp. 153 (the famous sermon *Veneranda dies*) and 273]. Moralejo-*Calixtinus*, p. 559, n. to line 4, and BravoLozano-*Guía*, p. 136, n. 210, misread Vielliard-*guide*, pp. 96–97, n. 3: she is not advocating the interpretation *crucecitas de pescados*. It is Conant-*Santiago* (p. 52, n. 4) who does so: "'Little crosses of fish' – conceivably cockle shells marked so, or made into, crosses." Du Cange-*Glossarium* knows *crusilla* as the diminutive of *crux, -cis*, in the sense of "little crosses." David-Jacques (2:54, n. 2) derives *crusilla* from the Latin *crusia* (Spanish *concha*, French *coquille*, English *cockle*) "shell" or "cockleshell"; hence *crusilla* (small shell).

The adoption of the cockleshell as emblem of Santiago as well as of his pilgrims must be traced back, first of all, to the general appeal that shells have exercised upon human imagination ever since prehistoric times. Children collect shells on the seashore, and so does everybody else. Second, Santiago de Compostela is at a short distance from the sea, and hence an association of St. James with shells that are found in such abundance on the beaches of the ocean seems only natural. Third, the tradition of Santiago holds that the beheaded body of the saint together with its severed head was placed in a boat, which charted miraculously its course from Joppa to Iria Flavia (Padrón) (see above, n. 153). Fourth, a particular pilgrimage tradition associates a miracle of St. James with the shells. A French knight drowning in the sea is pulled out by Santiago: the knight is all covered with shells. The thaumaturgic power of the cockleshell is otherwise attested in the miracle number 12 of Book 2 of the *Liber*. As it often happens in similar circumstances, once the diffusion of the Santiago shell became fairly extensive and its wearing by pilgrims common practice, symbolic meanings were attached to it. The most widespread of these relies on the notion that the Santiago shell is always represented with its convex side out and its grooves downwards: from here an analogy is made to the back of the hand and the fingers engaged in works of mercy. Paradoxically, the popular voice for the cockleshell, Latin *veneria*, Spanish *venera*, Portuguese and Gallego *vieira*, derives from *Venus, -eris*, on the strength of the goddess' own birth in the sea.

Shells were, of course, a much-traded commodity in Santiago and specifically at the two transept esplanades. Their commercialization was governed by episcopal as well as papal ordinances. LópezFerreiro-*Santiago* (5:38–40, 98, and Appendix, 109 and passim) and Moralejo-*Calixtinus* (p. 599, n. to line 4) speak of a specific regulation which, around 1200, limited the licensed merchants of cockleshells to a total of one-hundred of which twenty-eight were attached to the cathedral while the rest were independent. See for the bibliography on this famous symbol, (apart from López Ferreiro-*Santiago* 2:57–58, and VázquezParga-*pereg* 1:129–35) among the recent studies, Treuille-*Coquille*, CosteMess-*Coquille*, Cohen-*signa*, Cohen-*Pilgrimage*, Köster-*Pilgerzeichen-muscheln*, and Köster-*Pilgerzeichen*; see also pp. 57–59 above. *Intersigna* of the text is amended by Conant-*Santiago* (p. 52, n. 5) *in insignia*.

445. *Botas de vino* in Spanish: so Moralejo-*Calixtinus*, p. 559. Bonnault-*Compostelle*, p. 202, translates as *bous*, "a large wine flask."

446. And not "invocatory medals" as Conant-*Santiago*, p. 52, translates: cf. Vielliard-*guide*, p. 97, n. 5. Shoes were a fundamental practical implement of the pilgrims.

447. Latin *pera*, Italian *scarsella*, Provencal *sporta*, French *panetière* or *escarcelle*, Spanish *escarcela*. See above, p. 57, for its symbolic

significance; also, Herbers-*Jakobsweg*, pp. 64–65 and nn. 24–25 on p. 65.

448. Medicinal herbs of all sorts, which we see today too in provincial markets across Spain. On the whole, the list of the articles on display reflects present-day practices. Strangely, at this point at least, the *Guide* does not mention the *azabacheros* (see below, n. 451), most of whom were at the north portal.

449. This is the Camino Francés, the so-called French pilgrimage road itself outside the city and leading to, or being in the vicinity of, the Porta Francigena (cf. above, n. 366). Private initiative provided there the basic services for those who could afford them.

450. I could find no indication, even approximate, of the actual measurement meant here.

451. This is the Portal de la Azabachería (cf. Moralejo-*Calixtinus*, p. 379, n. to line 8; and n. 431 above) so called after the *azabache*, the obsidian, out of which figures of Santiago, cockleshells, as well as other insignia were carved and subsequently commercialized at this location. The portal facade here described is no longer extant. It was demolished in the eighteenth century and replaced by the present neoclassical one. Some of the original Romanesque reliefs have been inserted into the upper section of the Portal de las Platerías. The double entrance described here and thereafter parallels the two entrances of the Portal de las Platerías. For the hypothetic reconstruction of the north portal, see LópezFerreiro-*Santiago* 3:115–21; Moralejo-*fachada norte*; Durliat-*porte France*; and Moralejo-*portails cathédrale*.

452. If indeed so, then the disposition of the jamb structure of the north portal varies from the one we have at the Platerías which has been preserved to our day largely intact: there we have three upright shafts on the extreme right of the double portal, three on the extreme left, and five between the entrances: that is to say, there is one shaft in common to both entrances, and on the whole a grand total of eleven. If the description of the north portal given in the *Guide* is indeed faithful, then the two portal entrances on the north side were flanked on the level of the jambs by a total of thirteen columns. On the one hand, it seems strange to think that the two transept facades could have received such a different treatment at the formal level of the jambs; on the other, the thirteen shafts of the north portal do correspond to the symbolic representation of Christ with the College of the Apostles: the Lord, indeed, is represented above the central column as the subsequent text tells us (cf. n. 453 below as well as the bibliography of n. 451.

453. *Dominus in sede majestatis* in the text, in short, the *Maiestas Domini*, the Lord in Majesty. This relief is inserted now in the south facade, above the archivolts, in what is a large repository of

dismantled reliefs from the west and the north facades. Cf. Moralejo-*portails cathédrale*, pp. 93–94.

454. Probably, as if sustaining the mandorla around the enthroned Christ.

455. *Stricto sensu*, only Adam: though Eve too will be punished, it is Adam who bears the collective responsibility for the Fall. LópezFerreiro-*Santiago* (3:117, n. 1) reports that this relief had been inserted above the entrance door of a house in the Pitelos district of Santiago (cf. Vielliard-*guide*, p. 98, n. 1). Today it is in the museum of the cathedral (cf. Moralejo-*portails cathédrale*, pp. 94–95).

456. *In alia persona* in the text, meaning perhaps "in another effigy." This relief has been transferred to the south facade, above the left archivolt (cf. Vielliard-*guide*, p. 99, n. 2; and Moralejo-*portails cathédrale*, p. 95.

457. *In ciborio* in the text, here surely with the meaning of "tympanum."

458. Moralejo-*portails cathédrale* proposes, pp. 95–96, to identify this scene with two barely distinguishable figures above the left archivolt of the Portal de las Platerías.

459. The months of the year were represented in the Middle Ages in two modalities: the Labors of the Months and the Zodiacal Signs. It is the latter that we had on the north facade. Sagitarius, which represents November, is inlaid above the left archivolt of the facade of the Platerías. A fragment of Pisces, which represents February, is in the museum of the cathedral (Moralejo-*portails cathedrale*, p. 96); as are other fragments.

460. Common apotropaic motif, always symmetrically disposed.

461. We find the same arrangement at the Portal del Perdón of San Isidoro in León. Within the portal as a whole, Peter and James hold a privileged central position.

462. Of probable apotropaic meaning too. On the portal of the church of Santa María in Carrión de los Condes we have also four bull heads just under the lintel of the entrance. But in Carrión the bulls refer to the local story of the virgins saved by the redoubtable animals. It is not clear what could have been their raison d'être in the Cathedral of Santiago.

463. This is the Portal de las Platerías, that is to say, of the *plateros*, (the silversmiths), on the strength of their many shops found even today in the immediate vicinity of the portal. The sculptural program, as well as individual reliefs destined for this facade, respond to various stylistic resolutions among which the most significant has been traced back to one Esteban, master sculptor of the cathedral before the turn of the eleventh century and perhaps

THE PILGRIM'S GUIDE TO SANTIAGO

a little bit afterwards too. This same Esteban would subsequently become the master builder of the cathedral of Pamplona. On the jambs of the right doorway there is an important inscription that refers to the beginning of the cathedral in the year MCXVI of the Hispanic era (1078 of the Christian era), a date which, however, may be read also as MCXLI (1103): cf. n. 570 below; and Moralejo-*Calixtinus*, p. 570, n. to line 5. Needless to say, interpretations abound.

Apart from the original sculptures of this portal, on the upper section of the facade there are a large number of figures and fragments *de remploi,* reused, which originally were located on the other major portals and which, as a consequence of the baroque programs, have been dismantled and relocated above the Portal de las Platerías. The description that the author of the *Guide* offers of the original pieces of this portal does not always correspond to what we find there today. There have occurred along the centuries deteriorations, eliminations, replacements, and additions that have considerably altered the original program extant in the twelfth century. Moreover, many have maintained that the observations and descriptions of the author of the *Guide* have, at times, been simply inaccurate and erroneous (cf. LópezFerreiro-*Santiago*, 3:96–114, and 117; KingsleyPorter-*Pilgrimage* 2:16–17; GómMor-*románico*, p. 132; and Vielliard-*guide*, p. 101, n. 2). For a bibliography of pertinent works on the Portal de las Platerías, see the list given above at n. 388, and in particular Naesgaard-*Compostelle*, pp. 11–18; and Moralejo-*portails cathedrale*, pp. 98–100. Furthermore, see two more works not quoted above: Deschamps-*Languedoc Espagne* and Gaillard-*Compostelle León.*

464. This is the lower register of the right tympanum. *Dominica Traditio* of the text, the Betrayal of the Lord, may serve as a generic definition only. According to the details provided hereafter, which however do not always correspond to what we have presently, a considerable portion of the Passion cycle is represented here. At any rate, the Betrayal as such may be applied to the very first scene on the right only, a scene that represents a programmatic overlapping of the Kiss of Judas and the Detention of Christ.

465. This is the central scene with two executioners on the right side tying Christ to the column.

466. Once again two executioners in the act of whipping Christ. These are behind the Lord, to the left.

467. There are serious questions concerning this scene. An individual is seated in a sort of a wicker chair of the kind used for the graphic description of the paralytic healed by Christ. If this figure is indeed Pilate, then he is seated on the wrong throne. The person standing in front of him is unhaloed and in his pose and

complexion he looks rather like one of the guards, particularly close to the one tying the hands of Christ. If the seated figure is indeed Pilate, then the standing figure must be one of the guards, and the episode might thus convey Luke 23.13, "Pilate then summoned the chief priests and the leading men and the people." Another interpretation has also been advanced: the setting of the crown of thorns (Matthew 27.27–31; Mark 15.16–20). Two further points of interest must be mentioned: on the extreme left there is still another scene which looks like one of the miracles of Christ, the Healing of the Blind: this might have been a scene inserted later from another portal; and whether we have a Pilate or the Crown of Thorns scene, the episodes are out of accepted order: customarily the sequence progresses from left to right and starts with the Kiss and the Detention. In fact, the Adoration of the Magi above has the Magi enter from the left (cf. Naesgaard-*Compostelle*, pp. 11–17 and 58–60; and Moralejo-*portails cathédrale*, p. 99).

468. The left portion of the upper register of the tympanum is chipped away and, on the whole, in a lamentable condition. Only two of the three Magi, in genuflected pose, are visible. The star is just above and between the two Magi. There are at least two, and perhaps even three angels, though not all of them belong to the Magi episode. Perhaps the angel flying in the center of the scene is the "admonishing" angel of the *Guide*; the one on the extreme right, on the other hand, just above the scene of the Kiss and Detention, seems to bear a crown of martyrdom in his hands.

469. Of these four figures, only one is an apostle, St. Andrew, on the right jamb of the left entrance; the figure facing him is generally identified as Moses; the one on the left jamb of the right entrance, is perhaps the High Priest Melchizedek; and, finally, facing the latter, there is a figure of a woman with a lion cub, originally from the north portal (cf. Vielliard-*guide*, p. 101, n. 2; Moralejo-*portails cathédrale*, p. 100; and Durliat-*Jacques*, pp. 339–40 and 349).

470. The scene of the Three Temptations of Christ on the left tympanum, from a different atelier than the tympanum of the Betrayal (Naesgaard-*Compostelle*, p. 16) is disposed on both the lower and the upper registers of the tympanum.

471. The figure of Christ in the extreme left position seems to correspond to the Temptation of the Kingdoms of the World (on the mountain). The other two temptations are arranged in a vertical sequence farther to the right. The order of the Temptations given in the *Guide* (Temple, Bread, Kingdoms) does not correspond either to the order in Matthew 4.1–10 (Bread, Temple, Kingdoms) or to that in Luke 4.13 (Bread, Kingdoms, Temple); also, it is questionable whether it fits at all the order on the tympanum.

472. Matthew 4.11. Only one of the angels is presently visible.

473. Above the jamb figures, in the corners just below the bottom of the tympana.

474. Above the central column of the portal. Probably added after 1120 only (Naesgaard-*Compostelle*, p. 17).

475. The text is somewhat confusing at this point: "in introitu dextrali, scilicet ad dexteram" is rather repetitive, for it does not intend to say that five columns are to the right of the right entrance, but that there are altogether five columns at the right entrance, to the right of the central column; and the same for the left entrance. For each doorway there are thus three columns on the outer side and three on the inner side, while the central column, between the two doorways, is common to both. The middle column as well as those in extreme right and left positions are of marble and bear superimposed human figures on three registers. These figures are, in all certainty, prophets and apostles, though their more precise identification, apart from St. Peter and perhaps of Moses, is problematic. The traditional differentiation between prophets and apostles – the former with scrolls or phylacteries and the latter with books – is not maintained here. The four middle columns are of granite and are twisted. The four last ones are also of granite but plain.

476. This striking figure has been variously interpreted as the personification of luxury or lust, or perhaps a metaphor for the great whore of Babylon, "the harlot who rules enthroned beside abundant waters" (Apocalypse 17.1). Moralejo-*portails cathédrale*, p. 98, attempts to find a correlation with Eve, "the mother of death." Be that as it may, however, it seems certain that the designation it gets in the *Guide* as "the adulterous woman" is nothing but a metaphor, rendered the more poignant by the final rhetorical exclamation.

477. In reality, above the two archivolts of the tympana, for what follows is on the upper facade proper of the portal. This portion of the facade was used – until as late as the nineteenth century (Durliat-*Jacques*, p. 340–42) – as a kind of repository or collection gallery for sacred art that for one reason or another had been removed from its original location. Little wonder, therefore, that we find scarce authentic correspondence between the *Guide*'s description and the present state of the facade.

478. The Christ figure we presently have in the very middle of the facade is a Compostela version of a Gothic modeling from the early thirteenth century (Durliat-*Jacques*, p. 341): it came to replace the one described by the *Guide*. Peter, on the other hand, is still on the facade, but not at his assigned place, immediately to the left of the Lord (if the author of the *Guide* speaks indeed of the point of

view of Christ!) but close to the far left corner of the gallery of images. The dimensions of Peter, no less than those of some other apostolic figures on the facade, give us the parameters for the original figure of James the Greater: the figure we have to the right of Christ, between two pruned trees that the *Guide* calls cypress (Mâle-*XII*, p. 293), was, to be sure, part of a Transfiguration scene of the original west facade and came to replace the Santiago of the south facade in the last third of the twelfth century, in the wake of the completion of the Portal de la Gloria by Master Mateo in 1188. There is also a hypothesis according to which the transferral of at least some of the reliefs could have occurred earlier (cf. below, n. 480).

479. These are still in place, one to the right and one to the left of each archivolt.

480. This is the principal portal of the cathedral. All that follows in this description was demolished in the last third of the twelfth century at the time of the erection of the Pórtico de la Gloria. Most of the sculptural pieces got lost; some became reused; some are preserved otherwise. Moralejo-*portails cathédrale* (pp. 100–103) surmises that the original Romanesque portal had never been actually completed; subsequent to the popular insurgence of 1117 against Queen Urraca and the ecclesiastical prelates, as well as the ensuing rampage, destruction and fire in the cathedral, the reliefs of the west portal might have been, at least in part, dismantled and transferred to the south portal (Conant-*Santiago*, p. 25, and n. 3 on the same page). It has been remarked that the *Guide*'s description of the Transfiguration is not really factual and concrete, and relies mostly on the corresponding biblical passages (Matthew 17.1–9, and in particular 2–3; and Luke 9.28–36, and in particular 31). During the general baroque interventions in the cathedral in the eighteenth century and the construction of the magnificent facade of El Obradoiro (1738–50), some further Romanesque sculptural work must have conceivably been removed from the facade.

481. Note the author's hesitance to engage in actual description.

482. The Transfiguration is usually a two-level composition with Christ flanked by Moses and Elias on the upper level, and the three apostles, – Peter, James and John – on the lower one. There are, however, twelfth-century tympanum compositions in which, due to space considerations, the whole scene takes place on a single level (Charité sur Loire). We do not know for sure where the exact location of the Transfiguration was on the facade. We only know that this portal too had two entrances and hence, with all certainty, two tympana. The sheer size of St. James on the south portal, however, which, as we have seen, belonged to the

Transfiguration of the main portal, precludes a complex scene on a tympanum that could not have been much larger than any of the tympana of the south portal. It stands to reason, therefore, to conjecture that the Transfiguration, the central iconographic program on the facade, was located above the tympanum.

483. Represented, probably, by a hand emerging from the clouds.

484. This figure too, horned and climbing out of a cloud, appears on the south portal, though it is not mentioned by the *Guide*.

485. Today on the south portal.

486. The use of the future in the text, *habiture sunt*, is probably indicative of the fact that not all of them were raised at the time. The left tower of the west facade was, on the whole, never completed.

487. The north portal.

488. The four towers of the transept facades were the smallest and the shortest (cf. Conant-*Santiago*, pl. IV).

489. These were extremely large, serving later as base for the large baroque facade of *El Obradoiro*.

490. *Due super singulas vites*: really meaning, one above each of the two corkscrew staircases. For *vites*, see Du Cange-*Glossarium*, s. v.; and Moralejo-*Calixtinus*, p. 563, n. to line 16. LópezFerreiro-*Santiago* (3:94 and n. 2 of the same page) located the staircases, and hence the towers that once were above them, in the corners formed by the transept and the main triple nave of the cathedral, that is to say, at the two western corners of the crossing. With all probability, at those points there were stairs both descending to the old cathedral and ascending into the towers.

491. This was a lantern tower, later replaced by a dome.

492. This seems to be an overstatement. Conant-*Santiago* (p. 54, n. 4) states that "in the walls, only the facing is of cut stone, the vault is...of rubble, and the core of the rest of the building...as well." By now, the cut stones on the exterior face of the walls are considerably deteriorated.

493. Medieval frescos usually executed with a single layer of plaster or intonaco.

494. In the text, *teolis et plumbo*. Cf. Du Cange-*Glossarium*, s. v. *teolica* from *tegula* for "roof" (Moralejo-*Calixtinus*, p. 563, n. to line 21). LópezFerreiro-*Santiago*, 3:140–41, interprets *teolis* as "roofslates." The *Historia compostelana*, p. 201, reports that a considerable portion of the roof of the cathedral was covered with wood planks and straw, *miricis et tabulis*. Should we understand here thatched roof as used until recently in Cebrero? [Used now again. (Ed.)]

495. Reinforces, on the level of various aspects of the cathedral, what had been suggested earlier concerning the towers (cf. n. 486 above).

496. There is no reason to translate it as "chapels" (Conant-*Santiago*, p. 55; Vielliard-*guide*, p. 106, n. 1).

497. The nine altars that are being listed here starting with that of San Nicolás, correspond to the five chapels that open from the ambulatory and the four on either side of the east wall of the transept. The altar of San Nicolás, dedicated in 1102, has long disappeared: it was located in what today is the passageway to the Corticela (see n. 387 above). St. Nicholas is, of course, one of the most popular saints in the Mediterranean countries. Bishop of Myra, Anatolia, his remains were the object in 1087 of a famous *furta sacra* that took them to Bari in southern Italy. Perhaps due to his specific role as patron of travelers and pilgrims, he ended up playing an important role in the city of Santiago. He is also the patron of the University of Compostela (cf. Moralejo-*Calixtinus*, p. 564, n. 6). As Vielliard-*guide* (p. 106, n. 2) appropriately suggests, a specific study of the original Romanesque chapel and altar assignments would be more than justified.

498. The altar of Santa Cruz, the Holy Cross, together with its chapel, became superseded in the early sixteenth century by that of the Concepción or the Prima (Moralejo-*Calixtinus*, p. 564, n. to line 6). Vielliard-*guide* (pp. 106–7, n. 3) conjectures that a fragment of the *lignum crucis* (literally, the Wood of the Cross, that is to say, the True Cross) might have been venerated in the chapel. Tradition maintains that Pope Calixtus II presented the Sanctuary of Cebrero (see pp. 285–86) with a fragment of the *lignum crucis*; he might have presented the Cathedral of Compostela with another fragment (Vielliard-*guide*, pp. 106–7, n. 3).

499. The altar and chapel of Santa Fe, St. Foy, was also rededicated in the sixteenth century to San Bartolomé. The chapel, however, underwent only minimal transformations (Moralejo-*Calixtinus*, p. 564, n. to line 5). St. Foy, virgin and martyr, is, of course, one of the most popular saints on the pilgrimage route to Compostela. See pp. 241–44.

500. The chapel of San Juan Evangelista also became considerably amplified in the sixteenth century, though its original Romanesque structure is, in part, still preserved. Santa Susana is its new titular saint. St. John the Evangelist, brother of Santiago, needs hardly a justification for being included among the saints of the cathedral.

501. On the chapel of San Salvador, the Holy Savior, today of the Rey de Francia, the French King, see above, n. 393. Its location bears a triple emphasis and a double centralization in the economy

of the basilica: it is the easternmost chapel; originally the largest one; and it is flanked by the chapels of the two apostles who, together with James the Greater, constitute the prestigious inner circle of the College of Apostles. Furthermore, Peter, James and John also appear on the very facade of the cathedral, in the Transfiguration (see above, nn. 478, 480, and 482).

502. The chapel of San Pedro, the Prince of the Apostles, with its altar, dedicated in 1102, has kept its original Romanesque structure. It has repeatedly changed its allegiance: in the sixteenth century it was known as the Chapel of Doña Mencía de Andrade, and today, as that of Nuestra Señora de la Azucena – of the Lily or of the Magistral (following Moralejo-*Calixtinus*, p. 564, n. to line 6).

503. The chapel and altar of San Andrés, Peter's brother, the last of the apse, was demolished and absorbed into the large baroque chapel of the Virgen del Pilar (1711–22) or of the Monroya (Moralejo-*Calixtinus*, 564, n. to line 6).

504. The chapel and altar of San Martín, on the south transept, was, as that of San Andrés, also absorbed into the chapel of the Pilar in the early eighteenth century. In the early twelfth century, the relics of San Fructuoso, archbishop of Braga in the seventh century, were translated to Santiago, also a *furta sacra,* and deposited in the chapel of San Martín which thence was also known as chapel of San Fructuoso (Herbers-*Jakobsweg,* p. 149, n. 334). St. Martin, needless to say, was among the most famous saints in general and on the pilgrimage road in particular. See also pp. 257–59.

505. The altar and chapel of San Juan Bautista, the last of the nine altars in the radiating chapels or on the east wall of the transept, and the second in the south transept, also fell victim of the vast baroque redecoration of the early eighteenth century: in its place the Puerta Real or Quintana was opened (cf. Sánchez/Barreiro-*Santiago* 1:93, 97, 99–100, 110; LópezFerreiro-*Santiago* 3:138).

506. This was only an altar, and not a chapel. Its location was on the level of the colonnade that separates the chancel from the ambulatory towards the east. That is the reason that its position is defined as being between the altar of Santiago – the high altar of the cathedral – and that of San Salvador, the central easternmost chapel. On Mary Magdalene, see above nn. 206 and 208, as well as pp. 259–61.

507. It is not clear where the faithful would be situated for these masses: perhaps in the ambulatory around.

508. The triforium or gallery of the basilica, as pointed out in n. 409 above, served also as night shelter for pilgrims in times of great crowds. Vielliard-*guide,* p. 107, nn. 9 and 10, proposes the thesis that the three altars of the gallery might have been located

on the inner side of the west facade, in part relying on a Carolingian tradition demanding one or more altars dedicated to angels, and in particular to St. Michael, at that side of the church. But, why were these altars located towards the west? I propose the following: the archangels, and so Michael, might have conceivably been connected to general notions of guardianship of the church. The sinners, the penitents, and the catechumens, confined to the parvis of the church beyond its west end, had to be prevented from unduly entering the house of the Lord; for this task, again, the archangels were highly qualified. As to the other altars, these must have simply followed suit. Cf. also, for different views, J. Vallery-Radot, "Notes sur les chappelles hautes dédiées à saint Michel," *Bulletin monumental* 88 (1929): 453–78; and Williams-*Camino*, p. 272. Conant-*Santiago* (p. 55) thinks that the three altars were located "in the apse gallery, and above the portals."

509. It is not clear which San Benito, Benedict, is meant here: whether the one of Nursia (Norcia in Umbria), the founding father of western monasticism (480–543), or the one of Aniane, the great reformer of French monastic discipline in France (c. 750–821). The former is by far the more celebrated; but the latter is connected to Saint-Guilhelm-le-Désert and hence to the pilgrimage road to Compostela. There are other alternatives too.

510. As to St. Paul, he is apostle *sensu lato* only: considered as the Apostle of the Gentiles, we find him often on the roster of the College of the Apostles as the replacement for Judas Iscariot. As to St. Nicholas of Myra/Bari, he has already one of the transept chapel-altars dedicated to him. It seems unlikely, but not impossible, that a second altar could have also been dedicated to him within the essentially nonliturgical ambiance of the triforium used as sleeping quarters for the pilgrims (cf. n. 409 above). For further arguments in favor of Nicholas of Bari, based on the use of the responsory for St. Nicholas on the feast of the Apostle Santiago, cf. BravoLozano-*Guía*, p. 139, n. 224. There is, however, a second lesser-known St. Nicholas of Trani, a coastal city north of Bari, a saintly figure who had some fame among seamen. A late twelfth-century bronze door, by Barisanus, is dedicated to him [W. Melczer, *La Porta di Bronzo di Barisano da Trani a Ravello*, (Cava de' Tirreni, 1984) p. 116, n. 2]. This St. Nicholas was also a bishop and, most importantly for us, was called *pellegrino*, pilgrim. This might be the reason for having an altar dedicated to him, precisely, within the sleeping quarter of the pilgrims.

511. The reference, I take, is to the chapel of the twelfth- and early thirteenth-century episcopal palace adjacent to the north tower of the west facade.

512. Practice from early Christian to later medieval times dictated that a relic of relevance be placed under the particular altar assigned to it, in precisely determined vertical orientation to the center of the altar slab. Such a spatial connection between relic and altar assured a two-way ideologico-theological relationship: the relic was granted a mystic participation in the eucharistic mystery; and the eucharistic mystery was attested by the living presence of the relic. The witnessing to the eucharistic mystery finds a correlative in the martyr-saint's *confessio* – his acknowledgment of Christ immediately preceding his martyrdom proper. And the *confessio*, at its turn, is the paleo-Christian term used for the *martorion*, the reliquary tomb, and ultimately for the receptacle hollowed out in the altar slab for the relic (cf. WW-*Kirchenlexikon* 3, s. v.).

513. "Jacet, arca marmorea reconditum, in obtimo arcuato sepulcro" in the text. For terms similar to *arca marmorea*, cf. Moralejo-*Calixtinus*, pp. 392 and 394. LópezFerreiro-*Santiago* (1:161–73 and 287–309) argues for a connection with Galician *mámoas* (tombs); Conant-*Santiago* (p. 55, n. 3) calls it, inexplicably, "imaginary"; Plötz-*Jacobus* (pp. 99–104) finds a relationship with *achaia marmarica*; cf. also Williams-*Camino*, p. 274.

514. See above, pp. 2–3.

515. On Theodemir, bishop of Iria Flavia (800–847), cf. López Ferreiro-*Santiago* 2:11–20 and 27–28; subsequent to the discovery of the tomb of Santiago and the foundation of the city of Santiago de Compostela in the first third of the ninth century under Alphonso II the Chaste (789–842), bishop of Santiago. Theodemir's sepulchral inscription has recently been found in the cathedral (cf. DíazDíaz-*calixtino*, p. 16, n. 7).

516. It is not quite clear why Theodemir would have liked to move it. One plausible explanation is that he might have wished to effect a *translatio* to Iria Flavia, the place of his bishopric, and once this proved, for some reason, impossible, he moved the bishopric to Santiago.

517. A passage parallel to two others we have found in chap. 8 above, concerning the life and the destiny of the relics of St. Giles (pp. 98–102) and St. Leonard, (pp. 105–7). Cf. also Herwaarden-*Jacobus*, p. 112, n. 109, on places with claims of possessing some relic of the saint. On the presence of relics in Saint-Sernin of Toulouse and elsewhere, cf. LópezFerreiro-*Santiago* 2:20–29.

518. Candles were particularly important objects in the economy of churches and especially of large reliquary churches. Candle craftmanship, both in wax and in tallow, was one of the most important trades along the route. Offerings of candles were quite common, and often enough gigantic candles, whose weight matched the weight of the individual on whose behalf the

particular saint was invoked, were donated to churches and sanctuaries. I myself have seen some such candles in sanctuaries devoted to the *Virgen Peregrina* in southern Galicia.

519. The small altar itself becomes a relic: appropriately so, on the strength of its proximity to another relic, the earthly remains of Santiago. Cf. pp. 1–7 above.

520. That is to say, based on the calculations of n. 400 above, 1 palm = 0.21 m, $1.05 \times 2.64 \times 1.54$ m. The altar is large and particularly wide. The twelfth-century altar of Saint-Sernin for instance, which seems an appropriate comparison, is 2.23 m long by 1.34 m wide.

521. As the small altar becomes a relic (cf. n. 519) so the large one turns into a reliquary. We have occasionally instances of such procedure: a major example, though a late one, is Bernini's bronze *Cathedra Petri* enclosing the early Christian ivory throne of Peter. LópezFerreiro-*Santiago* (1:307–9 and 277–85) as well as Moralejo-*Calixtinus* (p. 566, n. to line 5), whom I follow here, studied the problem of the altars. They recognize three successive monuments. Of the first altar little has come down to us: the excavations of 1878 at the tombs of the disciples in the cathedral brought to light fragments of a granite column and two marble slabs that might have belonged to this first altar. A second altar (perhaps a pre-Romanesque) was later built. We do not know whether this second altar did also enclose the first one, though probably it did. Finally, Diego Gelmírez, in the course of his general restoration works, erected in 1105 the third altar here described, at which point the second altar was transferred to the church of San Pelayo de Antealtares (cf. above, n. 386). For a different interpretation, cf. Herbers-*Jakobsweg*, p. 151, n. 345.

522. For the antependium – altar front, see below nn. 525–33. LópezFerreiro-*Santiago* (3:236) offers a reconstruction of the altar with its silver antependium and ciborium. Ambrosio de Morales, the seventeenth-century librarian and archivist of the cathedral, seems to confirm the above (LópezFerreiro-*Santiago* 3:231–39). The silver antependium was melted down at the end of the seventeenth century, at a time when the one that still exists today was executed (Vielliard-*guide*, p. 111, n. 1).

523. The liturgical cloth for the altar is calculated so that on the sides it hangs over about 94 cm, stopping 10.5 cm before ground level, and on the front and back it hangs over only 21 cm.

524. This *paliotto* or frontal, the cover for the altar front, of 147×273 cm, is calculated so that it rests on the altar surface to a depth of 40 cm, while on each side it overhangs by about 10 cm. Otherwise, it covers totally the altar front.

THE PILGRIM'S GUIDE TO SANTIAGO

525. Early and high medieval altar fronts, antependia, belong, next to the reliquaries, to some of the most splendidly executed and lavishly decorated art works that have come down to us across the centuries. The gold and silver plated, embossed, partly cast, bejewelled, niello-filled, enamelled altar fronts are among the highest realizations of medium-sized, non-carvable figural representations. The golden antependium of Aachen or of Milan and the silver antependium of Città di Castello are able to provide us with an idea of the splendor that the silver altar front of Santiago must have irradiated in its day. The section heading of the *Guide* speaks of silver alone; but the text discusses the noble metals in term of gold and silver: certain cast portions might have been executed in gold.

526. The text reads *in quo sunt*. Gramatically, *quo* refers to the antecedent *tronus*, but in a wider sense it may refer to the altar front as a whole. It does not make sense to speak of the elders "in the throne": hence, "around," or "surrounded by."

527. Apocalypse 4.4 (Jerusalem Bible) reads: "Around the throne in a circle were twenty-four thrones, and on them I saw twenty-four elders sitting...." The Apocalypse does not mention right or left.

528. Apocalypse 5.8. The phials are interpreted by some Church Fathers as receptacles for the gathering of the condensated prayers of the faithful.

529. Apocalypse 4.3 and 4.6. This is the *Maiestas Domini* composition – the Lord in Majesty – which rigorously demands that the Evangelists, in their animal symbols (tetramorph; described in Apocalypse 11.6), be placed in unmediated proximity to the throne of the Lord: that is to say, there is nothing between the throne and the tetramorph but the mandorla of light. The elders of the Apocalypse, therefore, must be located outside the *Maiestas Domini* representation, and not on the mandorla around Christ. In the reconstruction of Moralejo-*Ars sacra* (p. 238, fig. 2) the elders are in the mandorla. See the description of the scene in Moralejo-*Ars sacra*, pp. 204–10.

530. Such a disposition we find, for instance, on the early twelfth-century tympanum of Carennac.

531. Under "flowers," the author of the *Guide* might mean phitomorphic, that is to say, plant motives in general.

532. For Diego Gelmírez, see above, pp. 22–23. The inscription provides the clue for the dating of the work. As Gelmírez was elected to the episcopal dignity in 1100 and was consecrated in 1101 (Vielliard-*guide*, p. 111, n. 3; and Moralejo-*Calixtinus*, p. 2, n. to line 1, and p. 567, n. to line 5) LópezFerreiro-*Santiago* (1:307–9) proposes the year 1105 for the altar front. Herbers-*Jakobsweg* (p.

153, n. 348) arrives at different dates: 1098, 1099, and 1103 respectively.

533. The 75 silver marks correspond (cf. LópezFerreiro-*Santiago*, 3:234) to *arroba y media*, that is to say, some 17 kg silver. The 75 marks, however, are the total expense for the work, not merely the cost of the silver. There is also gold, possibly jewels, enamel, as well as labor, no matter how poorly paid. But even taking into consideration 17 kg of silver for the front alone, that seems hardly adequate to cover such a vast surface including figures at least the heads of which were cast metal (similar to the technique used on the reliquary casquet of San Millán de la Cogolla).

534. Alphonso VI (1072–1109), king of León and Castilla, and his son-in-low Count Raymond of Bourgogne, later of Galicia, brother of Pope Calixtus II, first husband of Doña Urraca, daughter of Alphonso VI (cf. above pp. 16–18; and farther Moralejo-*Calixtinus*, p. 567, n. to line 8, and Herbers-*Jakobsweg*, p. 153, n. 349). Vielliard-*guide* (p. 113, n. 1) identifies the king with Alphonso VII, el Batallador, who is also Alphonso I of Aragón. The king and the court are relegated to the bottom of the inscription as a temporal frame only for the work of Gelmírez.

535. *Cimborius* in the text, here in the accepted meaning of "baldachin." For attempts at a reconstruction of the ciborium, extant until the later fifteenth century, cf. LópezFerreiro-*Santiago* 3:236; and Moralejo-*Ars sacra*, pp. 210–21 and fig. 5.

536. LópezFerreiro-*Santiago* (3:236) interprets the paintings and drawings as enamel and niello work.

537. Square in its ground plan. These are the usual specifications of the ciboria from the early Christian period on: particularly important instances that have fortunately come down to us are the ciboria in Sant'Apollinare in Classe in Ravenna and those in Rome – San Clemente and San Paolo fuori le Mura.

538. That is to say, the intrados of the vault.

539. Paul mentions the three well-known Theological Virtues in 1 Corinthians 13.13; and then, in Galatians 5.22–23, he speaks of nine other virtues which, *stricto sensu*, are the "fruits of the Spirit." The latter are the Virtues of the Holy Ghost here represented in the form of female personifications. For somewhat different views, cf. Moralejo-*Ars sacra*, p. 214, n. 84; and Herbers-*Jakobsweg*, p. 153, n. 352.

540. In the Byzantine fashion; as we find such iconography, for instance, in San Vitale in Ravenna. By "summit" is meant the center of the vault.

541. A well-known image of the Lamb of God, but never, as far as I remember, on a throne, rather, in a roundel of wreath as, for

instance, in the Mausoleum of Galla Placidia in Ravenna or, closer to our interests, on the Portal del Cordero in San Isidoro, León. The *tronum* of the text may be a metaphorical designation only.

542. That is to say, eight. That number is otherwise too habitual in Byzantine art: so the prophets/apostles of Galla Placidia in Ravenna.

543. In the spandrels above the capitals.

544. Also in the spandrels. *Stricto sensu,* only one is a prophet, in fact, the greatest prophet of the Old Testament – Moses; the others are the famous Three Patriarchs of the Hebrew nation who often appear as a prefiguration of the Trinity: so, for instance, on the twelfth-century bronze door of Bonanno in Monreale [W. Melczer, *La Porta di Bonanno a Monreale* (Palermo, 1987) pp. 112–14].

545. The *rotulos* are the phylacteries or scrolls which, in an old iconographic tradition, are assigned to prophets. It is not clear to what prophecies the reference here is: there are indeed some doubts concerning the identity of the three patriarchal figures. It cannot be excluded that the author of the *Guide,* seeing phylactery-holding figures, thought of prophets and then assigned names at random without consulting the inscriptions, confusing thereby prophets with patriarchs. Figures such as Isaiah, Ezekiel, Zechariah, Micah, and others are the ones usually quoted for their messianic prophecies subsequently interpreted by Christian exegetes as referring to Christ. The disposition of the figures – prophets on the sides and angels on the front and back – is also unusual, though possible.

546. *Per circuitum* in the text. It could be interpreted as signifying literally "in circle," or, in a generic sense, "seated round about." Conant-*Santiago* (p. 56) and we too have opted for the latter; Caucci-*Guida* (p. 130) for the former (*in cerchio*); Vielliard-*Guide* (p. 113) and Herbers-*Jakobsweg* (p. 155) also for the latter, but more outspokenly (*tout autour du ciborium* and *rund um das Ziborium* respectively). Henceforth the text will speak of "sides," confirming the generic meaning assigned to *per circuitum,* and determining the square-based alternating truncated pyramids and parallelepipeds that form the outer roof line of the ciborium.

547. Moralejo-*Ars sacra* (p. 218) draws a parallel to the illumination on fol. 4 of the *Codex* of Compostela. Such was, anyhow, the standard representation of apostles in the Romanesque period, cf. W. Melczer, *La Porta di Bronzo di Barisano da Trani a Ravello* (Cava de' Tirreni, 1984), pp. 95–110.

548. *In coopertura vero desuper* in the text. These seem to be on the highest register of the roofing, just underneath the silver ball. There are, however, some questions here: cf. below, n. 552. Moralejo-*Ars sacra,* pp. 221–23, notes the similarity of the language

used by the author of the *Guide* both in the description of the portal of the Platerías and in that of the ciborium.

549. The evangelists seem to be located on the corners of the roofline, above the level of the apostles.

550. *Propriis similitudinibus* in the text, that is to say, in their tetramorphic image.

551. The *Historia Compostelana* (I, xviii, in Flórez-*Sagrada* 20:52) speaks of the *Cibolium* as made of *auro argentove*. From here that Vielliard-*guide* (p. 114, n. 2) and Herbers-*Jakobsweg* (p. 155, n. 354) interpret *depictus* as enamel work; Moralejo-*Ars sacra* (p. 212), on the other hand, conceives of it also as painted wood. Nor should it be excluded that the structural portion of the ciborium might have been built, as usual, in stone and marble; if so, then the intrados of the vault might have been frescoed.

552. There is a major problem here: this triple arcade seems to rest on a triangular base – how to explain otherwise the triple orientation? God the Father is represented oriented towards the west, the main nave; if the other two arches are oriented as described, then the three arches either do not form a closed triangle, which is odd, or they form a rectangular triangle two sides of which, with the Father and the Holy Spirit, are at right angles to each other, while the side with Christ facing towards the south-east is the hypothenuse of the triangle – and this is no less odd. Conant-*Santiago* (p. 183, n. 2) refers to some discrepancy in the orientation of the present cathedral if compared to that of the ninth-century church, but that problem has no bearing on the orientation of the triple arch on the ciborium. Whether God the Father and Christ are standing or enthroned, in either case in a niche, is another problem.

553. Common symbol of the universal dominion of Christianity.

554. As in Isaiah 11.2–3: wisdom, understanding, counsel, fortitude, knowledge, piety, and fear of the Lord. These Gifts are intended for the sanctification of those who receive them.

555. *Balani* in the text. My translation follows Vielliard-*guide*, p. 115, who relies on E. Forcellini, *Totius Latinitatis Lexicon* (Padua, 1864–67); Moralejo-*Calixtinus* (p. 568, n. to line 26) proposes *mirobalano* on questionable grounds.

556. The Gifts of the Holy Spirit are superimposed thus upon the Twelve Apostles, one on each two. It is a convenient overlapping of two basic theologico-historic notions.

557. Alphonso I el Batallador, the Warlike, king of Aragón and Navarra (1104–34).

558. Perhaps in the early 1130s (Conant-*Santiago*, p. 57, n. 3).

559. In a high-standing cathedral as such of Santiago, such exclusive practices are to be expected.

560. Pope Paschal II issued in the time of Bishop Gelmírez a privilege on behalf of the Cathedral of Santiago: according to this privilege – except for the pope, bishops and archbishops – only those could celebrate mass at the tomb of James or at the apostolic altar upon whom a particular cardinalate was bestowed. Such cardinalate, limited to seven in number at any given moment, did not include any of the prerogatives otherwise due to cardinals. This meant that there were two kinds of canons in the Cathedral of Santiago: the cardinal-canons who were presbyters of the chapter of the cathedral and the rest of the canons who were merely deacons.

The date of Paschal's privilege is variously reported: the *Historia Compostelana*, 1, chap, 45 (Flórez-*Sagrada* 20:93–94) gives the year 1109; Vielliard-*guide* (p. 116, n. 5), the year 1104; and Herbers-*Jakobsweg* (pp. 156 and 358), relying on Jaffé-*Regesta* (n. 6208), the year 1108. Cf. also Vones-*Compostellana*, pp. 269 and 287; and Fletcher-*Gelmírez*, p. 170. Herbers-*Jakobskult* (p. 94) notes a document of 1101 in the same matter, probably spurious. The privilege of the special cardinalates lasted well into the nineteenth century. On various hierarchical and administrative aspects of the chapter of canons of Santiago, cf. LópezFerreiro-*Santiago* 5:155–76. On the reaction of the Italian pilgrims at the curious privilege, cf. Caucci-*Guida*, p. 131, n. 70.

561. We know of no such privilege (cf. Herbers-*Jakobsweg*, p. 156, n. 359).

562. Starting with López Ferreiro, everybody has been wondering whether this Bernard is not indeed identical with the treasurer Bernard, chancellor of Alphonso VII and responsible for the execution of the fountain at the north portal (cf. above, n. 440). LópezFerreiro-*Santiago* (3:37–45) and Vielliard-*guide* (p. 117, n. 1) answer in the affirmative; Moralejo-*Calixtinus*, (p. 569, note to line 15); Herbers-*Jakobsweg* (p. 157, n. 360); and BravoLozano-*Guía*, (p. 141, n. 238) following S. Portela Pazos (*Anotaciones al Tumbo A de la Catedral de Santiago*, Santiago, 1949, pp. 87–97), on the strength of the adjective *senex*, propose that the stonecutter is the father of the treasurer. Cf. also Williams-*Camino*, p. 283.

Three further points may, in our judgment, strengthen the argument for the stonecutter as the father of the treasurer: first, the stonecutter is termed *mirabilis magister* a qualifier more suited to a craftsman than to an administrator; second, the fountain of Bernardus the treasurer is dedicated "ad mee et animarum meorum parentum remedium," for the salvation of my soul and of that of my parents. The father of the treasurer had to be a man of considerable and even extraordinary achievements so as to deserve such outspoken praise (cf. above, n. 440); and third, the text of the *Guide* clearly differentiates between the *Didascali lapicide*, the stonecutters, who come first, and the administrators, *ministrantibus fidelissimis*, who are mentioned later.

563. This second master stonecutter has not been identified. Vielliard-*guide* (p. 117, n. 2) on the strength of the name, suggests for him, no less than for Bernard, a French origin. The argument is strong though not conclusive.

564. Evidently, rank-and-file stonecutters.

565. If "Wicart" is indeed a patronymic (see below, n. 567), then it is probably a corruption of Guichard (or Guiscard), and hence a Frenchman, at least in origin (David-*Jacques* 12:212–13, n. 2). This individual is not designated with any particular dignity or function.

566. *Domno canonice Segeredo*, translated by Vielliard-*guide* (p. 117) as *maître du chapitre* and by Moralejo-*Calixtinus* (p. 570) as *prior de la canónica*. Whether this individual is identical with one, a treasurer, documented between 1077 and 1097 (Vones-*Compostellana*, p. 550) is questionable. Segeredo died before 1111 (LópezFerreiro-*Santiago* 3:37, n. 2; and David-*Jacques* 12:212, n. 2).

567. *Abbate domno Gundesindo* in the text, who died around 1111 (cf. in the previous note the bibliography concerning the death of Segeredo). Unfortunately, little is known about these three administrators. There has been some question whether "Wicart" is a patronymic at all: LópezFerreiro-*Santiago* (3:36–37) suggests the possible reading of *vicario*, vicar, an additional title to be added to Segeredo's priorship. But there are difficulties here too, for while prior and abbot were recognized dignitary positions at the chapter of Santiago, vicar was not (David-*Jacques* 12:212, n. 2). The abbot was the president of the canons and also the responsible for the ongoing daily liturgy (cf. David-*Jacques* 12:212, n. 2; and Fletcher-*Gelmírez*, p. 168 ff.). The last two names, Segaredo and Gundesindo, are Hispanic patronymics of perhaps Visigothic derivation.

568. Alphonso VI, actually king of León and Castilla. Died in 1108.

569. This is Diego Peláez, bishop of Santiago from 1070 to 1088. The qualifier *strenuissimo milite* is probably a pointer at the politico-military confrontations in which Peláez was involved, not the least with Alphonso VI himself: the latter threw him into prison for some fifteen years (*Historia Compostelana*, 1, ii , in Flórez-*Sagrada* 20:15) Cf also Moralejo-*Calixtinus*, p. 570, n. to line 3.

570. "In the era" refers to the Hispanic computation (cf. above, n. 463), which is 38 years ahead of the common Christian one, and thus corresponds to the year 1078. A most important date which,

in spite of some adverse critical interpretation, has withstood the wear and tear of time. This same date recurs twice more within the monuments of Santiago: in the *Historia Compostelana*, 1, lxxviii (in Flórez-*Sagrada*, 20:138) with the precise indication of the day, *V idus julii*, July 11; (although elsewhere, 3, i, in Flórez-*Sagrada*, 22:473, n. 1, the year 1082 appears); and on the left jamb of the right entrance of the Portal de las Platerías, with an identical indication of the year and day. Cf. Moralejo-*Calixtinus*, p. 570, n. to line 5; and Herbers-*Jakobsweg*, p. 157, n. 367.

571. This is Alphonso I el Batallador, the Warlike, known also as Alphonso VII, king of Aragón and Navarra (1104–34). The computation is erroneous for it gives the year 1137 for the death of the king, or, reckoning backwards from the year of his actual death, 1075 for the beginning of the cathedral.

572. Henry I, king of England, nicknamed Beauclerk , the fourth and youngest son of William I, reigned between 1100 and 1135. An equally erroneous reckoning: 1140 and 1073 respectively (see n. 571 above).

573. Louis VI le Gros, the Fat, king of France between 1108 and 1137. The erroneous calculations: 1141 and 1074 respectively (see above, n. 570). The concordances with the dates of death of the three kings are, with near certainty, interpolations. For all the above, see Whitehill-*Date Santiago*; David-*Jacques* 12:211–15; as well as, in general, Vielliard-*guide*, p. 119. n. 1; Moralejo-*Calixtinus*, pp. 570–71, n. to line 5; and Herbers-*Jakobsweg*, p. 157, n. 367. In the chapel of San Salvador (cf. nn. 393 and 501 above) there is an important inscription, albeit mutilated, concerning the consecration of the basilica based on the date of its foundation: "trigeno anno post dominice incarnationis milleno septuageno quinto tempore quo domus est fundata iacobi," thirty years after the year 1075 of the Incarnation of the Lord, the date in which the church of Santiago was founded. This date, 1105, is confirmed by the consecration of the altar of Gelmírez in the same year (cf. LópezFerreiro-*Santiago* 3:40-42, and Moralejo-*Calixtinus*, pp. 570–71, n. to line 5).

574. That is to say, taking the year 1078 as base, the year 1122. The reference must be to the architecture of the basilica, a credible but fairly strenuous schedule. But even so, "from first to last stone" ought to be taken metaphorically.

575. Perhaps a reference to the chains of prisoners in the hands of the infidels.

576. Ideologically cogent; otherwise, in terms of the physical relief accorded by the miracles, an ambivalent statement.

577. Cf. similar list of miracles, n. 147 above, as well as Kriss-*viator*, p. 15.

578. The long paragraph on miracles ends in a propagandistic note: *munera...deferentes*, "bringing gifts," is the central thought here.

579. Calixtus II, pope 1119-24.

580. Diego Gelmírez, the great promoter of Compostela and its cathedral: see above, n. 532, and pp. 22–23. Elected bishop of Santiago in 1100, and archbishop from 1120 to his death in 1140.

581. Luke 10.1-17. The explicit parallel with the Seventy-Two Disciples of Christ invites a correlation between Christ and Santiago. All this cannot but further dignify the cathedral. In the light of the large size of the chapter, documented from 1102 on, the above discussed distinction of the canons between cardinals and deacons becomes more understandeable (cf. above, n. 560, as well as LópezFerreiro-*Santiago* 3:249–58; Biggs-*Gelmírez*, p. 241; and Fletcher-*Gelmírez*, pp. 167–69).

582. See above, nn. 358 and 359. No transmitted rule for canons by Isidore came down to us, only a rule for monastic life: cf. López Ferreiro-*Santiago* 3:253, 5:121, n. 2; Herbers-*Jakobuskult*, p. 162. LópezFerreiro-*Santiago* (2:45) interprets it as a reference to the "text of the divine office and to the distribution of the Canonical Hours."

583. That is to say, the offerings. This was, and still is, an economic matter of the greatest importance to judge by the complexity of the operation described.

584. For every week there were, it seems, seven or twelve hebdomadiers, that is to say canons to whom the week's offerings were assigned. With seven canons per week, in thirteen weeks the list was exhausted and a new round would start; if, on the other hand, the number of canons was twelve per week, then the round lasted six weeks only. Cf. Biggs-*Gelmírez*, p. 241, and Helbers-*Jakobsweg*, p. 159, n. 377.

585. In the singular in the text though, evidently, it should be in the plural. Cf. n. 584 above.

586. It must be said that the sharing in the economic benefits responded to a sense of overall justice tempered by carefully considered Aristotelian hierarchical prerogatives.

587. This is the ancient Hospital del Apóstol Santiago located on the north side of the north parvis of the cathedral, that is to say, facing the Portal de la Azabachería (cf. above, nn. 431 and 451, and in particular LópezFerreiro-*Santiago*, 3:193 and 4:145, and Moralejo-*Calixtinus*, p. 379, n. to line 9). This hospital was specifically destined for poor pilgrims.

588. The turn of phrase seems to indicate that the injunction to re-
serve the tithe for the poor was indeed not really, or at least not at
all times, observed.

589. Saint-Léonard in Limoges.

590. Characteristically for the author of the *Guide*, for whom the
yardstick rests always in matters French, the welfare poor pilgrims
receive in Santiago de Compostela is highlighted by an exemplum
of one of the most famous pilgrimage churches on French roads.

591. This occurs *ex more*. That is to say, there are rules and regulations sanctioned by ordinances; and others, by consuetudinary practice.

592. This phrase too, as above at n. 588, seems to point at ongoing
infractions of the economic regulations concerning the just sharing
of the cathedral's benefits and, in particular, the tending to the poor
pilgrims.

593. The subject of this chapter ought to be understood perhaps as
an afterthought to the *Guide* as a whole and, in particular, to the
long Chapter 9 on the Cathedral of Santiago to which, thematically
speaking, Chapter 10 also belongs. This last chapter provides an
occasion to the author of the *Guide* to return once again to the two
main preoccupations of the earlier portions of the text: on the one
hand pilgrimage and saints; and on the other, France. Indeed, all
three miracles narrated below occur on French soil and hence, im-
plicitly, to Frenchmen. It shall not escape us that the text mentions
first the *peregrini...redientes* and only then the *advenientes*. The in-
voluntary accent lies, here too, on the country of return, France.

594. Matthew 10.40. The passage within which the quotation of Matthew is embedded constitutes a most significant proportional relation: the pilgrims are to Santiago, as Santiago (and the other apostles)
are to Christ. The anomalous treatment of the Disciples at Emmaus
in Santo Domingo de Silos (see above, p. 68) is related to such a
proposition, though it goes much beyond it.

595. The wrath of God in these accounts expresses itself in miraculous occurrences that punish those who do not abide by the mandate to appropriately welcome the pilgrims. The stories are what
Herbers-*Jakobsweg* (p. 150, n. 383) calls *Strafwunder*, that is to say,
miracles concerning the punishment of the sinner and the concomitant reward/safety of the pilgrim.

596. In the department of Air, on a subsidiary feeder route of the
via podense in direction of Geneva.

597. The trade of the merciless personage has not been chosen at
random: Lyon has been, well until the Renaissance, the most important textile center of France. Hence the weaver and the torn linen.

598. There is no sure way of telling which of the half a dozen towns and villages that bear that name is meant here. Due to the proximity of one or the other of the pilgrimage roads in France, the reference might be to a town in the Aveyron, not too far from Conques or to another called Villeneuve-d'Agen, or to still another, Villeneuve-sur-Lot, not far from Agen. It will be remembered that, through the relics of St. Foy, Agen, and Conques are clearly related.

599. Here the pilgrim himself becomes the thaumaturge, he who exercises the power of miracles.

600. *Corde penitens* in the text. The woman is allowed to repent of her sin, though she is not allowed to make amends for it.

601. The usual condition of the poor becomes the condition of the better-off classes too at the end of the pilgrimage. The text describes them as *heroes Galli*, probably military noblemen, hence knights.

602. The last of the three miracles takes place in the very region to which the author of the *Guide* has been repeatedly associated throughout the entire account. This can hardly happen by chance. Furthermore, the city is described, as this is only to be expected, in some detail: a citizen, Gautier, is mentioned of whom, however, we know nothing; the church of Saint-Porchaire, reconstructed in the sixteenth century, still keeps its original eleventh-century belltower and portal. Even today, the streets around the church belong to the most typical ones of this well-preserved medieval city.

603. The Rue Saint-Porchaire, one of the busiest in the city.

604. Evident hyperbole.

605. Partly because of their status as pilgrims, but partly perhaps because of being knights.

606. Though mostly the poor, as forcefully argued above, Chapter 10.

607. *Codex quartus* of the text. Looking at the manuscript, one realizes that the "in" of *quintus* was eventually transformed into the "ar" of *quartus*, as we have it now. The book was indeed the fifth portion of the *Codex* until the seventeenth century when Book IV, the *Pseudo-Turpin*, was excised from the manuscript.

608. That is to say, authenticated and approved.

609. Whitehill-*Liber*, p. xlii, stresses the significance of this last emphasis that Cluny receives at the very conclusion of the *Codex* (cf. pp. 18–19 above, as well as n. 3 above).

Santiago. Cathedral of Santiago. Pórtico de la Gloria.
St. James. Late XII C.

HAGIOGRAPHICAL REGISTER

CAESARIUS OF ARLES: (Lat. and Engl.; Fr.: Césaire; It.: Cesario), the fifteenth bishop of Arles, was a man who gained fame of sanctity through a judicious combination of high-standing ecclesiastical as well as lay political statesmanship, strenuous pastoral work exercised beyond the call of duty and, with all probability, as it transcends indirectly from his biography, a warm and engaging personality. From a number of official documents as well as from the *Vita sancti Caesarii* (*ActaSS* Aug. 6:50–83; Migne-*PL* 67:1007–42; and *MG-Mer* 3:457–501), probably a collective work whose main architect was Bishop Cyprien of Toulon, we gather a fairly accurate description of his life. The subdued and moderate tone of the narrative and the frank mentioning of moments of failure of the saint are an indication of the reliability of the *Vita*.

Caesarius is born around 470 in the surroundings of Chalon-sur-Saône into a moderately well-to-do Gallo-Roman family which owned a few slaves. At the age of eighteen Caesarius begs the bishop of Chalon, St. Silvestre, to be admitted into the local clerical life where he spends the next two years or so. At the end of that period, under less than clear circumstances, Caesarius abandons his parents and the place of his upbringing and sets out for Lerins in whose monastery he spends some time, presumably a few years. At Lerins, Caesarius must have shown a degree of responsibility, for he is made cellarer of the monastery during a particularly intense period of his formation: in fact, he engages in excessively long hours of study which debilitates him to the point that he is sent to Arles for medical advise and perhaps even cure.

To the patristic formation acquired in Lerins, Caesarius adds now in Arles some literary and rhetorical studies with an African rhetorician named Pomerius, without ever being able however to establish a sound classical background for his education. For that, perhaps, he had altogether started too late.

In Arles Caesarius enters also into the circle of Bishop Eone who shows an evident predilection for the studious youth. Aware of family ties between them, Eone procures the final transfer of Caesarius to Arles and confers upon him, in succession, the diaconate, the priesthood, and the priorship of a monastery on an island of the Rhône. When Eone dies in 503, Caesarius becomes his natural successor. Caesarius's bishopric will last 40 long years, a period in which the now Arlaisian prelate by adoption will know how to demonstrate a great sense of realism combined to a relentless pastoral work at the grassroots level.

The politico-ecclesiastical scenario was not among the most propitious: the Visigoths until 507, the Ostrogoths until 536, and the Merovingian Franks thereafter – the wheels of power passed in succession from hand to hand. The Arian controversy made things no easier. Caesarius, a Catholic by upbringing, had to exercise all his diplomatic skill as well as his common sense in order to survive. And survive he did. On the vast political and ecclesiastical scene, Caesarius was a vigorous advocate for the primacy of Arles over Vienne and for the re-establishment of the prefecture of the city; the latter he obtained from Theodoric. On the pastoral level, Caesarius was one of the most popular preachers of the Latin Church and the founder of a monastery of nuns of which his sister Caesaria became the abbess. For the same monastery Caesarius wrote a *Regula ad virgenes* of a particularly rigorous *clausura* later on changed for the Rule of St. Benedict.

Side by side with his statesmanship obligations, Caesarius knew how to exercise steadily and with a sense of profound devotion the pastoral care vis-à-vis his flock: the indigents, the sick, the homeless, the refugees (he himself had been one), the fugitives, the prisoners – these were the continuous subjects and objects of his care. That Caesarius operated with a great measure of conviction and sincerity one may deduce also from the popular traditions associated to the miracles attributed to him. On one occasion Caesarius is said to have enclosed a sea wind in his glove in order to let it out in a dry valley and thereby to render it fruitful. It is not the kind of story told on somebody distant and aloof.

Caesarius's *dies natalis* fell on August 27. The year was 543.

O. F. Arnold, *Caesarius von Arelate und die gallische Kirche seiner Zeit* (Leipzig, 1894); A. Malnory, *St. Césaire, évêque d'Arles, 503–43* (Paris, 1894); M. Chaillan, *St. Césaire* (Paris, 1912); S. Cavallin, *Literarhistorische und textkritische Studien zur Vita S. Caesarii Arelatensis* (Lund, 1934); J. Fassy, *St. Césaire d'Arles* (Paris, 1939); J.-Ch. Didier, "Cesario," in *BSS*; G. de Plinval, "Césaire d'Arles," in *DHGE*; P. Lejay, "Cesaire d'Arles," in *DTC*; H. G. J. Beck, "Caesarius of Arles, St.," in *NCE*.

CAPRAIS: The *Martyrologium of Usuard* quotes, for October 20, St. Caprais, martyr of Agen. His execution took place under Maximien, around the year 303. Most details of his life, so far as known to us, are incorporated as subsidiary narratives in the account of the life of St. Foy. In the *Historia Francorum*, 6.12 and the *De gloria martyrum*, 1.52 of Gregory of Tours, there is a further account of Caprais, this one patterned after that of Symphorien of Autun. Caprais is made here a bishop and a church is dedicated to him. It is doubtful whether he ever was a bishop. The narratives on the life of St. Foy report that Caprais, in order to escape the persecutions of Diocletian, retreated into a cave. Once he learned of the martyrdom of St. Foy though, he surrendered to the judge Dacien who first tried in vain to induce him to apostatize and then consigned him to the executioners. While Caprais was being tortured, two brothers, Primo and Felician, converted and were decapitated together with St. Foy and Caprais himself on October 6. It is not clear why his feast is assigned to October 20. The supplement to the *Martyrologium Hieronymianum* gives the same date.

BHL nos. 234-35; *ActaSS* Oct. 8:815–23; Duchesne-*Fastes*, 2:114–46; R. Van Doren, "Caprais," in *DHGE*; A. Amore, "Caprasio," in *BSS*; see also the entry on St. Foy.

CLEMENT: (Lat.: Clemens; Fr.: Clément; It.: Clemente), saint and pope, the first of that name, but of dubious ranking in the ancient sources. Tertullian (*Liber de praescriptione haereticorum* 32: Migne-*PL* 2:45) makes Clement the immediate successor of Peter; Irenaeus (*Adversus Haereses* 3.3.3: Migne-*PG* 7:849) places him as the fourth bishop of Rome, after Linus and Anacletus; Eusebius (*Historia Ecclesiastica* 3.15.34: Migne-*PG*, 20:249, 285) puts him into third place; so do too Augustin (*Epistola* 53, *ad Generos* 2: Migne-*PL*. 33:196), Optatus of Milevis (*De schismate Donatistarum* 2.3: Migne-*PL* 11:948) and others, writing indistinctly Clet or Anaclet. As to Jerome, he oscillates between Tertullian and Irenaeus in a matter that aroused many intellectual passions well into the later Middle Ages. That is also the reason that several belletristic attempts have been made in order to reconcile the above disparate positions: having been ordained by Peter, Clement might have given his place to Linus and recuperate his rights after the death of Anacletus or Cletus; or, Peter might have governed *together* with Linus and Anacletus – and hence Clement would still turn out to be the direct successor of the first bishop of Rome.

Two might have been the reasons that made the figure of Clement, after that of the Apostles, one of the most imposing and significant in Christian history: the long and beautiful letter in Greek, surely authentic, addressed to the Corinthians (*Prima Epistola*, Migne-*PG* 1:201–328). This is a document of the first rank of importance that tells us as much of the early history of the Church, of Rome's relations with dispersed Christian communities, of the gradually emerging Christian methods proper of biblical exegesis, of the notion of Roman authority in the early

Church – as it speaks to us of Clement himself: a man fully conscious of both, his position and his duties, reasonably detached already from the not-long-ago still-practiced Hebrew traditions, at home in Stoic philosophy, and sympathetic, in some ways at least, to the Rome of his times. This is somewhat of a surprise if we take into consideration that his life must have overlapped with Domitian's reign (G. Bardy, "Clément de Rome," in *DHGE*). The form and the tone of the letter, furthermore, measured and constructed under the sign of moderation – these are among the cherished classical Roman cultural ideals – is firm and at the same time gentle: it persuades without coercing.

The second reason that made the later fortunes of St. Clement's reputation is, without any doubt, his legendary *Passio* (*ActaSS* 2:19–22). Though assuredly a late compilation, these accounts captured, as in a magnetic hold, the imagination of the masses over the centuries. According to the *Acta*, Emperor Trajan threw Clement into prison for the many conversions the latter had effected among the Roman aristocracy; later on, upon his refusal to sacrifice to the pagan gods – a staple feature in Christian hagiography – he was exiled. The locus of the exile was determined by Roman economic necessities: the mines of the Chersonese, today Crimea, on the shores of the Black Sea. Since Clement continued to exercise his ministry of evangelization as well as his pastoral duties among the Christian prisoners working in the mines, by imperial orders he was thrown into the Sea of Azov with an anchor tied to his neck. Once the act of martyrdom was over, the sea retreated disclosing the locus of the tragic event together with the tomb of Clement. Every year henceforth, on the anniversary of his *dies natalis*, the sea so retreated allowing the faithful to visit his tomb and to pray at it. The deeper folkloric reverberations that this legend has evoked among the masses over the centuries may be appreciated by observing the eleventh-century frescoes in the lower church of San Clemente in Rome: popular gusto here takes hold of the narrative of the martyrdom converting the hagiographic material into a profoundly appealing partly melodramatic and partly farcical play.

A later narrative has St. Cyril effect the *translatio* of the remains of St. Clement to Rome, where the relics are welcomed with exultation. The feast of St. Clement is celebrated on November 23.

W. Scherer, *Der erste Klemensbrief* (Regensburg, 1902); F. Gerke, *Die Stellung des ersten Klemensbriefes innerhalb der Entwicklung der altchristlichen Gemeindeverfassung und des Kirchenrechts* (Leipzig, 1931); E. Caspar, *Die älteste römische Bischofslisten* (Berlin, 1926); G. Bardy, *Théologie de l'Église, de Saint Clément de Rome à Saint Irénée* (Paris, 1945); P. Franchi de' Cavalieri, "La leggenda di San Clemente papa e martire," *Note agiografiche* 5 (1915): 1–40; H.

Campenhausen, *Kirchliches Amt und geistliche Vollmacht* (Tübingen, 1953); W. W. Jaeger, *Early Christianity and Greek Paideia* (Cambridge, MA, 1961); S. Sanders, *L'hellénisme de Saint Clément de Rome et le paulinisme* (Louvain, 1943); A. Ehrhardt, *The Apostolic Succession in the First Two Centuries of the Church* (London, 1953); G. Zannoni, "Clemente I," in *BSS*; H. Dressler, "Clement I, Pope, St.," in *NCE*; G. Bardy, "Clément de Rome," in *DHGE*; Delehaye-*légendes*, 96–116.

DIONYSIUS: The ms. lat. 2291 of the Bibl. Nat. of Paris (also, in Duchesne-*Fastes* 2:469) contains a list of bishops. Dionysius (Lat.; Fr.: Denys; It.: Dionigi) figures among them as the first bishop of Paris. Gregory of Tours confirms the same (*Historia Francorum* 1.30, Migne-*PL* 71:177) within the frame of a larger story: during the times of Emperor Decius (249–51), seven missionary bishops were dispatched from Rome to Gaul. One of these was Dionysius, who was destined for Paris. The chronological imprecision and the evident numerological symbolism belie the oral tradition on which Gregory's account rests. It may be reasonable to suppose that within the wider time-frame of the third century a number of missionaries had indeed been sent to Gaul and that Dionysius, even if not necessarily the first missionary in Paris, might have been the organizer of its ecclesia (R. Aubert, "Denys," in *DHGE*).

Gregory's account in the *Historia Francorum*, expanded and embellished in the *De gloria Martyrum* (chap. 71), speaks also of the death of martyrdom of Dionysius by sword. A ninth-century anonymous narrative *passio, Post beatam et gloriosam* (*BHL* no. 2178), speaks of Dionysius in terms of a *cephalophorus* saint, that is to say, one who, after being beheaded, picks up and carries his own head. According to a still later *passio*, Dionysius, in fact, carried his head to the place of his burial. The locus of Dionysius' martyrdom, on the other hand, is conveyed as the *mons martyrum*, that is to say, what we know today as the hill of Montmartre.

On the first burial of Dionysius we know very little. The *Vita Genovefae*, written perhaps a little after the year 500, speaks of a basilica built by St. Geneviève (died in 519) over the tomb of Dionysius in the *vicus Catulliacus*, north of Paris. There have, however, been other pretenders too to the honor of erecting a church over Dionysius' tomb: Venantius Fortunatus (*Carmina* 1.11) speaks of Amelius, bishop of Bordeaux, as one who built a chapel over the tomb.

From the seventh century on the fortunes of Dionysius turned ever more spectacular: around 624 King Dagobert founded an abbey under Dionysius' patronage and next to his funerary basilica. About a century later the pretension emerged gradually in monastic quarters of St.-Denys that their saint actually did not come to Paris under Decius, but about two centuries earlier, sent by Pope Clement, variously viewed as the second, the third, or the fourth bishop of Rome (see the entry on Clement of Rome). The oldest *passio* of Dionysius, the *Gloriosae* (*BHL* no. 2171), rewritten in the eighth century, as well as other documents not always trustworthy, contain this affirmation.

In the ninth century we arrive to the crowning *inventio* of this relentless process of exaltation by antedating. The Byzantine Emperor Michael had sent in 827 a precious manuscript to Louis the Pious containing the works of one thought of as Dionysios the Areopagite, the Athenian disciple of St. Paul. The manuscript ended up in the hands of Hilduinus, abbot of St.-Denys (died in 840). The learned abbot translated the texts and, in the *Vita S. Dionysii* (Migne-*PL* 106:15; *BHL* no. 2175; *ActaSS* Oct. 4:695–767) identified the saintly first bishop of Paris with the disciple of St. Paul. The chain of wishful identifications acquired subsequently an unexpected intermediate link: the texts Emperor Michael had sent to Louis were actually written by a Syrian monk between 480 and 530 – hence the term Pseudo-Areopagite applied to their author. Surprisingly enough though, these texts – *De coelesti hierarchia, De mystica theologia, De divinis nominibus,* and others – were destined to become among the most famous and seminal Neoplatonic writings of the Christian Middle Ages.

Fantastic as the identification of St. Dionysius with the disciple of St. Paul might have been, such was the medieval predilection for analogical rapprochements and etymological reasoning and so persevering and convincing the French argumentation that Hilduinus' theory entered even the *Breviarium Romanum*. The feast of Dionysius is celebrated on October 9.

ActaSS Oct.4:696–855; E. Griffe, *La Gaule chrétienne à l'époque romaine* (Paris, 1947), 1:71–75, 89 ff., 110; I. Levillain, "Saint Trophime et la mission des Sept en Gaule," *Revue de l'histoire de l'Église de France* 13 (1927): 145–89; H. Moretus-Plantin, "Les Passions de St. Denys," in *Mélanges Cavallera* (Paris, 1948), pp. 215–30; R. Loenertz, "La légende de St. Denys l'Aréopagite. Sa genèse et son premier témoin," in *AnBoll* 69 (1951): 217–37; Delehaye-*martyrs*, 358–59; R. Bossuat, "Traditions populaires relatives au martyre et à la sepulture de St. Denys," *Le Moyen Age* 62 (1956): 479–509; R. Aubert, "Denys," in *DHGE*; C. de Clercq and P. Burchi, "Dionigi, Rustico ed Eleuterio," in *BSS*; B. Kötting, "Dionysius v. Paris," in *LTK3*.

DOMINGO DE LA CALZADA: Hermit and saint, was born in Viloria, near Burgos, sometime in the first half of the eleventh century. He started his life, as nearly everybody else on the plains of Castilla la Vieja, as a shepherd. We know hardly anything more of his early life, not even the year of his birth. Having received a rudimentary education in the monastery of Valvanera, today in the province of Logroño, he tried in vain to gain entry into monastic life by applying for admission into the famous monastery of San Millán de la Cogolla, also in the province of Logroño, close to the plains of Castilla. The rejection of his application must have been a shock for Domingo. It is not clear whether the refusal was due to his poor intellectual preparation or to his physical deformity of which, however, we know no details. A crucial influence on the life of Domingo was exerted by Gregory of Ostia, the papal legate, whose close companion Domingo became, henceforth following Gregory in his apostolic mission all across northern Spain. After a while, Gregory ordained the eager disciple: Domingo was now a priest.

Gregory's death in 1044 signalled a radical change in the existence of Domingo. In fact, he retired at that point in life to a somewhat distant and particularly inhospitable region of Castilla, east of Burgos. There, on the banks of the Oja River, close to the pilgrimage road that ran a little bit further to the north, he established a hermit's residence dedicating the rest of a very long life to the assistance of pilgrims. Having erected a humble hut for himself, a chapel dedicated to Our Lady, and a hospital for pilgrims, Domingo embarked upon the most important aspect of his work, the maintenance, repair, and occasionally the building of the pilgrimage road. From here he acquired the onomastic attribute that henceforth he bore, "de la Calzada," that is to say, of the *causeway*, in reference to the transitable surface of the road. Particularly important undertakings of Domingo were the bridges that he spanned across rivers, brooks, or ravines, of which the most famous is the stone bridge over the Oja River.

The hermetic aspect of his life though seemed to considerably suffer as a consequence of the above feverish activities as well as of the profound influence he gradually gained upon the inhabitants of the region who early enough were attracted to his personality: in time, they settled around his humble dwelling – an archetypal practice that favored the physical proximity of saintly figures or their relics. From here first the village and later on the town of Santo Domingo de la Calzada came into being during the crucial years of the last third of the eleventh century. This otherwise too, was marked by a drive for consolidation and *repoblación*, that is to say, resettlement of the territories regained from Islam. Since these territories were all in the northern tier of the peninsula, crossed, as by a vertebral column, by the pilgrimage road to Santiago, it is evident the extent to which the welfare work of Domingo coincided with the interests of Alphonso VI, king of

Castilla. In fact, Alphonso, thus gratified in his overall geopolitical orientation, actively cooperated with Domingo in the resettlement of the town in his name and supported in many ways his road construction and maintenance works.

When Domingo died in 1109, at a very ripe age that must have been at least octogenarian, he was buried in the church of Santo Domingo de la Calzada which, a little later, was upgraded, together with the churches of Nájera and Calahorra, to cathedral dignity.

The details of the sanctification and canonization of Domingo are somewhat unclear. His feast is celebrated on May 12, the day of his death. Domingo's thaumaturgical exploits were already well known during his lifetime: that was one of the reasons for people to flock around him and to settle in his vicinity. With his death and burial, his relics, in the Cathedral of Santo Domingo de la Calzada, became the object of popular devotion. The famous episode of the unjustly hung French pilgrim rescued by a saint, and the concomitant story of the roasted rooster and chicken that, as a confirmation of the miracle, stood up in the frying pan and started to crow – is sometimes attributed to St. Domingo, while at other times, to St. James himself.

Santo Domingo de la Calzada, anyhow, the saint and the town, appropriately capitalized on the attribution touching them, wherefrom the popular couplet took rise: "Santo Domingo de la Calzada, / donde la gallina cantó después de asada," that is to say, where the chicken sang after having been roasted. This is not the only instance of such overlapping of thaumaturgical prerogatives in Christian hagiography in general and on the road to Santiago de Compostela in particular. If anything, it strengthens the holistic notion of the miraculous act, as well as that of the essential unity of the pilgrimage road.

ActaSS May 3:166–79; VázquezParga-*pereg* 2:162–69; Huidobro Serna-*peregrinaciones*, 804–34; J. González Tejada, *Historia de Santo Domingo de la Calzada* (Madrid, 1702); J. Fernández Alonso, "Domingo de la Calzada," in *BSS*; C.-M. Molas, "Dominique de la Calzada," in *DHGE*.

EUTROPIUS: A long-standing tradition makes of Eutropius (Lat. and Engl.; Fr.: Eutrope; It.: Eutropio), the first bishop of Saintes in the region of Saintonge in central-western France. This pious tradition wants him to be a first-century personage, a contemporary of Dionysius, sent to Gaul by Pope Clement considered, without much historical verification, the successor of Peter (see the entries for Dionysius and for Saturninus). His historical bishopric, in fact, ought to be situated considerably later, perhaps towards the end of the third century. It was not before the sixth century though that two or three converging accounts contributed to bring the figure of Eutropius into sharper devotional focus as well as to establish for him a securer historical frame: in the early second half of the century, Bishop Léonce of Bordeaux restored or repaired the funerary chapel of the saint as well as completed the construction of the basilica of St. Vivien in the city; next, a poem by Venantius Fortunatus, bishop of Poitiers (died 609), written around 567, celebrated the occasion; and finally Gregory of Tours (539–93) wrapped up the story of the saint with an account of his martyrdom.

Fortunatus, in *Carmina*, 1.12, speaks of Eutropius as the first bishop of Saintes, "urbis Sanctonicae primus fuit iste sacerdos," and in 1.13 he makes mention of the *Eutropitis aula*, the dwelling place of the saint, in terms of his funerary chapel, "cum qua templa tenet sanctus habitando quiete." It was this funerary chapel that Bishop Léonce had repaired, and whose completion, with all probability, served as the occasion for Fortunatus' poem of celebration of 567. The poet mentions the pastoral dignity of Eutropius, but says nothing of his martyrdom. This was to be the task of Gregory of Tours towards the end of the century: in his *De gloria Martyrum*, 55, Gregory made a place for Eutropius among the martyrs of the Faith. His story included a general account of the *translatio* of the relics of the saint from the suburban funerary chapel to the newly completed basilica. This occurred under Bishop Palladius (died in 600).

Particularly important in Gregory's account is the episode of the recognition of the visible signs of Eutropius' martyrdom. Having completed the *translatio*, two high-ranking ecclesiastics, in an act of *impromptu* historical verification, raised the lid of the sarcophagus and glanced, with astonishing eyes, at the parted skull of the saint. The following night Eutropius himself appeared in a dream to the two churchmen confirming that the parted skull is indeed the proof of having died a martyr's death. Eutropius's martyrdom became registered in the various martyrologies for April 30.

The four personages whom we find thus in various capacities in the sixth century around Eutropius – Léonce, Fortunatus, Gregory and Palladius – greatly contributed to consolidate, dignify, and historicize the figure of Eutropius. In fact, the devotional cult of his relics, after the sixth century, spread rapidly in the Saintonge and the Guyenne due also, to a considerable measure, to the *via turonense* that connected the region of Saintonge with Santiago. The vast network of the pilgrimage roads channeling the pilgrims towards far-away Galicia, was beneficial not merely to the cult of St. James, but also to the reliquary churches on the way: these were constantly fed by fresh streams of pilgrims.

The many transformations-corruptions that the name of Eutropius underwent from the sixth century on (Estropi, Estroupiel, Ytrope, etc.) are a sure sign for his popularity. They contributed also to associate him, in the popular imagination, by means of false etymology, with the cure of particular illnesses. So, deriving from "Estropi" (*torpor, -is; torpidus;* Fr.- *torpeur;* Engl.: torpor) Eutropius became the healer of the cripple; and from "Ytrope" (*hydrops, -opis; hydropicus*), the healer of the dropsical. The profound wound on his skull, on the other hand, made Eutropius the doctor of migraines and headaches in general. During the War of Religions the bones of Eutropius were dispersed and partly burned, except for a few fragments taken to Vendome and except for the skull: this was for a while kept in Bordeaux and later returned to Saintes.

Gallia christ 2:1054; *ActaSS* Apr. 3:733–36; Gregory of Tours, *De gloria Martyrum* 56, in Migne-*PL* 71:756–57; Venantius Fortunatus, *Carmina* 1.12–13, in Migne-*PL* 88:76–77; L. Audiat, *Saint Eutrope. Ier évêque de Saintes, dans l'histoire, la légende, l'archéologie* (Paris, 1887); *BHL* nos. 2784–88; *AnBoll* 20 (1901): 333; Delehaye-*martyrs*, 104 and 394; B. de Gaiffier, "Les sources de la passion de saint Eutrope de Saintes dans le 'Liber sancti Jacobi,'" *AnBoll* 69 (1951): 57–66; [Madame] Lamontellerie, "S. Eutrope de Saintes. Exemple de pérennité et d'évolution des croyances chrétiennes," *Bulletin de la Société de mythologie française* 32 (1958): 99–137; E. Griffe, "Eutrope," in *DHGE*; J. Houssain, "Eutropio," in *BSS*.

EUVERTE: Euverte (Fr.; Lat.: Evortius or Evurtius), bishop of Orleans. According to the *Vita Aniani* (*MG-Mer,* 3:108–9), the times of Euverte fall in the first half of the sixth century. We know but little of his life. He was responsible for the first church *intra muros* of Orleans, dedicated to the Holy Cross. Euverte was the predecessor to Aignan in the episcopal see of Orleans; the latter continued the building program and further expanded the church of the Holy Cross first erected by Euverte.

We know nothing concerning the circumstances of his death. The feast of St. Euverte is celebrated on Sept. 7.

BHL nos. 2799–2800; *ActaSS* Sept. 3:446–62; J. de la Martinière, "Les origines chrétiennes d'Orléans," Revue *d'histoire de l'Église de France* 25 (1934): 1–25.

FACUNDO AND PRIMITIVO: Facundo (Lat.: Facundus; It.: Facondo) and Primitivo (Lat.: Primitivus) are either mentioned together or only Facundo appears with a history, a *patrocinium*, and a cult of his own. Of Primitivo we know nothing at all. In a distant village of Galicia, *Acci* or *Guadix*, there is an inscription dated 652 that commemorates the deposition of relics of both saints. Their cult, at this early stage, must have been strictly local. Neither the *Orationale* of Tarragona nor that of Silos mentions them. The tenth- and eleventh-century Hispanic and Hispano-Mozarabic liturgical calendars, on the other hand, set their festivity on November 27. It is the *Martyrologium of Usuard* that introduces the saints into the non-Hispanic world.

The diffusion of churches dedicated to Facundo and Primitivo, or to Facundo only, in Spain is restricted within the borders of ancient Gallicia which, at the time, reached well into present Portugal and went towards the east as far as the plains of Castilla. Of such cult sites, what later became known as Sahagún was by far the most significant (Sanct Facund → Sant Fagund → San Fagún → Safagún → Sahagún). Alphonso III had settled shortly after 870 a community of refugee monks from Córdoba on the site of the martyrdom of the two saints. This place, called *Domnos sanctos*, eventually developed into an abbey dedicated to the saints; at least twice destroyed by the Saracens and as many times rebuilt anew, the abbey became, by the later eleventh century, under the impact of the calculated policies of Alphonso VI (1065–1109), the power center of the Cluniac reformed Benedictine monasteries in Spain, something like the Spanish Cluny. Its sphere of influence was considerable, including many subordinate churches and monasteries. Most importantly, lying on the *via francigena*, commanding a particularly tight relationship with Cluny, it developed in time a double allegiance: on the one hand, to Santiago de Compostela and the effort of the *Reconquista* under the leadership of St. James; on the other, to the Carolingian involvement in that same *Reconquista* and especially in the alleged expedition of Charlemagne into Spain and actually as far as Sahagún. This last tradition thrived on the strength of its ideological and poetic force creating, among others, the local legend of the slain French paladins' flowering spears (Whitehill-*Liber* 4:8; Moralejo-*Calixtinus* 4:8; Vielliard-*Guide*, chaps. 3 and 8. Also, see the entry on Roland).

Biographical data concerning the two saints is scanty. Their very existence in Roman times has enjoyed wide acceptance, but the details of their passion are less than clear. The earliest texts that narrate their martyrdom are two manuscripts of the tenth century from Cardeña and Silos respectively, the first in the B.L. in London (Ms. Add. 25,600), and the second in the B.N. in Paris (n. acq. lat. 2,180). These texts depend heavily upon the *passiones* of other saintly personages, particularly the *passio* of Felix of Gerona

THE PILGRIM'S GUIDE TO SANTIAGO

(*BHL* no. 2864), to whose hymn, *Fons Deus vitae perennis*, the hymn dedicated to Facundo and Primitivo, *Fons Deus aeterna pacis*, is no doubt closely related.

The core of the narrative tells of one Atticus who organizes a convocation on the banks of the Cea River in honor of the idols of Galicia, in which Facundo and Primitivo refuse to participate. At the end of a violent confrontation, which includes attempts at ugly coercion, the two are decapitated. This happened "sub Attico et Pretextato consulibus." The graphic description of Molanus' addition to the *Martyrologium of Usuard* conveys the events in a surprisingly dramatic epilogue: "In Gallaecia iuxta fluvium Cejam, natalis sanctorum Facundi et Primitivi martyrum, quibus, post multa supplicia superata, duae coronae ab angelis delatae sunt. Quod Atticus praetor accipiens: Capita, inquit, amputentur, ne sit locus coronis" (J. Guerra, "Facundus," in *BSS*). The account defines the birth of the saints, as customary, in terms of their martyrdom; furthermore, their overcoming martyrdom is understood in terms of their stoically supporting the physical pains involved in the torments; and the unexpected epilogue leaves the reader in suspense concerning the cause of death: this may be interpreted to have set in either as a consequence of the martyrdom or at the moment of the decapitation.

The details of the passion must have been worked out by a professional hagiographer, apparently after the consecration of the church of Sahagún in 935. The topographic localization of the martyrdom in Gallicia responds to the ancient borders of the region. As to the family and the social condition of the saints, these are only in part determined: there is no reason in any event to suppose that they were brothers; the military background might have been superimposed upon the saints' biographies otherwise too culled from the passion of the Saints Emeterius and Caledonius. The assignation of the date of the martyrdom by some to the times of Marcus Aurelius, and by others to those of Diocletian, is tentative.

The localization of the original reliquary tombs is uncertain too. The *Passio* speaks of a place "in finibus Gallaeciae, super ripam fluminis, cui nomen est Ceia, secus stratam," which has been identified with the *Domnos sanctos* of Sahagún. Documents of later dates (a diplomata of Ramiro II of 945) claim that tombs had been in existence before the settlement of the monks of Córdoba by Alphonso III; and the twelfth-century anonymous chronicle of Sahagún maintains that these tombs were Visigothic. From the twelfth century on the relics underwent several successive local *translationes*. Presently they are preserved in the church of San Juan, also in Sahagún. A competing localization of the relics of Facundo and Primitivo in the cathedral of Orense may be the

240

result of an interested reading of the township of Cea in the diocesis of Orense, in which there is a church dedicated to Facundo, as identical with the banks of the Cea *in finibus Gallaeciae* of which the *Passio* of the saints speak to us.

Vives-*Calendarios* 2 (1949): 119–46, 339–80; 3 (1950): 145–61; Vives-*Inscripciones*, n. 307; R. Escalona, *Historia del real monasterio de Sahagún* (Madrid, 1782); W. Fernandez Luna, *Monografía histórica de Sahagún* (León, 1921;) *BHL* nos. 2820–21; Hübner-*Inscriptiones*, n. 175; GómMor-*mozárabes*, pp. 202–6; GómMor-*Cat León*, pp. 343–61; Fábrega-*Pasionario*, 1:64–67, 2:46–56; J. Guerra, "Facundus," in *DHGE*; J. Fernández Alonso, "Facondo e Primitivo," in *BSS*.

FOY: The particularly large number of extant manuscripts conveying the account of the passion of St. Foy (Lat.: Fides, –is; Engl.: Foy or Faith; It.: Fede) witness to the extraordinary popularity of the saint in central and southern France as well as in northeastern Spain. There seems to be little doubt that such popularity is ascribable to two main reasons: on the one hand, Foy's tender age at the time of her martyrdom; and on the other, the meaning of her name – faith – which must have greatly impressed the imagination of the popular audience. The many accounts of the passion of the saint may be reduced to two main recensions: one of these has its source in a tenth-century manuscript in the B.N. of Paris (ms. lat. 5301, fols. 328r–329v), while the other, also in a tenth-century manuscript of the École de Médecin of Montpellier (H 152, fols. 231v–237v). It is from the second recension that the most common and widespread account of the passion derives, the *Passio SS. Fidis et Caprasii* (*BHL* nos. 2928–38). The dating of her martyrdom cannot be determined with further exactitude: it is variously put either under the persecutions of Maximianus in 286–88 or as a consequence of the persecutions of Diocletian initiated in 303.

The legend of Foy's passion is told with gusto and a predilection for colorful details. Foy was born in Agen, in southwestern France, from pagan parents. She was brought up by a Christian wet-nurse who also had her baptized by Caprais, a man considered as the first known bishop of Agen. The girl soon showed precocious signs of virtuous mind and heart: she made vows of virginity and preached publicly the beauties of the Christian religion.

Thereupon many citizens of Agen converted to the true Faith. With the arrival of Dacien, most Christians, including Bishop Caprais, took refuge in the nearby town of Pompéjac. Foy, on her part, barely twelve years old at the time, valiantly confronted the Roman officials refusing to sacrifice to the pagan deities. "I am ready to undergo no matter what torments you would choose for me," said the young girl. Dacien did not tarry for long: he had her tied to a brass grid and even had the fire started underneath. At the site of such cruelty many bystanders converted, ready to face martyrdom at their turn. Caprais too, advised of Foy's martyrdom, hurried to confess, that is to say to proclaim, his Faith. The double passion of Foy and Caprais was soon crowned by one and the same martyrdom: both were beheaded, whether on the same day or not remains an unresolved question. The *martyrologia* record October 6 for St. Foy and October 20 for St. Caprais.

The narrative of the *Passio* soon became complemented by a set of further episodes, amplifications, and colorful additions: next to the two saints, others too follow in the glorious path of martyrdom – so Alberta, the sister of Foy, two brothers of Caprais, Primus and Felicianus, and no less than 500 neophytes. The martyrdom of Foy becomes tainted with the stigma of denigration and defilement, since she is whipped and dragged to the temple to be raped; miraculous intervention, however, forestalls some of these schemes: the temple caves in at the right moment and a dove puts out the flames under the brass grid.

The earthly remains of St. Foy found a first resting place outside the walls of Agen, at the site of her martyrdom, in a modest funerary chapel built by Bishop Dulcidius in the fifth century. But they did not remain there for long. The relics became the object of one of the most famous cases of *furta sacra* of the Middle Ages to which the youthful saint, according to the accepted principles operating in such matters, consented. The abbey of Conques, founded towards the beginning of the ninth century and richly endowed subsequently by the French monarchs, tried unsuccessfully to acquire the relics of St. Vincent, the deacon-martyr of Zaragoza, at the time in Valencia. The monks of Conques, on their return from Valencia, empty-handed, learned about St. Foy and devised a way to get hold of her relics. One of them, Ariviscus, having remained in Agen for a few years and having worked himself into the confidence of the local ecclesiastical hierarchies, on the day of Epiphany of the year 866 broke the lid of the tomb and fled with the precious remains of the young saint. On January 14th of that year the relics of St. Foy were triumphantly escorted into the abbey church of Conques. A document of the year 883 cites St. Foy as the patroness of the abbey.

A number of building programs followed, each on a further grandiose scale than the preceding one, in order to provide the precious relics with the appropriate ecclesiastical and architectural frame of reference. Étienne II, abbot of Conques (942–84), initiated the building of a first spacious basilica in 942; a second basilica, this time triple-naved, was erected by Abbot Hugues in the second half of the tenth century; and a third abbey church, the splendid structure we know today, was begun by Abbot Odolric between 1041 and 1050. The relics of the saint, in the meanwhile, did not lie still either. The skull of Foy was enclosed into a precious head-reliquary donated to the abbey by Charles the Bold; this head-reliquary was subsequently placed upon an enthroned *Maiestas* from Auvergne that Abbot Étienne had procured for the abbey. During the Wars of Religion, walled in, the relics escaped destruction. The remoteness of Conques in the Massif Central helped to preserve the relics through the Revolution.

More importantly for the hagiographic history of the relics, these proved to be, from the beginning, most efficiently miraculous: at one point, the saintly remains could not be moved from one location to the next – the principle of the irremovability of the relic without its consent; at another, the legs of Abbot Hugues, badly bruised in the course of hauling stones for the construction of the abbey church, were healed by saintly mediation. Such instances, however, were considered nothing but the initial stages only of her miraculous interventions. As the reputation of her thaumaturgical powers spread, so too her many miracles increased. There was nothing new in such a course of events: Christian, and not merely Christian, history has from its earliest times known the trend: the more that miracles were desired, the more they happened. Regarded as the "Illuminated" for having rendered vision to a blind man whose eyes had been torn out, Foy was henceforth considered especially efficient in healing the blind, in having sterile women conceive, and particularly, in the liberation of prisoners. The many shackles and chains hung all over the Abbey Church of Conques witness to the miracles of the liberation of Christian prisoners in Saracen captivity; also, the various books of the *Liber miraculorum S. Fidis* testify to these and other miracles. This *Liber*, modeled upon similar medieval books of miracles, proves particularly rich. The first two books were the work of one Bernard of Angers in the early eleventh century; the last two books were composed in Conques towards the end of that century.

To the great appeal that a young martyr girl must have had upon the popular imagination, one must add the particularly favorable geographic situation of Conques on the *via podense* that leads to Santiago: a combination of these factors made of St. Foy, over the centuries, one of the most beloved saintly figures on the route to St. James, and of Conques, to our own days, perhaps the single most haunting site on the pilgrimage route. The magnificent architecture of the Romanesque abbey church, its famous tympanum, its historiated capitals, and its superb collection of

Kleinkunst in the Treasury constitute one of the richest medieval ensembles anywhere in Europe.

The relationship between the great abbey and the Hispanic *Reconquista* was particularly tightly woven: devotion to the young saint was strong in Navarra, Aragón, and Cataluña; a former monk of Conques became, by the end of the eleventh century, bishop of Barbastro and of Roda in Aragón; Pedro I, king of Aragón, after the victory of Barbastro, placed his reign under the *patrocinium* of St. Foy; the great abbey of the Rouergue had particularly numerous possessions in Navarra: among others, the church and the hospital of Roncesvalles. A Spanish tradition speaks of a *translatio* of her remains to San Cugat del Vallés (cf. Croiset-*Année* 5:913).

Passio SS. Fidis et Caprasii, in *BHL* nos. 2928–38 and in *ActaSS* Oct. 8:823–25; the *translatio*, in *BHL* nos. 2939 and in *ActaSS* Oct. 3: 294–99; in *BHL* no. 2091 and in *ActaSS* Oct. 3:289–92; the *Liber miraculorum S. Fidis*, in *BHL* nos. 2942–61; A. Bouillet and L. Servieres, *Ste. Foy vierge et martyre* (Rodez, 1900) (with translation of the *Liber miraculorum*); P. Alfaric and E. Hoepffner, *La chanson de Ste. Foy* (Paris, 1926), 2 vols; J. Daoust, "Foy," in *DHGE*; Durliat-Jacques, pp. 44–79.

FRONT: St. Front (Fr.; Lat.: Frontus and later Fronto; It.: Frontone), according to tradition, the first bishop of Périgueux, enjoyed a fundamentally regional cult limited to the Dordogne and to Périgueux. The origin of the cult of St. Front is lost in the early days of the Merovingian Périgord. Gregory of Tours does not mention him, while the author of the life of St. Géry does it *en passant* for the sake of his own hero (*AnBoll* 7 [1888]: 394). The oldest *Vita* of St. Front, in barbarous Latin, has been preserved in two manuscripts (*AnBoll* 48 [1930]: 343–60); it was composed in pre-Carolingian times, and it is a somewhat hasty and less-than-thoughtful assemblage of disparate fragments not always hanging logically together. (See Croiset-*Année* 5:382.)

Born of Christian parents in Linocassium, Lanquais in the Dordogne, and having learned to read the Psalms, Front goes to live the hermit's life with two companions. Persecuted by Squirius, a Roman *praeses* – governor – he leaves for Egypt. On his way back, on the strength of the miracles he had performed, Front was consecrated bishop of Périgueux by St. Peter in Rome, and was sent home with the mission of converting his compatriots. A companion, George, dies on the route, whereupon Front returns to Rome and, given the staff of Peter, resurrects his companion to life. In the light of this miracle many pagans convert. Seventy of these are made Front's disciples and, once back in Périgueux, they all become the victims of Squirius' persecution. Withdrawn with his disciples to a solitary retreat, Front and the faithful company suffer hunger. An angel compells Squirius to send them food on seventy camels. Once these return, Squirius himself converts and is baptized by St. Front. The last portion of the account has been borrowed from the story of another saint with a similar name, Frontonius.

Several episodes and aspects of the story are rather incongruous and ill-matched: the flight into Egypt as well as the camels seem to belong to a different story superimposed upon that of Front; the miracles that led to his consecration are never clarified; the mission Front is given to convert his compatriots hardly corresponds to the account of his baptism; the episode of George seems to be another overlapping.

Perhaps because of such and similar discordances, towards the tenth century a second *Vita* was composed by one Gauzbert, co-bishop of Limoges (Paris, B.N., ms. lat. 5365, in *AnBoll* 75 (1957): 351–65). This version of Front's life is considerably simplified; its structure is made reasonably logical. The early mentioning of Squirius is eliminated as is the Egyptian stay altogether. And the end of the narrative stresses the pastoral work of Front: impressed by the conversion of Squirius, the pagans of the city also convert while Front and his disciples build churches for the introduction of Christian cult. In a still later text of the eleventh century (*BHL* nos. 3183 and 3185, the latter in *ActaSS* Oct. 11:407–13) Front is made one of the original Seventy-Two Disciples of Christ.

On the foundations of a sixth-century church erected in honor of St. Front, a new tenth-century church was built by the archbishop of Bourges, Aymon in 1047. Partly burned down in 1120, it was reconstructed once again in the magnificent ground plan, elevation, and dimensions as we see it today. The elaborate reliquary tomb structure erected in 1077 by the monk Guinamound of La Chaise-Dieu in imitation of the round tomb of the Holy Sepulcher in Jerusalem, was destroyed in 1575 in the course of the Wars of Religion. In the year 1261 a recognition of the body of St. Front was effected by Bishop Pierre de Saint-Astier in order to corroborate the integrity of the relic. The memory of St. Front is celebrated on October 25.

From the tenth century on the collegiate church of St. Front became the burial site for the bishops of Périgueux. In the seventeenth century the church of St. Front was declared the cathedral of the city supplanting the old church of Saint-Étienne-de-la-Cité.

ActaSS Oct. 11:392–414; Duchesne-*Fastes* 2:87–88, 130–34; *BHL* nos. 3182–88, 8286; M. Coens, *La vie ancienne de S. Front de Périgueux*, in *AnBoll* 48 (1930): 324–60; Quentin-*martyrologues*, p. 221; J. Lavialle, *Reliques de saints conservées dans la basilique S.-Front* (Périgueux,

1902); J. Roux, *La basilique S.-Front de Périgueux* (Périgueux, 1920); R. Aubert, "Front," in *DHGE*; H. Claude, "Frontone," in *BSS*.

GENESIUS OF ARLES: A fifth century *passio*, the *Acta primorum martyrum sincera* (*BHL* no. 3304) as well as an anonymous sermon (*BHL* no. 3305) of the same epoch, are the oldest accounts on Genesius of Arles (Lat. and Engl.; Fr.: Genès; It.: Genesio). According to these sources, Genesius was a young catechumen who had entered the Roman militia with the functions of notary or stenographer. Once the imperial persecutions reached the region of Arles (of Diocletian according to most, but possibly of Decius), caught by apprehension and fear, Genesius went into hiding. Some time later, he asked to be baptized; but the local bishop, assuming that the young catechumen, if arrested by the authorities, would not be able to resist the pains of torture, declined to administer him the baptismal rites. One day, in spite of his hidings, Genesius was detained by his persecutors on the banks of the Rhône. Trying to escape from them, he threw himself into the current and swam across to the other shore. There, however, he was immediately caught, arrested, and executed. The Christians of the area, impressed by the young catechumen's martyrdom, erected an altar on the site *cruoris vestigia*, and translated his remains to this side of the shore, to be buried in the famous cemetery of Alyscamps. Genesius belongs to the typology of the *cephalophorus* saint, that is to say, one who, after being decapitated, carries his own head. (One of the more famous instances of this typology is St. Dionysius.) Genesius' martyrdom falls early in the fourth century, probably in the year 303 or 308.

The description in the *Acta* and elsewhere of the two locations – of the martyrdom and of the inhumation – correspond well to the topographic realities of Trinquetaille and Arles; also, it corresponds well to the various memorials and monuments erected at the two sites: the altar, a mulberry-tree, a marble column, and the Basilica of St.-Genès extant to our own day.

The *Martyrologium Hieronymianum* (463–65, 650) mentions for Genesius a *dies natalis* for August 25, and for the consecration of his basilica, December 16. The cult of Genesius rapidly took deep roots in Arles and even beyond its region. A significant aspect in the saint's appeal lies no doubt in the very story of his martyrdom, a story at one and the same time credible and realistic (Genesius is afraid, he escapes, hides, throws himself into the river, the bishop declines to baptize him) as well as edifying (Genesius is a young catechumen studying to become a new convert, he asks for baptism). It is significant that Venantius Fortunatus speaks of Arles in terms of *Urbs Genesii*, singling out Genesius from among a number of other famous alternatives (Trophimus, Caesarius,

Hilary). The relics of the catechumen-saint are considered by Prudentius (*Peristephanon*, 4.35) *praepollens*, that is to say, highly powerful and efficacious. St. Apollinaris of Valence witnesses to pilgrims who desire to be buried in the vicinity of the saint and thus wait in his shadow for the Resurrection. It should be also remembered that a number of Paleochristian sarcophagi in Arles are decorated on their short end by the head of a youth in whom one has seen an evocation of Genesius. The saint, as only natural, has been considered particularly efficacious in rescuing the faithful from the perils of drowning.

Beyond the region of the Rhône, St. Genesius has struck deep roots particularly in Spain and Italy: the sacramentary of Vich and a Hispanic abridgement of the *Martyrologium Hieronymianum* witness to these ultramontane interests.

ActaSS Aug. 5:123–36; *MartRom*, 359; S. Cavallin, "S. Genès le notaire," *Eranos* (Göteborg) 43 (1945): 150–75; F. Benoît, *Les cimitières suburbains d'Arles* [Studi di antichità cristiane, 11 (Vatican City, 1935), pp. 4–12]; B. von der Lage, *Studien zur Genesius Legende* (Berlin, 1898–99); O. Franchi de' Cavalieri, *S. Genesio di Arelate, S. Ferreolo di Vienne, S. Giuliano di Brivas*, in *Note Agiografiche* 8 (Studi e Testi, 65), (Vatican City, 1935), pp. 203ff.; S. Prete, "Genesio," in *BSS*; R. Aubert, "Genès d'Arles," in *DHGE*.

GILES: There are several early lives of Giles (Fr.: Gilles; It.: Egidio; Lat.: Aegidius), saint, hermit, and abbot. The oldest is a cumbersome and overcomplicated narrative, the *Vita Sancti Aegidii* (*BHL* no. 93; *ActaSS* Sept. 1:299–303. For the various editions, see J. Pycke, "Gilles," in *DHGE*), full of anachronisms and inverisimili-tudes, written in the tenth century by a monk of the Abbey of St.-Gilles on the Petit Rhône, not too far from Arles. The authorship is at times attributed to Fulbert of Chartres, but with no better justification than the fact of the latter's having composed an office for St. Giles (Migne-*PL* 141:343). According to the *Vita*, Giles is born in Athens of high-standing and pious parents. Once he becomes an orphan, he travels to Marseilles – we suppose by ship – and subsequently initiates a life of hermitage and solitude which would henceforth be characteristic of his ways in the world. At first Giles spends some years in the company of Caesarius, bishop of Arles; next he goes to live in a grotto on the banks of the Gard, accompanied by the hermit Vérédème; finally, he retires completely from the world into absolute solitude on the delta of the Rhône in the company of wild animals only. Among them is a doe who feeds him daily with her milk. Up to this point the life of Giles is an ever-deepening spiritual exercise in introspection.

Here, however, a first change of scenario takes place. A Gothic king – the Visigothic King Wamba – on a hunting party, is pursuing a frail doe, that turns out to be Giles's faithful companion. The terrified doe takes refuge naturally enough next to the saint. At this point a stray arrow shot by the king wounds Giles, but he accepts no help; instead, he proposes to the king the foundation of a monastery. His wish is immediately granted, and Giles becomes the abbot of the new settlement. Here a second change of scenario occurs: Giles sets out for Orleans where Charlemagne confides to him having committed some grave sin, the nature of which, however, the emperor does not disclose. At a subsequent mass, an angel reveals to Giles the nature of the sin while at the same time gives assurances of absolution on behalf of the monarch. Yet another change of scenario takes Giles to Rome: there he sues for direct pontifical protection for his monastery in order to ensure its desired independence.

Giles died on September 1. It is hardly possible, however, to determine, even approximately, the year of his death. It oscillates, depending on the authority consulted, between the last third of the seventh and the first third of the eighth century. His life is a paradigm of the devout's progression from hermitage to monasticism.

The chronological incongruities of the narrative cannot be glossed over: St. Caesarius died in 543; King Wamba, around 670; Charlemagne, in 814. There is no way to correlate these dates. But the real difficulties lie elsewhere: in 514 Caesarius had sent a delegation to Rome which included a certain Abbot Aegidius, whom some have readily identified with St. Giles (Mabillon-*Annales Benedicti*, 1:99-100). But such an early date, apart from not squaring with the dates of the other people of the account, does not fit the late *patrocinium* of St. Giles at the monastery of Gard: early tenth-century documents speak of a "monasterium sancti Petri in Gothia" only. Besides, while the tomb of St. Giles is a Merovingian sarcophagus, the inscription on it is of the tenth century; and furthermore, the older papal bulls in the cartulary of St. Giles are apocryphal, of late fabrication. Indeed, most signs point to a tenth-century retroactive chronicling whose aim is to shore up the standing of the monastery of Saint-Gilles-du-Gard with the dignity that antiquity lends: it is within such an ideological frame that the figure of a hermit, who might have lived sometime in the sixth or perhaps the seventh century, turned into one of the most widely revered saints of the Middle Ages.

The ample diffusion of the devotion to St. Giles in various regions of France, in central and mideastern Europe, as well as in England generated a large number of early translations, as well as rearrangements of his *Vita*, a pattern which we do not find, as a rule, with most other saints. True that Saint-Gilles-du-Gard lies both on the road to Santiago – the *via tolosana* – and on that to Rome; and furthermore it lodges on the bottom of the north-south axis which, along the Rhône, reaches the northern plains and Paris. The ample diffusion of Giles' fame and, more significantly, the deep devotion of his devotees, however, cannot be explained away with only the pilgrimage routes or with the conveniently drawn in Hispanic (King Wamba) and Carolingian (Charlemagne) figures who play such prominent roles in the story. Even less can it be explained away on the strength of the great splendor that the abbey church and its monastery attained between the eleventh and the thirteenth centuries: indeed, St.-Gilles became one of the seminal radiating centers of monastic culture in the South. There have also been attempts at looking for an answer to the sudden diffusion and unusual depth of the saint's cult in connections with the Gregorian Reform, or with the network of Benedictine abbeys. But none of these has really made a convincing argument.

It might not be amiss to remember at this point that the city, all around the abbey, at some point with 40,000 inhabitants, was in the centuries of Romanesque culture an enterprising and bustling trading center, with an active port on the Petit Rhône, the small arm of this important river, an international marketplace and fair of the first order. Under such circumstances, the central message of the legend of Giles – the nourishing doe and the wounded saint – might have travelled far and fast on the wings of popular imagination and oral culture. In Chartres, the scene of the doe is represented thrice: twice on stained glass windows and once on the south portal. The moving episode of the trembling doe taking refuge with Giles, itself generated the thaumaturgical specialization of the saint, famous for curing, precisely, mental imbalances and illnesses, paranoia, irrational proclivities, the fear of the unknown and of the night, even the fear of loneliness. The traits of softness, gentleness, and meekness might have been conjugated in the mind and the heart of the popular audience with the reciprocal tenderness displayed by Giles and the doe, an affective relationship suggesting filial, paternal, and particularly maternal trends. Such deep-seated perception, readily assimilated, might ultimately be responsible for the profound influence of Giles across most of western Europe.

The date of Giles' death, September 1, is recorded in both the *Martyrologium Romanum* and in that of Usuard. The particular relationship of Giles with St. James is evident in at least three aspects of the French saint's story: the locale of the hermitage between Arles and Gelonne, on the *via tolosana*; the Wamba episode – probably an offshot of the Visigothic king's campaigns in Septimania and his conquest of Nîmes; and the Charlemagne interlude.

ActaSS Sept. 1:284–304; *Martyrologium Usuardi*, in Migne-*PL* 124: 423–28; E.-C. Jones, *Saint Gilles. Essai d'histoire littéraire* (Paris, 1914); F. Brittain, *St. Giles* (Cambridge, 1928); N. Pétourand, *L'iconographie de la chasse de Saint Gilles* (Lyon, 1949); L. Gnadinger, *Eremitica. Studien zur altfranzösischen Heiligenvita des 12. und 13. Jahrhunderts* (Beihefte zur Zeitschrift für romanische philologie 130), (Tübingen, 1972); P. Viard, "Egidio," in *BSS*; J. Picke, "Gilles," in *DHGE*.

HILARY OF POITIERS: Hilary (Fr.: Hilaire; It.: Ilario; Lat.: Hilarius), saint, bishop of Poitiers, Doctor of the Church, one of the greatest seminal thinkers of the early Western consolidation of the Roman Catholic Church. Hilary was born in Poitiers between 310 and 320 of a socially high-standing family, which provided him with a sound classical and philosophic education. Hilary was converted to Christianity in his formative years, though we do not know exactly when, apparently as a direct consequence of his readings in the Holy Scriptures (Venantius Fortunatus, *Vita*, 1.3, in Migne-*PL* 9:183–200). Such an intellectual trend in his conversion suits well the highly speculative bent of his mind that will later generate the great exegetical and theological masterpieces of his career – with good reason he has been called the Athanasius of the West.

Married and the father of a daughter Abra, Hilary was shortly after 350 elevated to the episcopal see of his city. Already in this first portion of his adult life he wrote extensively; among many other works he composed the oldest extant Matthew commentary in Latin, the *Commentarium in Matthaeum*, a work of important numerological symbolism. Cf. J. Doignon, *Hilaire de Poitiers avant l'exil. Recherches sur la...foi épiscopale en Gaule au milieu du IVe s."* (Paris, 1971); and also by Doignon, *Hilaire de Poitiers. Sur Matthieu. Introduction. Texte critique...* (Paris, 1978–79). There seem to be no traces of classical influence in these early works.

Ardently engaged in the Arian controversy, Hilary was exiled in Phrygia by Emperor Constantius II, an exile which lent him the occasion to deepen his thoughts concerning Eastern Trinitarian thinking. From this cogitation his great speculative masterpiece, *De Trinitate*, as well as other writings, would eventually issue. A constantly creative mind, Hilary generated ideological restlessness in the East too: it was not without reason that he was termed "discordiae seminarium et perturbator Orientis" (Sulpicius Severus, *Chronicorum* 2.45.4, in Migne-*PL* 20:155). Released from exile, Hilary spent some time in Italy (360–53) and in Milan he engaged in a second battle against Arianism: his *Liber contra Auxentium* belongs to this epoch. Back in Poitiers, he ended his days in 367, occupied to the end with exegetical work. Throughout his writings, Hilary demonstrates a sharply focused speculative mind of unusual analytic power though not quite severed from underlying topical as well as current historico-political considerations.

The earthly remains of Hilary were buried between the tombs of his wife and his daughter, in a funerary chapel that, considerably later, became Saint-Hilaire-le-Grand. The subsequent destiny of his relics is uncertain. Saint-Denys near Paris and Saint-George of Le Puy claimed at one point to possess at least some of his remains, the latter, apparently, with good reason. Hilary's veneration and the tradition of his miracles are circumscribed mainly to the central-western regions of France, and mainly to the Poitou.

The most represented miracle of St. Hilary – the rising of the ground under the saint to allow him to appear on the same level as the other bishops who had deprived him of his seat – is also of intellectual import. Other miracles include the expulsion of the serpents from the island of Gallinaria and the resuscitation of a dead child: this last one follows already the line of customary miraculous saintly interventions.

In Poitiers, apart from Saint-Hilaire-le-Grand, there is a second church that remembers him, Saint-Hilaire-le-Celle, erected at the site of his dwelling. Hilary's *dies natalis* is celebrated on January 13.

BHL nos. 3885–909; *ActaSS* Jan. 1:790–803; G. Giamberardini, *S. Ilario di Poitiers e la sua attività apostolica* (Cairo, 1956); P. Galtier, "Saint Hilaire, trait d'union entre l'Occident et l'Orient," *Gregorianum* 40 (1959): 609–23; M. Meslin, *Hilaire de Poitiers* (Paris, 1959); P. Galtier, *Saint Hilaire de Poitiers, le premier docteur de l'église latine* (Bibliothèque de théologie historique), (Paris, 1960); G. Morrel, "Hilary of Poitiers: a Theological Bridge between Christian East and Christian West," *Anglican Theological Review* 44 (1962): 312–16; U. C. Brennecke, *Hilaire von Poitiers und die Bischofsopposition gegen Konstantius II. Untersuchungen zur dritten Phase der arianischen Streites* (Patristische Texte und Studien 26), (Berlin, 1984, pp. 337–61); A. Quacquarelli, "Ilario," in *BSS*; R. Aubert, "Hilaire," in *DHGE*; S. J. McKenna, "Hilary of Poitiers, St.," in *NCE*.

HONORATUS: Honoratus (Lat., Eng., Ger.; Fr.: Honorat; It.: Onorato), first abbot of Lérins and bishop of Arles, might have been born in Trier (E. Brouette, "Honoratus," in *LTK3*) sometime in the last third of the third century. That he was the offspring of a consular family we gather from the funerary sermon preached by Hilary of Arles, his successor in the episcopal see. Baptized in his early youth, Honoratus left his native country together with his brother Venantius and his mentor Caprasius, with the idea of searching for a more perfect realization of the Christian life. After an apparently short stay in Marseille, they embarked for Greece, where Venantius died. Honoratus, himself ill, returned to Provence and on the advice of Bishop Leontius of Fréjus, established himself on a serpent-infested island of the Lérins group, off the southern seacoast near Cannes. It is not clear under whose economic protection Honoratus founded, around 410, what would later become the famous monastery of Lérins. The monastery and the school of Lérins became, in the fifth and sixth centuries, one of the most vigorous spiritual and intellectual centers of Gaul whose influence irradiated throughout the whole of Western Christendom (cf. D. Misonne, "Lérins," in *LTK3*, s. v.)

In 427 Honoratus somewhat reluctantly accepted the calling to ascend to the episcopal see of Arles in the wake of the assassination of Bishop Patroclus. It is not quite clear whether between Patroclus and Honoratus there was not a brief bishopric of Euladius. At any rate, barely able to reestablish the bishopric authority and the overall harmony in the city, Honoratus died in 429, as we are told, exhausted by his relentless pastoral work and by his absorbing ecclesiastical preoccupations.

Honoratus was inhumed in the famous cemetery of Alyscamps. The later-erected church over his tomb is now secularized. In 1392, during the Hundred Years' War, his remains were transferred for safe-keeping to Lérins (Veillard-*guide*, p. 35, n. 6) amidst splendid celebrations, the echoes of which have reached us in the so-called *sanctus transitus* – strangely enough, not *translatio*. With the secularization of the abbey in 1788, the relics of Honoratus were divided among various churches, one of which is the cathedral of Grasse.

The *Martyrologium romanum* mentions Honoratus on January 1. His *patrocinium* – the cult extended by his devotees – rests on the perception of a sincere and godly life spent in search of his own Christian realization as well as in the fulfillment of his ecclesiastical and pastoral duties vis-à-vis his fold. His cult is centered in Arles and the surrounding areas.

ActaSS Jan. 2:379–90; Hilary of Arles, *Vita S. Honorati*, in Migne–*PL* 50:1249–72; *BHL* nos. 3975–79; F. Bonnart, *St. Honorat. de Lèrins* (Tours, 1914); S. Cavallin, *Vitae SS. Honorati et Hilarei episcoporum arelatensium* (Lund, 1952); H. G. J. Beck, "Honoratus of Arles, St.," in *NCE*; G. Mathon, "Onorato," in *BSS*; E. Brouette, "Honoratus," in *LTK3*.

ISIDORE OF SEVILLE: The life of Isidore (Eng., Fr.; Lat.: Isidorus; Sp.: Isidoro) of Seville, the great encyclopedist of the early Middle Ages, has been transmitted to us through a copious tradition collected in breviaries and elsewhere (*ActaSS* Apr. 1:327–64). His Romanized parents had to leave Cartagena, *Cartago nova*, around 554, driven out by the Byzantine authorities; they settled in Visigothic Seville, taking with them Leandro and Fulgentius, two older brothers of Isidore, and Florentina, his sister. Of these, Leandro became achbishop of Seville; Fulgentius, bishop of Astigi (Ecija), and Florentina entered a cloister. Isidore must have been born in Seville between 560 and 570. With the passing away of the parents, Leandro assumed the duties of *pater familias* and attended to the education of young Isidore. He was probably sent to an episcopal school; his frequenting a monastic school too, on the other hand, is questionable.

The incredibly vast and many–sided corpus of his writings, which makes of him the first great encyclopedist of the Middle Ages, suggests that Isidore must have been foremostly an autodidact, absorbing the material of his learning from whatever source with monastic punctiliousness and constancy. In the *De officiis ecclesiasticis* Isidore offers a much-needed handbook of Visigothic liturgy; in the *Regula monachorum* he presents a synthetic program culled from Eastern and Western monastic traditions; in the *Historia Gothorum* Isidore attempts to reconcile the native Romanized population with the Visigothic one and thereby to establish the foundations of a Hispanic national church; in *Sententiarum libri tres*, his most significant theological work, Isidore treats mainly moral questions of both general and topical interest. The fortune of his name, however, is attached to the *Etymologiae* or *Origines* which is a broad etymological encyclopedia – one of the most vital bridges between the ancient and the medieval worlds.

Isidore succeeded his brother Leandro in the archiepiscopal see of Seville around the year 600. Judging from his *Sententiae*, in which he reviews the strenuous and demanding schedule of a bishop, he must have taken his pastoral duties with devout abnegation and high earnestness. The demands of public life took him to various Visigothic church councils, the Second Provincial of Seville, and the Fourth National of Toledo in 633. The imprint of Isidore on this last council was profound and lasting: the liturgical unity of the Visigothic Church became reaffirmed, and an *opusculum*, the *Ordo de celebrando concilio*, attributed to Isidore himself, laid down the principles and the mechanism for subsequent convocations. Having exercised the episcopate for some forty years, Isidore prepared himself with appropriate Christian care and humility for his own *transitus* which, by then, was close:

having distributed his personal belongings, wearing a sackcloth, and having offered, according to the Visigothic rite, public penance *in extremis*, Isidore died in 636 at the ripe age of nearly 80 years. The details surrounding his death have been faithfully preserved by the testimony of a witness.

Little is known of his original burial site. An old tradition of the eighth century wanted his remains to be resting between those of his brothers (Paris, B.N. ms. lat. 8093); a later one looked for his tomb in Santiponce (Old Sevilla). The memory of his death on April 4 is variously recorded: the famous *Martyrologium of Usuard* of the third quarter of the ninth century takes up Isidore on that date, and subsequently we find the saint in many calendars and *martyrologia* as well as old litany cycles.

From the eleventh century on Isidore's fame as an erudite sage became superseded by that of a thaumaturge, though without ever obliterating his impact on the encyclopedic tradition. In the year 1063 the remains of Isidore were transferred to León in a celebrated *translatio* recorded in the *Translationis Isidori* (Flórez-*Sagrada* 9:406–12), whose details are well known through the *Chronicon* of Silos too. In the summer of that year the troops of Ferdinand I of León had reached the domains of the *taifa* sovereign of Sevilla who, in view of the impending danger to his city, offered a deal: the remains of the martyr Santa Justa against the withdrawal of the Leonese army. Ferdinand agreed. At that point, however, Isidore himself appeared in a miraculous intervention and dislodged the martyr in favor of himself. On December 21 of that year the Basilica of León, which until then had been dedicated to St. Pelayo, was reconsecrated to Isidore, and the next day the feast of the *translatio* took place (*ActaSS* Apr. 1:353–64).

The relics of St. Isidore, in their new Leonese habitat and enclosed in a stupendously precious silver reliquary casket extant to our own days, carried the fame of the broad thaumaturgical powers of the saint. Close to the last stretch of the road to Santiago, Isidore mightily contributed to the notion of the magnificence of the miracles that were awaiting the pilgrims of the Jacobean itinerary; at the same time, in a reciprocal way, Isidore benefited also from the towering influence of St. James. Isidore's miraculous appearance on horseback leading the Christian army of Alphonso VII to the conquest of Baeza is an iconographic imitation of St. James' doing the same at the battle of Clavijo. Thus the famous iconography of the *Matamoros* – the slayer of the Moors – is borrowed for more or less holy purposes, a phenomenon quite recurrent along the pilgrimage route.

DíazDíaz-*Index*, pp. 28–47; F. Arévalo, *Sancti Isidori Hispalensis episcopi opera omnia* (Rome, 1797–1803); the same in Migne-*PL* 82–

84; F. Arévalo, *Isidoriana* (Rome, 1797); the same in Migne-*PL* 81; J. Pérez de Urbel, *San Isidoro de Sevilla* (Barcelona, 1940); L. Araujo-Costa, *San Isidoro de Sevilla* (Madrid, 1942); H. Beeson, *Isidor-Studien* (Munich, 1913); P. Séjourné, *Le dernier Père de l'Église, Saint Isidore de Séville. Son rôle dans l'histoire du droit canonique* (Paris, 1929); J. Fontaine, *Isidore de Séville et la culture classique dans l'Espagne wisigothique* (Paris, 1959); A. Viñayo González, "Isidoro," in *BSS*; K. Baus,"Isidor, Erzbishof von Sevilla," in *LTK3*; R. Schmid, "Isidore of Seville," in *SHE*.

LEONARD: Of Leonard (Fr.: Léonard; It.: Leonardo; Ger.: Leonhard; Lat.: Leonardus) of Noblat near Limoges, saint and confessor, nothing is known until the eleventh century. Hagiographers before that date ignore him. A first mention of St. Leonard we find in an incidental remark of Ademar of Chabannes (Migne-*PL* 141:69) within a piece of writing concerning the head of St. John the Baptist supposedly found in 1017 at Saint-Jean-d'Angély in the Poitou in the central-western portion of Gaul. The faithful flocked from all over to admire such stupendous *inventio*. At this point *Leonardus confessor, in Lemovicino* is mentioned. There is a second document in the form of a letter sent by a cleric of Limoges to Bishop Fulbert or Fulbertus of Chartres asking the prelate whether he was acquainted with some *vita* of St. Leonard (Migne-*PL* 141:273). We know of no answer to this letter.

A suspicious *Vita sancti Leonardi* (*BHL* no. 4862; suppl., p. 194, no. 4862a) appeared, as if from nowhere, around 1030: this *vita* is so full of distrustful details that it must be a total fabrication. Indeed, it is considered such. The Bollandists' comment to the *Martyrologium romanum* thinks it *fabularum plena* (B. Cignitti, "Leonardo," in *BSS*); furthermore, confrontation with hagiographic material has shown an unusual amount of borrowings from the lives of St. Remigius and St. Calais.

Leonard is born in Gaul under Emperor Anastasius in the early sixth century. His parents were of high-standing nobility to the point that Clodoveus, king of the Franks (481–511) officiated at the baptism as his godfather. (Cf. Croiset-*Année* 6:115; and Voragine-*Légende*, pp. 583–87.) Having refused to enter the army, Leonard followed St. Remigius of Reims and emulated him in the exercising of charity vis-à-vis prisoners. In fact, the liberation of prisoners became the focal point of his later thaumaturgical operations. One day crossing the forest of Pavum near Limoges, Leonard finds the queen in birth pangs. The saint's prompt intervention makes her deliver a healthy babe. Clodoveus, who was hunting in the vicinity, is overwhelmed: he bestowes upon the saint that portion of the forest which Leonard would be able to circumscribe while riding on an ass.

Leonard puts himself promptly to work: he builds an oratory dedicated to Our Lady and an altar dedicated to St. Remigius; next, he digs a well that miraculously fills with water. He also names the place *Nobiliacum* in deference to Clodoveus, *nobilissimo rege*. Soon Leonard's name rides on the wings of fame: many come to reside in the vicinity of the saint; soon a village springs up, Saint-Léonard-de-Noblat. The sick and the handicapped flock to his place. Prisoners in far off lands invoke his name. Having given evidence of his Faith through his pious pastoral work, without suffering martyrdom – hence he is known as confessor, Leonard dies on November 6, around the middle of the sixth century.

In part due perhaps to the pseudo-realistic tenor of his *Vita*, in part to the prominent role that the king is made to play in it, and in part to the very pilgrimage road on which Noblat lies, Leonard became very rapidly and, precisely during the crucial eleventh and twelfth centuries of Romanesque culture, one of the best known international saintly figures. In line with the dictates of medieval analogical thinking, Leonard's hermit-like retirement and isolation might be at the root of his later fame as liberator of prisoners. In fact, the liberation of captives became his thaumaturgical specialty and the springboard of his fame. In the freeing of prisoners though there was competition from other quarters: St. Domingo de Silos, St. Domingo de la Calzada, and St. James himself. But Leonard stood his ground.

The fame of St. Leonard of Noblat was particularly widespread in France and southern Germany, as the special protector of the military engaged in the endless crusade with the infidels. Knights, crusaders, the members of the military orders and soldiery of various kinds were among his fervent devotees. Strangely, in southern Germany Leonard became also the patron of the fields and the protector of the peasants.

The fact that the geographical area of his devotees was particularly developed in Bavaria, Würtenberg, and Austria brings to mind with further pointedness the significance of the international connections of the *via lemovicense* with the so-called *Oberstrasse* that collected pilgrims precisely from the south-German areas and from Austria. In this respect, it is noteworthy to recall that a new and enlarged *Vita* of Leonard with an elaborate list of miracles, composed towards the end of the eleventh or the beginning of the twelfth century, was written by Bishop Walram of Naumburg in Saxony, precisely in a distant German province (*BHL* nos. 4872–4872a, 4872b–4873; Migne-*PL* 159:993–994).

Apart from being the specific saint of prisoners in chains, in a curious paradox, Leonard became also the patron saint of chainmakers and generally speaking of iron workers. The underlying justification lies in the notion of the saint's offering protection against bandits and highwaymen.

BHL nos. 4862–79; *ActaSS* Nov. 3:139–209; L. Montesano, *Vita di San Leonardo detto il Limosino* (Monopoli, 1925); I. Biossac, *Saint Léonard ermite en Limosin* (Saint-Léonard-de-Noblat, 1960); S. Mastrobuoni, *Opera S. Leonardo di Siponto* (Manfredonia, 1960–61); A. M. Zimmermann, "Loenhard," in *LTK3*; B. Cignitti, "Leonardo," in *BSS*.

MARTIN OF TOURS: Martin (Eng., Fr.; It.: Martino), bishop of Tours, saint and confessor is, without any doubt, among the greatest and most firmly established figures in Christian hagiography. The two solid sources for Martin's *vita* are Sulpicius Severus' *Vita* and the notices in Gregory of Tours' *Historia Francorum*. His early life is shrouded in chronological uncertainties though not in substantive inconsistencies. He is born of pagan parents sometime around 316–317 in Sabaria, Pannonia, presently Szombathej, Hungary. His father was a veteran of the Roman army, a military tribune subject to fairly constant official transfers. Before long we see Martin in Pavia, among the hopeful catechumens of the important imperial city, and at fifteen years of age, enrolled already in the army, in the imperial guard of Constantius and later on of Julian. In the meanwhile Martin is baptized (Sulpicius Severus, *Vita* 2.3). Sometime later, if not the most important event of his life, certainly the one destined to become the most famous and the most widely represented one takes place: the dividing of his cloak with a beggar. It is this act of charity at the gates of Amiens that eventually turned paradigmatic for Martin, fueled by the sound common sense and imagination of later generations. His discharge from the army occurred, according to the *Vita*, in Worms around 355 – but possibly earlier, for soon afterwards his own discipleship to St. Hilary of Poitiers began to absorb his attention, a discipleship that would henceforth leave an indelible mark on his life.

In rapid succession, prompted by his Christian zeal always directed towards concrete evangelizing, thaumaturgic or exorcising goals, we see Martin back in Pannonia and later in Italy. In Pannonia he converts his mother, fails to persuade his father, and leads a bitter combat against the prevalent Arian heresy; in Italy, after an uneasy sojourn in Milan, Martin embraces the hermit's life on the island of Gallinaria off the coast of Genoa. In the meanwhile, in 360, since Hilary had just come back from exile, Martin joined him in Poitiers. His priestly ordination and his establishment in Ligugé, near Poitiers, of probably the first Gallic monastic settlement follow. It is from Ligugé that his fame as thaumaturge was destined to acquire ever-wider echoes. In 371, in spite of the resistance of the local clergy, Martin is elevated to the episcopal see of Tours (Sulpicius Severus, *Vita* 9; Gregory of Tours, *Historia Francorum* 1.48; 2.14; 10.31).

It is from this point on that the great pastoral labor of Martin will attain ever-wider constituencies and strike ever deeper roots. In the face of the barely primitive Christianization of most of the central regions of Gaul, Martin engages himself in an all-out campaign directed at stamping out pagan superstitions and hybrid cult practices. The word of Christ is brought to the out-of-the-way countryside, which was most of it. At the same time, Martin founds monasteries: in the first line at Marmoutier just outside Tours, which eventually becomes a crucible in the formation of Christian ecclesiastic leadership. The farther regions of Gaul are not neglected either, primarily the valley of the Loire; neither are Paris and Vienne. His indefatigable labor engages him in a measured defense of Priscillian, in numerous imperial visitations to Trier and elsewhere, and in stressful conflicts with the Spanish bishops.

Martin dies, characteristically for the office he was holding, during a pastoral visitation at Candes in 397. The cult of Martin, broad and deeply rooted in his own time, only grew with his death. Martin is one of the first official confessor-saints, that is to say, saints who did not die a death of martyrdom but who proclaimed their Faith in Christ through their works. Over his tomb a small chapel was erected by his successor in the episcopal see, Brice. After 461 this was superseded by a larger church at whose site, in the eleventh century, the magnificent Romanesque pilgrimage church of St. Martin was built, which subsequently during the Revolution was almost totally destroyed. The relics of Martin were dispersed, as far as we know, three times: in the ninth century, during the Wars of Religion, and in 1793. Needless to say, being at the fountainhead of one of the four French roads that lead towards Santiago de Compostela greatly contributed to the spreading of the cult of the saint. Outside France the devotion to St. Martin is particularly widespread in Spain, especially in the north, alongside the route to Santiago: a large number of churches are dedicated to him, like San Martín of Frómista, one of the most precious Romanesque structures on the route. No less famous is he in Italy and Germany. His feast is celebrated on November 11.

BHL nos. 5510–5666; Sulpicius Severus, *Vita S. Martini*, in *CSEL* 1:109–216; Gregory of Tours, *Historia Francorum*, 1.36–38, 43, in Migne-*PL* 71:179–81, 184–86; E. C. Babut, *Saint Martin de Tours* (Paris, 1913); H. Delehaye, "Saint Martin et Sulpice Sévère," *AnBoll* 38 (1920): 5, 136; P. Monceaux, *Saint Martin* (Paris, 1926); J. Leclercq, *Saint Martin et son temps* (Rome, 1961); É. Griffe, *La Gaule chrétienne à l'époque romaine* (Paris, 1947, 1:199–220); H. G. J. Beck, "Martin of Tours, St.," in *NCE*; J. Fontaine, "Martin," in *LTK3*; É. Amann, "Martin de Tours,"in *DTC*; M. Liverani, "Martino," in *BSS*.

MARY MAGDALENE: The Gospels know three figures whose personalities and characters considerably overlap: the anonymous sinner who wipes the feet of the Lord with her abundant hair (Luke 7.36–50); Mary of Bethany, the sister of Martha and Lazarus who, during the supper in Bethany, among other acts of piety, pours forth a precious perfume on the head of Christ (John 12.1–8; Matt. 26.6–12; Mark 14.3–9); and Mary Magdalene who, once freed from demons (Luke 8.2; Mark 16.9) proceeds with her companions – the *myrrhophorae* – to the sepulcher of Christ which proves to be empty, and later enjoys the privilege of being the first mortal to see the resurrected Christ. No matter how shaky Gregory the Great's historical argumentation must have seemed to later exegetes, it was his notion of a single Mary Magdalene subsuming her colleagues that triumphed all through the Middle Ages (cf. V. Saxer, "Le culte de Marie-Madeleine...").

But East and West soon parted ways: while the former saw the tomb of Mary Magdalene in Ephesus and effected a *translatio* of her relics to Constantinople, a course of events dutifully recognized from the beginning of the tenth century on, the latter followed the dictates of an eminently French tradition which involved the whole household of Lazarus. The raised Lazarus with Martha and Mary (the Mary Magdalene of the Gregorian identification) and a host of other saints including Maximinus, emigrate to Provence. Marseille and Aix are full of their memories. A sub-tradition has Mary Magdalene and her party put to shore at Saintes-Marie-de-la-Mer. The cult of Lazarus' household, anyhow, did not find its ultimate station in Provence, but in Bourgogne. The relics of Lazarus, according to this French tradition, were finally laid to rest in Autun; and those of Mary Magdalene, after an intermediate stop in Aix or perhaps in Saint-Maximin, in Vézelay. Secondary relics of Mary ended up in Exeter in Cornwall and in Halberstadt in Saxen-Anhalt. In the eleventh century, collegiate churches were erected in her honor in Verdun and Besançon. As to the cavern of Sainte-Baume, it claimed to possess her head.

It was within such parameters that Vézelay became one of the great power centers of reformed Benedictine monastic life as well as of devotional cult of Mary Magdalene. The abbey of Vézelay had been established in the middle of the ninth century by one Girard of Vienne for Benedictine nuns; later on it became restructured for the use of monks under the patronage of the Virgin

Mary. Under Abbot Geoffroy of Vézelay (1037–52) a profound meta-
morphosis took hold of the abbey: first, the Cluniac Reform was
introduced, and thereupon a change of *patrocinium* from the Virgin
Mary to Mary Magdalene was established. Since the second of these
changes entailed giving up a special relationship with the Virgin
herself, the new patronage could not be set in place without appropriate compensatory factors, both psychological and theological. The
bodily relics of Mary Magdalene constituted such an overwhelm-
ingly persuasive factor: so, Vézelay claimed in the eleventh century
to possess the entire body of the saint.

The central period of flourishing lasted in Vézelay throughout
the whole of the twelfth and the thirteenth centuries, during which
period the shrine became the focus of a triple avenue of interests,
often strongly interwoven: the cult of Mary Magdalene, the crusading zeal against the infidels, and the cult of St. James with the
concomitant pilgrimage to Santiago. With time, the first and the
third of these orientations became preeminent, and thus Vézelay
turned into the fountainhead of the third of the French roads, the
via lemovicense, leading to Santiago.

The account of the later saintly life of Mary Magdalene had been
promoted by a number of texts that are part of the earlier quoted
French-Provençal tradition. One of these, the *Vita apostolica* (*BHL* no.
5489), tells the story of Mary's apostolate in Provence and her death
and burial in the basilica of St. Maximin; another text, the *translatio
posterior*, narrates the *furta sacra* perpetrated by one, the monk Badilon,
who took her body to Aix-en-Provence; from there it was subsequently transferred to Vézelay. According to the text, this occurred
in the year 749. On the whole, the narratives concerning Mary
Magdalene are fantasy rich, most of them construed long *post fac-
tum* of any possible events, and actually during the very period of
the ascendancy of Vézelay, as an appropriate justification for its newly
acquired *patrocinium*. Indicative of the devotion of which she had
become the object in France, is Mary Magdalene's role in the French
epic tradition: cf. Bédier-*épiques* 2:67–92.

The celebration of Mary Magdalene's feast falls on July 22.

For the the antique sources, see V. Saxer, "Les saintes Marie de Béthanie
et Marie de Magdala dans la tradition liturgique et homilétique
d'Orient," in *Revue des sciences religieuses* 32 (1958): 1–37; also by Saxer,
"Le culte de Marie-Madeleine en Occident des origines à la fin du moyen-
âge," *Cahiers d'archéologie et d'histoire* 3 (Auxerre-Paris, 1959). See, further, É.-M. Faillon, *Monuments inédits sur l'apostolat de sainte Marie-
Madeleine en Provence* (Paris, 1848; 2d ed., 1865); A. Chérest, *Vézelay. Étude
historique*, 3 vols. (Auxerre 1863–68); L. Duchesne, "La légende de sainte
Marie-Madeleine," *Annales du Midi* 5 (1893): 1–33; P. Plaine, "Remarques

critiques sur une étude de M. l'abbé Duchesne intitulée...," *Revue du monde catholique*, ser. 6, 7 (1895): 273–90, 436–47; M. Sicard, *Sainte Marie-Madeleine, la tradition et la critique (sa vie, histoire de son culte)*, 3 vols. (Paris, 1910); A. Pissier, *Le culte de sainte Marie-Madeleine à Vézelay* (Saint-Père-sous-Vézelay, 1923); E. Vacandard, "De la venue de Lazare et de Marie-Madeleine en Provence," *Revue des questions historiques* 100 (1924): 257–305; V. Saxer, "L'origine des reliques de sainte Marie-Madeleine à Vézelay dans la tradition historiographique du Moyen-Âge," *Revue des sciences religieuses* 29 (1955): 1–18; V. Saxer, "Maria Maddalena," in *BSS*.

MAXIMIN: The story of Maximin (Eng., Fr.; It.: Massimino; Ger. and Lat.: Maximinus), saint and bishop of Arles, is closely related and, in the first portion of his *vita*, actually included in the French tradition of Lazarus, also known as the Provençal tradition. According to this narrative, sometime after the raising of Lazarus, he and his two sisters, usually identified as Mary Magdalene and Martha (see entry on Mary Magdalene), boarded a ship and sailed to southern Gaul. It was the year 45 of our era. Some of these accounts include also, as companions of Lazarus, the Seventy-Two Disciples of Christ: one of these is identified with Maximin. The main participants of this evangelizing exodus found subsequently ample occasion for their apostolizing zeal as well as sanctification: Mary Magdalene ended up in Vézelay, and Lazarus himself in Autun. As to Maximin, he set out energetically all over southern Provence preaching, converting, making disciples, and finally becoming, sometime in mid-life, the first bishop of Aix. We do not know when he died or how. It seems to be certain though that there was no martyrdom involved.

There are problems concerning the relics of St. Maximin: for a while Vézelay pretended to possess them; so did also the little village of St.-Maximin in the circuit of Brignoles, department of Var, which claimed also that it was guarding the remains of Mary Magdalene, St. Sidoine, and others [E. M. Faillon, *Monuments inédits sur l'apostolat de sainte Marie-Madeleine en Provence*, (Paris, 1848, 2:665)]; finally, Billom, in the circuit of Clermont, also claimed to have the remains of the saint (ibid., 2:685–88). Once the position of Mary Magdalene in Vézelay became sufficiently consolidated, the Vézelayan pretensions concerning St. Maximin were all but abandoned. The ultimate Provençal resting place for Maximin may be justified on account either of his overlapping some other saintly figure at home in Provence, or of his largely legendary apostolic activities in southern Gaul. If so, it stands to reason to postpone the actual pastoral work of St. Maximin to the fourth century, the time of the probable establishment of the diocese of Aix.

The date of St. Maximin's feast is also variously rendered: the missals and breviaries of Aix speak of June 7; the *Breviarium* of Vézelay, on the other hand, proposes June 8. The latter date is picked up by the *Martyrologium romanum* (N. Del Re, "Massimino," in *BSS*).

G. Morin, "Saint Lazare et saint Maximin; données nouvelles sur plusieurs personnages de la tradition de Provence," *Mémoires de la Société nationale des antiquaires de France* 56 (1895): 27–51; H. Leclercq, "Maximin (Saint)," in *DACL*; J.-R. Palanque, "Les premiers évêques d'Aix-en-Provence," in *AnBoll* 67 (1949): 377–83; J. Rath, "Aix," in *LTK3*.

ROLAND: Roland (Eng., Fr.; It.: Orlando) had already been, probably before the eleventh century, the object of a widespread popular cult whose two earliest epicenters were in Blaye, near Bordeaux, and in Roncesvalles. A tradition lost in the even earlier tenth century wants Roland and his closest companions, Olivier and Bishop Turpin, to be laid to rest in three sarcophagi subsequently preserved in the church of St.-Romain in Blaye. The third sarcophagus, on the other hand, was at times thought to contain the remains of Aude la Belle, sister of Olivier and promised bride of Roland. This second attribution, of considerably later date than the first one, closed a romantic triangle left out of sight by the earlier version.

The Roncesvalles or Roncevaux tradition is, possibly, even older. An incursion of Charlemagne's army into Spain – based historically on an assistance mission to the emir of Zaragoza – becomes rewritten as a complex campaign against the armies of the infidel chieftain Marsile. On the way back into France, while crossing the Pyrenees at the Pass of Roncesvalles, a second reinterpretation occurs: Basque irregulars trying to bite into the rearguard of the Carolingian army are described as Islamic forces in an all-out onslaught against the Christians. The border skirmish becomes an epic battle. Charlemagne, for his part, does not participate directly in the military engagement. This is handled by Roland, Olivier and the paladins who, in the rearguard of the army, offer a heroic resistance in the face of the infidels' infinite numerical superiority. Important for the Christian imprint of the story is Roland and his friends' death: their heroic death becomes Christian sacrifice, martyrdom. Unlike the exploits of an Achilles or an Aeneas, the epic feats of Roland must necessarily end, as the earthly life of martyrs for the sake of their Faith, in self sacrifice. It is such sacrificial immolation that will lend Roland and his companions their aura of sanctity.

If Blaye is then the place where the earthly remains of the paladins lie, Roncesvalles is the site of the exploits themselves, where
Roland's sword, Durendal, split a mighty rock and where his horn,
the Olifant, emitted, far too late to ensure any effect on the necessary
outcome, its last tragic call. Even more importantly, Roncesvalles is
at the heart of the epic stories later collected and consolidated in the
Chanson de Roland. Riding on the wings of the most famous of medieval stories, it is little wonder that Roland became an international
hero, the epitome of Christian knighthood: in Spain he appears on
capitals – as the famous relief in Estella's Royal Palace – battling the
awesome giant Ferragus; in Italy he turns into a predilect person of
local heroic stories and, by the sixteenth century, even of the most
amorous of all heroic stories: in fact, in the absolute best-seller of the
Renaissance, Ariosto's *Orlando Furioso*, he is the main character. Even
more importantly, in Germany Roland becomes the emblematic figure of municipal civic liberties, the guardian of well-being and perhaps also of order: in city halls and municipalities, for instance in
Halberstadt, we find the hero of Roncesvalles in gigantic dimensions guarding the entrance or watching over things from some stra-
tegically appropriate corner.

The legend of the flowering lances on the fields of the Cea River
at Sahagún, believed to be the lances planted by Charlemagne's
paladins (Cf. Whitehill-*Liber* and Moralejo-*Calixtinus* 4:8, as well
as the *Guide*, chaps. 3 and 8), is a mythical transposition upon the
far-away Leonese fields, not without Freudian connotations, of the
Carolingian involvement in the *Reconquista*.

Roland's crucial role in what became for Western perceptions
the mother of all Christian battles, must be conjugated within a
multiple historical scenario destined to an unusually long and glorious fortune in the centuries to come: it made of Charlemagne *the*
paladin of Christian warfare against the infidels; it established the
Pyrenees as the border of Christian Europe; it pretended, and attained to, a main role in the Hispanic *Reconquista*; and finally, it
claimed for Roncesvalles a privileged key position on the pilgrimage road to Santiago de Compostela.

Roland and his companions were never canonized. Their sanctification must be understood in terms of popular devotion only.
Such extra-official and essentially popular trends, however, have
played a significant role along the path of Western Christian devotion. The Three Holy Kings were never canonized either: originally in St Eustorgio in Milan, their precious relics were later, in
the wake of a clamorous military *furta sacra*, translated to Cologne on the Rhine where one of the most stupendous Gothic
cathedrals was erected to house them. Not unlike Roland, Olivier

THE PILGRIM'S GUIDE TO SANTIAGO

and the other paladins, to our own day the Three Holy Kings continue to be the object of a warm and widespread popular devotion.

Bédier-*épiques*; C. Jullian, "Épopée et folklore dans la Chanson de Roland," *Revue des études anciennes* 18 (Jan.–March 1916): 31–51; E. Faral, "La chanson de Roland" – *Étude et analyse* (Paris, 1933); J. Horrent, "La chanson de Roland" *dans les littératures française et espagnole au moyen âge* (Paris, 1951); R. Menéndez Pidal, "La chanson de Roland" *y el neotradicionalismo* (Orígenes de la épica románica), (Madrid, 1959); G. F. Jones, *The Ethos of the "Song of Roland"* (Baltimore-London, 1963); P. Le Gentil, *La Chanson de Roland* (Paris, 1967); F. G. Holweck, *A Biographical Dictionary of the Saints* (St. Louis-London, 1924, p. 862); M. C. Celletti, "Rolando, Oliviero," in *BSS*; C. Jullian, "La tombe de Roland à Blaye," *Romania* 25 (1896): 161–73.

ROMANUS OF BLAYE: St. Romanus (Fr.: Romain; It.: Romano) is the subject of two closely interconnected *vitae*, the one as little reliable than the other [*Vita S. Romani presbyteri et confessoris apud Castrum Blaviae quiescentis*, in *AnBoll* 5 (1886): 177–91; *Vita brevior*, in *AnBoll* 26 (1907): 52–56]. In these accounts we learn of Romanus's southern and actually African origin. This seems to be suggested by the itinerary he followed on his way to Blaye – Narbonne, Toulouse, Bordeax. Narbonne, on the coastline, suggests a landing from North Africa. In the earliest mention of St. Romanus, by Gregory of Tours (*De gloria confessorum* 46, in Migne-*PL* 71:863), we learn of another connection which, if historically veracious, carries the highest significance: St. Martin is mentioned as having buried Romanus. Such a connection with Martin would place Romanus well into the fourth century. This notice lends further authority to the account of the *vitae* according to which Martin was also Romanus's ordaining priest. St. Martin's intervention at two crucial moments of Romanus's career – ordination and burial, might have its ultimate raison d'être in the Jacobean connection of Tours and Blaye: both lie on the *via turonense* that leads to Santiago.

The account of the burial, on the other hand, does not necessarily imply that Martin was present at Romanus's actual death. This seems highly unlikely given the distances involved. Gregory's narration suggests that the more famous saint might have come specifically for Romanus's funeral. An even more plausible course of events, at this point only speculative, might have been the following: sometime after the death and burial of Romanus, St. Martin might have journeyed to Blaye for a first *translatio* of his remains to a more dignified sepulcher. Technically

speaking, the date of Romanus's feast, November 24, should refer to his actual death, possibly first burial. If Martin's later intervention holds, however, then it is plausible that the recorded date
remembers the intervention of the famous bishop of Tours.
The largely opaque personality of Romanus becomes thus highlighted by the presence of St. Martin. A second, and no less significant, upgrading of his public appeal occurs through Romanus's
connection with Roland. Since Roland was never officially canonized, there could have been no church in his name. Roland's burial,
together with his companions, in the church of St.-Romain at Blaye
(see article above on Roland) serves thus the devotion of which the
paladin of Charlemagne is the object no less than it bolsters the
public image of Romanus himself. The bond with the mythical figure of Roland catapults St. Romanus into the mainstream of the
Carolingian lore so vigorously present on the road to Santiago.
Otherwise too Romanus fits well the social parameters of the pilgrimage road: he is a patron saint of travelers and particularly of
sea travelers. It will be remembered that many British pilgrims dis-
embarked either north of Bordeaux in the region of Blaye or south
of the city around Mimizan, proceeding thence on foot to Santiago.
    We know nothing concerning the grounds on which the *vitae*
speak of Romanus as confessor. He might have undertaken some
specific pastoral work about which we are ignorant; also, the ap-
pellation might carry honorific connotations in a general sense only.
Some relics of St. Romanus are preserved in St.-Denys.

BHL nos. 7306, 7307, 7308; C. Jullian, "La tombe de Roland à Blaye,"
Romania, 25 (1896): 161–73; J. Marilier, "Romano," in *BSS*.

SATURNINUS: Saturninus (Lat., Engl. and Germ.; Fr.: Saturnin
or Sernin; It.: Saturnino), first bishop of Toulouse, saint and martyr
of the Church, is one of the key figures along the route to Santiago.
We know nearly nothing of Saturninus before his arrival at
Toulouse. According to the *Missale Gothicum*, he came from the East.
The oldest source concerning him is also one of the most ancient
documents regarding the Gallican Church: a fifth-century sermon
written, at the latest, in 430 for it mentions the bishopric of
Exuperius, the *Passio Sancti Saturnini* (*BHL* nos. 7495–96). This *Passio*
refers in stark, simple but trustworthy terms to the details of
Saturninus's later life and mainly of his passion.
    Saturninus arrives in Toulouse under the consulate of Decius
and Gratus, at a time when the temples were glorying in pagan
sacrifices and Christian communities were scarce, minuscule, and
dispersed. This must have been around the year 250. It is not clear
under what circumstances or when he became bishop. It seems

THE PILGRIM'S GUIDE TO SANTIAGO

that the episcopal dignity is employed in his regard as an honorific title. Oblivious to pagan proclivities dominating the people, Saturninus sets out to spread the Gospel throughout the city. As he proceeds from place to place, the oracles of the false divinities fall silent before him to the greatest consternation of the local priests and the crowds gathered to consult them. Furious with Saturninus who at one point passes in front of the capitol, the priests, unable to make their gods speak, incite the populace against the bishop. The crowd, turned ugly and brutal, seizes Saturninus: now he ought to sacrifice a bull on the altar of the gods to appease their wrath. But Saturninus answers that he has nothing to fear from the false deities who are nothing but demons: to the contrary, it is the demons that fear him, the Christian bishop. At that the enraged populace ties him with a rope, attaching its free end to the neck of a bull: spurred by the reckless and uncontrolled mob, the infuriated bull rushes down the steps of the capitol dragging after him the body of the saint. His bones fractured, his head smashed, Saturninus dies (M.-O. Garrigues, "Saturnino," in *BSS*).

The close of the story is brief: the bull escapes; the crowd, becalmed by the cathartic process, disperses; the body of Saturninus, left on the road, is found by two saintly women who, in order to prevent desecration – a preoccupation deriving from the older Hebrew tradition – bury it in a deep tomb.

The circumstances of the martyrdom carry a double connotation: on the one hand, the bulls evoke certain aspects of the *tauromachia* present to our own days in the south of France, let alone in Spain; on the other hand, the flight of stairs of the capitol recalls the monumental power of Rome. The Christian treatment of these two elements is highly symbolic; and in both cases the ensuing interpretation is not devoid of paradox: the bulls drag Saturninus to his death – which is, however, *dies natalis*, the beginning of eternal life; and being hurled down from the capitol corresponds to spiritual ascension to heaven. The treatment of the details of the martyrdom by the author of the *Guide* appears almost textually in the *Legenda aurea* (cf. Voragine-*légende*, p. 680).

Saturninus's martyrdom, as conveyed in the *Passio*, does not seem to point to an organized persecution, as those engineered by Decius or somebody else. Instead, it carries the hallmark of a grass-root tumult, perhaps instigated by the pagan priesthood, perhaps only assisted or guided by it once the popular forces, pretty much uncontrolled, were already in motion.

The account of the early history of Saturninus, however, willl soon take a novel turn. In Arles, Bishop Patroclus, around the second decade of the fifth century, had been strenuously working on upgrading the status of St. Trophimus, the first bishop of Arles.

For the early saintly figures, this always meant the rearrangement of history, and, in particular, the receding of the saints' dates as far back as possible. In the case of St. Trophimus, Patroclus's theory was that the first bishop of Arles had actually been despatched by St. Peter himself. A concomitant aspect of this move – no less important than the exaltation of Trophimus – was to bolster the claims of Arles for primacy over the rest of Gaul. This design, however, was evidently too grandiose to succeed, and Bishop Patroclus had to shelve his plans. In the next century however, St. Caesarius, the fifteenth bishop of Arles, picked up matters where they had been left by his tempestuous predecessor, and offered, in the frame of his famous work, *De Trinitatis Mysterio* (Ed. Morin, Maretioli, 1942, 2:179) a broader and more palatable version of the same theory: renouncing from the outset the unrealistic notion of the primacy of Arles, he sustained the apostolocity of Trophimus, but he cleverly smoothed its rough edges and made it more palatable by making Trophimus part of a group of four, one of whom was St. Saturninus of Toulouse. Since the theory stemmed from such an authorized source as Caesarius, and since, judiciously enough, it was embedded in an anti-Arian tract, it enjoyed wide acceptance.

It is not quite clear where the original burial place of the saint was. One speaks of a pagan necropolis on the north side of Toulouse, on the way towards Cahor [M. Labrousse, *Toulouse antique* (Paris, 1968, p. 556)]. Pious tradition holds that the topographic location of the much later church of Notre-Dame-du-Taur evokes the original site of the tomb. It is there that, around 360, Bishop Hilary erected Saturninus's first memorial chapel, probably a wooden construction, all traces of which have long vanished. In the meanwhile, however, the cult of the saint grew, both in depth and in extension. By the end of the fourth century Bishop Silve decided to erect an appropriate reliquary church for Saturninus – no doubt as a response to the increasing popular devotion to the saint. This work was completed by his successor Exuperius: by the beginning of the fifth century the *translatio* of the relics was effected from the original tomb to the new basilica [E. Griffe, *La Gaule chrétienne à l'époque romaine*, (Paris, 1964, 1:48–52)]. The archeological remains of this basilica, in particular a large apse, have been found underneath the magnificent eleventh-century Romanesque reliquary pilgrimage church which, though it is far from its pristine form, we admire today.

By the tenth, eleventh, and twelfth centuries, the devotion to Saturninus took on a wider national character, almost always connected to the pilgrimage road to Santiago. Evidence of devotion to Saturninus is dense in various regions of France, quite apart from the area of Toulouse: the whole Mediterranean seashore traversed, as a matter of course, by the *via tolosana*; the areas crossed by the *via podense* and the *via lemovicense*, that is to say, the next two itineraries farther to the north; still farther away, the Parisian region. Outside France, Spain witnesses to important monuments and iconographic relationships in the cult of the saint. A Hispanic tradition, in fact, claims his presence in Pamplona and Toledo (cf. Croiset-*Année* 6:648; and Moralejo-*Calixtinus*, p. 532 and n. to line 10). The *Martyrologium Hieronymianum* evokes Saturninus twice: on November 29 for the martyrdom, and on October 30 for the *translatio* of Exuperius. That the cult of Saturninus had ever since the earliest times deep-seated popular foundations, one may deduce from the very name of the saint: Sernin, from *Cerni*, is a popular, endearing diminutive of Saturninus.

N. Bertrandi, *Gesta Tholosanorum* (Toulouse, 1515, fols. XLII–XLV^v; *Passio* (of St. Saturninus), *BHL* nos. 7495–96, 7498–99, 7499b, 7505, 7507, 7507b; M. J. Maceda, *Actas sinceras...de los santos Saturnino, Honesto y Fermín* (Madrid, 1798, pp. 243–69); Gregory of Tours, *Historia Francorum*, 1.30; 6.12; 10.29; *De gloria Martyrum*, 47, 65; *De gloria Confessorum*, 20, in Migne-*PL* 71:177, 385, 560, 748, 763, 842; O. de Gissey, *Histoire de Saint Saturninus, évêque de Toulouse* (Toulouse, 1628); R. Dayde, *L'histoire de Saint-Sernin* (Toulouse, 1661); M. de La Tour, "Examen des actes du martyr de saint Saturnin," *Revue des sciences ecclésiastiques* 2 (1862): 160–77; M. de La Tour, *Vie de saint Sernin disciple de Saint Pierre, évêque de Toulouse et martyr...*, (Toulouse, 1864); Quentin-*martyrologues*, pp. 185, 448, 483; L. Saltet, "Le commencement de la légende de saint Sernin," *Bulletin de littérature ecclésiastique* 23 (1922): 30–60; L. Levillain, "Saint Sernin," *Revue d'histoire de l'Église de France* 13 (1927): 145–89; M.-O. Garrigues, "Saturnino," in *BSS*; G. D. Gordini, "Saturninus," in *LTK3*.

TROPHIMUS: The story of Trophimus (Eng., Lat., Ger.; Fr.: Trophime; It.: Trofimo), saint and confessor, and probably the first bishop of Arles, is lost in the night of the past. Almost everything is tentative in the accounts of his life. His name is Greek, but this does not signify that he could not have been from the region of Arles, as many Greek names were current on the northern shores of the Mediterranean and particularly in southern Gaul. There is a good possibility, on the other hand, that Trophimus might have indeed come from one of the Judeo-Christian or perhaps even one of the Christian colonies of the East. Such a view is supported by Gregory of Tours. According to his account (*Historia Francorum*, 1.28–30: Migne-*PL* 71:175–77), Trophimus came to Arles together with St. Saturninus and others not before the persecutions of

Decius, that is to say, around the year 250. There are, however, other texts that set his coming at an unspecified earlier time.

Pope Zosimus, whose pontificat falls between 417 and 418, favored the primacy of Arles over the rest of Gaul and nominated Bishop Patroclus of Arles, not without the latter's inspiration and instigation, metropolitan of the provinces of Vienne and Narbonne. In a famous letter Zosimus speaks of the first bishop of Arles as of an individual sent from Rome, and he terms him the evangelizer of Gaul (Migne–*PL* 20:665–66). Later in the fifth century, an unrealistic ensemble of 450 bishops of the province of Arles declare that they believe that Trophimus had been sent by Peter to Gaul and speak of him as the greatest glory of the southern provinces. Evidently, the movement initiated by Bishop Patroclus to make the bishop of Arles the primate of Gaul was acquiring momentum. St. Caesarius adds his authoritative voice to this trend: in the *De Trinitatis Mysterio*, the fifteenth bishop of Arles makes of Trophimus, in the company of Saturninus and two other saintly figures, a *discipulus apostolorum* (cf. the note on St. Saturninus). The *Martyrologium* of Ado of Vienne (Quentin-*martyrologues*, pp. 303, 451, 503) identifies Trophimus as a disciple of Paul.

As we know little concerning Trophimus's identity, we are also ignorant about his death and his tomb. One document speaks of the burial of his remains in the suburban cemetery of Notre-Dame, today St.-Honorat of Alyscamps. This, however, must not have been his first tomb. From Notre-Dame his relics were translated before 972 to the cathedral of St. Stephen. A little later Trophimus became co-patron saint of the cathedral. *Martirologia* and lectionaries kept careful track of such an evolution: Trophimus soon ended up as *confessor Christi* and the exclusive patron saint of the cathedral, dislodging Stephen.

An Arlesian lectionary of the middle of the twelfth century (Paris, B.N., ms. lat. 783) compiles these as well as other, mostly legendary, sources offering a nearly full *vita*. Having become the disciple-companion of Paul subsequent to the latter's conversion, Trophimus follows his master until he, Trophimus, falls ill in Miletus: it is an attack of gout which will later make him protector of those who suffer from such and similar ailments. Once re-established, Trophimus follows Paul to Spain. At that, Peter intervenes and sends him to evangelize Gaul. Strangely enough, these sources speak little of Trophimus's pastoral work in Arles or elsewhere and mention nothing of his becoming bishop.

In spite of the many incongruencies and the endless modifications and upgradings that he was made object of, the cult of St. Trophimus is fully recognized by the Church. His feast is celebrated on December 29. The story of his many *translationes* is no less complex than that of his life. We know of at least two removals of his relics: the first, from Notre-Dame in the Alyscamps to the cathedral; and a second, in 1152, from the cathedral to the magnificent Romanesque church where we find them today in an appropriately built *confessio.*

Gregory of Tours, *Historia Francorum* 1.28–30, in Migne-*PL* 71:175–77; Ado of Vienne, *Chronicon*, in Migne-*PL* 123:179; *Martyrologe d'Arles-Toulon*, Bibl. Vatic., ms. Reg. lat. 540, f. 185; *Sacramentarium ecclesiae Arelatensis*, Paris. B.N., ms. lat. 2810, f. 2; *Lectionnaire d'Arles*, Paris, B.N., ms. lat. 5295; W. Gundlach, *Der Streit der Bisthümer Arles und Vienne um den Primatus Galliarum* (Hannover, 1890); G. de Manteyer, "Les légendes saintes de Provence et le martirologe d'Arles-Toulon," in *Mélanges d'archéologie et d'histoire de l'École Française de Rome* 17 (1897): 467–89; L. Royer, "Arles," in *DHGE*; L. Levillain, "Saint Trophime confesseur et metropolitain d'Arles et la mission des sept en Gaule," *Revue d'histoire de l'Église de France* 13 (1927): 145–89; M.-O. Garrigues, "Trofimo di Arles," in *BSS* with an ample bibliography; W. Bohne, "Trophimus," in *LTK3.*

WILLIAM OF AQUITAINE: William (Fr.: Guillaume; Ger.: Wilhelm; It.: Guglielmo; Lang d'Oc: Guilhem; Lat.: Wilhelmus) known variously as of Aquitaine, of Gellone, or of Orange, is an endearing saintly figure on the route to Santiago: he exemplifies within his earthly career the two traditional aspects of Christian life, the active and the contemplative. Son of the count of Thierri and of Aude, daughter of Charles Martel, William is closely related to the royal Carolingian house: in fact, Charlemagne confers upon him in 790 the title of duke of Toulouse and marquis of Septimanie. The titles of nobility showered upon him, however, are no gratuitous presents: they correspond to the continuous preoccupation of the emperor to clear his western borders infested by the incursions both of Muslim regulars and of Basque irregulars. In fact, the rest of the active life of William will be spent in these military undertakings: he pushes back the Basques as far as Fazensac; is defeated by Hisham I at Villedaigne; and conquers Barcelona in 801. Named marquis of Spain on the strength of this last feat, his ambitions at that point lie already elsewhere.

Following in the footsteps of a Hispano-Visigothic Count Benedict who had founded the monastery of Aniane, he establishes, with the help of the monks of the same Aniane, the monastic community of Gellone. Before long, he bestowes upon the new settlement part of his own personal wealth and soon after decides to take up monastic habits. It is the year 806. William dies six years later in the odor of sanctity (*Vita Guillelmi*, in *ActaSS* May 6:154–73; *Vita S. Wilhelmi*, in *BHL* no. 8916).

The monasteries of Aniane and Gellone are a short distance from each other; and the relative influence of the former on the latter has ever since the earliest accounts of the life of William been an uneasy bone of contention. While the *Vita S. Wilhelmi*, written in 1120–30, does not make mention of either Benedict or Aniane, the *Vita S. Benedicti Anianensis* (Mabillon-*Acta* 4/1:191–226) has been rearranged at a later date in order to emphasize the dependence of Gellone on Aniane.

Subsequent to William's death, it was probably Charlemagne who had his remains placed in a marble sarcophagus of Aquitaine, partly destroyed during the Revolution. It was in the twelfth century that the abbey took the name of Saint-Guilhem-le-Désert. William's *dies natalis* falls on May 28. A day for the *translatio* is also remembered, March 5. On that day of the year 1139, the right arm of the saint – the best of his active years and hence evoked with special veneration – was placed into a separate reliquary, known subsequently as the *bras de vermeil*. St.-Sernin of Toulouse, one of the largest repositories of relics in the Middle Ages, had a portion of William's body since the year 1139.

William's warfare in and around Orange made him the central hero of the cycle of *chansons de geste* that carry his name, *La Chanson de Guillaume*; he is, at the same time, a secondary though important figure in many other Carolingian heroic poems (cf. Bédier-*épiques* 1:60–205). The many Hispanic and specifically anti-Moorish connections of William, the prominent Carolingian relationships of his story, and the cycle of *chansons de geste*, became compounded with the traditions of St. James and of Charlemagne on the southernmost pilgrimage route. Their overall force made of William one of the most virile but at the same time one of the most popular saintly figures of the road to Santiago.

L. Clarus, *Herzog Wilhelm von Aquitanien...* (Münster, 1865); J. E. Saumade, *Soldat et moine. Vie de S. Guillaume du Désert* (Montpellier, 1878); L. P. Tisset, *L'abbaye de Gellone des origines au XIIIe s.* (Paris 1933); V. Saxer, "Le culte et la légende hagiographique de S. Guillaume de Gellone," in *Mélanges Louis -Geste Carolingien* 2:565–89; M. Rouche, "Guillaume (Saint), dit de Gellone," in *DHGE*; R. Van Doren, "Guglielmo," in *BSS*.

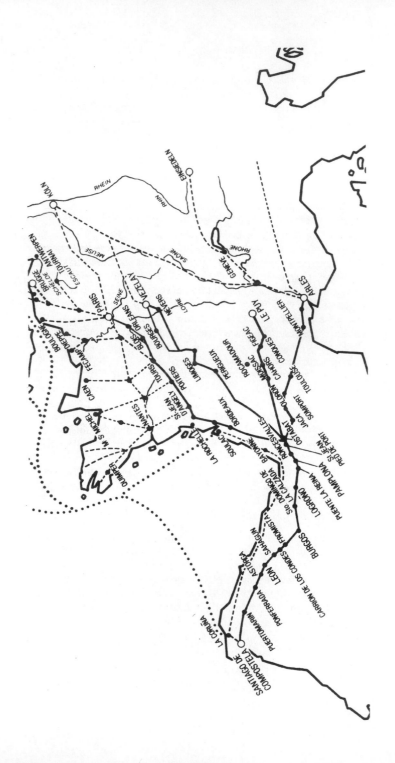

GAZETTEER

AGEN. The classical Aginnum, on the Garonne, located in a particularly lush and fruitful portion of the alluvial plain. The city knew many vicissitudes in the post-Roman era during the successive invasions and incursions of Goths, Huns, Burgundians and Saracens.

AISELA, see ESLA.

AIX-EN-PROVENCE. On the river Ars and at a short distance from Marseille, is the classical Aquae Sextiae founded in the second century BC by Sextius Calvinus, from whom the city took the name. Aix evokes also, most importantly, the thermal waters for which it is justly famous. The city was flourishing during the Empire and during the centuries of the pilgrimages, a period which partly coincided with the great Provençal revival.

ALAVA. In the province of Vitoria, one of the three provinces of the Basque Country.

ALTAPORCA, see ATAPUERCA.

ALTERDALLIA, see TARDAJOS.

ALYSCAMPS. A site of bewitching atmosphere and haunting evocations that never fails to impress the visitor. Tradition maintains that it was consecrated by St. Trophimus and that Christ himself had appeared for the occasion. Actually, its origins hark back to prehistoric times in which it was a burial ground. Subsequently, the Gallo-Roman and later on the paleo-Christian necropolis capitalized on the already extant tradition: this relied on the sharp bend that the Rhône describes at this point as well as on the strong current that tends to cast ashore whatever driftwood floats downstream. It was so that barges, boats, and barrels, which in the past carried corpses to be buried, put to shore in the vicinity of the famous cemetery. Often a coin was stuck between the teeth of the corpse to make the gravediggers' effort worthwhile. Dante mentions the Alyscamps in *Inferno* 9.112–15. The church of Saint-Honorat and Saint-Genès in the Alyscamps presents Carolingian wall structures together with various later interventions (cf. Benoît-*cimitières*, pp. 32 61); Vielliard-*guide*, p. 35, n. 7, and Moralejo-*Calixtinus*, p. 525, n. to line 7.)

ANJOU. Anjou, the ancient Andecavi, with its capital Angers, watered by the Loire, lies in one of the most prosperous regions of the west of France.

ARAGÓN, REGION. One of the largest historico-cultural territories in Spain extending south of the Pyrenees on mid-ground between Navarra and Catalonia and watered by the Aragón and mainly the Ebro; the latter serves as its fluvial and economic axis. The name Aragón derives from the homonymous river.

ARAGÓN, RIVER. An important affluent of the Ebro, the Aragón brings to it the abundant waters of a good portion of the southwestern Pyrenees. Through the valley of Canfranc, the Aragón descends from the Somport towards Jaca, at which point it changes course from south to west. It continues thus towards the west until past the not-too-long-ago completed artificial lake of Yesa. By Sangüesa it turns once again towards south-southwest to reach finally the upper valley of the Ebro southeast of Logroño. Apparently, the country took the name from the river, and from the country, the kingdom of Aragón.

ARCOS. Los Arcos, the Arcus of the text, and the Urancia of the *Pseudo-Turpin* (Whitehill-*Liber* 1:304). The town is of Roman origin. A legislation of 1175 by Sancho VI el Sabio set the Franks and the autochthonous population on the same legal foot. The parish church of Santa María, originally of the twelfth century, has suffered subsequent interventions up to the baroque. There is an old bridge on the Odrón, repaired in the eighteenth century. The hospice harks back to the thirteenth century (VázquezParga-*pereg* 2:146–48).

ARLES. The ancient Arelas or Arelate, lies on the Rhône, at a point in which the river describes a loop-like turn. In the center of a fruitful plain, not too far from the sea, the city became, after 412, the metropolitan see for the whole of Gaul. See also Moralejo-*Calixtinus*, p. 474, note to line 21. On the famous cemeteries of Arles, see Benoît-*cimitières*.

ASTORGA. The site of Astorga, the Osturga of the *Codex*, on a height of 868 m, was in all probability an Iberian settlement of the Amacos, of the Astures, or of the Ligures. Romanized under the name of Asturica Augusta, it was an important strategic center controlling the mining region to the north and the west, and qualified by Pliny as *urbe magnifica*. No less than six military roads converged upon it, one of which, coming from Bordeaux, is parallel to, and often lying underneath or identical with, the Camino Francés, the French road, leading to Compostela. Razed to the ground by Theodoric in 459, in the eighth century it was occupied by Muslim armies: in the wake of the occupation, it rapidly lost population until the process of resettlement started again in the mid-ninth century, only to be devastated once again by Al-Mansur at the end of the tenth century. Within the late

Roman walls an eleventh- and twelfth-century cathedral was erected marking the importance of the city at the confluence of the Camino Francés with the Ruta de la Plata, the Silver Route proceeding from the south.

Demolished in the fifteenth century and rebuilt subsequently in late Gothic style, little is left of the original Romanesque structure except a late eleventh-century Virgen de la Majestad, (Virgin in Majesty). There is a late Santiago Peregrino between the merlons of the battlement above. Particularly famous were the city's Hospital de las Cinco Llagas – the Hospital of the Five Wounds – whose bare walls are in part still standing, the Hospital de San Esteban y San Feliz (Stephen and Felix), and the Hospital de San Juan (John) erected in 1178 but completely rebuilt in the eighteenth century. A pervading tradition at several sites of the Camino claims the presence of St. Francis, though no documentary evidence exists. The saint is said to have been staying at the Hospital de San Juan and, in recognition for the hospitality received, established the Convento de San Francisco, next to which there were two further hospices. An important diocesan museum in the cathedral with Romanesque polychrome wood statues of the Virgin and Child, and a Museo de los Caminos (of the Roads) complete Astorga's presence in an epicentric position in Roman, medieval, but also in later times. The city is also the capital of the Maragatería, a regional folkloric entity in its own right.

ATAPUERCA. The Altaporca of the text, owes its renown to a historic battle in which Ferdinand I of Castilla vanquished his brother García de Navarra in 1045. The outcome of the battle signaled the historic destiny of Castilian ascendance.

AUXERRE. The ancient Altisiodurum or Autisiodurum, on the Yonne River, today capital of the department of Yonne. An important Roman city, it was Christianized in the third century. Two important church councils were held in Auxerre: in 578 and in 1098. Auxerre might have been chosen for the parting of the brethren, for the city is, coming from Italy, on the way to Paris; the route to Saintes, on the other hand, though shorter via Lyons and Clermont, is easier via Auxerre, Tours, and Poitiers.

BARBADELO. The Barbadellus of the *Codex*, refers to a parish church west of San Miguel, Santiago de Barbadelo. (Cf. Valiña-*Camino*, p. 156 and map on p. 157.)

BAYONNE. The Baiona of the text, from the Basque *baia ona*, a good bay, the most important city in the French Basque region.

BELIN. Once a Gallo-Roman settlement, the small village lies some 50 km southwest of Bordeaux, in the region of the Landes. Bédier-*épiques* (3:340–41) reports of a pilgrim's hospice which was once in the village; elsewhere (vols. 3 and 4 passim), Belin is registered as a place of importance in various *chansons de geste*, and particularly in the *Garin le Loherain* of the end of the twelfth century.

BELORADO. The Belfuratus of the text, on the River Tirón, was once on the borderline between Castilla and Navarra. The *Poema de Fernán González*, couplet 68, tells us so: "aquesta vylla era en cabo del condado." this town was at the end of the county. According to Moralejo-*Calixtinus*, p. 504, n. 1, it had a district of Franks.

BERNESGA. On the east side of León, but well within city limits, flows the Bernesga, the Bernesgua of the *Codex*, considerably larger than the Torio. It also descends from the Cordillera, the mountain chain, at Puerto de Pajares, and it empties into the Esla.

BISCARELLUS, see VISCARRET.

BISCARETUM, see VISCARRET.

BLAYE. The ancient Blavia, on the right bank of the Gironde, some 50 km north of Bordeaux.

BORCE. Village in the diocese of Oloron on the French side of the Pyrenees. Unlike Ostabat, it had never attained any prominence in the economy of the Camino.

BORDEAUX. The ancient Burdigala on the Garonne, at only some 25 km from the Gironde, was in Roman times the capital of Aquitania, and throughout the Middle Ages and the Renaissance continued to enjoy a position of uninterrupted prominence. While legend wants Bordeaux to have been already evangelized in the first century by St. Martial, we only have documentary evidence of a bishopric in the city in the early fourth century: a Bishop Orientalis from Bordeaux is mentioned at the Council of Arles of 314.

BORDELAIS. The region of Bordeaux, immediately south of the Saintonge, famous for its wines which the author of the *Guide* does not forget to mention.

BURBIA. The Burbia, Burdua of the text, is a small stream that flows through Villafranca del Bierzo and empties into the Sil.

BURGOS. Born along the Arlanzón around the year 854 as a characteristic *burgo*, that is to say, a settlement underneath a castle, raided by the Moors and resettled by the initiative of Diego Porcelos, Burgos knew a rapid development. It was the epicenter of the Castilian consolidation of economic and political power. Already in 920 Burgos became a city, with Fernando (Ferdinand) I the capital of the novel kingdom of Castilla, and with Alphonso VI an episcopal see supplanting Oca and others.

The city stands in many ways under the sign of the pilgrimage. The Cid himself is reported to have gone to Santiago de Compostela: "Ya se parte Don Rodrigo que de Vivar se apellida para visitar Santiago, andando va en romería," (there departs Don Rodrigo whose family name derives from Vivar, to visit Santiago, there he goes in pilgrimage). In Burgos, several generic hospitals for pilgrims, the Puente de los Malatos (the bridge of the sick) and the cemetery for pilgrims with a chapel dedicated to San Amaro, the French pilgrim who settled in Burgos, speak to us of the city's organic link with the pilgrimage route. So too does the Hospital del Rey (the king's hospital), founded by Alphonso VIII and built in High Renaissance style: it contains sculptural representations of Santiago Peregrino and of Santiago Matamoros (slayer of the Moors), *lux et honor Hispaniae,* as well as beautiful sixteenth-century relief carvings by Juan de Valmaseda with scenes of pilgrimage. The church of San Lesmes, formerly of San Juan, was founded by Alphonso VI in 1074: it brings home the Cluniac connections of the city. Adelmo or Lesmes was a French Cluniac monk who went to Santiago and on the way back, at the insistence of Constance of Burgundy, wife of Alphonso VI, remained in Castilla in order to consolidate the new Roman liturgy. San Lesmes became, by the sixteenth century, the patron of the city.

The metropolitan cathedral of Santa María was initiated in 1221 in the new Gothic style. It is one of the great monuments of its kind, although heavily overlaid with later interventions. In the chapel of Santiago, of the sixteenth century, there are at least three Santiagos of which two are *Matamoros.* There are of course many other important monuments in the city.

CACABELOS. The Carcavellus of the text, on the river Cua, was erected on the terrain of the more ancient Bergidum. It belonged to the bishopric of Santiago de Compostela and Bishop Gelmírez rebuilt it around 1108 (GómMor-*Cat León*, pp. 57–62, 394–95; Moralejo-*Calixtinus*, p. 505, n. 3).

CAMPUS LEVURARIUS , see LIBUREIRO.

CANFRANC. Once insignificant; today a fashionable winter resort.

CARCAVELLUS, see CACABELOS.

CARCERA, see VALCARCE.

CARRIÓN DE LOS CONDES. The Roman Lacobriga – the Karrionus of the *Codex*, in the province of Palencia, on the left bank of the River Carrión – is a first rate agricultural center within fertile and well-watered plains. Called in the Middle Ages Santa María del Carrión, it was a particularly important town of up to 12,000 inhabitants ruled by the powerful family of the Beni Gómez, the sons of Gómez, so called by the Muslims (Moralejo-

Calixtinus, p. 504, n. 3). In the eleventh century, in the times of the Cid, two sons of Gómez were held responsible for having perpetrated the famous affront against the daughters of the Campeador. In the twelfth century the city was divided into two by a wall and each of the two districts was governed by one of the Gómezes (MenéndezPidal-*Cid*, p. 172).

The church of Santa María del Camino, or de la Victoria, is a twelfth-century Romanesque structure with subsequent Gothic and baroque interventions. Its portal shows a twelfth-century Herod cycle as well as a program deriving from the legend of the tribute of the one hundred maids and the liberating bulls (VázquezParga-*pereg* 2:213). There are also further sculptures on the portal. The church of Santiago, on the other hand, has one of the most splendid Romanesque facades of Spain: the medieval arts and crafts, the Twelve Apostles, and an overwhelming Maiestas Domini complete the composition. The monastery of San Zoil or Zoilo was an important Benedictine settlement subject to Cluny and already sponsored in the eleventh century by the counts of Carrión, Don Gome Díaz and his consort Teresa (VázquezParga-*pereg* 2:214). Romanesque sepulchral tombstones of the Infants of Carrión are in the nave of the abbey church. The town had many hospices and hospitals. One of these, "de la Herrada," of the Horseshoe, was situated opposite the church of Santa María; it had a large bucket at its entrance with wine for the thirsty pilgrims. Another hospice, next to the church of Santiago, manned by the Templars, has its pointed entrance arch still standing. Carrión must have had a considerably important *aljama*, Jewish district: Rabbi Dom Shem Tob was a native of the city. The presence of Charlemagne in Carrión is attested by the epic poem *La prise de Pamplune* (the conquest of Pamplona) (VázquezParga-*pereg* 2:214).

CARRIÓN, RIVER. The Karriona of the *Codex*, an affluent of the Pisuerga, watering Tierra de Campos. The Carrión streams through the town of Carrión de los Condes and flows towards the south, to Palencia.

CASTAÑEDA. The Castaniolla of the *Codex*, became renowned because of its ovens: limestones carried by the pilgrims from Triacastela were fired there, and the lime thus obtained was subsequently hauled with wagons to Santiago (LópezFerreiro-*Santiago* 3:27). We know of similar arrangements that combined the useful with the pious: Saint-Pierre-sur-Dive. Vielliard-*guide* (p. 9 and n. 4 on the same page), follows Bédier on the toponym Castañola; so does also King-*way James* (2:482). LópezFerreiro-*Santiago* (3:27), on the other hand, recognizes Santa María de Castañeda in the vicinity of Arzua. Cf. also VázquezParga-*pereg* 2:319–20.

CASTRA SORECIA, see CASTROGERIZ.

278

CASTRO SARRACIN, see SARRACIN.

CASTROGERIZ. The Castra Sorecia of our text was built on the foundations of a Visigothic fortress, Castrum Sigerici. It is an eminently lineal town, the longest of its kind along the route. In 974 Count Garcí Fernández granted the community of ecclesiastics of Santa María del Manzano probably the first *fuero* – municipal legislation – in Castilla. Castrogeriz prides itself in a particularly rich artistic ensemble. The Colegiata de la Virgen del Manzano – Virgin of the Apple – originally of the ninth century, was rebuilt at the beginning of the thirteenth by Doña Berenguela la Grande in a Romanesque-Gothic transitional style. Its portals are of considerable interest. The Museo de Santo Domingo holds archeological findings of considerable importance. No less than four hospices are still documented for the town in the fifteenth century.

CEA. The Cea, Ceya of the text, sometime found also as Ceia or Ceión, flows by Sahagún. It is an affluent of the Esla and it marks the western limit of the Tierra de Campos. It signals also a politico-military border, for it marked, with Ferdinand I, the westernmost expansion line of Castilian dominance, and with Sancho el Mayor, of Navarrese advance.

CEBRERO. El Cebrero, O Cebreiro in gallego, the Portus montis Februarii of the *Codex*, a 1298 m high mountain crest rather than a pass, lies on the Atlantic-Cantabrian watershed line. *Februarii* stands for *Zebrarii* or *Ezebrarii* of the *Historia Silense* (p. 57), from which derives *cebro*, "savage or untamed ass," which once was abundant in the region (Moralejo-*Calixtinus*, p. 505, n. 4). It was a welcome pilgrim's refuge from the ninth century on, for it is situated over a string of villages and hamlets on the original Galician route to Santiago (Goicoechea-*Rutas*, pp. 598–600). The site is documented in 1072 as church and pilgrim's hospital. Alphonso VI turned it over to the monks of Saint-Geraud d'Aurillac subsequently affiliated to Cluny. From 1487 on the Benedictines of Valladolid took over the governance of the refuge. It is one of the most haunting sites on the pilgrimage road. The local dwellings of elliptical groundplan, stone walls and thatched roofs – *pallozas* – loom somber and large on the windswept height.

The priory of Santa María la Real is a high-sounding name for a humble chapel although of considerable size, restored not too long ago thanks to the labor of love of the recently deceased Elías Valiña Sampedro, the faithful and self-effacing local parish priest who did so much for the revitalization of the road to Compostela. The present structure of the eleventh century was erected over an earlier one of the ninth century. It contains a twelfth-century polychrome Virgin and Child wood statue, and equally twelfth-century chalice and patena which were used at the time of the famous fourteenth-century Eucharistic miracle known, precisely, as the "miracle of Cebrero" or, owing to Wagner's interest in the subject, the *Santo Graal Gallego*, "the Galician Holy Graal." The Catholic Monarchs in 1486, on their way to Compostela passing through Cebrero, left a precious reliquary for the preservation of the miraculous blood. The pilgrim's refuge, also restored by Father Elías, is open to pilgrims. Piedrafita del Cebrero, some 5 km further to the north, lies at a somewhat lower pass.

CIZE. The Pass of Cize, Port de Cize in French, Puertos Cisereos or Puerto de Cize in Spanish, portus Cisere or portus Ciserei in Latin, is a complex set of valleys, canyons, and mountain passes that were already part of the old Roman military road joining *Burdigala*, that is to say Bordeaux, with *Asturica Augusta*, Astorga in far away León. The pass, *porz de Sizre* in the *Chanson de Roland* (v. 583) and *puerto de Sitarea* in the *Poema de Fernán González* (couplet 137d), *stricto sensu*, on a climb of 879 meters, joins the valleys of Cize on the French side with that of Roncesvalles on the Hispanic one. The climb on the French side starts at Saint-Jean-Pied-de-Port on the Nive, or better, at Saint-Michel, further upstream, and reaches, not without great effort, the *Alto de Ibañeta*, the Ibañeta Heights, from which it descends towards Roncesvalles. The *Codex* considers the possibility of avoiding the steep climb by taking a milder path through the valley of Valcarlos on the Petite Nive. The climb for the pilgrims, even in favorable weather conditions, must have been strenuous to say the least. Cf. Valina-*Camino*, pp. 22–27.

CONQUES. Conques is situated deep in the gorges of the Rouergue, department of Aveyron, in one of the most authentically preserved medieval sites of the Massif Central. The splendid basilica of Sainte-Foy of Conques is the smallest, but probably the most harmonious, of the large pilgrimage churches on the route to Santiago de Compostela. See Mortet-*Architecture* 1:47-50; Bouillet-*Conques*; Aubert-*Conques*; Deschamps-*Conques-Sernin*; Bernoulli-*Conques*; Fau-*chapiteaux Conques*; Gaillard-*Rouergue*; Gaillard-*Foy*; Fau-*Conques*; Bousquet-*Conques*; Durliat-*Jacques*, pp. 44–79 and 417–44.

CORBIGNY. In the department of Nièvre, in the proximity of Vézelay, was a Benedictine monastery established in 864 by Egila, abbot of Flavigny. In the late eleventh and early twelfth centuries the relics of one Leonard were brought to the abbey (Cottineau-*Répertoire*, pp. 870–71; Moralejo-*Calixtinus*, p. 534, n. to line 21).

CUA. An affluent of the Sil.

CUEVAS. Couas must be Cuevas which today is no township anymore. It is signaled as a quarter of Viana, a town of notable importance already established by Sancho el Fuerte as an avant-garde defense bastion of Navarra. Through Viana flows a small stream called La Presa. It is somewhat strange that the *Guide* chooses to ignore a town of the importance of Viana.

EBRO. The Ebro, the Ebra of the text, marked the frontier line between Navarra and Castilla, as it today marks the frontier between Navarra and La Rioja. Its rich and abundant stream is amply recognized by the *Codex* which takes notice, in particular, of its rich fishery.

EGA. The Ega, the Aiega of the text, receives, for a change, a good press. It descends from the mountains of Andia and empties into the Ebro. A popular saying gathers the healthy and positive attitude towards this and other rivers, though not without an misogynist bias: "Ega, Arga y Aragón hacen al Ebro varón," "make the Ebro male."

ESLA. The Aisela in the text, and according to Moralejo-*Calixtinus* (p. 512, n. 1), in an ancient *graphia*, Astura, is born by Peña Prieta in the Picos de Europa of the Cantabrian mountain chain, and it empties into the Duero near Zamora. It carries, like the Pisuerga, abundant water.

ESTELLA. The city in the Comunidad de Navarra, on the Ega river, corresponds to the ancient Lizarra. The present name, Estella, seems to evoke the Milky Way and hence a Carolingian connection with the pilgrimage road to St. James: the Dream of Charlemagne (see p. 20 above). There is, however, no certainty in such an assumption. Sancho Ramírez, in the tenth century, displaced the original pilgrimage road some 3 km to the south to have it pass through the city. In 1090 he enacted legislation favoring the settlement of Franks in the district of San Martín, the commercial center of the city. Estella, otherwise too a royal residence, flourished due, among other things, to a liberal legislation that favored commerce and exchanges. This last line of economic interest resulted in the drawing up of a famous *tabla de cambios*, an exchange list, quite rare in the Middle Ages. In Estella, Navarrese, Franks, and Jews were living in somewhat segregated communities, actually city quarters. The later Middle Ages saw a steady deterioration in the civic coexistence of the various ethnic groups. The year 1328 registers a violent pogrom. Calamities followed: in 1348 there was an outbreak of the bubonic plague, as a consequence of which some 70% of the inhabitants died; in 1475 the Ega River flooded most city districts.

Estella remains one of the most impressive layouts of medieval urban topography and, together with Toledo, one of the richest ensembles of authentic medieval monuments in Spain. The district of San Miguel, the Puente de la Cárcel or Bridge of the Prison, lately reconstructed, the pilgrims' hospital of San Lázaro, the Rúa

– the pilgrimage road traversing axially the city, the Plaza de San Martín, San Pedro de la Rúa, the Portal de San Nicolás or del Castillo – all these jointly testify to the above medieval past. The Palacio de los Reyes de Navarra, the royal palace of the kings of Navarra, of the twelfth century, which is among the oldest extant civic structures in Spain, merits particular mention. It boasts a splendid capital of Roland and Ferragut, a further proof of the city's Carolingian connection. Remarkable monuments are San Pedro de la Rúa (of the Road), of the twelfth century, with a transitional Romanesque-Mudejar portal, a Romanesque cloister, and an impressive fortified belltower; the church of Santo Sepulcro (Holy Sepulcher), that shows the splendid archeological remains of its Romanesque nave and apse, a richly carved later Gothic portal, and a rare twelfth-century stone sculpture in the round of Santiago Peregrino; and finally the facade of the church of San Miguel in Excelsis that displays one of the richest Romanesque relief programs anywhere. There are many more monuments in the city.

FERREIROS. There is a Ferreiros, the Ferreras of the *Codex*, before Puertomarín. At the place where it appears in chap. 3 of the itinerary, however, it seems to be out of sequence. Moralejo-*Calixtinus*, p 506, n. 5, proposes for it a place in the township of El Pino, close to Arzúa.

FONCEBADÓN. The Portus Montis Yraci of the *Codex* is the Pass of Foncebadón on Monte Irago. (See also Irago below, p. 290). On the pass, on a height of 1500 m, there is an additional artificial hill of about 5 m height. In a prehistoric tradition lost in the night of the past, probably of mystic-celestial import, the heap of stones was accumulated over the centuries by pilgrims and peasants who attained the pass. From the summit a splendid vista opens up upon the valleys of the Bierzo. The region was, since the sixth century, a hub of hermit life fostered by San Fructuoso, San Fabián, San Sebastián, and others. As to Foncebadón itself, today it is a shadow of its past importance. It lies in the middle of a particularly rough portion of the route – between Rabanal and Villafranca del Bierzo – with only ruins of the eleventh-century church and hospice founded by the hermit Guacelmo.

FRANCAVILLA, see VILLAFRANCA

FRÓMISTA. Or better, Frómista del Camino, in the province of Palencia, is settled on a plain which in prehistoric times knew a Celtic tribe, the Vacceos. The present name derives from the Latin Frumesta, itself from *frumenta*, abundance of grain. Burned down and all but obliterated during the Islamic domination, its resettlement in the tenth century was so successful that during the

Romanesque era and even subsequently Frómista became one of the richest towns of the Camino de Santiago.

The Benedictine abbey church of San Martín – the only structure left over from the once powerful monastery – was founded in 1066 by Doña Mayor, wife of Sancho el Mayor of Navarra and daughter of Count Sancho García. In 1118 the monastery became affiliated to the Cluniacs of Carrión. The suspiciously neat aspect of the present-day church belies extensive restoration works executed around 1893 according to the criteria of Violet-le-Duc prevailing at the time in Europe. But even so, the triple apse, the octagonal drum sustaining the dome, and what is left of the splendid original capitals and modillions, as well as what may be deduced from the unfortunately over-restored architectural sculptures – cannot but command admiration. The harmony and the equilibrated feeling of space make of San Martín one of the most celebrated Romanesque masterpieces in Spain. Some of the disassembled original capitals are presently preserved in the Archeological Museum of Palencia. The Gothic church of Nuestra Señora or Santa María del Castillo (of the castle) is erected on the site of a fortification. Of the many hospices, the hospital of Santiago and the *aljama*, the Jewish quarter, little is left. San Telmo, patron of seafarers, was born in the town.

FURNELLUS, see HORNILLOS DEL CAMINO.

GARONNE. The Garona of the text is the Garonne, one of the longest (575 km) and richest of the French rivers. It is born in the valley of Arán in Spanish territory and it makes its first 40 or so km in Spain. In a northwestern course, it waters St.-Gaudens, Toulouse, Agen, Bordeaux, and, joined by the Dordogne, forms one of the most spectacular estuaries of Europe, the Gironde. High tide penetrates up to 130 km upstream into this fluvial system. Pilgrims and others crossing the Garonne or the Gironde had to use ferries or boats.

GASCOGNE. The Gasconica of the text, is the ample territory that extends south of the Garonne between the ocean and the Languedoc to the east. The Novempopulanie of Roman times, this vast, racy, and, in many ways, sui generis country takes its name from Vascon (the Vaccaei of Pliny), an evident reference to the Basque country to the south, on both sides of the Pyrenees.

HORNILLOS DEL CAMINO. The Furnellus of the *Codex*, is on the River Hormaza. It possesses archeological remains of the Benedictine monastery of San Lázaro and of a later hospice for pilgrims. San Lázaro was sponsored by various monarchs.

IRAGO. Early twelfth-century documents speak, in a place called in the vulgar "Fonssabatón," or nearby, of an "alberguería de Irago," a "convento de Irago" and of a "Hospital de San Juan de

Irago." Cf. VázquezParga-*pereg* 2:280; and BravoLozaro-*Guia*, p. 96, n. 19.
ITERO DEL CASTILLO. The Pons Fiterie of the Latin text corresponds to the present-day Itero del Castillo, of the Castle. The toponym utilized by the *Codex* makes reference to the bridge on the important Pisuerga River, as well as to the borderline condition of the place. Fiterie, in fact, from the Latin *fictus*, fixed, went into the Spanish *hito*, in the sense of landmark, milestone, limit. It stands for the western borderline of early Castilla with the Palentino, the region of Palencia. In the outskirts of the town, the road crosses the Pisuerga River on a monumental bridge of eleven arches, often reconstructed, which was originally built by Alphonso VI. Nearby there was once a hospice founded by Cistercian monks and later manned by the Knights of St. John of Jerusalem. Not too far away there is the Romanesque-Gothic hermitage of San Nicolás.

JACA. Of pre-Roman origins, Jaca derives from Iak, itself from Iaccetani or Iacetanos, an Iberian ethnic group. The Romanization of the city, Iacetania, took advantage of the sharp bend of the Aragón River which at this point changes direction from a southward to a westward course. Conquered by Islam in 616, the Dyaca of the documents in Arabic, the territories of Jaca were liberated by Count Aznar Galindo (dies in 838), and the city became an important focus of the *Reconquista*. Ramiro I, natural son of Sancho el Mayor, made it the capital of the newly forged kingdom of Aragón in 1035, transferring the episcopal seat from still occupied Huesca. In 1063 his son, Sancho Ramirez, upgraded the town to the category of *urbs*. With *fueros* (statutes and laws), municipal legislation granted in 1077, and an important mint for the crown of Aragón, Jaca continued as capital until the reconquest of Huesca in 1096.

The beginnings of the famous Cathedral of San Pedro goes back to the last years of the reign of Ramiro I who died in 1063 in the battle of Grans. At the time of his death the transept and the triple apse were just about finished. Sancho Ramirez continued the works adding to the structure a triple nave and a massive narthex with a fortified tower above. In the dome of the crossing possible Mozarabic influences have been detected. Of particular importance are the sculptures on the portals and on the capitals: the western tympanum carries a symbolic program; but the southern porch and portal bear highly developed figural representations with a marked sense of volume. The monument is a centerpiece in Kingsley Porter's theory of the irradiation of Hispanic Romanesque sculpture (KingsleyPorter-*Pilgrimage*). The cathedral preserves the relics of Sant'Orosia or Eurosia, a noble maiden from Bayonne whose hands and feet were cut off in 714. Her martyrdom came to symbolize the resistance against the Moors. The devotion to her, as protectress of the harvest, is widespread in Spain and northern Italy.

Nowadays a particularly rich diocesan museum is attached to the cathedral. In it Romanesque mural paintings deriving from churches and chapels in the Pyrenees, demolished or severely deteriorated, are displayed observing in each case the volume and configuration of the original ambiances. In the convent of the Benedictines (*las Benitas*) there is a magnificent Romanesque sarcophagus of Doña Sancha (died 1095) and a polychrome Romanesque sculpture of the Savior; in the Church of Santiago, a Romanesque capital functions as baptismal font.

KARRIONA, see CARRIÓN.

KARRIONUS, see CARRIÓN DE LOS CONDES.

LANDES. The Landes, the Syrticus ager (from *syrtis, -is,* "sand banks"; *ager, agri,* "field") of the Romans, is the westernmost portion of the Gascogne, running from Bordeaux to Bayonne, bordering on the ocean. It is a territory of mobile sand dunes and marshland of over 150 km in length, scarcely populated, that the pilgrims of the *via turonense* had to traverse in order to get to Saint-Jean-Pied-du-Port. The Landes is the nearest thing in France to a desert. For the pilgrims it was certainly, along with the formidable mountain passes of the Pyrenees, the central Castilian meseta, and the Leonese-Galician orographic system, one of the most strenuous portions of the route. British pilgrims, landing at Mimizan halfway down the coastline, also traversed a good portion of the Landes.

LARRASOAÑA. The Ressogna of the *Codex,* on the Arga River.

LEGIO, see LEÓN.

LEÓN. The Legio of the *Codex,* which corresponds exactly to the etymology of the name, *Legio VII Gemina,* the Seventh Roman Legion encamped on its territory, lies between the rivers Torio and Bernesga. Emperor Servius Sulpicius Galba founded the city by land grants to his legionaries. Conquered by Islam in the early eighth century (714 or 717), reconquered, lost, and definitively reconquered by Ordoño I and Alphonso III in 882, León became the capital of the kingdom of León under Ordoño II and remained so between 909 and 1037 when it became annexed to Castilla by Ferdinand. The brushfire of Al-Mansur reached León in 987, but soon after, the resettlement with Mozarabs from Toledo and Córdoba initiated a general political and economic recovery of the city. The political ascension of Castilla, however, further underlined by the reconquest of Toledo in 1085, tended to work against the continued dominant position of León.

By far the most important single monument of León, from the vantage point of the pilgrimage road, is San Isidoro. The pre-Romanesque church had a previous dedication to St. John the Baptist and to San Pelayo, a child-saint from Córdoba. In 1063, however, the relics of St. Isidore of Seville (see Hagiographical Register) were transferred, through an appropriate political deal by Ferdinand I and his consort Doña Sancha. Concurrently, between 1056 and 1067, the first building campaign on the new Romanesque Real Basílica de San Isidoro had started. Towards the end of the century, Doña Urraca, daughter of the monarch, considerably amplified and enriched it. In 1147, Doña Sancha, daughter of Urraca, entrusted the basilica to regular canons of the Order of St. Augustine. Soon the chapter was elevated to the rank of an abbey. In the twelfth century the canons of the Colegiada de San Isidoro founded a hospice for poor pilgrims, later on transferred to the care of the Franciscans. Most importantly, the narthex of San Isidoro became converted into a *Panteón Real*, a royal pantheon of the kings of León. Some twenty-three royalties have been buried there. The fabric of San Isidoro and the pantheon constitutes one of the most impressive ensembles of Romanesque art anywhere. The tympanum del Cordero, (of the Lamb) and that of del Perdón (of Forgiveness), both on southern portals, are relief sculpture of the highest quality. The vaulting of the pantheon has probably the finest Romanesque mural painting anywhere in Europe. The ivory carvings and the embossed silver plaques of the reliquary casket of St. Isidore in the museum above are breathtaking.

The cathedral of Santa María de la Regla, the *pulchra leonina*, on the other hand, constitutes a superb instance of thirteenth-century French Gothic on Spanish soil. Built upon Roman thermal baths and two churches, a tenth-century Mozarabic and an eleventh-century Romanesque, the cathedral is prodigal in Jacobean evocations: Santiago Peregrino figures on the portal, in the homonymous chapel, and on a magnificent stained-glass window, as well as in the Museo Catedralicio, the Museum of the Cathedral. There is also an important pilgrimage scene on a Gothic funerary monument. The column underneath the portal figure of Santiago has been consumed by the touching devotion of generations of pilgrims. Next to the church of Santa Ana there was a cemetery of pilgrims as well as a lepers' hospital.

Otherwise too León was particularly rich in hospitals and hospices: no less than seventeen of these are registered in the later Middle Ages. The Order of Santiago was given its main headquarters in the sixteenth century in the Monasterio de San Marco, a remarkable Renaissance structure. It once housed a large hospital for pilgrims. Today there is an important museum of sacred art in it. The *Guide's* enthusiasm for the city, "urbs regalis et curialis cunctisque felicitatibus plena," a royal and courtly city, full of all sorts of happiness, is well justified. A few kilometers west of the city is the Sanctuary of the Virgen del Camino – the Virgin of the Route – standing for an old tradition, albeit in modern garb. The Virgen del Camino is the patroness of both León and its province.

LIBUREIRO. The Campus Levurarius of the text, the ancient Campus Leporarius or Field of Hares, has a transitional Romanesque church of Santa María, an old bridge over the Rio Seco, the Dry River, and the remains of a pilgrim's hospital. Cf. Moralejo-*Calixtinus*, p. 506, n. 4.

LIMOGES. The ancient Rastiatum and later Augustoritum, the place became the headquarters of the Gallic nation of the Lemovices, wherefrom its Merovingian name of Lemovicas, and from which its present one is derived. The city was justly famous in the twelfth century and thereafter for its magnificent enamel production.

LIMOUSIN. Limousin is the territory around Limoges, capital of the Haute Vienne.

LINARES DEL REY. Or Liñares, the Linar de Rege of the *Codex*, where there is a twelfth-century parish church of San Esteban (Stephen).

LOGROÑO. The Grugnus of the *Codex*, today the capital of the autonomous region of La Rioja (name deriving from the Rio Oja, the Oja River). The origins of the place go back to the Iberian tribes of the Uarracos and perhaps to the Roman Vareia. Muslim forces occupied it for a while in the eighth century. The importance of the settlement was conditioned by the Ebro River which is navigable, precisely, up to Logroño. The city developed in the wake of the Camino: Alphonso VI granted its *fueros*, municipal legislation, and, around 1095, embarked upon a program of resettlement geared upon attracting Franks and others to the town. The imposing bridge of twelve arches built by San Juan de Ortega (1080–1163) took advantage of an already extant structure. The Rúa Vieja (Old Road) and the Rúa Mayor (Major Road) signal the itinerary for the pilgrims that traverse the city.

The imperial church of Santa María del Palacio still preserves some archeological vestiges of its twelfth-century origin. Emperor Alphonso VII, in 1130, donated a palace to the Order of the Holy Sepulcher, which then undertook the building of the church. The thirteenth-century Gothic belltower harks back to indigenous Romanesque belltowers in the Poitou, in south-western France. The present version of the Church of Santiago el Real is of the fourteenth or fifteenth century. Over its south portal there are a

Santiago Peregrino of 1662 and a Santiago Matamoros of 1737. On its *retablo mayor* – the main altarpiece – there is a wood polychrome figure of Santiago Peregrino. The *Con-Catedral* (Co-Cathedral) of Santa María la Redonda is presently of the fifteenth century. It is however built upon a twelfth-century polygonal (octagonal?) church such as that of Eunate or Torres del Río. The Romanesque-Gothic church of San Bartolomé prides itself in excellent Gothic reliefs representing episodes of the life of St. Bartholomew. Seventeen km from Logroño lies the legendary Clavijo, where Ramiro I of Asturias defeated, with the help of Santiago Matamoros, Abd el-Rahman II (Abderraman) on May 23, 844. This was the first major military intervention of St. James. Many more would follow. (Cf. SánchezAlbornoz-*Clavijo*.)

LOIRE. The largest and longest of the French rivers and the most important too for its history, the Loire flows first towards the northwest and, from Orleans on, towards the west, emptying into the Atlantic after a 1,000 km course.

MANSILLA DE LAS MULAS. Mansilla of the Mules – the Manxilla of the text, perhaps for *mansionella*, small mansion or dwelling – in the province of León, lies on the banks of the Esla with a bridge over it. It was settled in 1181 by Ferdinand II, and it has kept in part its medieval walls. It had once a large number of churches and at least three hospices (GómMor-*Cat León*, p. 460). The famous Mozarabic monastery of San Miguel de Escalada is in the vicinity.

MARSEILLE. On the shores of the Mediterranean, capital of the department of the Bouches-du-Rhône, the classical Massilia, has been since Roman times one of the most active ports and trading centers of the entire southern-European coastline.

MÉRIDA. The ancient Emerita Augusta, was capital in Roman times of the westernmost portion of the peninsula, Lusitania. Magnificent monuments have come down to us from its Roman splendor. The city was particularly active in the later Roman Empire, with a garrison of up to 90,000 men, and rapidly became an important center for the propagation of Christianity as well as Mithraism. The city was granted the archiepiscopal dignity still under the Visigoths, a standing kept henceforth under Islamic rule too until 1120: hence the politico-military qualifier *in terra Sarracenorum* (cf. Moralejo-*Calixtinus*, p. 571, n. to line 19). The transference of the archiepiscopal see to Compostela occurred at two consecutive moments: a bull of 1120 signed by Calixtus authorized a temporary transference of the archbishopric limited until such a time when Mérida would be reconquered; a second document of 1124 extended the newly acquired dignity *sine die*. Indeed, shortly after the reconquest of Mérida in 1228, the ancient city became entrusted to the Order of Santiago and to the apostolic cathedral of Compostela. For the documents, cf. Jaffé-*Regesta*, ns. 5823 and 7160; Robert-*Bullaire Calixte*, n. 146; Mansilla-*pontificia*, n. 63; and further, LópezFerreiro-*Santiago* 3:528 and 4 (Appendix): 3–5; Moralejo-*Calixtinus*, p. 571, n. to line 19; and Herbers-*Jakobsweg*, p. 159, n. 374.

MIÑO. The Minea River of the *Codex*. Born in the mountains of northern Galicia, the Miño descends southwards traversing Lugo and Orense. At the latter city, however, it turns sharply towards the west-northwest forming the deep cleavage that presently marks the border with Portugal. See also Puertomarín below.

MOLINASECA. The Siccamolina of the text, is a typical village of the Bierzo with slate roofing on the houses, located within a rich hydrographic network. The Meruelo flows next to the town with an originally Romanesque bridge over it, the Boeza streams somewhat farther on, and finally the River Sil, abundant in water, still farther away. A pilgrims' hospice was established in Molinaseca in the early sixteenth century, although there might have been some earlier facilities on the site. Cf. VázquezParga-*pereg* 2:285–86.

MONREAL. The Mons Reellus of the *Codex*, has a two-arched early Gothic pilgrimage bridge over the Elorz. In the parish church of San Martín there is a thirteenth-century image of the Virgin.

NÁJERA. In the province of Logroño in La Rioja, it was successively a Roman *castrum*, a Visigothic settlement, and a Muslim town. Islamic culture gave the town its present name: Naxera, an Arabic toponym signifying "site among rocks." On the slopes of a hill crowned by a castle and delimited by the river Najerilla, affluent of the Ebro, it was reconquered in 923 by Ordoño II. Sancho III el Mayor of Navarra made it a stopover on the pilgrimage route which, previously, passed through the Vascongadas, a region further to the north; also, he minted there some of the earliest coins in Christian Spain. His son, García "el de Nájera" (the one from Nájera), did much to promote and develop the city. Nájera was capital of Navarra until 1076 when La Rioja was joined to Castilla by Alphonso VI who took political advantage of the endemic Navarrese internecine rivalry. The Castilian king promoted public works connected with the road, facilitated the settlement of an important Jewish community, and fostered mercantile activities in many ways.

The pilgrims' bridge over the Najerilla, the Puente de Peregrinos, was built or perhaps only restructured by San Juan de Ortega in the twelfth century. There was a hospital next to it variously known as of Santiago, of San Lázaro, or *de la cadena*, of the chain. Santa Maria la Real, the great abbey church with hospice, was founded in 1032 by Don García I, king of Navarra, son of Sancho el Mayor. The place for the abbey was determined by a "hunting chance," a medieval topos frequently employed in the topographic definition of a sacred site. In this case the king's falcon, pursuing a dove, chanced upon a cave with an image of the Virgin with a vase of lilies in front of her. From here derives the name for the oldest Spanish knightly order, the Orden de Caballería de la Terraza (the Knights of the Jar). The Romanesque church was consecrated in 1056 under the monastic order of St. Isidore. In 1079, however, Alphonso VI placed it into Cluniac hands. A royal pantheon of the kings of Navarra, Castilla and León is also part of the ensemble which, disappointingly, was heavily gothicized in the fifteenth century and further overhauled with plateresque interventions in the sixteenth. A twelfth-century Romanesque tomb of Doña Blanca of Navarra, with striking figural representations, has been preserved.

NAVARRA. A territory pressed against the northwestern Pyrenees, it was inhabited originally by the Basques or Vascons, the Vaccaei of Pliny. The name derives from the Basque *Navarros*, the inhabitants of the low lands, a reference, by contrast, to the Pyrenees. There have been important ethnic-political connections with French Navarra and the Bearn region north of the Pyrenees. Navarra is an essentially green land that contrasts with the brown, yellow, and gray of the Hispanic meseta.

NÎMES. The capital of the department of Gard, the classical Nemausus, was one of the most flourishing cities of Gallo-Roman civilization and particularly of the ancient Gallia Narbonensis. Its arena, Temple of Diana, and Maison Carrée are justly famous. Whether its first bishop, documented around the year 394, was indeed one Felix, is questionable.

NIVE, see SAINT-JEAN-PIED-DE-PORT.

OCA. The Forest of Oca, the nemus Oque of the *Codex*, was at the time a particularly taxing portion of the road due to both its mountainous terrain and its woodland of difficult penetration. Its original extension went from Nájera to Burgos. From the last third of the eleventh century all of it belonged to Castilla; and it constituted an especially significant scenario for Alphonso VI's policies of Castilian supremacy, resettlement, and promotion of the pilgrimage road. The Forest of Oca reaches its highest elevation at the Pass of Pedraja (1150 m).

ORANGE. The classical Arausio, in the department of Vaucluse, close to Avignon, boasts a Roman theater and a triumphal arch in honor of Augustus as part of its ancient heritage.

ORBEGA, see ORBIGO.

GAZETTEER

ORBIGO. The Orbega of the *Codex*, both the bridge over the homonymous river and the hospital next to it once administered by the Order of St. John of Jerusalem, were significant in the Middle Ages. Their subsequent fame, however, rests on the knightly challenge that one Suero de Quiñones proclaimed in the Holy Compostela Year 1435. Such a Holy Year occurs whenever July 25, the feast of St. James, falls on a Sunday. Quiñones' challenge, in the name of his lady and of Santiago, consisted in his determination to sustain a joust, assisted by seven companions only, against whomever would accept it and with no limitations in the number of his opponents. An international assemblage of 58 knights (some speak of 300) accepted the challenge of Quiñones who, needless to say, wrapped up the day in resonant triumph (LópezFerreiro-*Santiago* 7:144–55; VázquezParga-*pereg* 2:263–67; Caucci-*Guida*, p. 79, n. 10).

ORLEANS. Established on the ruins of Cenabum or Genabum, nearly demolished by Caesar in 52 BC for having initiated an anti-Roman rebellion with the slaying of the metropolitan merchants, Orleans reappears under Emperor Aurelianus with the name Aureliani, a toponym that it will henceforth preserve. Resting on a geographically important bend of the Loire, Orleans was destined to play a significant historical role in the annals of France. From the fourth century on there has been a bishopric in the city, later on turned into the capital of the department of Loiret. On the church of the Holy Cross, later cathedral, cf. G. Chenesseau, *Sainte-Croix d'Orléans*, Paris, 1921, 2 vols. In the text there is a sign of the cross after "Sancte," for "Holy Cross."

OSTABAT. Some 13 km southwest of Saint-Palais and some 18 km before Saint-Jean-Pied-de-Port, Ostabat has lost its past standing, and today is an insignificant village; but it was once an important gathering point with hospices, hospitals, and inns.

OSTURGA, see ASTORGA.

PALAS DE REY. The medieval Pallatium Regis, according to tradition, was founded by King Witiza (701–9). There are a considerable number of monuments within the limits of the township. The parish church of San Tirso is a Romanesque construction built in the twelfth century over earlier structures.

PAMPLONA. The ancient Pompuelo, after its founder Gnaeus Pompeius around 75 BC, was for centuries the capital of the kingdom of Navarra, and today, of the *Comunidad Foral*, the jurisdictional community of Navarra. The Roman fortified town was erected upon earlier Iberian foundations. In the fifth century it fell under Visigothic rule and in the eighth, under Islamic dominion, until finally in the ninth century it became capital of Navarra. Sancho III el Mayor bestowed privileges upon pilgrims and others who settled in the city. In the Middle Ages there were three independent sections in the city, each with its own walls, whose inhabitants were usually quarreling among themselves: the Navarrería, for the autochthonous inhabitants; the Burgo de San Cernin and the Burgo Nuevo de San Nicolás, both inhabited by Franks and others favored by the resettlement legislations. It was not before 1423 that Charles III the Noble unified the three districts.

The present Gothic cathedral was built upon a twelfth-century structure on which Maestro Esteban, whom we know from the Portal de las Platerías of the Cathedral of Santiago, must have also worked. The splendid capitals, in the Museo de Navarra, among the most beautiful within the Romanesque repertory, testify to the splendor of the original church. There was a Hospital de San Miguel, St. Michael, next to the cathedral, with fifty beds, that offered food and shelter to the pilgrims for three days in a row. The Iglesia de San Cernin, or St. Saturninus, in the homonymous district, is a thirteenth-century church-fortress. Apart from the rich Museo de Navarra, there is also an important diocesan museum.

PÉRIGUEUX. In the region of Périgord, it is the ancient Vesunna or Petragoricas (Petragoricum, Petricorium), once the headquarters of the Gallic tribe of the Petracorii. Capital of the hauntingly beautiful department of Dordogne, Périgueux used to be divided into two portions: the *Cité* and the Puy-St.-Front where the reliquary cathedral rises.

PISUERGA. Pisorga in the text, in Spanish is masculine, el Pisuerga, though one finds also Pisorica. It is a large and important river that mouths into the Duero, carrying a surprisingly large volume of water. Hence the popular saying: "El Duero lleva la fama, y el Pisuergo lleva el Agua," "The Duero carries the fame, while the Pisuerga carries the water." It is born in the north in the Cantabrian Mountains on the present border between Palencia and Santander. The course of the river signaled for centuries the much-contested borderline between Castilla and León. Its importance is, however, foremost economic: it constitutes the western borderline in probably the most fruitful portion of the Castilian meseta called, precisely, Tierra de Campos, literally, Earth of Fields. It must be pointed out that in the vast stretch between the Ebro and the Pisuerga, the *Codex* names none of the streams that from the north descend towards the meseta.

POITIERS. The ancient Limonum and later on Pictavi, capital of the historical region of the Poitou and more recently, of the department of Vienne, one of the best and most authentically preserved medieval cities of central-west France. Splendid Romanesque monuments give witness to its glorious past: Saint-

Hilaire, Notre-Dame-la-Grande, Sainte-Radegonde. See pp. 256–58 above, on Hilary.

POITOU. The Pictavi or Pictones, an ancient people of Gaul, of probably Celtic origin, gave the name to the region of Poitou in central-western France, south of the Loire. A gentle and generous region, the famous city of Poitiers is its capital. The *via turonense* links the region with both Tours and Santiago.

PONFERRADA. In the province of León, this city is in an iron-ore region already appreciated and exploited in Roman times. The classical name of the place, *Inter amnium Flavium*, makes reference to the rivers Sil and Boeza that flow together by the city (*inter + amnis, -is*, "stream"). The present name, as well as the one used by the *Guide*, Ponsferratus, refers to a bridge with iron balustrade built towards the end of the eleventh century by the bishop of Astorga, Osmundo, to facilitate the passage of pilgrims (cf. Flórez-*Sagrada* 16:58–69, 499–50; and VázquezParga-*pereg* 2:291–98). The masculine ending of *Ponsferratus* is quite unusual, as against the normal feminine *Pons ferrata*. The process of resettlement of the town was initiated under Ferdinand II, who handed the place over to the Templars in 1185. There is a local devotion to the Virgen de la Encina (of the Oak) recalling her miraculous appearance in an oak grove, devotion that lately spread all over the Bierzo.

The Templar's castle-convent is a remarkable structure stemming from the end of the twelfth century with Romanesque, Gothic, and Renaissance elements blended together. The structure is presently much degraded. The Hospital de la Reina (of the Queen) was established by the Catholic Monarchs in 1498. Local people have been helping themselves quite liberally to its stones. The sixteenth-century Basílica de la Virgen de la Encina has been erected upon an earlier structure. In it there is a Romanesque cross from Santo Tomás de las Ollas. A considerable number of Visigothic, Mozarabic, and Romanesque monuments are in the vicinity. The Hermitage of Valdesantiago and the Hospital de Columbrianos speak of Jacobean devotion.

PONS FITERIE, see ITERO.

PONS MINEE, see PUERTOMARÍN.

PONSFERRATUS, see PONFERRADA.

PORMA. An affluent of the Esla.

PORTOMARIN, see PUERTOMARÍN.

PORTUS MONTIS YRACI, see FONCEBADON.

PORTUS MONTIS FEBRUARII, see CEBRERO.

PUENTE LA REINA. Pons reginae, a bustling medieval town throughout the pilgrimage centuries, owes its importance and its name to the magnificent bridge of five arches over the Arga which to our own days proclaims the vitality of the pilgrimage road. The construction of the bridge is attributed, though with some doubts, to Doña Mayor, wife of Sancho III, el Mayor, of Navarra (1004-35). Alphonso I, el Guerrero (the Warlike) fostered the development of the town granting in 1121 land donations to new settlers. To an eleventh-century Iglesia del Crucifijo (Church of the Crucifix) of the Templars, a large hospital was added in the fifteenth century. The church houses a fourteenth-century wooden Christ figure brought along, according to the tradition, by a German pilgrim. The Iglesia de Santiago, of the late twelfth and thirteenth centuries, on the calle Mayor leading to and from the bridge, has an interesting late Romanesque portal. In its interior, a polychrome wood *Santiago Peregrino* (Santiago in his iconography as a pilgrim) of the seventeenth or eighteenth century as well as baroque Santiago scenes on the altar welcome the visitor. Cf. VázquezParga-*pereg* 2:124-29 and Passini-*Compostelle*, pp. 14-21.

PUERTOMARÍN. Or Portomarín, the Pons Minee of the text, in the province of Lugo, lies on both banks of the Miño. It is the Roman Pons Minei or Portus Minei or Pons Minee, the bridge or the ford of the Miño. Chronicles of the ninth and tenth century call it *locum Portomarini* (Flórez-*Sagrada* 18:328; LópezFerreiro-*Santiago*, appendices, 2:192–94. A famous early medieval bridge over the Miño, rendered even more famous by Doña Urraca de Castilla's demolishing it in her struggle against her ex-husband, Alphonso el Batallador, the Warlike, was reconstructed around 1120 by Pedro el Peregrino, Peter the Pilgrim (see above, p. 146, n. 37), another of the pilgrimage road builders. Next to the bridge there was also an important hospital for pilgrims. In 1962 the waters of the Belesar reservoir covered Puertomarín, including the medieval bridge and the hospital. Other monuments, such as the church of San Pedro, were disassembled and reconstructed at the town's new site. At times, when the reservoir is low, the submerged bridge re-emerges from the waters. Many more twelfth-century monuments, such as the monastery of Santa María Loyo of the Templars, have long been lost.

RABANAL. Actually Rabanal del Camino, the Raphanellus of the *Codex*, on the climb towards the pass of Foncebadón. Its parochial church of the Asunción is of the thirteenth century. In it there is a polychrome wood statue of *Santiago Peregrino*. Archeological vestiges of the hospital de San Gregorio are located in the vicinity of the church.

REDECILLA DEL CAMINO. The Radicellas of the *Codex* has a parish church with a splendid Romanesque baptismal font in the form of a fortified city. Mozarabic and Byzantine influences are detectable on the font.

RESSOGNA, see LARRASOANA.

RHÔNE. Just north of Arles this river divides into two branches, the Rhône and the Petit Rhône. Arles lies on the eastern shore of the main branch of the Rhône which thence flows south to the sea. The Petit Rhône, on the other hand, turns to the west-south-west in direction of Saint-Gilles and thence takes to the sea.

RONCESVALLES. The villa Runcievallis of the text is an evident magnification. There is no town or even village, and probably there never was one: one finds only ecclesiastical or related structures. Roncesvalles, Roncevaux, or Orreaga in the Basque language, at a height of 950 m, is a fundamental point of the pilgrimage road to Santiago for being, precisely, at the crossroads of the Jacobean and the Carolingian traditions. The episode of Charlemagne's lending a helping hand to the Saracens of Zaragoza dictated by the political expedience of the moment, and the subsequent rout inflicted upon his rearguard by Basque irregulars were later turned inside out by Carolingian, French, and Cluniac interests: the emperor, Roland, and his paladins were made into the ultimate heroes of the Christian resistance against the Muslim infidels. Cf. VázquezParga-*pereg* 2:83–108; Moralejo-*Calixtinus*, p. 503, nn. 1 and 2; and above, p. 77, n. 42

In 1132 the bishop of Pamplona, Sancho de Larrosa, founded the original Real Colegiata de Nuestra Señora de Roncesvalles or Real Casa de Roncesvalles at a short distance from the height of Ibañeta and a little bit downward the valley on the Hispanic side. Here the site was somewhat sheltered, and the obvious reason for the move was to obviate the inclemencies of the pass. The Colegiata, a church governed by canons, was manned, precisely, by regular canons of St. Augustine who depended, until 1219, on Somport, and henceforth on the chapter house of the cathedral of Pamplona. The actual church was initiated in 1209 and consecrated around 1219 by Sancho el Fuerte who is buried in the Sala Capitular, the chapter house, together with his spouse Clemencia. The complex structure is made up of church, hospital, abbey, cloister, and chapter house. In the Gothic church there is a fourteenth-century polychrome wood carving of the Virgin of Orreaga who is the object of a local cult. The chapel of the Sanctus Spiritus (twelfth century?), called also the Silo of Charlemagne, is the oldest structure of Roncesvalles. It contains an *ossarium*, a communal grave variously interpreted as the remains of pilgrims or of the paladins of Charlemagne. The chapel of Santiago or of the Pilgrims is from the beginning of the thirteenth century The local museum contains an evangelistary of the kings of Navarra of the twelfth century. Cf. E. Lambert, "Roncevaux," *Bulletin Hispanique* 37 (1935): 417–36; and Bédier-*épiques* 3:297–327.

RONCEVAUX, see RONCESVALLES.

RUNA. The confusion of the text, quoting Runa at chap. 6, is both substantive and formal. There is no stream called Runa anywhere nearby. Bédier-*épiques* (3:293–94) maintains that Runa might be another name for the Arga. A second inaccuracy of the text makes the Runa flow by Puente la Reina. At that point, instead, there is an insignificant stream, the Ilzarbe, that empties into the Arga. Pamplona, on the other hand, is watered by the Arga, engrossed upstream by the Ilzsma. Moralejo-*Calixtinus* (p. 510, n. 8) suggests that Runa may derive perhaps from Iruna, the Basque name of Pamplona. Be that as it may, the Arga is the common fluvial denominator of Pamplona and Puente la Reina.

SAHAGÚN. Or Sahagún de Campos (of the fields), in the province of León, is today a ghost of its splendid past. At a height of over 800 m, on the left bank of the River Cea, Sahagún corresponds to the ancient Camata of the Romans. Its present name is a contraction of Sanctus Facundus, San Fagún, a martyr of Roman times (see pp. 245–47). The banks of the Cea were the scenario of a legendary battle between the army of Charlemagne and the infidel giant Aigolando: the spears of the slain Christian knights, who obtained the palm of martyrdom, bloom now at the site in miraculous recollection of that glorious event. The legend of the blooming spears, not without erotic connotations grafted upon heroic ones, is recorded in Book 4, chap. 8 of the *Liber Sancti Jacobi*, the *Historia Turpini*, that is to say, the *Pseudo-Turpin* (MeredithJones-*Karoli*, pp. 108–13; Whitehill-*Liber* 1:308–9).

The Monasterio de los Santos Facundo y Primitivo was founded in 872 by Alphonso III the Great and was much favored by subsequent monarchs. Alphonso VI made it into nothing less than the centerpiece of French and Cluniac influences in Spain, developing it thereafter into the most powerful reformed Benedictine abbey in the kingdom (VázquezParga-*pereg* 1:224). The pilgrims' hospital of the abbey had 60 beds and was supplied annually with 2,000 *fanegas* (Spanish bushels) of wheat; the *cuba de Sahagún* was a famous bucket in which pilgrims could satiate their thirst at will. The abbey had legal and de facto jurisdiction over more than 90 monasteries and churches.

The Cluniac import of the legend of the blooming spears is reinforced by a second tradition according to which it was Charlemagne who had founded the town. The pathetically bare remains of the abbey church, as well as those of San Tirso and San Lorenzo, reveal a particular Romanesque-Mudejar workmanship in brick. In the Museo de las Madres Benedictinas de Santa Cruz there are the sepulchral tombs of Alphonso VI and of his consort as well as a representation of the Virgen Peregrina (the Virgin as Pilgrim), by Luis Roldán (seventeenth century), an effigy that created a secondary Jacobean tradition of its own (Moralejo-*Calixtinus*, p. 420, n. 10).

SAINT-GILLES-DU-GARD. Saint-Gilles-du-Gard lies to the west of the Petit Rhône, between this small branch of the river and the city of Nîmes. It the early Middle Ages it was among the best known and most active commercial centers of Provence.

SAINT-JEAN-D'ANGÉLY. Twenty-six km from Saintes, in the department of Charente-Inférieure in the Poitou, it was the site of an important Carolingian abbey that became the nucleus of a town in the eleventh century.

SAINT-JEAN-DE-SORDE. On the Oloron and not far from its *embouchure* into the Pau, it actually lies between the two streams. It had a tenth-century Benedictine abbey of importance. Cf. M. Dumolin, "L'abbaye Saint-Jean de Sorde," *Bulletin monumental* 94 (1935): 5–28 and Vielliard-*guide*, pp. 20–21, n. 1. The two water sources are differentiated: the first is a *gaver*, from the vulgar Latin *gabarus*, and which entered French as *gave*, that is to say, "brook," the Gave d'Oloron; the second, *flumen*, "river," the Pau. Today both streams are considered *gaves*.

SAINT-JEAN-PIED-DE-PORT. At the confluence of the Nive and the Petite Nive, Saint-Jean-Pied-de-Port, the Imus Pyrenaeus, the Lower Pyrenees, was precisely for a long time the capital of the Basse-Navarre. It became French only in the seventeenth century. Saint-Michel-Pied-de-Port, on the other hand, 2 km from Saint-Jean, is on the Nive, to the south. The climb along the Nive is milder and easier than along the Petite Nive where the present route proceeds to Arneguy and Valcarlos.

SAINT-LÉONARD DE NOBLAT. On the river Vienne, in the Haute-Vienne.

SAINT-MICHEL-PIED-DE-PORT, see SAINT-JEAN-PIED-DE-PORT.

SAINTES. The ancient Santones, later on Mediolanum Santonum, on the Charente River, today in the department of Charente-Inférieure or Maritime in central-west France. In classical and medieval times Saintes was an extraordinarily flourishing center becoming one of the most active cities of the Saintonge and of Aquitaine.

SAINTONGE. The ancient Santones or Santoniensis tractus, between the Aunis, the Angoumois, and the Poitou on the north and the east, and the Atlantic and the estuary of the Gironde on the west and the south. The *via turonense* obligatorily traverses it.

SALA DE LA REINA. The Sala Regine of the *Codex*. It has not been identified. Cf. Moralajo-*Calixtinus*, p. 506, n. 4. Perhaps it was connected to the township of Palas de Rey.

SALADO. A short stream, the Rivus Salatus, the salty river, flows actually at a short distance east from Lorca. It originates in the Sierra de Andia in the north and it empties into the Arga.

SAMOS. It is remarkable that the *Codex* makes no mention either of Samos or of Sarria. In the former there was at the time already a very old Abadía de los Santos Julián y Basilisa which, in the twelfth century, adhered to Cluny. Presently, a sixteenth-century structure is standing there built after the fire of 1558.

SAN MIGUEL. It is not clear where San Miguel, the villa sancti Michaelis of the text, lies. Perhaps it is nothing more today than an abandoned house west of Sarria (cf. Valiña-*Camino*, p. 155 and map on p. 157). For the alternatives, cf. Moralejo-*Calixtinus*, p. 506, n. 3.

SANTIAGO DE BOENTE. The Sanctus Jacobus de Boento of the text, lies in the township of Arzúa.

SANTO DOMINGO DE LA CALZADA. Or Santo Domingo of the Causeway, the Sanctus Dominicus of the *Codex*, is an important station of the route on the Oja River. The town is inextricably linked to the homonymous saint and to his public works (see Hagiographic Register). Such activities were, on the other hand, in the best interests of Alphonso VI, preoccupied in the *castellanización* of the region, in turning the territory Castilian, for which purpose the fostering of the pilgrimage route to Santiago was one of the principal means.

The town of Santo Domingo de la Calzada itself was born as a consequence of such activities, around 1120–25, when a few houses were built around his tomb. Initially Burgo de Santo Domingo, the place rapidly rose to episcopal eminence (1227). Its Colegiata (church governed by a college of canons) became a cathedral and the diocese assumed the expanded name of Calahorra-Santo Domingo de la Calzada. The original Romanesque-Gothic transitional structure of the Catedral del Salvador (of the Savior), began around 1158, has lost much of its former shape. It was a typical reliquary pilgrimage sanctuary with ambulatory, radial chapels, and triforium. The rather late tomb-reliquary of the saint, the *monumentum*, is interconnected with the church and the crypt. A particularly famous episode related to the cathedral is the pious legend of the French pilgrim hanged on the strength of false testimony and subsequently resuscitated by the saint; the story, of the rooster and the chicken, on the other hand, is intended to prove the veracity of the first miracle (see p. 242). In deference to the French pilgrim hanged, French co-nationals have held the tradition in great respect. Feeding the rooster and the chicken, which are constantly kept in the cathedral, became with time a nearly liturgical *obbligato*: it is supposed to ensure eventually reaching Santiago. There is an old pilgrimage bridge spanned across the Oja River: it was built by Santo Domingo.

SAR. The Sar originates between Monte del Gozo (see above, p. 148, n. 50) and Meijonfrío or Meixonfrio; the Sarela, at the village of Peregrina. The two rivers meet at Laraño, near Santiago. After having left the municipal boundaries of Santiago, the Sar traverses the valley of Mahía and touches Iria Flavia and Padrón emptying into the Ulla at Puentecesures (I have followed here Moralejo-*Calixtinus*, p. 550, n. to line 6). The Sar is famous for the monastery of Santa Maria del Sar established by Gelmírez in 1136. More importantly for the pilgrimage lore, however, tradition holds that the unmanned boat with the relics of St. James, following a ría, actually the estuary of the Ulla, put to shore at Iria Flavia, presently Padrón, at the point where the Sar empties into the Ulla; thence the disciples transported the precious relic along the Sar towards the north to what would eventually become Compostela (Caucci-*Guida*, p. 115, n. 43).

SARELA, see SAR.

SARRACIN. Castro Sarracin, the castrum Sarracenicum of the *Codex* remembers the historic Islamic presence in the toponym. The site amounts to a hill with a castle on its top above the village of Vega de Valcarce (GómMor-*Cat León*, p. 483; Moralejo-*Calixtinus*, p. 505, n. 3).

SARRIA. In Sarria there were at least two twelfth-century churches, hence a place of considerable importance on the Camino. See above, p. 304, under Samos.

SICCAMOLINA, see MOLINASECA.

SIL. The Sil carries a large amount of water to the Miño. It collects the streams of the Bierzo within a rich water basin with large iron-ore layers. The valley of the Sil was called Vallis Viridis, Valverde, that is to say the Green Valley.

SOMPORT. Summus portus, known in the *Codex* as Portus Asperi (1632 m), though considerably higher than the pass of Cize at Roncesvalles, was considered less dangerous due to the banditry in the narrow passes of the latter. Of great importance in the earlier centuries of the pilgrimage, it decayed later on in favor of Roncesvalles, which was able to offer a historico-legendary connection of the greatest significance: the stories and the locale of Charlemagne's exploits. Cf. above, pp. 19–20.

TARDAJOS. The Alterdallia of the text, is a village in the proximity of Burgos.

TORIO. The Turio of the text, Torio in Castilian, is a small stream that flows just east of León, in the outskirts.

THE PILGRIM'S GUIDE TO SANTIAGO

TORRES DEL RIO. This famous town has a splendid twelfth-century octagonal church that bears precise architectural relations with the Templars' church of Eunate. A peculiarity of the church of Torres del Rio lies in the rib structure of the dome which, in precisely defined Islamic fashion, avoids the centerpoint. We find a similar structure on the other side of the Pyrenees, in the pilgrims' refuge church of Hôpital-Saint-Blaise as well as, of course, on the magnificent Islamic domes of the Great Mosque of Córdoba. The river, which here entered the toponym, is the Linares.

TOULOUSE. The Roman Tolosa, on the Garonne, capital of Aquitaine, the Aquitania of the Romans, that is to say, the country of the waters, an allusion to the magnificent hydrographic system of the basin of the Garonne and its affluents. This most important city in the southwest of France dominates its fruitful plains. The southernmost of the French routes to Santiago, the *via tolosana*, takes its name from the city, a splendid centerpiece of Romanesque culture. Cf. the article on St. Saturninus of Toulouse, pp. 272–75.

TOURS. The ancient headquarters of the Roman Turones – the name for the people of the Gallia lugdunense – Tours was known in classical times as Caesarodunum. In the early Middle Ages the city was already the capital of the historic region of the Touraine. One of the most important stopovers on the road to Santiago, Tours lies on the northernmost of the four French routes leading towards the Pyrenees, and gave its name to this route, the *via turonense*. The city has always been a cultural center of the first magnitude within the provinces of France. Nestled on the banks of the Loire, Tours is in the midst of one of the most fertile and beautiful regions of France. In effect, it is "the garden of France." See above, pp. 263–65.

Vielliard-*guide* (p. 17) translates *Turonica* as Tours, the city; Moralejo-*Calixtinus* (p. 514), and BravoLozano-*Guía* (p. 3), as Touraine, the region; strictly speaking, however, Touraine is *Turonicum, -i*, while the city, Tours, is either *Turones, -um* (masc. pl.) or *urbs Turonica*. It is the latter that we have in chap. 6 of the text with the elision of *urbs*. Hence it is correct to translate for the city and not for the region.

TRIACASTELA. In the province of Lugo, on a height of 860 m, this town once knew considerable affluence. The origin of the name is unknown. It is not clear either who was responsible for the foundation of the monastery-castle dedicated to the saints Peter and Paul. The parochial Church of Santiago has a Romanesque apse (VázquezParga-*pereg* 2:320–22). A representation of Santiago is on the main altar and on an allegedly twelfth-century processional cross. Archeological remains of various hospitals, of a prison for pilgrims, and numerous graffiti, some of which show a cock (*gallus*) which belies its French (Gallic) authorship, speak of a busy frontier town in the distant past. It was in Triacastela that pilgrims were in the habit of picking up a large block of limestone and transporting it as far as Castañeda in order to obtain from it the necessary lime for the construction of the cathedral for the apostle. Those who did so were appropriately called *petríferos*, that is to say, bearers of stones.

TRINQUETAILLE. Trinquetaille lies on the western shore of the Rhône, between the two branches of the river. The origin of the settlement goes back to pre-Roman times. Bédier-*épiques* (3:103) considers it a *faubourg* of Arles. Vielllard-*guide* (p. 37) so translates the *vicus* of the text. It is, however, more appropriate to render it as village.

URANCIA, see LOS ARCOS.

VALCARCE. The Carcera of the text, effectively, runs in its own valley, the Vallis Carceris, from Piedrafita towards the southeast.

VALCARLOS. Vallis Karoli, the Valley of Charlemagne, along the Petite Nive. It starts a little before Arnéguy and climbs up to a few kilometers before the Puerto de Ibañeta, the Ibañeta Pass. Cf. Valina-*Camino*, p. 27. See also the article on Roland, above, pp. 268–70.

VALVERDE, see Sil.

VÉZELAY. Vézelay rises on a prominent hill in the department of Yonne, district of Avallon.

VILLAFRANCA. The Francavilla of the *Codex*, is actually Villafranca de Montes de Oca, the Auca of the Romans. It was an episcopal see from Visigothic times until 1075. The resettlement policies of the Castilian monarchs brought Frankish settlers into town, from which its name derives. An old monastery of San Felix is documented in Villafranca (cf. Serrano-*Burgos*, 2:15, 211, 215; VázquezParga-*pereg* 1:474, 2:171). Villafranca marked the beginning of the painful crossing of the Montes de Oca, the forest of Oca, a difficult terrain full of underbrush and thickets (see Oca, above).

VILLAFRANCA DEL BIERZO. Villafranca del Bierzo, in its present full name, was the Roman Bergiolum. It lies at the confluence of the rivers Burbia and Valcarce and is the last major stopover before the valley and the pass of Valcarce. In the twelfth century it was known as Vico Francorum or Villa Francorum on account of the large number of French pilgrims who had been given settlement facilities by Alphonso VI. In its time it had up to five hospices of which one remains at present: the Colegio de la Divina Pastora (Divine Shepherdess). Of the hospice of Santiago and of that of San Lázaro only the name is left. The eleventh-century Cluniac monastery of Santa María de Cluniaco was later largely Gothicized. The Iglesia de Santiago was erected in 1186 by the bishop of Astorga. It preserves a late Romanesque portal, the Portal del Perdón, with historiated capitals, at which pilgrims who found it impossible for one reason or another to continue to Santiago were entitled to the same spiritual benefices as those they were to receive at the tomb of St. James. As elsewhere along the road, a tradition has been kept alive according to which the thirteenth-century Gothic-Mudejar church of San Francisco was founded by the saint himself (cf. López-*San Francisco*, passim). The city has preserved to our own days a tangible sense of history.

VILLANOVA. Or Vilanova, the Villanova of the text, according to Moralejo-*Calixtinus*, p. 506, n. 5, is another name for the town of Arzúa.

VILLAROYA. The Villa Rubea of the *Codex*.

VISCARRET. In Viscarret, Biscaretum, or Biscarellus, there was once a hospital for pilgrims. Hardly a trace of it is visible today.

VIZCAYA. In the province of Bilbao, one of the three provinces of the Basque Country.

Puente la Riena, Navarra. Pilgrims' bridge. Late XI C.

BIBLIOGRAPHY

I: SOURCES AND REFERENCE WORKS

ActaSS — *Acta Sanctorum.* Ed. Bollandus, et al. Antwerp, 1643– .

AnBoll — *Analecta Bollandiana.* Ed. H. Delehaye, P. Peeters, M. Coens, and B. de Gaiffier. Paris-Brussels, 1882– .

BHL — *Bibliotheca hagiographica latina antiquae et mediae aetatis.* Ed. Socii Bollandiani. 2 vols. Brussels, 1898–1901; supplement. Brussels, 1911.

Bruyne-*esthétique* — Bruyne, E. de. *Études d'esthétique médiévale. Époque romane.* Bruges, 1946.

BSS — *Bibliotheca Sanctorum.* Ed. Istituto Giovanni XXIII, Pontificia Università Lateranense. Rome, 1961– .

Carré-*Coruña* — Carré Aldao, E. "Provincia de la Coruña," in *Geografía General del Reino de Galicia.* Barcelona, 1932, 2:954–94.

CCh — *Corpus Christianorum seu nova patrum collectio.* Turnhout-Paris, 1953– .

Corominas-*Br dicc* — Corominas, J. *Breve diccionario etimológico de la lengua castellana.* 3rd ed. Madrid, 1973.

Cottineau-*Répertoire* — Cottineau, L. H. *Répertoire topo-bibliographique des abbayes et prieurés.* 2 vols. Mâcon, 1935–39.

Croiset-*année* — Croiset, J. *Exercices de piété pour tous les jours de l'année....* 12 vols. Lyon, 1713–20.

CSEL — *Corpus scriptorum ecclesiasticorum latinorum.* Ed. Academia Vindobonensis. Vienna, 1866– .

DACL — *Dictionnaire d'archéologie chrétienne et de liturgie.* Ed. F. Cabrol and H. Leclerq. 15 vols. Paris, 1907–53.

DavidsonDunn-Wood-*Pilgrimage* — Davidson, Linda Kay, and Maryjane Dunn-Wood. *Pilgrimage in the Middle Ages: A Research Guide.* New York: Garland, 1993.

DHGE — *Dictionnaire d'histoire et de géographie ecclésiastiques.* Ed. A. Baudrillart. Paris, 1912–77.

DíazDíaz-*Index* — Diaz y Díaz, C. *Index scriptorum latinorum Medii Aevi hispanorum.* Madrid, 1959.

DTC — *Dictionnaire de théologie catholique.* Paris, 1903–50.

Dubois-*martyrologe Usuard* — Dubois, J., ed. *Le martyrologe d'Usuard.* Brussels, 1965.

Du Cange-*Glossarium* — Du Cange, Ch. *Glossarium Mediae et Infimae Latinitatis* (1883–87). 10 vols. Graz, 1954.

Duchesne-*Fastes* — Duchesne, L. *Fastes épiscopaux de l'ancienne Gaule.* 3 vols. Paris, 1907–15.

Fábrega-*Pasionario* — Fábrega Grau, A. *Pasionario hispánico.* 2 vols. Madrid, 1953–55.

Fita-*codex* — Fita, P. F., and J. Vinson. *Le Codex de Saint-Jacques de Compostelle (Liber de miraculis S. Jacobi) Livre IV.* Paris, 1882. Also in *Revue de linguistique et de littératures comparées* 15 (1882): 1–20, 225–70.

Flórez-*Sagrada* — Flórez, E. *España Sagrada. Teatro geográfico histórico de la Iglesia de España.* 27 vols. Madrid, 1747–72.

Gaiffier-*Breviarium Apostolorum* — Gaiffier, B. de. "Le Breviarium Apostolorum (*BHL,* 652). Tradition manuscrite et oeuvres apparantées." *AnBoll* 81 (1963): 89–116.

Gallia christ — *Gallia christiana (nova).* 16 vols. Paris, 1715–1865.

Gams-*Kirchengeschichte Spanien* — Gams, P. B. *Kirchengeschichte von Spanien.* 2 vols. Regensburg, 1862; rpt. Graz, 1956.

GarcíaVillada-*Historia eccl Esp* — García Villada, Z. *Historia ecclesiástica de España.* Madrid, 1929.

Hämel-*Pseudo Turpin* — Hämel, A., ed. *Der Pseudo-Turpin von Compostela, aus dem Nachlass von A. de Mandach.* Bayerische Akademie der Wissenschaften phil.-hist. Klasse 1. Munich, 1965.

Historia compostelana — *Historia compostelana.* Ed. E. Falqué Rey. *CCh* 70. Also in Flórez-*Sagrada* 20.

Hübner-*Inscriptiones* — Hübner, A. *Inscriptiones Hispaniae christianae.* Berlin, 1871.

Jaffé-*Regesta* — Jaffé, Ph. *Regesta Pontificum Romanorum.* 2nd ed. Leipzig, 1885–88.

LchI — *Lexikon der christlichen Ikonographie.* Ed. E. Kirschbaum and W. Braunfels. 8 vols. Rome-Freiburg-Basel-Vienna, 1974.

Lex-Mitt — *Lexikon des Mittelalters.* Munich-Zurich, 1980– .

Lipsius-*apokryphen Apostel* — Lipsius, P. A. *Die apokryphen Apostelgeschichte und Apostellegenden.* 2 vols. Braunschweig, 1883–84.

LTK3 — *Lexikon für Theologie und Kirche.* Ed. M. Buchberger, J. Höfer, K. Rahner. Freiburg im Breisgau, 1957–65.

Mabillon-*Acta Benedicti* — Mabillon, J. *Acta sanctorum ordinis S. Benedicti.* 9 vols. Paris, 1668–1701; Venice, 1733–40 (6 vols).

Mabillon-*Annales Benedicti* — Mabillon, J. *Annales ordinis S. Benedicti (480–1157).* 6 vols. Paris, 1703–39; Lucca, 1739–45.

Mansilla-*pontificia* — Mansilla, D. *La documentación pontificia hasta Inocencio III (965–1216).* Rome, 1955.

MartRom — *Martyrologium Romanum.* Ed. H. Delehaye *et al.* Brussels, 1940.

MenéndezPelayo-*heterodoxos* — Menéndez y Pelayo, M. *Historia de los heterodoxos españoles.* 2 vols. Madrid, 1917.

BIBLIOGRAPHY

MG— Monumenta Germaniae historica inde ab a. c. 500 usque ad a. 1500. Hannover-Berlin, 1826– ; *MG-Ep: Epistolae; MG-Le: Leges; MG-Mer: Rerum Merovingicarum.*

Migne-*PG—Patrologia Graeca.* Ed. J.-P. Migne. 161 vols. Paris, 1857–66.

Migne-*PL—Patrologia Latina.* Ed. J.-P. Migne. 221 vols. Paris, 1878–90.

Moralejo-*Calixtinus—* Moralejo, S., C. Torres, and J. Feo. *Liber Sancti Iacobi. Codex Calixtinus.* Santiago de Compostela, 1951.

NCE — New Catholic Encyclopaedia. New York, 1966– .

Perdrizet-*calendrier —* Perdrizet, P. *Le calendrier parisien à la fin du moyen âge d'après le bréviaire et les livres d'heures.* Paris, 1933.

PérezUrbel-*monjes —* Pérez de Urbel, J. *Los monjes españoles en la Edad Media.* 2 vols. 2nd ed. Madrid, 1933–34.

Quentin-*martyrologues —* Quentin, H. *Les martyrologues historiques du Moyen-âge.* Paris, 1908.

Réau-*Iconographie—* Réau, L. *Iconographie de l'Art chrétien.* 11 vols. Paris, 1955–59.

Robert-*Bullaire Calixte—* Robert, U. *Bullaire du pape Calixte II.* 2 vols. Paris, 1891.

Romero/alia-*Calixtino —* Romero de Lecea, C., J. Guerra Campos, and J. Filgueira Valverde. *Libro de la Peregrinación del Códice Calixtino.* Facs. ed. Madrid, 1971.

Sanders-*Beati —* Sanders, H. A., ed. *Beati in Apocalypsis Libri XII.* Rome, 1930.

SHE — The New Schaff-Herzog Encyclopedia of Religious Knowledge. Ed. S. M. Jackson. New York-London, 1911.

Vielliard-*guide —* Vielliard, J. *Le guide du pèlerin de Saint-Jacques de Compostelle.* Paris, 1938; 2nd ed., 1950; 5th ed., 1984.

Voragine-*légende—* Voragine, Jacques de. *La légende dorée.* Ed. T. de Wyzewa. Paris, 1925.

Whitehill-*Liber —* Whitehill, W. M. *Liber Sancti Iacobi – Codex Calixtinus.* 3 vols. Santiago de Compostela, 1944.

WW-Kirchenlexikon — Wetzer und Weste's *Kirchenlexikon.* Ed. J. Hergenrötker and F. Kaulen. Freiburg im Breisgau, 1884.

COLLECTIVE WORKS: MÉLANGES, FESTSCHRIFTEN, EXHIBIT CATALOGUES

*Jacques Quête sacré-*Dupront— *Saint-Jacques de Compostelle. La Quête du sacré.* Ed. A. Dupront. Turnhout, 1985.

Martial-Limoges — L'art roman à Saint-Martial de Limoges. Exhib. cat. Limoges, 1950.

Mélanges Louis-geste carolingien — Mélanges René Louis: La Chanson de geste et le mythe carolingien. 2 vols. Saint-Père-sous-Vézelay, 1982.
Pèlerinage biblique classique — Les Pèlerinages de l'Antiquité biblique et classique à l'Occident médiéval. Ed. M. Simon. Études d'histoire des religions. Paris, 1973.
Pèlerinage-Fanjeaux — Le pèlerinage. Cahiers de Fanjeaux 15. Toulouse, 1980.
Pèlerins chemins Jacques-LaCoste Messelière — Pèlerins et chemins de Saint-Jacques en France et en Europe du x⁰ siècle à nos jours. Ed. R. de La Coste-Messelière. Exhib. cat. Paris, 1965.
Pellegrinaggi culto santi-Todi — Pellegrinaggi e culto dei santi in Europa fino alla 1ª crociata. Convegno del centro di studi sulla spiritualità medievale 4. Todi, 1963.
Pellegrinaggio Europa-Padova — Il pellegrinaggio nella formazione dell'Europa. Aspetti culturali e religiosi. Padova, 1990.
Pellegrinaggio Letteratura Jacopea-Perugia — Il Pellegrinaggio a Santiago di Compostella e la Letteratura Jacopea. Convegno internazionale di Studi, Perugia, 1983. Perugia, 1985.
Pistoia cammino Santiago — Pistoia e il cammino di Santiago. Una dimensione europea nella Toscana medioevale. Convegno Internazionale di Studi, Pistoia, 1984. Perugia, 1987.
Portico Gloria — O Portico da Gloria e o seu temp. Exhib. cat. Santiago de Compostela, 1988.
Santiago-Europalia — Santiago de Compostela: Mil ans de pèlerinage européen. Europalia. Gand, 1985.
Santiago-Madrid — Santiago en España, Europa y América. Madrid, 1971.
Santiago Routes-Bamberg — The Santiago de Compostela Pilgrim Routes. A Council of Europe congress organized in cooperation with the Deutsches Komitee für Denkmalschutz and the Deutsche St.-Jakobus Gesellschaft, Bamberg, 1988. Strasbourg, 1989.
Soulac-Médoc-Jacques — Soulac et le Médoc dans le pèlerinage de Saint-Jacques de Compostelle. Ed. J. Warcollier. Exhib. cat. Soulac, 1975.
Wallfahrt-Grenzen — Wallfahrt kennt keine Grenzen. Ed. L. Kriss-Rettenbeck and G. Möhler. Munich-Zurich, 1984.

HISTORICAL AND CRITICAL LITERATURE

Abecassis-hébraique juif — Abecassis, A. "Les Lieux saints, pèlerinage hébraique, pèlerinage juif," in *Les Pèlerins de l'Orient et les Vagabonds de l'Occident.* Cahiers de l'Université de Saint-Jean-de-Jérusalem 4. Paris, 1978, pp. 45–66.

BIBLIOGRAPHY

Ahlsell-*peintures Rabastens* — Ahlsell de Toulza, G. "Les peintures murales de la chapelle Saint-Jacques dans l'église Notre-Dame du Bourg à Rabastens-sur-Tarn," in *Pèlerinage-Fanjeaux*, pp. 43–55.

Alcolea-*Santiago* — Alcolea, S. *La catedral de Santiago*. Madrid, 1948.

Apraiz-*representación caballero* — Apraiz, A. "La representación del caballero en las iglesias de los caminos de Santiago," *Archivo Español de Arte* 46 (1941): 384–96.

Arié-*España musulmana* — Arié, R. *España musulmana*. In *Historia de España* 3. Ed. M. Tuñón de Lara. Barcelona, 1982.

Arrondo-*Rutas jacobeas* — Arrondo, E. G. *Rutas jacobeas. Historia, Arte, Caminos*. Estella, 1971.

Aubert-*Conques* — Aubert, M. "Conques-en-Rouergue," in *Congrès archéologique de France, 100ᵉ session. Figeac, Cahors et Rodez, 1937*. Paris, 1938, pp. 458–523.

Aubert-*Hospice Pons* — Aubert, M. "Hospice des pèlerins à Pons." in *Congrès archéologique La Rochelle, 1956*. La Rochelle, 1958, pp. 229–33.

Aubert-*Sernin* — Aubert, M. *Saint-Sernin*. Paris, 1930.

Aurora-*Caminho portugues* — Aurora, Conde d'. *Caminho portugues para Santiago de Compostela*. Braga, 1965.

Babelon-*Violence* — Babelon, J. "Le Thème de la violence dans l'iconographie de Saint Jacques le Matamore," in *Actes du 94e Congrès National des Sociétés Savantes* (Pau, 1969). Paris, 1971, pp. 333–47.

BaltarDomiguez-*médicos peregr* — Baltar Domíguez, R. "Algunos aspectos médicos de las peregrinaciones medievales a Compostela," in *Actas del XV Congreso Internacional de la Historia de la Medicina, Madrid-Alcalá, 1956*. Madrid, 1959, 2:33–52.

Barbero/Vigil-*orígenes sociales Reconquista* — Barbero, A., and M. Vigil. *Sobre los orígenes sociales de la Reconquista*. 2nd ed. Barcelona, 1984.

BarreiroSomoza-*Gelmírez* — Barreiro Somoza, J. "Gelmírez Diego." *Gran Enciclopedia Gallega* 15:231–56, s.v.

Barret/Gurgand-*Jakobspilger* — Barret, P., and J.-N. Gurgand. *Unterwegs nach Santiago. Auf den Spuren der Jakobspilger*. Freiburg-Basel-Vienna, 1982.

Barret/Gurgand-*Priez Compostelle* — Barret, P., and J.-N. Gurgand. *Priez pour nous à Compostelle*. Paris, 1978.

Baumer-*Wallfahrt Metapher* — Baumer, I. "Wallfahrt als Metapher," in *Wallfahrt-Grenzen*, pp. 55–64.

Bautier-*Charlemagne Espagne* — Bautier, R. H. "La campagne de Charlemagne en Espagne (778). La réalité historique." Actes du Colloque de Saint-Jean-Pied-de-Port, 1978. In *Bulletin de la Société des Sciences, Lettres et Arts de Bayonne* 135 (1979): 1–51.

Bédier-*épiques* — Bédier, J. *Les légendes épiques. Recherches sur la formation des Chansons de Geste.* 4 vols. Paris, 1912; 3rd ed. 1929; rpt. Paris, 1966.

Bennassar-*Saint Jacques* — Bennassar, B. *Saint-Jacques-de-Compostelle.* Paris, 1971.

Benoît-*cimitières* – Benoît, F. *Les cimitières suburbains d'Arles dans l'antiquité chrétienne et au Moyen Âge.* Rome-Paris, 1935.

Berlière-*pèlerinages judiciaires* — Berlière, V. "Les pèlerinages judiciaires au moyen âge," *Revue Bénédictine* 7 (1890): 520–26.

Bernoulli-*Conques* — Bernoulli, Ch. *Die Skulpturen der Abtei Conques-en-Rouergue.* Basler Studien für Kunstgeschichte 13. Basel, 1956.

Biggs-*Gelmírez* — Biggs, A. G. *Diego Gelmírez. First Archbishop of Compostela.* Diss., Catholic University, Washington, 1949; rpt., as *Diego Gelmírez.* Vigo, 1983.

Bishko-*Cluniac Priories Galicia* — Bishko, Ch. J. "The Cluniac Priories of Galicia and Portugal: Their Acquisition and Administration, 1075–ca.1230," *Studia Monastica* 7 (1965): 305–56.

Bishko-*Fernando I Cluny* — Bishko, Ch. J. "Fernando I y los orígenes de la alianza castellano-leonesa con Cluny," *Cuadernos de Historia de España* 47–48 (1969): 31–135; 49–50 (1969): 50–116.

Bishko-*Frontier* — Bishko, Ch. J. *Studies in Medieval Spanish Frontier History.* London, 1980.

Bishko-*Monastic* — Bishko, Ch. J. *Spanish and Portuguese Monastic History 600–1300.* London, 1984.

Boglioni-*Pèlerinages religion populaire* — Boglioni, P. "Pèlerinages et religion populaire au Moyen Age," in *Wallfahrt-Grenzen*, pp. 66–75.

Boissonade-*croisades françaises Espagne* — Boissonade, P. "Les premières croisades françaises en Espagne. Normands, Gascons, Aquitains et Bourguignons (1018–1302)." *Bulletin Hispanique* 36/1 (1934): 5–28.

BonetCorrea-*Jacques baroque* — Bonet Correa, A. "Le chemin et la cathédrale de Saint-Jacques de Compostelle à l'époque baroque," in *Santiago-Europalia*, pp. 61–69.

BonetCorrea-*Santiago* — Bonet Correa, A. *Santiago de Compostela. Die Wege der Pilger.* Freiburg-Basel-Vienna, 1981. Also as *Santiago de Compostela. El camino de los peregrinos.* Barcelona-Madrid, 1985.

Bonnault-*Compostelle* — Bonnault d'Houët, baron de. *Pèlerinage d'un paysan picard à Saint-Jacques de Compostelle au commencement du XVIIIᵉ siècle.* Montdidier, 1890.

Boshof-*Armenfürsorge* — Boshof, E. "Untersuchungen zur Armenfürsorge in fränkischen Reich des 9. Jahrhunderts," *Archiv für Kulturgeschichte* 58 (1976): 265–339.

Bosl-*Mobilität* — Bosl, K. "Die horizontale Mobilität in der europäischen Gesellschaft im Mittelalter und ihre Kommunikationsmittel," *Zeitschrift für bayerische Landesgeschichte* 35 (1972): 40–53.

Bottineau-*Jacques* — Bottineau, Y. *Les chemins de Saint-Jacques.* Paris, 1964.

Bouillet-*Conques* — Bouillet, A. "Sainte-Foy de Conques, Saint-Sernin de Toulouse, Saint-Jacques de Compostelle," *Mémoires de la Société des Antiquaires de France* 53 (1893): 117–28.

Bousquet-*Conques* — Bousquet, J. *La sculpture à Conques aux XIe et XIIe siècles.* 2 vols. Lille, 1973.

BravoLozano-*Guía* – Bravo Lozano, M. *Guía del peregrino medieval.* Saghún, 1989.

Brown-*Saints* — Brown, P. *The Cult of Saints. Its Rise and Function in Latin Christianity.* Chicago, 1981.

Brückner-*Pilger* — Brückner, W. "Pilger, Pilgerschaft," in *LchI* 3, cols. 439–42.

Brückner-*Wallfahrtswesen* — Brückner, W. "Zur Phänomenologie und Nomenklatur des Wallfahrtswesen und seine Erforschung. Wörter und Sachen in systematisch-semantischen Zusammenhang," in *Volkskultur und Geschichte: Festschrift für J. Dünninger.* Berlin, 1970, pp. 384–424.

Burger-*Rolandienne* — Burger, A. "La question rolandienne. Faits et hypothèses," *Cahiers de civilisation médiévales* 4 (1961): 269–91.

Burger-*Roland Turpin Guide* — Burger, A. "Sur les relations de la Chanson de Roland avec le récit du faux Turpin et celui du Guide du pèlerin," *Romania* 73 (1952): 242–47.

Cabanot-*débuts romane* — Cabanot, J. *Les débuts de la sculpture romane dans le Sud-Ouest de la France.* Paris, 1987.

Cabanot-*décor Sernin* — Cabanot, J., "Le décor sculpté de la basilique Saint-Sernin de Toulouse." Sixième colloque international de la Société française d'archéologie, Toulouse, 1971. *Bulletin Monumental,* 1974, pp. 99–145.

Campo-*medicina Santiago* — Campo, L. del. "La medicina en el camino de Santiago," in *Actas de la Semana de Estudios Medievales, Estella.* Pamplona, 1966.

Camps-*románico* — Camps, E. *El arte románico en España.* Barcelona, 1935.

Cannata-*insigne* — Cannata, P. "Divisa e insigne del romeo in relazione al pellegrinaggio romano," in *L'Arte degli Anni Santi. Roma 1300–1875.* Exhib. cat. Milan, 1984, pp. 46–57.

CarroCelada-*Picaresca via* — Carro Celada, E. *Picaresca, milagrería y milandanzas en la via láctea.* Madrid, 1971.

Castro-*España historia* — Castro, A. *España en su historia. Cristianos, moros y judíos.* Buenos Aires, 1948.

Caucci-*chemin italien* — Caucci von Saucken, P. G. "Le chemin italien de Saint-Jacques," in *Jacques Quête sacré-Dupront*, pp. 63–75.

Caucci-*Guida* — Caucci von Saucken, P. G. *Guida del pellegrino di Santiago. Libro quinto del Codex Calixtinus.* Milan, 1989.

Caucci-*itinerari italiani* — Caucci von Saucken, P. G. "La via francigena e gli itinerari italiani a Compostella," in *Wege der Jakobspilger.* Santiago Routes-Bamberg Congress. Tübingen, 1989.

Caucci-*Testi italiani Santiago* — Caucci von Saucken, P. G., *et al. Testi italiani del viaggio e pellegrinaggio a Santiago de Compostela.* Perugia, 1983.

Cauwenbergh-*pèlerinages expiatoires judiciaires* — Cauwenbergh, E. van. *Les pèlerinages expiatoires et judiciaires dans le droit communal de la Belgique au moyen-âge.* Louvain, 1922.

Cetto-*Miègeville* — Cetto, A. M. "Explication de la Porte Miègeville de Saint-Sernin de Toulouse," in *Actes du XVIIᵉ Congrès international d'histoire de l'art. Amsterdam, 1952.* La Haye, 1955, pp 147–58.

Charpentier-*Jacques mystère* — Charpentier, L. *Les Jacques et le mystère de Compostelle.* Paris, 1971.

Chelini/Branthomme-*chemins Dieu* — Chelini, J., and H. Branthomme. *Les chemins de Dieu.* Paris, 1982.

Chocheyras-*Jacques* — Chocheyras, J. *Saint-Jacques à Compostelle.* Rennes, 1985.

Cocheril-*ordres militaires* — Cocheril, M. "Essai sur l'origine des ordres militaires dans la Peninsule Ibérique," *Collectanea ordinis Cisterciensium reformatorum* 20 (1958): 346–61, 21 (1959): 302–29.

Cohen-*Pilgrimage* — Cohen, E. *In the Name of God and of Profit. The Pilgrimage Industry in Southern France in the Late Middle Ages.* Diss. Brown University, Providence, 1977.

Cohen-*Roads Pilgrimage* — Cohen, E. "Roads and Pilgrimage. A Study in Economic Interaction," *Studi medievali* 21 (1980): 321–41.

Cohen-*signa* — Cohen, E. "'In haec signa': Pilgrim-Badge Trade in Southern France," *Journal of Medieval History* 2 (1976): 193–214.

Conant-*Santiago* — Conant, K. J. *The Early Architectural History of the Cathedral of Santiago de Compostela.* Cambridge, MA, 1926.

Constable-*Monachisme pèlerinage* — Constable, G. "Monachisme et pèlerinage au Moyen Ages," *Revue historique* 258 (1977): 3–27. Also in *Religious Life and Thought.* London, 1979, pp. 3–27.

BIBLIOGRAPHY

Constable-*Opposition Pilgrimage* — Constable, G. "Opposition to Pilgrimage in the Middle Ages," *Studia Gratiana* 19 (1976): 125–46. Also in *Religious Life and Thought*. London, 1979, pp. 125–46.

CorderoCarrete-*Peregrinos mendicantes* — Cordero Carrete, F. R. "Peregrinos mendicantes," *Cuadernos de Estudios Gallegos* 17 (1962): 83–89.

CorderoCarrete-*Veneras cruces Santiago* — Cordero Carrete, F. R. "Veneras y cruces de Santiago (?) en la heráldica inglesa," *Cuadernos de Estudios Gallegos* 6 (1951): 205–19.

Costa-*cabeça Santiago* — Costa, A. de Jesús da. "Quem trouxe a cabeça de Santiago de Jerusalém para Braga-Compostela?," *Lusitania Sacra* 5 (1960–61): 233–43.

Crozet-*cavalier victorieux pèlerinage* — Crozet, R. "Le thème du cavalier victorieux sur les routes de pèlerinage," *Compostelle* 29 (1971).

Damonte-*Firenze Santiago* — Damonte, M. "Da Firenze a Santiago de Compostella. Itinerario di un anonimo pellegrino nell'anno 1477," *Studi medievali* 13/2 (1972): 1043–71.

Daux-*chansons pèlerins* — Daux, C. *Les chansons des pèlerins de Saint-Jacques (paroles et musique)*. Montauban, 1899.

Daux-*Pèlerinage confrérie* — Daux, C. *Pèlerinage et confrérie de Saint-Jacques de Compostelle*. Paris, 1898; rpt.: Geneva-Paris, 1981.

David-*Gulice Portugal* — David, P. *Études historiques sur la Galice et le Portugal du VIᵉ au XIIᵉ siècle*. Paris-Lisbon, 1947.

David-*Jacques* — David, P. *Études sur le Livre de Saint-Jacques attribué au pape Calixte II*. Lisbon, 1946–49. Extracted from *Bulletin des Études portugaises et de l'Institut français au Portugal* 10 (1945): 1–41; 11 (1947): 113–85; 12 (1948): 70–223; 13 (1949): 52–104.

Davies-*Compostela* — Davies, H. and M. H. Davies. *Holy Days and Holidays. The Medieval Pilgrimage to Compostela*. London-Toronto, 1982.

Defourneaux-*Français Espagne* — Defourneaux, M. *Les Français en Espagne au XIᵉ et XIIᵉ siècles*. Paris, 1949.

Delaruelle-*Piété populaire* — Delaruelle, E. *La Piété populaire au Moyen Age*. Turin, 1975.

Delehaye-*légendes* — Delehaye, H. *Les légendes hagiographiques*. 4th ed. Brussels, 1955.

Delehaye-*martyrs* — Delehaye, H. *Les origines du culte des martyrs*. 2nd ed. Brussels, 1933.

Delisle-*Jacobi* — Delisle, L. "Note sur le recueil intitulé De miraculis sancti Jacobi," *Le Cabinet historique* 24 (1928): 1–9.

Deschamps-*Conques Sernin* — Deschamps, P. "Étude sur les sculptures de Sainte-Foy de Conques et de Saint-Sernin de Toulouse et leurs relations avec celles de Saint-Isidore de León et de Saint-Jacques de Compostelle," *Bulletin monumental* 100 (1941): 239–64.

Deschamps-*Languedoc Espagne* — Deschamps, P. "Notes sur la sculpture romane en Languedoc et dans le nord de l'Espagne," *Bulletin monumental* 82 (1923): 305–51.

DíazDíaz-*antigua literatura* — Díaz y Díaz, M. C. "Estudios sobre la antigua literatura relacionada con Santiago el Mayor," *Compostellanum* 11 (1966): 621–52.

DíazDíaz-*calixtino* — Díaz y Díaz, M. C. *El Códice calixtino de la catedral de Santiago. Estudio codicológico y de contenido.* Santiago de Compostela, 1988.

DíazDíaz-*escuela* — Díaz y Díaz, M. C. "Problemas de la cultura en los siglos XI–XII. La escuela episcopal de Santiago," *Compostellanum* 16 (1971): 187–200.

DíazDíaz-*Jakobus Legende Isidor* — Díaz y Díaz, M. C. "Die spanische Jakobus-Legende bei Isidor von Sevilla," *Historisches Jahrbuch* 77 (1958): 467–72.

DíazDíaz-*literatura jacobea anterior* — Díaz y Díaz, M. C. "La literatura jacobea anterior al códice Calixtino," *Compostellanum* 10 (1965): 639–61.

DíazDíaz-*litt. jacobite* — Díaz y Díaz, M. C. "La littérature jacobite jusqu'au XIIᵉ siècle," in *Santiago-Europalia*, pp. 165–71.

Domke-*Frankreichs Santiago* — Domke, H. *Frankreichs Süden. Im Bannkreis der Pyrenäen. Wege nach Santiago.* Munich, 1983.

Domke-*Spaniens Santiago* — Domke, H. *Spaniens Norden. Der Weg nach Santiago.* Munich, 1973.

Dossat-*Types pèlerins* — Dossat, Y. "Typs exceptionnels de pèlerins: l'hérétique, le voyageur déguisé, le professionnel," in *Pèlerinage-Fanjeaux*, pp. 207–25.

Douais-*Trésor Sernin* — Douais, C. *Documents sur l'ancienne province de Languedoc.* 3 vols. Paris-Toulouse, 1901–6.

Duchesne-*Jacques Galice* — Duchesne, L. "Saint Jacques en Galice," *Annales du Midi* 12 (1900): 145–79.

Dünninger-*Wallfahrt* — Dünninger, H. "Was ist Wallfahrt? Erneute Aufforderung zur Diskussion um eine Begriffs-bestimmung," *Zeitschrift für Volkskunde* 59 (1963): 221–32.

Dupront-*Puissances pèlerinage* — Dupront, A. "Puissances du pèlerinage: perspectives anthropologiques," in *Jacques Quête sacré-Dupront*, pp. 173–252.

Dupront-*Sacré* — Dupront, A. *Du Sacré. Croisades et pèlerinages. Images et languages.* Paris, 1987.

Durliat-*construction Sernin* — Durliat, M. "La construction de Saint-Sernin de Toulouse au XIᵉ siècle," *Bulletin monumental* 121 (1963): 151–70.

Durliat-*cryptes Sernin* — Durliat, M. "Les cryptes de Saint-Sernin de Toulouse, bilan des recherches récentes," in *Les Monuments historiques de la France* 17 (1971): 25–40.

Durliat-*Espagne* — Durliat, M. *L'art roman en Espagne.* Paris, 1962.

Durliat-*Jacques* — Durliat, M. *La Sculpture Romane de la Route de Saint-Jacques.* Mont-de-Marsan, 1991.

Durliat-*Jacques art* — Durliat, M. "Les chemins de Saint-Jacques et l'art: l'architecture et la sculpture," in *Santiago-Europalia*, pp. 155–64.

Durliat-*Miègeville* — Durliat, M. "Les chapiteaux de la Porte Miègeville à Saint-Sernin de Toulouse," in *Économies et sociétés au Moyen Âge: Mélanges offerts à Édouard Perroy.* Paris, 1973, pp. 123–29.

Durliat-*Pèlerinages* — Durliat, M. "Pèlerinages et architecture romane," *Les dossiers de l'archéologie* 20 (1977): 22–35.

Durliat-*porte France* — Durliat, M. "La porte de France à la cathédrale de Compostelle," *Bulletin monumental* 130 (1972): 137–43.

Durliat-*Sernin* — Durliat, M. *Saint-Sernin de Toulouse.* Toulouse, 1986.

Dvornik-*Apostolicity Andrew* — Dvornik, F. *The Idea of Apostolicity in Byzantium and the Legend of Apostle Andrew.* Dumbarton Oaks Studies 4. Cambridge, MA, 1958.

EchevarríaBravo-*Cancionero peregrinos* — Echevarría Bravo, P. *Cancionero de los peregrinos de Santiago.* Madrid, 1967.

Engels-*Jakobusgrabes* — Engels, O. "Die Anfänge des spanischen Jakobusgrabes in kirchenpolitischer Sicht," *Römische Quartalschrift* 75 (1980): 146–70.

Ennen-*Stadt Wallfahrt* — Ennen, E. "Stadt und Wallfahrt in Frankreich, Belgien, den Niederlanden und Deutschland," in *Festschrift M. Zender.* Bonn, 1972, pp. 1057–75. Also in *Gesammelte Abhandlungen zum europäischen Städtewesen und zur rheinischen Geschichte.* Bonn, 1977, pp. 239–58.

EnríquezSalamanca-*Camino* — Enríquez de Salamanca, C. *El Camino de Santiago.* Madrid, 1991.

EnríquezSalamanca-*Pirineo aragonés* — Enríquez de Salamanca, C. *Por el Pirineo aragonés.* Madrid, 1988.

Erdmann-*Kreuzzugsgedankens* — Erdmann, C. *Die Entstehung des Kreuzzugsgedankens.* Stuttgart, 1935; rpt. Darmstadt, 1974. English trans. as *Origins of the Idea of Crusade.* Ed. M. W. Baldwin and W. Goffart. Princeton, 1977.

Fau-*chapiteaux Conques* — Fau, J.-C. "Les chapiteaux de l'église et du cloître de Conques," *Mémoires de la Société archéologique du Midi de la France* 24 (1956): 33–132.

Fau-*Conques* — Fau, J.-C. *Conques.* Zodiaque, Les Travaux des mois 9. Saint-Léger-Vauban, 1973.

FernándezAlbor-*delincuencia Camino* — Fernández Albor, A. "La delincuencia en el Camino de Santiago en la Edad Media," in *Pellegrinaggio Letteratura Jacopea-Perugia*, pp. 127–34.

FernándezCatón-*hospital Reyes Cat* — Fernández Catón, J. M. "El archivo del hospital de los Reyes Católicos de Santiago de Compostela," in *Inventario de Fondos, Universidad de Santiago.* Santiago de Compostela, 1972.

FernándezConde-*IglesiaAsturias* — Fernández Conde, F. J. *La Iglesia de Asturias en la alta edad media.* Oviedo, 1972.

FernándezConde-*medievo asturiano* — Fernández Conde, F. J. *Alta Edad Media. II: El medievo asturiano (siglos X–XII)*, in *Historia de Asturias.* Guijón, 1979, pp. 133–279.

Fichtenau-*Reliquienwesen* — Fichtenau, H. "Zum Reliquien-wesen im früheren Mittelalter," *Mitteilungen des Instituts für österreichische Geschichtsforschung* 60 (1952): 60–89. Also in *Beiträge zur Mediävistik.* Stuttgart, 1975, 1:108–44.

FilgueiraValverde-*Calixtino* — Filgueira Valverde, J. "Glosa a la 'Guía del Peregrino,'" in *Libro de la Peregrinación del Códice Calixtino.* Ed C. Romero de Lecea. Madrid, 1971, pp. 31–58.

FilgueiraValverde-*iconografía Santiago* — Filgueira Valverde, J. "La iconografía de Santiago y el grabado compostelano," *Cuadernos de Estudios Gallegos* 1/2 (1944): 185–202.

Finucane-*Miracles Pilgrims* — Finucane, R. C. *Miracles and Pilgrims. Popular Beliefs in Medieval England.* London-Melbourne-Toronto, 1977.

Fita-*Recuerdos* — Fita, P. F., and A. Fernández-Guerra. *Recuerdos de un viaje a Santiago de Galicia.* Madrid, 1880.

Fletcher-*Gelmírez* — Fletcher, R. A. *Saint James' Catapult. The Life and Times of Diego Gelmírez of Santiago de Compostela.* Oxford, 1984.

Gaiffier-*hagiographie iconologie* — Gaiffier, B. de. *Études critiques d'hagiographie et d'iconologie.* Subsidia hagiographica 43. Brussels, 1967.

Gaiffier-*pendu sauvé* — Gaiffier, B. de. "Un thème hagiographique: le pendu miraculeusement sauvé," *Revue Belge d'Archéologie et d'Histoire de l'Art* 13 (1943): 123–48.

Gaillard-*clunisienne* — Gaillard, G. "La pénétration clunisienne en Espagne pendant la première moitié du XIᵉ siècle," in Gaillard-*Études roman*, pp. 84–92; originally in *Bulletin du centre international d'études romanes*, 1960.

Gaillard-*Cluny Espagne* — Gaillard, G. "Cluny et l'Espagne dans l'art roman du XIᵉ siècle," in Gaillard-*Études roman*, pp. 93–98.

Gaillard-*commencements* — Gaillard, G. "Les commencements de l'art roman en Espagne," *Bulletin hispanique* 37/3 (1935): 273–308.

BIBLIOGRAPHY

Gaillard-*Compostelle León* — Gaillard, G. "Notes sur la date des sculptures de Compostelle et de León," *Gazette des Beaux-Arts* 6/1 (1929): 341–78.

Gaillard-*Études roman* — Gaillard, G. *Études d'art roman.* Paris, 1972.

Gaillard-*Foy* — Gaillard, G. "Une abbaye de pèlerinage: Sainte-Foy de Conques et ses rapports avec Saint-Jacques," *Compostellanum* 10 (1965).

Gaillard-*romane espagnole* — Gaillard, G. *Les débuts de la sculpture romane espagnole: León, Jaca, Compostelle.* Paris, 1938.

Gaillard-*Rouergue* — Gaillard, G. *Rouergue roman.* Zodiaque, La nuit des Temps 17. Saint-Léger-Vauban, 1963, pp. 25–185.

GarcíaÁlvarez-*Iriense* — García Álvarez, M. R. "El Cronicón Iriense," *Memorial Histórico Español* 50 (1963): 1–204.

GarcíaCortázar-*medieval* — García de Cortázar, J. A. *La época medieval.* In *Historia de España Alfaguara* 2. Madrid, 1977.

Garrison-*pèlerins juridique* — Garrison, F. "A propos des pèlerins et de leur condition juridique," in *Études d'histoire du droit canonique dédiées à G. Le Bras.* Paris, 1965, 2:1165–89.

Gavelle-*Tombes pèlerins* — Gavelle, R. "Tombes de pèlerins et souvenirs du pèlerinage de Compostelle," *Revue Comminges* 70 (1957): 155–62.

Geary-*coercition saints* — Geary, P. J. "La coercition des saints dans la pratique religieuse médiévale," in *La culture populaire au Moyen Âge.* Ed. P. Boglioni. Quebec, 1979, pp. 145–61.

Geary-*Furta Sacra* — Geary, P. J. *Furta Sacra. Thefts of Relics in the Central Middle Ages.* Princeton, 1978.

Geary-*humiliation saints* — Geary, P. J. "L'humiliation des saints," *Annales. Economies. Sociétés. Civilisations* 34 (1979): 27–42.

Geary-*Saint Shrine* — Geary, P. J. "The Saint and the Shrine. The Pilgrim's Goal in the Middle Ages," in *Wallfahrt-Grenzen*, pp. 265–73.

Georges-*pèlerinage Belgique iconographie* — Georges, A. *Le pèlerinage à Compostelle en Belgique et le Nord de la France, suivi d'une étude sur l'iconographie de saint-Jacques en Belgique.* Académie Royale de Belgique, Classe des Beaux Arts, Mémoires. 2 ser., 13. Brussels, 1971.

Gibert-*Libertades urbanas rurales León Castilla* — Gibert, R. "Libertades urbanas y rurales en León y Castilla durante la Edad Media," in *Les libertés urbaines et rurales du XIᵉ au XIVᵉ siècle.* Brussels, 1968, pp. 187–218.

Gibert-*reino visigótico* — Gibert, R. "El reino visigótico y el particularismo español," in *Estudios visigoticos* 1. Rome-Madrid, 1956, pp. 15–47.

Gilles-*Lex peregrinorum* — Gilles, H. "Lex peregrinorum," in *Pèlerinage-Fanjeaux*, pp. 161–89.

Goicoechea-*Cartografía* — Goicoechea Arrondo, E. *Cartografía del Camino de Santiago*. Estella, 1972.

Goicoechea-*Rutas* — Goicoechea Arrondo, E. *Rutas Jacobeas. Historia-Arte-Caminos*. Estella, 1971.

GómMor-*Cat León* — Gómez Moreno, M. *Catálogo monumental de España. Provincia de León*. Madrid, 1925.

GómMor-*mozárabes* — Gómez Moreno, M. *Iglesias mozárabes*. Madrid, 1919.

GómMor-*románico* — Gómez Moreno, M. *El arte románico español*. Madrid, 1934.

González-*Reconquista repoblación* — González, J. "Reconquista y repoblación de Castilla, León, Extremadura y Andalucía (siglos XI a XIII)," in *La Reconquista española y la repoblación del país*. Zaragoza, 1951, pp. 162–206.

Goyheneche-*Iconographie Jacques Basque* — Goyheneche, E. "Iconographie de Saint Jacques au Pays Basque," *Bulletin du Musée Basque* 29/3 (1965): 133–44.

Grabar-*Iconography* — Grabar, A. *Christian Iconography. A Study of its Origins*. Princeton, 1968.

Gruber-*Tagebuch Pilgers* — Gruber, R. *Tagebuch eines Pilgers nach Santiago de Compostela*. Linz, 1976.

GuerraCampos-*Bibl* — Guerra Campos, J. "Bibliografía (1950–1969). Veinte años de estudios jacobeos," *Compostellanum* 16 (1971): 575–712.

GuerraCampos-*sepulcro* — Guerra Campos, J. *Exploraciones arqueológicas en torno al sepulcro del Apóstol Santiago*. Santiago de Compostela, 1982.

Haase-*Apostel Evangelisten* — Haase, F. *Apostel und Evangelisten in den orientalischen Ueberlieferungen*. Neutestamentische Abhandlungen 9. Münster, 1922.

Hämel-*Überlieferung* — Hämel, A. "Überlieferung und Bedeutung des Liber Sancti Jacobi und des Pseudo-Turpin," *Sitzungsberichte der Bayerischen Akademie der Wissenschaften, phil.-hist.* Klasse 2. Munich, 1950.

Hefele/Leclercq-*Conciles* — Hefele, C. J., and H. Leclercq. *Histoire des Conciles*. Paris, 1910.

Heinzelmann-*Translationsberichte* — Heinzelmann, M. *Translationsberichte und andere Quellen des Reliquienkultes*. Typologie des sources du Moyen Âge occidental 33. Turnhout, 1979.

Hell-*Wallfahrt* — Hell, V., and H. Hell. *Die grosse Wallfahrt des Mittelalters*. Intro. by H. J. Hüffer. Tübingen, 1964; 3rd ed., 1979.

Herbers-*Jakobsweg* — Herbers, K. *Der Jakobsweg. Mit einem mittelalterlichen Pilgerführer unterwegs nach Santiago de Compostela*. Tübingen, 1986.

BIBLIOGRAPHY

Herbers-*Jakobuskult* — Herbers, K. *Der Jakobuskult des 12. Jahrhunderts und der "Liber Sancti Jacobi." Studien über das Verhältnis zwischen Religion und Gesellschaft in hohen Mittelalter.* Historische Forschungen 7. Wiesbaden, 1984.

HermannMascard-*reliques* — Hermann-Mascard, N. *Les reliques des saints. Formation coûtumière d'un droit.* Paris, 1975.

Herwaarden-*Jacobus* — Herwaarden, J. van. *O Roemrijke Jacobus bescherm uw volk. Pelgrimsgids naar Santiago.* Amsterdam, 1983.

Herwaarden-*James* — Herwaarden, J. van. "Saint James in Spain up to the 12th Century," in *Wallfahrt-Grenzen*, pp. 235–47.

Herwaarden-*Opgelegde Bedevaarten* — Herwaarden, J. van. *Opgelegde Bedevaarten. Een studie over de praktijk van oblegen van bedevaarten (met name in de stedelijke rechtspraak) in de Nederande gerunde de late meddeleuwen (ca. 1300–ca. 1500).* Amsterdam, 1978.

Herwaarden-*Origins Cult* — Herwaarden, J. van. "The Origins of the Cult of Saint James of Compostela," *Journal of Medieval History* 6 (1980): 1–36.

Heyne-*Hansestädten Santiago* — Heyne, B. "Von den Hansestädten nach Santiago. Die grosse Wallfahrt des Mittelalters," *Bremisches Jahrbuch* 52 (1972): 65–84.

Higounet-*chemins Jacques* — Higounet, Ch. "Les chemins de Saint-Jacques et les sauvetés de Gascogne," *Annales du Midi* 63 (1951): 293–304.

Hohler-*Jacobus* — Hohler, Ch. "A Note on Jacobus," *Journal of the Warburg and Courtauld Institutes* 35 (1972): 31–80.

Hotzelt-*Translationen Bayern* — Hotzelt, W. "Translationen von Märtyrerreliquien von Rom nach Bayern," *Studien und Mitteilungen des Benedicktinerordens* 53 (1935): 286–343.

Hotzelt-*Translationen Elsass* — Hotzelt, W. "Translationen römischer Reliquien ins Elsass," *Archiv für Elsässische Kirchengeschichte* 16 (1943): 1–18.

Howard-*Writers Pilgrims* — Howard, D. R. *Writers and Pilgrims: Medieval Pilgrimage Narratives and their Posterity.* Berkeley-Los Angeles-London, 1980.

Hüffer-*Jakobus Deutschland* — Hüffer, H. J. "Die spanische Jakobusverehrung in ihren Ausstrahlungen auf Deutschland," *Historisches Jahrbuch* 74 (1954): 124–38.

Hüffer-*Sant'Jago Deutschen* — Hüffer, H. J. *Sant'Jago. Entwicklung und Bedeutung des Jacobuskultes im Spanien und in dem Römisch-Deutschen Reich.* Munich, 1957.

HuidobroSerna-*peregrinaciones* — Huidobro y Serna, J. *Las peregrinaciones jacobeas.* 3 vols. Madrid, 1949–51.

JoinLambert-*Pèlerinages Israël* — Join-Lambert, M. "Les Pèlerinages en Israël," in *Pèlerinage biblique classique*, pp. 55–62.

Jugnot-*assistance Navarre* — Jugnot, G. "Le développement du réseau d'assistance aux pèlerins en Navarre (XIᵉ–XIIIᵉ siecles)." Actes congrès national des Sociétés savantes, Nantes, 1972. *Bulletin de philosophie et d'histoire*, 1978.

Jugnot-*chemins pèlerinage France* — Jugnot, G. "Les chemins de pèlerinage dans la France médiévale," in *L'homme et la route en Europe occidentale au Moyen Âge et aux temps modernes*. Auch, 1980, pp. 57–83.

Jugnot-*fondations augustiniennes* — Jugnot, G. "Deux fondations augustiniennes en faveur des pèlerins: Aubrac et Roncevaux," in *Assistance et charité*. Cahiers de Fanjeaux 13. Toulouse, 1971, pp. 321–41.

Jugnot-*pèlerinage droit pénal* — Jugnot, G. "Le pèlerinage et le droit pénal d'après les lettres de rémission accordées par le Roi de France," in *Pèlerinage-Fanjeaux*, pp. 191–206.

Jugnot-*via Podensis* — Jugnot, G. *Du Velay aux Pyrénées. La "via podensis" du Guide du pèlerin de Saint-Jacques de Compostelle*. 2 vols. Paris, 1981–83.

Kimpel-*Jakobus Ikon* — Kimpel, S. "Jakobus der Ältere," in *LchI 7*, cols. 23–39.

KingsleyPorter-*Leonesque* — Kingsley Porter, A. "Leonesque Romanesque and Southern France," *The Art Bulletin 8* (1926): 235–250.

KingsleyPorter-*Pilgrimage* — Kingsley Porter, A. *Romanesque Sculpture of the Pilgrimage Roads*. 10 vols. Boston, 1923.

King-*way James* — King, G. *The Way of Saint James*. 3 vols. New York-London, 1930.

Kirschbaum-*Grab Jakobus* — Kirschbaum, E. "Das Grab des Apostels Jakobus in Santiago de Compostela," *Stimmen der Zeit* 176 (1965): 352–62.

Kirschbaum-*Grabungen Santiago* — Kirschbaum, E. "Die Grabungen unter der Kathedrale von Santiago de Compostela," *Römische Quartalschrift* 56 (1961): 234–54.

Köster-*coquilles* — Köster, K. "Les coquilles et enseignes de pèlerinage de Saint-Jacques de Compostelle et des routes de Saint-Jacques en occident," in *Santiago-Europalia*, pp. 85–95.

Köster-*Pilgerzeichen* — Köster, K. "Mittelalterliche Pilgerzeichen," in *Wallfahrt-Grenzen*, pp. 203–23.

Köster-*Pilgerzeichen Muscheln* — Köster, K. *Pilgerzeichen und Pilgermuscheln von mittelalterlichen Santiagostrassen*. Neumünster, 1983.

Kötting-*Peregrinatio* — Kötting, B. *Peregrinatio religiosa. Wallfahrten in der Antike und das Pilgerwesen in der alten Kirche*. Forschungen zur Volkskunde 32–35. Münster, 1950.

BIBLIOGRAPHY

Kötting-*Reliquienverehrung* — Kötting, B. "Reliquienverehrung, ihre Entstehung und Formen," *Trierer Theologische Zeitschrift* 67 (1958): 321–34.

Kriss/Illich-*viator* — Kriss-Rettenbeck, L. and R., and I. Illich. "Homo viator – Ideen und Wirklichkeiten," in *Wallfahrt-Grenzen*, pp. 10–22.

Labande-*déplacement pèlerin* — Labande, E.-R. "Éléments d'une enquête sur les conditions de déplacement du pèlerin aux Xᵉ–XIᵉ siècles," in *Pellegrinaggi culto santi-Todi*, pp. 95–111.

Labande-*limina* — Labande, E.-R. "'Ad limina': Le pèlerin médiéval au terme de sa démarche," in *Mélanges R. Crozet*. Poitiers, 1966, pp. 283–91. Also in Labande-*Spiritualité*, no. 11, with original pagination.

Labande-*pèlerins* — Labande, E.-R. "Recherches sur les pèlerins dans l'Europe des XIᵉ et XIIᵉ siècles," *Cahiers de civilisation médiévale* 1 (1958): 159–69, 339–47. Also in *Labande-Spiritualité*, no. 12, with original pagination.

Labande-*Pellegrini crociati* — Labande, E.-R. "Pellegrini o crociati? Mentalità e comportamenti a Gerusalemme nel secolo XII," *Aevum* 54 (1980): 217–30.

Labande-*Spiritualité* — Labande, E.-R. *Spiritualité et vie littéraire de l'Occident. XIᵉ–XIVᵉ siècle*. London, 1974.

Lacarra-*arancel* — Lacarra, J. M. *Un arancel de aduanas del siglo XI*. Zaragoza, 1950.

Lacarra-*burguesía* — Lacarra, J. M. "La burguesía, fenómeno social en el camino," *Cuadernos historia* 16, 88 (1985): 12–18.

Lacarra-*Espiritualidad peregrinación* — Lacarra, J. M. "Espiritualidad del culto y de la peregrinación a Santiago antes de la primera cruzada," in *Pellegrinaggi culto santi-Todi*, pp. 113–45.

Lacarra-*Jacques économique* — Lacarra, J. M. "Le pèlerinage de Saint-Jacques: son influence sur le développement économique et urbain du Moyen Âge," *Bulletin de l'Institut français en Espagne* 46 (1950): 218–21.

Lacarra-*predominio Castilla* — Lacarra, J. M. "El lento predominio de Castilla," *Revista Portuguesa de História* 16 (1976): 63–81.

LaCosteMess-*abus pèlerinages* — La Coste-Messelière, R. de. "Édits et actes royaux contre les abus des pèlerinages à l'étranger (XVIIᵉ–XVIIIᵉ siècles) et perennité du pèlerinage à Saint-Jacques de Compostelle." Actes congrès national des Sociétés savantes, Pau, 1969. In *Bulletin philologique et historique* (Paris), 1972.

LaCosteMess-*accueil pèlerins Toulouse* — La Coste-Messelière, R. de, and G. Jugnot. "L'accueil des pèlerins à Toulouse," in *Pèlerinage-Fanjeaux*, pp. 117–35.

LaCosteMess-*chemin Poitou* — La Coste-Messelière, R. de. "Le grand chemin de St.-Jacques en Poitou," *Compostellanum* 10 (1965): 407–19.

LaCosteMess-*coquille* — La Coste-Messelière, R. de. "La coquille dans l'héraldique," in *Soulac-Médoc-Jacques*, pp. 53–58.

LaCosteMess-*Europe Jacques* — La Coste-Messelière, R. de. "L'Europe et le pèlerinage de St.-Jacques de Compostelle," in *Santiago-Madrid*, pp. 147–322.

LaCosteMess-*Fleurs lys coquilles* — La Coste-Messelière, R. de. "Fleurs de lys et coquilles Saint-Jacques. Rois et princes de France et le pèlerinage de Compostelle," in *Bulletin de la Féderation des Sociétés Savantes des Deux Sèvres.* Noirt, 1976.

LaCosteMess-*hospitaliers* — La Coste-Messelière, R. de. "Sources et illustrations de l'histoire des établissements hospitaliers du pèlerinage de Saint-Jacques de Compostelle," *Bulletin de la Société Historique des Deux Sèvres* 12 (1979): 183–216.

LaCosteMess-*hospitaliers pèlerins* — La Coste-Messelière, R. de. *Avec les hospitaliers et les pèlerins sur les chemins de Saint-Jacques.* Cadillac-sur-Garonne, 1967.

LaCosteMess-*routes* — La Coste-Messelière, R. de. "Importance réelle des routes dites de Saint-Jacques dans le pays du sud de la France et l'Espagne du Nord," *Bulletin philologique et historique* (Paris, 1972): 452–70.

LaCosteMess-*signe coquille* — La Coste-Messelière, R. de. "Sous le signe de la coquille, chemins de Saint-Jacques et pèlerins," in *Catalogue de l'exposition de Château-Thierry, 1983.* Ed. R. de la Coste-Messelière and C. Prieur. Paris.

LaCosteMess-*Voies compostellanes* — La Coste-Messelière, R. de. "Voies compostellanes," in *Jacques Quête sacré*-Dupront, pp. 37–62.

Ladner-*Viator* — Ladner, G. B. "Homo Viator. Medieval Ideas on Alienation and Order," *Speculum* 17 (1967): 233–59.

Laffi-*Viaggio* — Laffi, D. *Viaggio in Ponente a San Giacomo di Galitia e Finisterrae.* Bologna, 1681. Also ed. A. S. Capponi. Perugia, 1989.

Lambert-*Aymeric* — Lambert, É. "Aymeric" and "Aymeric Picaud," in *DHGE* 5, cols. 1291 and 1296–98.

Lambert-*cathédrale Toulouse* — Lambert, É. "La cathédrale de Toulouse," in Lambert-*médiévales* 2:149–74.

Lambert-*Compostelle* — Lambert, É. "La cathédrale de Saint-Jacques de Compostelle et l'école des grandes églises romanes des routes de pèlerinage," in Lambert-*médiévales*, 1:245–59.

Lambert-*médiévales* — Lambert, É. *Études médiévales.* 4 vols. Toulouse, 1956–57.

BIBLIOGRAPHY

Lambert-*Ordres confréries* — Lambert, É. "Ordres et confréries dans l'histoire de pèlerinage de Compostelle," *Annales du Midi,* 55 (1943): 369–403. Also in Lambert-*médiévales,* 1:127–44.

Lambert-*pèlerinage* — Lambert, É. *Le pèlerinage de Compostelle.* Paris-Toulouse, 1959.

Lambert-*Peregrinación* — Lambert, É. "La peregrinación a Compostela y la arquitectura románica," *Archivo Español de Arte* 59 (1943): 278–79.

Lambert-*pseudo Turpin* — Lambert, É. "L'historia Rotholandi du pseudo-Turpin et le pèlerinage de Compostelle," *Romania* 69 (1946–47): 362–87.

Lambert-*Pyrénées* — Lambert, É. "Les routes des Pyrénées atlantiques et les variations de leur emploi au cours des âges," *Pirineos* 7 (1951): 335–82. Also in Lambert-*médiévales,* 1:189–226.

Lambert-*Roncevaux* — Lambert, É. "Roncevaux et ses monuments," *Romania* 61 (1935): 17–54. Also in Lambert-médiévales, 1:159–87.

Lambert-*Roncevaux Cize* — Lambert, É. "Textes relatifs à Roncevaux et aux ports de Cize," in *Colóquios de Roncesvalles.* Zaragoza, 1956, pp. 123–31.

Lambert-*Roncevaux Roland* — Lambert, É. "Le monastère de Roncevaux, la légende de Roland et le pèlerinage de Compostelle." In *Mélanges de la Société toulousaine d'études classiques* 2 (1948): 163–78.

Lambert-*routes pèlerinage* — Lambert, É. "Le livre de Saint-Jacques et les routes de pèlerinage vers Compostelle," *Revue géographique des Pyrénées et du Sud* 14 (1943): 5–33.

Lastcyrie-*romane* — Lasteyrie, R. de. *L'architecture religieuse en France à l'époque romane.* Paris, 1912.

Layton-*Santiago* — Layton, T. A. *The Way of Saint James, or the Pilgrims' Road to Santiago.* London, 1976.

LeBras-*Pénitentiels* — Le Bras, G. "Pénitentiels," in *DTC* 12, s.v.

LeClerc-*Aimeric* — Le Clerc, V. "'Aimeric Picaudi de Parthenai,' Cantique et itinéraire des pèlerins de Saint-Jacques de Compostelle," in *Histoire Littéraire* 21. Paris, 1847, pp. 272–92.

Leclercq-*Mönchtum Peregrinatio* — Leclercq, J. "Mönchtum und Peregrinatio im Frühmittelalter," *Römische Quartalschrift* 55 (1960): 212–25.

Lejeune/Stiennon-*Roland* — Lejeune, R., and J. Stiennon. *La légende de Roland dans l'art du Moyen Âge.* 2 vols. Brussels, 1966.

Lelong-*Tours* — Lelong, Ch. *La basilique Saint-Martin de Tours.* n.p., 1986.

LéviProvençal-*España Musulmana* — Lévi Provençal, É. *España Musulmana (711–1031). La conquista, el Emirato, el Califato.* In *Historia de España* 4. Ed. R. Menéndez Pidal. Madrid, 1956.

321

Locard-*coquille pèlerins* — Locard, A. *Recherches historiques sur la coquille des pèlerins.* Lyons, 1888.

Löwe-*Peregrinatio*—Löwe, H. "Westliche Peregrinatio und Mission. Ihr Zusammenhang mit den länder- und völkerkundlichen Kenntnissen des früheren Mittelalters," in *Popoli e paesi nella cultura altomedievale. Settimane di studio del Centro italiano sull'alto Medioevo* 29/1. Spoleto, 1983, pp. 327–76.

LópezAlsina-*ciudad* — López Alsina, F. *La ciudad de Santiago de Compostela en la Alta Edad Media.* Santiago de Compostela, 1988.

LópezAlsina-*Tumbos* — López Alsina, F. "Los Tumbos de Compostela. Tipología de los manuscrítos y fuentes documentales," in *Los Tumbos de Compostela.* Madrid, 1985, pp. pp. 27–41.

LópezAydillo-*Santiago* — López-Aydillo, E. *Os miragres de Santiago.* Valladolid, 1918.

LópezCalo-*música peregrinaciones* — López Calo, J. "La música en las peregrinaciones jacobeas medievales," *Compostellanum* 10/4 (1965): 465–84.

LópezChavez-*camino portugués* — López Chavez Meléndez, J. M. *El camino portugués.* Vigo, 1988.

LópezFerreiro-*Pórtico* — López Ferreiro, A. *El Pórtico de la Gloria, Platerías y el primitivo Altar Mayor.* Santiago de Compostela, 1975; partial rpt. of 1891–92 ed.

LópezFerreiro-*Santiago* — López Ferreiro, A. *Historia de la Santa Apostólica Metropolitana Iglesia de Santiago de Compostela.* 11 vols. Santiago de Compostela, 1898–1911.

López-*San Francisco* — López, A. "El viaje de San Francisco a España," *Archivo Iberoamericano* 1 (1914): 369–90.

Louis-*Aiméri* — Louis, R. "Aiméri Picaud compilateur du Liber Sancti Jacobi," *Bulletin de la Société Nationale des Antiquaires de France* (1948–49): 80–97.

Ludwig-*Marschgeschwindigkeit* — Ludwig, F. *Untersuchungen über die Reise- und Marschgeschwindigkeit in XII and XIII Jahrhundert.* Berlin, 1897.

Lymann-*Eclecticism* — Lymann, Th. W. "The Politics of Selective Eclecticism: Monastic Architecture, Pilgrimage Churches, and 'Resistance to Cluny,'" *Gesta* 27 (1988): 83–92.

Lymann-*Miègeville* — Lymann, Th. W. "Notes on the Porte Miègeville Capitals and the Construction of Saint-Sernin in Toulouse," *AThe rt Bulletin* 49 (1967): 27–36.

Lyman-*Pilgrimage* — Lyman, Th. W. "The Pilgrimage Roads Revisited," *Gesta* 13 (1969): 30–44.

Lyman-*style Miègeville*— Lyman, Th. W. "Le style comme symbole chez les sculpteurs romans: essai d'interprétation de quelques inventions thématiques à la porte Miègeville de Saint-Sernin," *Cahiers de Saint-Michel de Cuxa* 12 (1981): 161–78.

Maes-*Finisterra* — Maes, L. Th. "Mittelalterliche Wallfahrten nach Santiago de Compostela und unsere Liebe Frau von Finisterra," in *Festschrift G. Kirsch*. Stuttgart, 1955, pp. 99–118.

Maes-*pèlerinages expiatoires* — Maes, L. Th. "Les pèlerinages expiatoires et judiciaires des Pays Bas Meridionaux à Saint-Jacques de Compostelle," *Boletín Universidad de Santiago* 51–52 (1948): 13–22.

MáizEleizegui-*arte jacobeo* — Máiz Eleizegui, L. *La devoción al Apóstol Santiago en España y el arte jacobeo hispánico*. Madrid, 1953.

Mâle-*fin Moyen Âge* — Mâle, É. *L'Art religieux de la fin du Moyen Âge en France*. 3rd ed. Paris, 1925.

Mâle-*XII* — Mâle, É. *L'art religieux du XII siècle en France*. Paris, 1922.

Mâle-*XIII* — Mâle, É. *L'art religieux du XIII siècle en France*. Paris, 1925. English trans. as *The Gothic Image: Religious Art in France of the Thirteenth Century*. D. Nussey, trans. New York, 1958.

Mandach-*chanson geste* — Mandach, A de. *Naissance et développement de la chanson de geste en Europe*. Geneva-Paris, 1961, vol. 1.

Mandach-*Pilgrim's Guide* — Mandach, A. de. "A Fresh Approach to the Pilgrim's Guide to the Way of St. James of Compostela," in *Santiago Routes-Bamberg*, pp. 37–47.

MansillaReoyo-*Disputas Toledo Barga Compostela* — Mansilla Reoyo, D. "Disputas diocesanas entre Toledo, Braga y Compostela en los siglos XII al XV," *Anthologica Annua* (Rome-Madrid) 3 (1955): 89–143.

MansillaReoyo-*metrópoli Compostela* — Mansilla Reoyo, D. "Formación de la metrópoli eclesiástica de Compostela," *Compostellanum* 16/1-4 (1971): 73–100.

Maraval-*Lieux saints* — Maraval, P. *Lieux saints et pèlerinage d'Orient*. Paris, 1985.

MariñoFerro-*Peregrinaciones símbolos* — Mariño Ferro, X. R. *Las Romerías / Peregrinaciones y sus símbolos*. Vigo, 1987.

Martinez-*camino jacobeo* — Martinez, T. *El camino jacobeo, una ruta milenaria*. Bilbao, 1976.

Martín-*Orden Santiago* — Martín, J. L. *Orígenes de la Orden Militar de Santiago (1170–1195)*. Barcelona, 1973.

Masson-*architecture hospices* — Masson, A. "Existe-t-il une architecture des hospices de Saint-Jacques?," *Revue historique de Bordeaux et du départment de la Gironde* 35 (1942): 5–17.

Mayer-*Kreuzzüge* — Mayer, H. E. *Geschichte der Kreuzzüge*. 4th ed. Stuttgart-Berlin-Cologne-Mainz, 1976. English trans. as *The Crusades*. J. Gillingham, trans. New York and Oxford, 1972.

Mayer-*románico*—Mayer, A. L. *El estilo románico en España*. Madrid, 1931.

McCulloh-*Cult Relics*—McCulloh, J. M. "The Cult of Relics in the Letters of Pope Gregory the Great. A Lexicographical Study," *Traditio* 32 (1976): 145–84.

McCulloh-*Papal Relic*—McCulloh, J. M. "From Antiquity to the Middle Ages: Continuity and Change in Papal Relic Policy from the 6th to the 8th Century," in *Pietas: Festschrift für B. Kötting*. Münster, 1980, pp. 313–24.

MenéndezPidal-*Cid*—Menéndez Pidal, R. *La España del Cid*. Madrid, 1929.

MenéndezPidal-*Roland*—Menéndez Pidal, R. *La chanson de Roland et la tradition épique des Francs*. Paris, 1960.

MeredithJones-*Karoli*—Meredith-Jones, C. *Historia Karoli Magni et Rotholandi ou Chronique du Pseudo-Turpin*. Paris, 1936; rpt. Geneva, 1972.

Mieck-*témoignages*—Mieck, I. "Les témoignages oculaires du pèlerinage à Saint-Jacques de Compostelle. Études bibliographiques (du XIIᵉ au XVIIIᵉ siècle)," *Compostellanum* 22 (1977): 1–32.

Mieck-*Wallfahrt Santiago*—Mieck, I. "Zur Wallfahrt nach Santiago de Compostela zwischen 1400 und 1650. Resonanz, Struktur-wandel und Krise," in *Spanische Forschungen der Görres-gesellschaft*. Ser. 1. Gesammelte Aufsätze zur Kulturgeschichte Spaniens 29. Münster, 1978, pp. 483–533.

Moralejo-*Agneau León*—Moralejo, S. "Pour l'interprétation iconographique du portail de l'Agneau à Saint-Isidore de León: les signes du zodiaque," *Cahiers de Saint-Michel de Cuxa* 8 (1977): 137–73.

Moralejo-*Ars sacra*—Moralejo, S. "'Ars sacra' et la sculpture romane monumentale: le trésor et le chantier de Compostelle," *Cahiers de Saint-Michel de Cuxa* 11 (1980): 189–238.

Moralejo-*fachada norte*—Moralejo, S. "La primitiva fachada norte de la catedral de Santiago," *Compostellanum* 14 (1969): 623–88.

Moralejo-*imagen*—Moralejo, S. "La imagen arquitectónica de la catedral de Santiago de Compostela," in *Pellegrinaggio Letteratura Jacopea-Perugia*, pp. 37–61.

Moralejo-*Jaca*—Moralejo, S. "Aportaciones a la interpretación del programa iconográfico de la catedral de Jaca," in *Homenaje a don José Maria Lacarre de Miguel....* Estudios medievales 1. Zaragoza, 1977, pp. 173–98.

Moralejo-*Notas Conant*—Moralejo, S. "Notas para una revisión de la obra de K. J. Conant," in K. J. Conant. *Arquitectura románica da catedral de Santiago de Compostela*. Santiago de Compostela, 1983, pp. 221–36.

BIBLIOGRAPHY

Moralejo-*patronazgo Gelmírez*—Moralejo, S. "El patronazgo artístico del arzobispo Gelmírez (1100–1140): su reflejo en la obra e imagen de Santiago," in *Pistoia cammino Santiago,* pp. 245–72.

Moralejo-*porche gloire*—Moralejo, S. "Le porche de la gloire de la cathédrale de Compostelle: problèmes de source et d'interprétation," *Les cahiers de Saint-Michel de Cuxa* 16 (1985): 97–110.

Moralejo-*portails cathédrale* — Moralejo, S. "Saint-Jacques de Compostelle. Les portails retrouvés de la cathédrale romane," *Les dossiers de l'archéologie* 20 (1977): 87–103.

Moralejo-*sculpture Jaca* — Moralejo, S. "La sculpture romane de la cathédrale de Jaca. État des questions," *Cahiers de Saint-Michel de Cuxa* 10 (1979): 79–106.

Morín/Cobreros-*camino iniciático* — Morín, J. P., and J. Cobreros. *El camino iniciático de Santiago.* 3rd ed. Barcelona, 1988.

Mortet-*architecture*—Mortet, V. *Recueil de textes relatifs à l'histoire de l'architecture en France au Moyen Âge, XIᵉ–XIIᵉ siècles.* Paris, 1911.

Moxó-*Repoblación España* — Moxó, S. de. *Repoblación y sociedad en la España cristiana medieval.* Madrid, 1979.

Mullins-*Santiago* — Mullins, E. *The Pilgrimage to Santiago.* London, 1974.

Murguía-*Gelmírez*—Murguía, M. D. *Diego Gelmírez. Ensayo crítico-biográfico.* La Coruña, 1898.

Naesgaard-*Compostelle* — Naesgaard, O. *Saint-Jacques de Compostelle et les débuts de la grande sculpture vers 1100.* Aarhus, 1962.

NeiraMosquera-*Santiago* — Neira de Mosquera, V. *Monografía de Santiago.* Santiago de Compostela, 1950.

Nicolas-*Saint-Gilles*—Nicolas, C. "Peintures murales et châsse de Saint-Gilles au XIIᵉ siècle," *Bulletin du comité de l'art chrétien* (Nîmes), 1908, pp. 108–14.

O'Callaghan-*Alfonso VI* — O'Callaghan, J. F. "The Integration of Christian Spain into Europe: the Role of Alfonso VI of León-Castile," in *Santiago, Saint-Denis and Saint Peter: the Reception of the Roman Liturgy in León-Castile in 1080.* Ed. B. Reilly. New York, 1985, pp. 101–20.

Osma-*Azabaches Compostelanos*—Osma, G. de. *Catálogo de Azabaches Compostelanos.* Madrid, 1915.

Oursel-*Compostella* — Oursel, R., F. Cardini, and D. Tuniz. *Compostella. Guida del pellegrino di San Giacomo. Storia di Carlo Magno e di Orlando.* Milan-Turin, 1989

Oursel-*garde Dieu*—Oursel, R. *Routes romanes: La Garde de Dieu.* St. Léger-Vauban, 1986. Also as *Peregrinos, hospitalarios y templarios.* Madrid, 1986.

Oursel-*pèlerins* — Oursel, R. *Les pèlerins du Moyen Âge.* Paris, 1963.

Oursel-*Routes saints* — Oursel, R. *Routes Romanes: La route aux saints.* St. Léger-Vauban, 1982. Also as *Le strade del Medioevo. Arte e figure del pellegrinaggio a Compostela.* Milan, 1982.

Oursel-*Routes solitudes* — Oursel, R. *Routes Romanes: La route aux solitudes.* St. Léger-Vauban, 1984. Also as *Caminantes y caminos.* Madrid, 1984.

Owen-*Roland* — Owen, D. R. *The Legend of Roland.* New York, 1973.

Pacaut-*Cluny* — Pacaut, M. *L'Ordre de Cluny.* Paris, 1986.

Pardo-*Camino* — Pardo, P., *et al. El Camino de Santiago.* Madrid, 1990.

Passini-*Camino* — Passini, J. *El Camino de Santiago.* Madrid, 1987.

Passini-*Compostelle* — Passini, J. *Villes médiévales du chemin de Saint-Jacques-de-Compostelle, de Pampelune à Burgos.* Paris, 1984.

PastorTogneri-*Gelmírez* — Pastor de Togneri, R. "Diego Gelmírez: une mentalité à la page. A propos du rôle de certaines élites de pouvoir," in *Mélanges offerts à René Crozet.* Poitiers, 1966, 1: 597–608.

Paulus-*Ablasses* — Paulus, N. *Geschichte des Ablasses im Mittelalter.* 2 vols. Paderborn, 1922–23.

Pellegrini-*curia Callisto II* — Pellegrini, L. "Cardinali e curia sotto Callisto II (1119–1124)," in *Contributi dell'Istituto di storia medioevale.* Milan, 1972, 2:507–56.

PérezUrbel-*comienzos Reconquista* — Pérez de Urbel, J., and R. Del Arco. *Los comienzos de la Reconquista (711–1038).* In *Historia de España* 6. Ed. R. Menéndez Pidal. Madrid, 1956.

PérezUrbel-*culto Santiago X* — Pérez de Urbel, J. "El culto de Santiago en el siglo X," *Compostellanum* 16 (1971): 11–36.

PérezUrbel-*himnos mozárabes* — Pérez de Urbel, J. "Origen de los himnos mozárabes," *Bulletin hispanique* 28/2 (1926): 113–39.

PérezUrbel-*Orígenes culto* — Pérez de Urbel, J. "Orígenes del culto de Santiago en España," *Hispania Sacra* 5 (1952): 1–31.

PérezUrbel-*Santiago* — Pérez de Urbel, J. *Santiago y Compostela en la Historia.* Madrid, 1977.

Piccat-*pellegrino impiccato* — Piccat, M. "Il miracolo jacopeo del pellegrino impiccato: riscontri tra narrazione e figurazione," in *Pellegrinaggio Letteratura Jacopea-Perugia*, pp. 287–310.

Plötz-*Ikonographie Jacobus* — Plötz, R. "'Benedictio perarum et baculorum' und 'coronatio peregrinorum.' Beiträge zu der Ikonographie des Hl. Jacobus im deutschen Sprachgebiet," in *Volkskultur und Heimat. Festschrift für Josef Dünninger zum 80 Geburtstag.* Würzburg, 1986, pp. 339–76.

Plötz-*Imago Iacobi* — Plötz, R. "Imago Beati Iacobi. Beiträge zur Ikonographie des Hl. Jacobus Maior in Hochmittelalter," in *Wallfahrt-Grenzen*, pp. 248–64.

Plötz-*Jacobus* — Plötz, R. "Der Apostel Jacobus in Spanien bis zum 9. Jahrhundert," in *Spanische Forschungen der Görresgesellschaft*. Ser. 1. Gesammelte Aufsätze zur Kulturgeschichte Spaniens 30. Münster, 1982, pp. 19–145.

Plötz-*Peregrini Palmieri* — Plötz, R. "Peregrini-Palmieri-Romei, Untersuchungen zum Pilgerbegriff der Zeit Dantes," *Jahrbuch für Volkskunde*, n.s. 2 (1979): 103–34.

Plötz-*Santiago peregrinatio* — Plötz, R. "Santiago-peregrinatio und Jacobuskult mit besonderen Berücksichtigung des deutschen Frankenlandes," in *Spanische Forschungen der Görresgesellschaft*. Ser. 1. Gesammelte Aufsätze zur Kulturgeschichte Spaniens 31. Münster, 1984, pp. 25–135.

Plötz-*Strukturwandel peregrinatio* — Plötz, R. "Strukturwandel der peregrinatio im Hochmittelalter. Begriff und Komponenten," *Rheinisch-westfälische Zeitschrift für Volkskunde* 26–27 (1981–82): 129–51.

Plötz-*Traditiones* — Plötz, R. "Traditiones Hispanicae Beati Jacobi. Les origines du culte de saint Jacques à Compostelle," in *Santiago-Europalia*, pp. 27–39.

PochGutiérrez-*inmunidad Peregrino* — Poch y Gutiérrez de Caviedes, A. "Un status de inmunidad internacional del peregrino jacobeo," *Compostellanum* 10/4 (1965): 333–406.

PortelaSandoval-*Santiago* — Portela Sandoval, F. J. *El camino de Santiago*. 3 vols. Madrid, 1971.

PrecedoLafuente-*Santiago Patrón* — Precedo Lafuente, M. J. *Santiago el Major, Patrón de España. Vida y culto*. Santiago de Compostela, 1985.

Reilly-*Church Reform Santiago* — Reilly, B. F. *The Nature of Church Reform at Santiago de Compostela during the Episcopate of Don Diego Gelmírez, 1100–1140 A.D.* Diss., Bryn Mawr College, 1966. (Diss. Abstr. XXVII, 1966–67, 4185-A 4186-A).

Reilly-*Santiago Saint Denis* — Reilly, B. F. "Santiago and Saint Denis: the French Presence in Eleventh Century Spain," *Catholic Historical Review* 54 (1968): 467–83.

RemuñánFerro-*Gremios compostelanos* — Remuñán Ferro, M. "Gremios compostelanos relacionados con la peregrinación jacobea," in *Pellegrinaggio Letteratura Jacopea-Perugia*, pp. 109–126.

Renquard-*étapes vitesse* — Renquard, Y. "Routes, étapes et vitesse de marche de France à Rome au XIIIe et au XIVe siècle d'après les itinéraires d'Eude Rigaud–1254 et de Barthélemy Bonis–1350," in *Studi in onore di Amintore Fanfani*. 6 vols. Milan, 1962, 3:403–28.

Richard-*pèlerinages* — Richard, J. *Les récits de voyages et de pèlerinages*. Typologie des sources du Moyen Âge occidental 38. Turnhout, 1981.

Richard-*relations pèlerinage*— Richard, J. "Les relations de pèlerinage au Moyen Âge et les motivations de leurs auteurs," in *Wallfahrt-Grenzen*, pp. 143–54.

Rodríguez Amaya-*metropolitana Emeritense Compostela*— Rodríguez Amaya, E. "La sede metropolitana Emeritense, su traslado a Compostela e intentos de restauración," *Revista de Estudios Extremeños* 5 (1949): 493–559.

Rodríguez/Ríos-*iconografía jacobea* — Rodríguez Bordallo, R., and A. M. Ríos Graña. "Aportación a la iconografía jacobea," in *Pellegrinaggio Letteratura Jacopea-Perugia*, pp. 219–24.

Roussel-*pelerinages* — Roussel, R. *Les pèlerinages à travers les siècles*. Paris, 1955; 2nd ed. 1972.

Rowling-*Everyday Life Travellers* — Rowling, M. *Everyday Life of Mediaeval Travellers*. London, 1971.

Sánchez Albornoz-*Clavijo* — Sánchez Albornoz, C. "La auténtica batalla de Clavijo," *Cuadernos de historia de España* 9 (1948): 94–139.

Sánchez Albornoz-*culto jacobeo* — Sánchez Albornoz, C. "En los albores del culto jacobeo," *Compostellanum* 1 (1971): 37–71.

Sánchez Albornoz-*España enigma* — Sánchez Albornoz, C. *España, un enigma histórico*. 3rd ed. Buenos Aires, 1971. Also as *Spain, a Historical Enigma*. Madrid, 1975.

Sánchez Albornoz-*Orígenes Asturias* — Sánchez Albornoz, C. *Orígenes de la nación española. Estudios críticos sobre la historia del reino de Asturias*. 3 vols. Oviedo, 1972–75.

Sánchez Albornoz-*reino astur-leónes* — Sánchez Albornoz, C. *La España Cristiana de los siglos VIII al XI: el reino astur-leónes (722–1037). Sociedad, economía, gobierno, cultura y vida*. In *Historia de España* 7/1. Ed. R. Menéndez Pidal. Madrid, 1980.

Sánchez/Barreiro-*Santiago* — Sánchez, F., and F. Barreiro. *Santiago, Jerusalén, Roma....* 3 vols. Santiago de Compostela, 1880–82.

Sánchez Cantón-*vida Galicia* — Sánchez Cantón, F. J. "La vida en Galicia en los tiempos del arte románico," *Cuadernos de Estudios Gallegos* 17 (1962): 182–201.

Sauerländer-*Conques* — Sauerländer, W. "Omnes perversi sic sunt in tartara mersi. Skulptur als Bildpredigt. Das Weltgerichtstympanon von Sainte-Foy in Conques," in *Jahrbuch der Akademie der Wissenschaft in Göttingen*. Göttingen, 1979, pp. 33–47.

Schimmelpfennig-*Heiligen Jahres* — Schimmelpfennig, B. "Die Anfänge des Heiligen Jahres von Santiago de Compostela im Mittelalter," *Journal of Medieval History* 4 (1978): 285–303.

Schmitz-*Bussbücher*— Schmitz, J. *Die Bussbücher und die Bussdisciplin der Kirche*. Magdeburg, 1883; 2nd ed. Halle, 1885.

Schmugge-*Kirche Gesellschaft* — Schmugge, L. "Kirche und Gesellschaft im Hochmittelalter," in *Jahres und Tagungsbericht der Görresgesellschaft, 1976*. Cologne, 1977, pp. 63–82.

Schmugge-*nationale Vorurteile* — Schmugge, L. "Über nationale Vorurteile im Mittelalter," *Deutsches Archiv für Erforschung des Mittelalters* 36 (1982): 439–59.

Schmugge-*Pilgerfahrt frei* — Schmugge, L. "'Pilgerfahrt macht frei' Eine These zur Bedeutung des mittelalterlichen Pilgerwesen," *Römische Quartalschrift* 74 (1979): 16–31.

Schmugge-*Pilgerverkehrs* — Schmugge, L. "Die Anfänge des organizierten Pilgerverkehrs im Mittelalter," *Quellen und Forschungen aus italienischen Archiven und Bibliotheken* 64 (1984): 1–83.

Schmugge-*Verpflegung Pilgern* — Schmugge, L. "Zu den Anfängen des organisierten Pilgerverkehrs und zur Unterbringung und Verpflegung von Pilgern in Mittelalter," in *Gastfreundschaft, Taverne und Gasthaus im Mittelalter*. Ed. C. Peyer and E. Müller-Luckner. Munich, 1983, pp. 37–60.

Schreiber-*Gemeinschaften* — Schreiber, G. *Gemeinschaften des Mittelalters. Recht und Verfassung, Kult und Frömmigkeit*. Münster, n.d.

Schreiber-*Wallfahrt* — Schreiber, G., ed. *Wallfahrt und Volkstum in Geschichte und Leben*. Düsseldorf, 1934.

Schreiner-*Discrimen* — Schreiner, K. "Discrimen veri ac falsi. Ansätze und Formen der Kritik an der Heiligen- und Reliquienverehrung des Mittelalters," *Archiv für Kulturgeschichte* 48 (1966): 1–53.

Schreiner-*Reliquienwesen* — Schreiner, K. "Zum Wahrheitsverständnis im Heiligen- und Reliquienwesen des Mittelalters," *Saeculum* 17 (1966): 131–69.

Secret-*Jacques* — Secret, J. *St.-Jacques et les chemins de Compostelle*. Paris, 1955.

Segl-*Cluniazenser* — Segl, P. *Königtum und Klosterreform in Spanien. Untersuchungen über die Cluniazenserklöster in Kastilien-León vom Beginn des 11. bis zur Mitte des 12. Jahrhunderts*. Kallmünz, 1974.

Segl-*Cluny Spanien* — Segl, P. "Cluny in Spanien. Ergebnisse und neue Fragestellungen," *Deutsches Archiv für Erforschung des Mittelalters* 33 (1977): 560–69.

SendinBlázquez-*Via Plata* — Sendin Blázquez, J. *Calzada y camino de Santiago. Via de la Plata*. Zamora, 1992.

Serrano-*Burgos* — Serrano, L. *El obispado de Burgos y Castilla primitiva, desde el siglo V al XIII*. 3 vols. Madrid, 1935–36.

Servatius-*Paschalis II* — Servatius, C. *Papst Paschalis II. Päpste und Papsttum 14*. Stuttgart, 1979.

SicartGiménez-*figura Santiago* — Sicart Giménez, A. "La figura de Santiago en los textos medievales," in *Pellegrinaggio Letteratura Jacopea-Perugia*, pp. 271–86.

SicartGiménez-*Santiago ecuestre* — Sicart Giménez, A. "La iconografía de Santiago ecuestre en la Edad Media," *Compostellanum* 27 (1982): 11–32.

Sigal-*marcheurs* — Sigal, P.-A. *Les marcheurs de Dieu. Pèlerinages et pèlerins au Moyen Âge.* Paris, 1974.

Sigal-*miracle* — Sigal, P.-A. *L'homme et le miracle dans la France médiévale (XIe–XIIe siècle).* Paris, 1985.

Sigal-*Miracle Gaule* — Sigal, P.-A. *Le Miracle aux XIe et XIIe siècles dans le cadre de l'ancienne Gaul d'après les sources hagiographiques.* 3 vols. Diss., University of Paris, 1981.

Sigal-*société pèlerins* — Sigal, P.-A. "La société des pèlerins," in *Jacques Quête sacré-Dupront,* pp. 125–57.

Sigal-*types pèlerinage* — Sigal, P.-A. "Les différents types de pèlerinage au Moyen Âge," in *Wallfahrt-Grenzen,* pp. 76–86.

Silvestre-*reliques* — Silvestre, H. "Commerce et vol de reliques au Moyen Âge," *Revue belge de philologie et d'histoire* 30 (1952): 721–39.

Simon-*antiquité chrétienne* — Simon, M. "L'antiquité chrétienne," in *Pèlerinage biblique classique,* pp. 97–115.

SoriaPuig-*camino Santiago* — Soria y Puig, A. *El camino a Santiago.* 2 vols. Madrid, 1992.

Spicq-*pérégrination NouvTest* — Spicq, C. *Vie chrétienne et pérégrination selon le Nouveau Testament.* Paris, 1972. Also as *Vida cristiana y peregrinación.* Madrid, 1977.

Stalley-*Pèlerinage maritime* — Stalley, R. "Pèlerinage maritime à Saint-Jacques," in *Santiago-Europalia,* pp. 123–28.

Starkie-*Santiago Pilgrims* — Starkie, W. F. *Road to Santiago. Pilgrims of St. James.* New York, 1957.

Steppe-*iconographie Jacques* — Steppe, J. K. "L'iconographie de Saint-Jacques le Majeur (Santiago)," in *Santiago-Europalia,* pp. 129–53.

Stokstad-*Santiago Pilgrimages* — Stokstad, M. *Santiago de Compostela in the Age of the Great Pilgrimages.* Norman, OK, 1978.

Stone-*cult Santiago* — Stone, J. S. *The Cult of Santiago.* London, 1927.

Stopani-*francigena* — Stopani, R. *La via francigena. Una strada europea nell'Italia del Medioevo.* Florence, 1988.

Stopani-*strade Roma* — Stopani, R. *Le grandi vie di pellegrinaggio del medio evo. Le strade per Roma.* Florence, 1986.

Stopani-*vie pellegrinaggio Medioevo* — Stopani, R. *Le vie di pellegrinaggio del Medioevo. Gli itinerari per Roma, Gerusalemme, Compostella.* Florence, 1991.

Stopani-*vie pellegrinaggio spedali* — Stopani, R. "Le grandi vie di pellegrinaggio nel medioevo: spedali lebbrosari e xenodochi lungo l'itinerario toscano della via francigena," in *Pistoia Cammino Santiago,* pp. 313–30.

BIBLIOGRAPHY

Storrs/CorderoCarrete-*Peregrinos ingleses* — Storrs, C., and F. R. Cordero Carrete. "Peregrinos ingleses a Santiago en el s. XIV," *Cuadernos de Estudios Gallegos* 20 (1965): 193–224.

Storrs-*Pilgrims England* — Storrs, C. *Jacobean Pilgrims from England from the Early XII to the Late XV Century.* Diss., University of London, 1964.

Sumption-*Pilgrimage* — Sumption, J. *Pilgrimage. An Image of Medieval Religion.* London, 1975.

Thompson-*godos España* — Thompson, E. A. *Los godos en España.* Madrid, 1971.

Thorel-*equipement pèlerin* — Thorel, O. *L'equipement d'un pèlerin picard à St. Jacques de Compostelle.* Amiens, 1909.

Töpfer-*Reliquien Pilger* — Töpfer, B. "Reliquienkult und Pilgerbewegung zur Zeit der Klosterreform im burgundisch-aquitanischen Gebiet," in *Vom Mittelalter zur Neuzeit: Festschrift H. Sproemberg.* Berlin, 1956, pp. 420–39.

TormoMonzó-*Galicia* — Tormo y Monzó, E. "La escultura en Galicia (siglo XII)," in *Cultura Española* 1 (1906): 171–82.

TorresLópez-*España Visigoda* — Torres López, M., *et al. España Visigoda.* In *Historia de España* 3. Ed. R. Menéndez Pidal. Madrid, 1956.

Treuille-*Coquille* — Treuille, H. "Crouzille et coquille," in *Soulac-Médoc-Jacques,* pp. 59ff.

Turner-*Image Pilgrimage* — Turner, V., and E. Turner. *Image and Pilgrimage in Christian Culture.* New York, 1978.

UbietoArteta-*destierro Peláez* — Ubieto Arteta, A. "El destierro del obispo compostelano Diego Peláez en Aragón," *Cuadernos de Estudios Gallegos* 6 (1951): 43–51.

UbietoArteta-*rito romano Aragón Navarra* — Ubieto Arteta, A. "La introducción del rito romano en Aragón y Navarra," *Hispania Sacra* 1 (1948): 299–324.

UbietoArteta-*Santa Cristina* — Ubieto Arteta, A. "Los primeros años del hospital de Santa Cristina del Somport," *Príncipe de Viana* 27 (1966): 267–76.

Urrutibéhéty-*Voies navarre* — Urrutibéhéty, C. *Voies d'accès en Navarre et carrefour des chemins de Saint-Jacques.* Bayonne, n.d.

Valdeón-*camino Santiago* — Valdeón, J., et al. *El camino de Santiago.* Madrid, 1990.

Valiña-*Camino* — Valiña Sampedro, E. *El Camino de Santiago. Guía del Peregrino.* León, 1985.

Valiña *Camino Compostela* — Valiña Sampedro, E. *El Camino de Santiago. Guía del Peregrino a Compostela.* Vigo, 1992. Rev. ed. of Valiña-*Camino.*

Valiña-*camino jurídico* — Valiña Sampedro, E. *El camino de Santiago. Estudio histórico-jurídico.* Madrid, 1971.

331

Valous-*cluniens* — Valous, G. de. "Les cluniens en Espagne," in *DHGE* 13, s.v.

Valous-*pénétration française* — Valous, G. de. "Les monastères et la pénétration française en Espagne du XIᵉ au XIIIᵉ siècle," *Revue Mabillon,* October–December 1940, pp. 77–97.

Vauchez-*spiritualité* — Vauchez, A. *La spiritualité du Moyen Âge occidental.* Paris, 1975.

VázquezParga-*Navarra* — Vázquez de Parga, L. "Aymeric Picaud y Navarra," *Correo erudito* 4 (1947): 113–14.

VázquezParga-*pereg* — Vázquez de Parga, L., J. M. Lacarra, and J. Uría Ríu. *Las peregrinaciones a Santiago de Compostela.* 3 vols. Madrid, 1948–49.

VázquezParga-*peregrinación iconografía* — Vázquez de Parga, L. "Algunos aspectos de la influencia de la peregrinación compostelana en la iconografía artística," *Compostellanum* 10 (1965): 449–63.

VázquezParga-*revolución comunal Compostela* — Vázquez de Parga, L. "La revolución comunal de Compostela en los años 1116 y 1117," *Anuario de Historia del Derecho Español* 16 (1945): 685–703.

Venece-*Pèlerinages chrétiens* — Venece, M. *Les Pèlerinages chrétiens du VIᵉ au XIᵉ siècle, leurs motifs et leurs influences sur le dogma et sur la vie chrétienne du haut Moyen Âge.* 3 vols. Diss., Gregorian University, Rome, 1955.

VicensVives-*España* — Vicens Vives, J. *Aproximación a la Historia de España.* Barcelona, 1952.

VillaamilCastro-*establecimientos beneficencia* — Villaamil y Castro, J. "Reseña histórica de los establecimientos de beneficencia que hubo en Galicia durante la Edad Media, y de la erección del Gran Hospital Real de Santiago, fundado por los Reyes Católicos," *Galicia Histórica* 1 (1901–2): 227–50, 289–312, 353–97.

ViñayoGonzález-*Caminos* — Viñayo González, A. *Caminos y peregrinos. Huellas de la peregrinación jacobea.* León, 1991.

Vogel-*pèlerinage pénitentiel* — Vogel, C. "Le pèlerinage pénitentiel," in *Pellegrinaggi culto santi-Todi,* pp. 39–94.

Vones-*Compostellana* — Vones, L. *Die "Historia Compostellana" und die Kirchenpolitik des nordwestspanischen Raumes 1070–1130. Ein Beitrag zur Geschichte der Beziehungen zwischen Spanien und dem Papsttum zu Beginn des 12. Jahrhunderts.* Kölner Historische Abhandlungen 29. Cologne-Vienna, 1980.

Ward-*Miracles* — Ward, B. *Miracles and Medieval Mind. Theory, Record and Event. 1000–1215.* London, 1982.

Ward-*Pórtico Gloria* — Ward, M. L. *Studies of the Pórtico de la Gloria at the Cathedral of Santiago de Compostela.* Diss., New York University, 1978.

Werckmeister-*Cluny* — Werckmeister, O. K. "Cluny III and the Pilgrimage to Santiago de Compostela," *Gesta* 27 (1988): 83–92.
Whitehill-*Date Santiago* — Whitehill, W. M. "The Date of the Beginning of the Cathedral of Santiago de Compostela," *The Antiquaries Journal* 15 (1935): 336–42.
Whitehill-*Romanesque* — Whitehill, W. M. *Spanish Romanesque Architecture of the Eleventh Century.* Oxford, 1941.
Wilckens-*Kleidung* — Wilckens, L. von. "Die Kleidung der Pilger," in *Wallfahrt-Grenzen*, pp. 174–80.
Williams-*Camino* — Williams, J. "La arquitectura del Camino de Santiago," *Compostellanum* 29 (1984): 267–90.
Williams-*Cluny* — Williams, J. "Cluny and Spain," *Gesta* 27 (1988): 93–101.
Williams-*León* — Williams, L. "San Isidoro in León: Evidence for a New History," *The Art Bulletin* 55 (1973): 171–84.
Williams-*Reconquest* — Williams, J. "Generationes Abrahae: Reconquest Iconography in León," *Gesta* 16/2 (1977): 3–14.
Williams-*Spain Toulouse* — Williams, J. "Spain or Toulouse? A Half Century Later: Observations on the Chronology of Santiago de Compostela," in *Actas del XXIII Congreso Internacional de Historia del Arte.* Granada, 1976, pp. 559–67.

Roncesvalles. Augustinian monastery and pilgrims' hospice. Original structure 1134–35. Rebuilt.

Toulouse. Cathedral of Saint-Sernin. Apse. Late XI C.

INDEX

Place names may also be found in the Gazetteer,
saints' names in the Hagiographical Register.

St. Euverte 108
St. Facundo 118
St. Foy 33, 34, 67, 103–4
St. Francis of Assisi 3
St. Fronto 107
St. Genesius 97
St. Géraud d'Aurillac 24
St. Giles 25, 98–102
St. Hilary of Poitiers 24, 33, 109
St. Honoratus 97
St. Ildephonsus 16
St. Isidore of León 67
St. Isidore of Seville 3, 108, 118, 131, 176; *De ortu et obitu patrum* 11
St. James 3, 5, 102, 118, 119, 125; and Carolingian tradition 20; as evangelizer of Spain 10, 12; as pilgrim 66, 68; as patron saint of Spain 12; as patron saint of *Reconquista* 18; body of, 126; cult of 7–14, 18, 19, 23, 29, 30, 65; evangelizing 9, 11; iconography of 63–70; in Gospels 7, 8; in Spain 10–11; martyrdom of 8, 9, 10, 29, 70; miracles of 29, 70; reliquary of 35; tomb of 13, 14, 21, 76; *translatio* of 12, 13, 29, 30
St. James the Lesser 12
St. John 5, 7, 10, 63, 64, 112, 125, 127; in Ephesus as apostolic see of 72
St. John the Baptist 3, 109–10
St. Leonard of Limousin 102, 105–7
St. Leonard of Noblat 25, 33
St. Martin of Tours 102, 108–9

St. Mary Magdalene 3, 25, 104–5
St. Mattheus 12
St. Matthew 96
St. Matthias 12
St. Maximinus 104
St. Michel 85
St. Nicholas of Bari 67
St. Paul 5, 10, 12, 19, 96, 123, 128; *Epistle to the Romans* 9
St. Peter 3, 5, 7, 10, 19, 63, 64, 69, 107, 114, 115, 123, 125; in Rome as apostolic see of 72; involvement in the Iberian peninsula 10
St. Philip 113
St. Primitivo 118
St. Romanus 117
St. Saturninus 25, 103
St. Seurin 117
St. Simon 113
St. Thaddeus 12, 113
St. Theodemir 127
St. Tiberius 103
St. Timothy 96
St. Trophimus 33, 96
St. William, confessor 102–3
stonecutters 130–31
streams and rivers, crossing of 46; see also bridges, ferrymen
Szentjákobfalva, Hungary 70
Szombathely, Hungary 24

T
Tabor Mountain 5, 6, 8, 64, 125
Tarbes 70
Tardajos 86
Tarik-Ibn-Zaid 14
Tatianus, *Diatessaron* 12

This 3rd Printing Was Completed on December 15, 1999
at Italica Press, New York, New York and Was
Set in Palatino and Charlemagne. It Was
Printed on 60-lb Natural Paper by
BookMobile, St. Paul,
Minnesota,
U. S. A.